MY WAR MEMOIRS

MY WAR MEMOIRS

BY

DR. EDUARD BENEŠ

CZECHOSLAVAK MINISTER OF
FOREIGN AFFAIRS

Translated from the Czech by

PAUL SELVER

GREENWOOD PRESS, PUBLISHERS
WESTPORT, CONNECTICUT

Originally published in 1928
by George Allen & Unwin, Ltd., London

First Greenwood Reprinting 1971

Library of Congress Catalogue Card Number 70-114467

SBN 8371-4763-8

Printed in the United States of America

AUTHOR'S PREFACE

THIS book contains a record of my war-time experiences. Life moves so rapidly that the approach of new political events is apt to make us forget the old ones too easily. Much of what I saw and heard during the war deserves to be remembered, and that is why I have decided to wait no longer, but to tell the story of our revolutionary movement now. This book will be supplemented by later works on the Peace Conference and on our post-war foreign policy, for my work during the war and subsequently as Czechoslovak Foreign Minister forms an inseparable whole.

This book does not contain the complete history of our revolutionary movement. It will be supplemented by others ; and I may add that I have not exhausted my own material. This book was written in fragments at a period when I was closely occupied both with home and foreign policy, and when there were difficult post-war problems to cope with. In many instances my remarks should be read in conjunction with President T. G. Masaryk's *World Revolution*,(1) which the present volume supplements by more detailed descriptions of various important episodes. I have written the book in my capacity as former General Secretary of the Czechoslovak National Council, and not as Czechoslovak Minister of Foreign Affairs.

Throughout the war I had ample opportunities of observing the extent to which our national cause was an inseparable factor in the leading events of the Great War and how it was affected by them. It is not possible to form a correct estimate of our revolutionary movement unless this fact is realized. In this book I have made this clear by narrating the details of our movement in relation to the general scope of the points at issue during the war. As regards the war itself, it was on such a vast scale that I have touched upon it only as it affects my narrative. Here and there I was compelled to repeat myself, because our movement had many ramifications, and was connected with events in the various States, which I deal with separately. This may tend to make my account clearer and more comprehensive.

I hope that the book will help to remove a number of political misunderstandings or ambiguities, as well as certain historical inaccuracies or erroneous statements which have accumulated during the last few years. It will at least, I think, reduce a number of matters under dispute to their right proportion. In any case, it is my wish to make clear what should not be doubtful to anybody, namely, that we never drew any distinction between our revolutionary movement at home and abroad, that we placed our diplomatic work on the same footing as the achievements of our troops, and that, in short, we look upon our revolutionary activities at home and abroad, in the council chamber and on the battlefield, as a single unified movement.

My chief endeavour has been to give an accurate account of facts, and in writing these memoirs I have been prompted by my attachment to our national cause and also by my attachment to the truth ; and I want the book to be not only a record of what happened, but also a lesson to be applied to our present and future political problems.

In conclusion, I should like to thank all those who have helped me to collect and arrange the material, etc. I am particularly grateful for the assistance rendered by Dr. A. Hartl, Dr. J. Werstadt, J. Papoušek, Dr. J. Opočenský, V. Škrach, and A. Babka.

EDUARD BENEŠ.

CONTENTS

V

CONTENTS

X

CONTENTS

PAGE

XX

TRANSLATOR'S NOTE

THE present version of the War Memoirs of Dr. Beneš has been prepared specially with a view to the interests of English and American readers. In selecting and preparing the material for this purpose I have been assisted by Mr. S. G. Hobson, the value of whose suggestions and advice I gladly take this opportunity of acknowledging.

The figures in parentheses throughout the text refer to notes appearing at the end of the book. Notes at foot of pages are indicated in the usual way.

P. S.

LONDON,
January 1928.

THE PRONUNCIATION OF CZECH NAMES

THE following notes will enable the English reader to understand the chief rules of Czech pronunciation:

a : as English u in but.
á : long a as the English ah.
ě : as English ye in yes.
í : as English ee in seen.
ů : a long final u, as English oo in root.
ej : as English ey in they.
c : as English ts in hats.
č : as English ch in church.
ch : as ch in Scottish loch.
ř : (at beginning or in middle of words) as r followed by the English s in measure; (at the end of words) as r followed by sh.
š : as English sh.
z : as English z
ž : as English s in measure.

The main accent is on the first syllable of words.

Examples : Beneš (Ben-esh) ; Kramář (Krum-ahrsh) ; Rašín (Rush-een) ; Šámal (Shah-mul) ; Štěpánek (Shtyep-ahnek).

MY WAR MEMOIRS

I

MY PREPARATIONS FOR WAR AND REVOLUTION

(a) MY POLITICAL PREPARATIONS

I

THE war surprised me, in one sense, and in another it did not. I had gone to Paris in 1905 at the age of twenty-one and had spent nearly a year there. Then I had stayed for several months in London and had returned to Paris for another year. In October 1907 I had gone for a year to the University of Berlin and devoted myself to a study of social conditions in Germany. Having returned to France (Paris and Dijon) for my law examinations, and having completed my studies there, I went back to Prague in September 1908.

I had gone abroad to study modern languages and prepare myself for a university professorship in this subject. My fondness for political matters, my bent for the study of social problems, and also material considerations, had caused me to turn to journalism, and from that to the study of law, political science, and sociology. I had occupied myself closely with philosophy while still at Prague in my first university year. As a young student who had been through hardships, who had had a difficult time during his studies, and who had been repelled by the political and social conditions at home, I was soon impressed by everything I saw in France and in Paris. I was greatly moved by the whole of the French and Parisian revolutionary tradition; I was carried away by the revolutionary and radical phraseology of the French Socialists, syndicalists, and other Left Wing parties; I was absorbed by the study of extremist movements, revolutionary syndicalism, French Socialism, anti-militarism, and anarchism, the French and Russian Revolutions with all their offshoots.

The endeavour to learn as much as I could abroad, and to acquire sufficient knowledge so that I could return home fully prepared for academic and public activity, urged me on to feverish labour to fathom rapidly the political, social, and cultural problems of France. From there I passed over to England, and subsequently also to Belgium, Italy, and Germany. The preparation of my thesis for a doctor's degree at the Dijon Faculty of Law compelled me at the same time to make a detailed study of the conditions in my own country and in Austria.

My stay in Paris brought me also among the Russian revolutionaries who had taken part in the first Russian Revolution of 1905, and my contact with them made a deep impression upon me. In 1906 and 1907 I visited their meetings at Paris, becoming a member of their societies. I began to make a close study of Russia and of Russian literature, both classical and revolutionary. After my return to Prague I kept in touch with the revolutionary Russians.

I was influenced by a number of political questions then current, which later affected my attitude towards the war. In France there was revolutionary syndicalism, the struggle for the separation of the Church and State, the struggle against the three years' military service, and anti-militarist propaganda. From these I drew the conclusion that on the whole France was pacifist. In England there was the discussion as to the economic future of England in case of war, the dispute between Liberals and Conservatives on the subject of Protection and the development of the German and English fleets. It was during my stay in London and Berlin that the most active discussion was taking place with regard to the development of the German fleet and the English policy of a "two-power standard." In Germany they were even then calculating that by 1920 their fleet would be equal in size to that of Great Britain.

The deepest impressions in these matters, however, were those which I formed in Berlin. The military parade, which was arranged in the summer of 1908 and at which I was present, overwhelmed me. The development of industry and railways, of the Prussian military and naval strength, compared with what I had seen at Paris and London in this respect, the mechanization of all public life under the influence of Prussian discipline, the atmosphere of constraint and the prevailing influence and authority of the military, aristocratic, and bureaucratic caste, affected me painfully because at that time I was unable to arrive at any clear conclusion as to what it was to lead to. I felt instinctively that it must end disastrously, and the effect which it produced upon me as a member of a small and neighbouring nation was a disturbing one.

I attributed the conditions in Germany to the non-political and herdlike character of the German people, their inadequate training in democracy, the lack of a revolutionary spirit in German Socialism, and the proneness to empty mechanical doctrinairism which never fully conformed with the demands of life and was either a convenient pretext for not doing anything practical or else led to a blind and fanatical pursuit of an *idée fixe*.

Thus I reached the study of Pan-Germanism, its theory and practice. In a theoretical respect I was interested by Lagarde, Treitschke, and Houston Stewart Chamberlain (and through him by Gobineau), while on the practical side I turned to Rohrbach, Rüdiger, and various Pan-German pamphleteers. I wondered what were the effects of the propaganda carried on by Rohrbach's group, which in hundreds of thousands of leaflets, booklets, and pamphlets popularized the Berlin–Bagdad scheme and demanded not only the development of the fleet, but also a large supply of aircraft.(2) In the pamphlets issued by Counsellor Martin during 1908 it was shown, for example, by diagrams, how, when, and within what time a German air fleet could land hundreds of thousands of troops near London, and how quickly it could transport similar forces to Constantinople, Bagdad, and the Persian Gulf. These matters both bewildered and provoked me, compelling me to reflect upon the political future of Germany, to make careful comparisons with what I had seen in England and France, and to occupy myself with the problems of war. Such, in general terms, is a synthesis of the external political impressions, with a direct or indirect bearing upon the war, which I brought back with me from my travels.

On the whole I became attached to France because of the tradition of the great revolution; the broad perspectives of its national history; its love for liberty of thought; for the fullness of its cultural life; for the abundance of its philosophical, scientific, literary, and artistic culture; for its traditional humanitarian, universal, and cosmopolitan tendency, which sought a genuine cult of humanity. I was also enormously attracted by the idealistic and revolutionary impulse underlying the social and socialistic thought and the practical movement of non-doctrinaire French Socialism.

England moved me profoundly by its impressive inner strength, which could be felt on all sides, by its harmony and order, by its development towards political and constitutional liberty, by its economic advance, by its endeavour in its national culture to form a harmonious human individuality, and by the strength of religious feeling and conscious religious life which even the average Englishman reveals. This practical experience of religious matters in England then led me to the study of philosophy and theory of knowledge, and also to an anti-positivist change of views on religion.

2

I returned from abroad strengthened in my original opposition to our political and social conditions. In comparison with England and France, and with Western Europe in general, Austria-Hungary, disorganized by its welter of nationalities, struck me as the prototype of a reactionary, aristocratic-bureaucratic State, resembling in many respects the reactionary, militaristic, and bureaucratic character of Germany, but without its administrative and financial order, without its inner strength and influence. I had felt repelled by Germany, but the Habsburg Empire repelled me more. The traditional anti-Austrian training of a Czech had caused all these feelings to take systematic shape from my youth onwards; I was instinctively a social and national malcontent when I left home. After some time, in 1907 and 1908, believing almost fanatically in the strength and influence of democratic principles, I expected that a change and a regeneration would result from universal suffrage in Austria. Nevertheless, I returned a convinced radical and revolutionary, even though my early training and the hardships of life had taught me at home before the war to suppress passions and sentiments, to master them by means of the intellect and to preserve a political calm and balance.

The long study of Socialism and social problems at home and abroad had strengthened the conviction in me that we were approaching a period when several fundamental problems concerning the structure of our society would be basically solved. The political struggle within the Austro-Hungarian Empire, the fight for universal suffrage, the Bosnian annexation crisis of 1908, the sway of absolutism in Bohemia and Croatia, convinced me that we were passing through a time of great political crisis, which would lead either smoothly or by cataclysms to fundamental changes.

In 1908 I had two further aims : to see Russia and to secure a living at home by obtaining a teaching post. I also thought of qualifying for a university professorship, spending some time in special academic work. Then, after adequate political preparation and training,—I reckoned that I should have to devote at least another ten years to self-education and political preparation,—I would make an attempt to enter politics. Accordingly, between 1908 and 1914, I studied political economy, sociology, and philosophy, preparing for my professorship and university duties. In the autumn of 1908 Professor Masaryk, who had followed the journalistic work I had done abroad, asked me to call upon him. He suggested that I should qualify for a university post in philosophy and sociology, promised me support, and gave me a number of hints for further work.

About the same time Dr. Fořt,[1] who was then a member of the Viennese Cabinet, also invited me to see him. He praised the work I had done abroad and invited me to join the Young Czech Party and to become one of its political workers. He pointed out the advantages which this would involve, the possibility of a comfortable existence and a career. I politely declined his offer. About the same time Dr. Šmeral,[2] the editor of *Právo Lidu*,[3] of which I had been a correspondent, and was still a contributor, asked me to pay him a visit. He was a leading figure in the party, and he indicated to me that if I would join the party and work for it he would look after my interests. Not wishing then to enter the domain of practical politics, I did not make any decision. Moreover, even at that time I maintained a certain reserve towards Dr. Šmeral, of whose views, which

[1] Dr. Joseph Fořt (b. 1850), a Czech politician and a prominent leader of the National Party of Liberal Thought. For a time was a Cabinet minister in the Austrian Parliament. After the war he took no part in political life.

[2] Dr. B. Šmeral (b. 1880), one of the leaders of the Czech Social Democrats, who, during the war, tended to pursue a policy of opportunism. After the establishment of the Czechoslovak Republic his activities in the Social Democratic Party were in the direction of Communism.

[3] *Právo Lidu (The People's Rights)*, the central press organ of the Czechoslovak Social Democratic Party. Founded 1891 and has appeared daily since 1900.

were strictly Marxist in theory, I did not approve. I continued, however, to be a contributor to *Právo Lidu* up to the beginning of the war, even after I had entered Masaryk's party. I had always been on good terms with the Social Democratic Party, in which I had close friends and excellent opportunities for working.

In the Progressive Party,[1] which I entered shortly afterwards, but in which, on the whole, I did little practical work, I belonged to a kind of moderate opposition. I had always been opposed to "diehard Realism," which seemed to me to lack political and vital qualities, besides being rigid, doctrinaire, and sometimes petty. In its essence it was non-revolutionary and non-radical, despite the fact that it was uncompromising in the forms it assumed. I worked with the younger men and sought a closer co-operation with the radical elements in our public life, aiming at the formation of a large group with progressive tendencies in political and social matters.

(b) MY PHILOSOPHICAL PREPARATIONS

3

My scientific and philosophical study during these years had confronted me with the necessity of adjusting the struggle within me to a definite philosophical attitude and system. This was what I had been striving after throughout my ten years of study and preparation. The four years of war supplemented in a practical manner what I had studied theoretically; they brought my theories into harmony with the realities of life.

When I joined the University I had already devoted some time to the study of Socialism and Masaryk's Realism. From this I had retained what I was then capable of absorbing. In the case of Realism this consisted more of the negative side, such as the objection to exaggerated nationalism, to demagogy, to jingoism, to superficiality in all political, literary, and social questions, the objection to political and literary romanticizing. It had provided me also with the realistic method of working. As regards Socialism, I acquired, above all, a leaning towards

---

[1] The Progressive (Realist) Party, founded 1900 from among the adherents of Professor Masaryk. It was recruited mainly from intellectual circles, and although not numerically strong it had a considerable influence on other parties.

positivism and materialism. My direct touch with Masaryk caused me to reflect upon the fundamentals of philosophic controversies. I was attracted by positivism, which rather led me away from Masaryk, who, however, continued to disturb and harass me by his destructive analysis of everything in positivism which I had regarded as philosophically sound.

My return to Prague, my preparations to take up a university post, and my work as a lecturer completed my philosophical development. Hacking my way through, so to speak, to settled views (Masaryk and his books helped me more than others), I gradually began to make these views hold good in metaphysics, ethics, psychology, and sociology. In the course of the war I transferred them from theory to practical politics. I always consciously practised politics in a scientific spirit, and if during and after the war I achieved any political successes, this was mainly due to the fact that I have always consistently applied my philosophy and my scientific method to political problems.

All these problems made me aware of the discrepancy between the culture and life of Western and Eastern Europe. It was a conflict with a noetic basis—the intellectualist West, the intuitivist and mystical East. I saw the two extremes clearly, and I formed a conclusion as to the proper relationship between them and as to their synthesis at which our nation in particular should aim.

From my earliest years the problem of religion had greatly attracted and disturbed me. Brought up as a strict Catholic, while still a boy I experienced—unconsciously and instinctively, perhaps—several phases of religious misgiving. School and university flung me into the opposite stream of religious negation, positivist opposition to religion and anti-clerical radicalism. My studies in France, England, and Germany—more particularly my experiences in England—had compelled me to seek new solutions. My internal struggle for a philosophic outlook, the study of Kant, Hume, Descartes, and Masaryk, had finally led me to adopt a positive attitude towards the problem of religion also. On this basis I had arrived at firm religious views accepting the belief in immanent teleology and in Providence as destiny.

On the philosophic side, therefore, I found myself on fairly firm ground in 1914. I felt myself sure in my philosophical and religious assumptions ; I had my clarified ethical views, based on the principle of full respect for mankind, and I had worked out in quite a detailed manner the ideas of critical realism in sociology and politics.

4

Thus, when the war broke out, its political meaning was, on the whole, obvious to me, while it was morally clear what I could, would, and must do. I never hesitated either for reasons of personal conviction or of practical political opportunism. From the very beginning one idea presented itself to me, and that was the consciousness of duty, the knowledge that the great moment had come when everybody who could and would accomplish something, must and would be an instrument of Providence in great and small things.

As far as political practice was concerned, I considered the conditions in our country so dislocated, and the leading circles in Vienna sufficiently alive to their own interests, that even on July 26, 1914, I was convinced that a way would be found to adjust matters and avoid war. From the beginning of the conflict with Serbia I felt that Austria-Hungary, being internally weak and having no centrifugal force amid its diversity of nations, would pay a severe penalty even for a victorious war. I therefore wondered what penalty it would pay if it lost a war engaged in by a number of Great Powers, whose centrifugal forces would certainly be greater than ever before. The penalty would undoubtedly be the loss of its political existence.

It also seemed to me that the war would result in a great social upheaval equal to a social revolution. During my stay abroad I had followed the results of Edward VII's diplomatic activity, and, at the same time, I had observed that French public opinion was, for the greater part, decidedly opposed to the propaganda of revenge. I believed in the possibility and even in the inevitability of an Anglo-German war which would be brought about mainly by economic competition, the German need for expansion, the German pressure upon Turkey and the Persian Gulf, and England's concern about her colonies and her naval mastery. But I was unable to form any clear conception of a war which would be entered into by Austria-Hungary and Russia, since I judged that the ruling classes of both those States were aware of the danger of a social revolution. At that time I was less well acquainted with their disputes about the Balkans and Balkan conditions.

That is why the war, for which Austria-Hungary was responsible in 1914, surprised me as an event of world politics, even though, in a political, philosophical, and moral respect I was prepared for it. I accordingly formulated the whole dilemma with which the Habsburg Empire was faced. Either it would come to an end through losing the war, or it would come to an end in a social upheaval and a revolution after the war. And it was in accordance with this alternative that our arrangements had to be made.

Such were the considerations which guided my action from the beginning of the conflict to its end. Now that the fateful moment had arrived I began, with a calm mind, determined to go to any length and to sacrifice everything, to carry out a revolution.

II

THE BEGINNINGS OF OUR REVOLUTIONARY MOVEMENT

(a) PROFESSOR MASARYK'S ACTIVITY

5

WHEN the first volleys were fired against Belgrade, I was spending my holidays in the country. The entry of England into the war meant, in my judgment, the certain defeat of Germany and accordingly, for the reasons already mentioned, the probable end of Austria-Hungary. I explained these views to my wife and my closest friends, and at the same time I expressed my determination to enter upon revolutionary activity against the Habsburg Empire for the purpose of hastening its end.

A few days later I went to Prague to see what impression the events had made on the ordinary people there, what views of the situation were taken by a number of my friends in the Progressive Party,[1] among the National Socialists,[2] and in Social Democratic circles. A week later I paid another visit to Prague and decided to apply for a passport. I had at once taken several eventualities into account; it would perhaps be a good thing to see what was going on abroad; it would perhaps be necessary to escape if I were called up for the army; or, finally, the necessity would perhaps arise of making good my escape should there be any revolutionary movement which would make it dangerous to remain at home.

I spent the month of August in a state of suspense, following events at home and on the Western front, paying weekly visits

---

[1] The Progressive (Radical) State Rights Party came into existence as a result of what is known as the Progressive movement in 1897. Its programme adhered consistently to the historic State rights, demanding the restoration of an independent Czech State. The leader of the party was Dr. Antonín Hajn, and before the war its press organ, *Samostatnost* (*Independence*), used to appear daily.

[2] The National Socialist Party came into existence in the same year as the Radical Progressive Party (1897), and it had the same political programme, for which, however, it aimed at securing support from among the masses. Its leader was V. Klofáč, and its organ the daily paper *České Slovo* (*The Czech Word*).

to Prague to see how it was reacting to events. I was in touch with the young Progressives, and I learnt also from the journalist Šašek that at the very beginning of August the young Radicals (later joined by the young Progressives) had met, had discussed the war, and had evinced the desire to do something. They wanted somebody to go abroad(3) and to send news home. I at once got into touch with a number of them.

It was about September 10th when I decided to join the staff of the newspaper *Čas* [1] and work there as an unpaid contributor. At the same time I intended to visit Professor Masaryk and tell him my opinion of what was taking place. I was exceedingly dissatisfied with the events and conditions at home. Among the leaders there were still marked traces of the quarrels due to the Šviha affair,[2] while public opinion was in a state of confusion. The arrests of a number of people (Klofáč,[3] for example) had, on the whole, not produced any reaction. With few exceptions the Press was behaving badly, expressing its fulsome approval of the mobilization, which had been accomplished without a hitch. Certain of the parties distinguished themselves in this respect to such a degree that it filled me with repugnance and shame. At the same time I was observing the advance of the Germans in the West and the first Austrian failures in Serbia. In spite of the overwhelming advance of the Germans on Paris, when I again recapitulated all my memories of Paris, of the spirit of France, of the moral qualities of the French people, I was filled with hope, if not with certainty, that the French would rally and hold out. And I felt that we could not continue in our present attitude, that the attitude of our Press and our passive policy were hopeless. Something would have to be done.

This was what I told Professor Masaryk whom I met while on my way to his house. The end of our long conversation on events at home, on the situation of Germany, France,

---

[1] *Čas* (*The Age*), the organ of the Realist Progressive Party. It was founded in 1886 and became a daily in 1900. It exerted considerable influence under the editorship of Dr. Jan Herben. Professor Masaryk and J. S. Machar, in particular, were its regular contributors. It was suspended at the beginning of the war, and after the war it was renewed for a short period (1920–23).

[2] Dr. Karel Šviha, the Parliamentary deputy of the National Socialist Party. In 1913 he was accused of being connected with the Austrian police, and he resigned his mandate.

[3] V. Klofáč ((b. 1868), founder and for many years the leader of the National Socialist Party. Was Minister of National Defence in the first Czechoslovak Government.

England, and Russia, which took place on that pleasant autumn day on the slope of Letná,[1] with its delightful view of the whole beauty of Prague, was that Professor Masaryk informed me that he had already started working and that we should therefore work together. He further told me that he was in touch with abroad and that he proposed very shortly to visit Holland. He added, however, that at the moment he was concerned about a number of his foreign friends whom the war had brought into an awkward situation. He also said that money was needed, and would be needed too, should we embark upon any political activity. Even at that time he expressed considerable fears about the ability of France to hold out, and he did not disguise his doubts with regard to Russia, in whose success he did not believe. He was quite hopeful about the English.

I at once went over my personal accounts and promised to provide financial help. In a few days I was able to supply Professor Masaryk with the first instalment of funds. We agreed that I should go regularly to the office of *Čas* and that my further work for the paper would develop in accordance with the views and plans which we exchanged.

6

In August 1914 Professor Masaryk proceeded on his first journey to Holland, where he got into touch with his English friends, Mr. Wickham Steed and Dr. Seton Watson. He wrote also to Professor Denis and gave him an account of the situation. On his return he called together the first meeting of his friends in the Progressive Party to tell them of his views and observations and to explain his plans to them. This meeting, like several of those which followed, was a focus from which later was formed what was known as the "Maffia."

This and the subsequent meetings, held at Dr. Bouček's house, were attended by Professor Masaryk and Dr. Bouček,[2] together with Dr. Herben[3]; the journalist Cyril Dušek[4]; Dr.

---

[1] Letná, a park in Prague on a hillside forming the left bank of the Vltava.
[2] Dr. V. Bouček, a Prague barrister and a member of the Realist Party. He was a deputy in the revolutionary National Assembly.
[3] Dr. Jan Herben (b. 1857), a prominent Czech author and journalist, editor-in-chief of *Čas*. He was a deputy in the revolutionary National Assembly, and later a senator of the National Democratic Party, which he left in 1925.
[4] Dr. Cyril Dušek (1882–1924), a journalist on the staff of *Čas*. After the war held diplomatic posts at Berne and Cairo.

Šámal[1]; Dr. Veselý[2]; Dubský, the publisher; and Pfeffermann, an engineer. Professor Masaryk explained in general outline his views about the war, referred to the action of our soldiers, criticized the measures adopted at Vienna, told us what he had learnt about food supplies, armaments, muddles in Vienna, Government plans for persecution, the policy of Archduke Frederick, Thun and Heinold. He urged the necessity for us to pursue a policy which would prevent our being crushed by the war and which would enable us to derive the greatest advantage from it. He also told us what he had seen and learnt in Holland. At the same time he gave us confidential reports from Vienna and even from Government circles such as the Ministries. We saw that he was in touch, on the one hand, with military men, and, on the other hand, with people who were well informed about the situation in the Government.

During subsequent meetings he showed us documents and confidential statements sent by Thun from Prague to Heinold, Minister of the Interior, and Prime Minister Stürgkh. Then there came reports on the ministerial councils, ministerial decrees, letters of Heinold and Stürgkh to Thun, reports sent to Archduke Friedrich's headquarters staff, statements on the political situation in the Czech territories, in Galicia and in the Jugoslav areas, together with reports which made it possible to form a judgment as to the further political plans of the Government and the Supreme Command.

I soon learnt more about the source of these reports. I frequently accompanied Professor Masaryk on his way home from the office of Čas. Gradually, and with some reserve, he told me things which he was unable to mention at the meetings. Thus I heard about his first conversations with Dr. Scheiner,[3] his conversations with other politicians, and also how he, together with Machar, had obtained the extremely valuable documents, to which I have already referred, through Kovanda, who was Heinold's servant and who had offered his services in this matter.

[1] Dr. P. Šámal (b. 1867), a Prague barrister and a politician belonging to the Realist Party. Was a prominent member of the "Maffia," and is now chief of President Masaryk's chancellery.

[2] Dr. F. Veselý (b. 1863), a barrister and politician belonging to the Realist Party. After the war was a member of the National Assembly, where he represented the National Socialist Party, and for a time was Minister of Justice.

[3] Dr. Josef Scheiner, Chairman of the Executive Headquarters of the Sokol Organization.

One day, at the beginning of November, Professor Masaryk suddenly called on me at my residence in Vinohrady. He told me that it was urgent to proceed at once to Vienna and obtain news from Machar.[1] I went the same day. I met Machar the next day in his house, and he told me all about Kovanda, who, during the night, was making typewritten copies of documents which Heinold was bringing home every day to keep himself informed about events and the political situation. The next day Machar introduced me to Kovanda at the Länderbank in order that we could arrange matters between ourselves personally according to our needs.

When Professor Masaryk could not go to Vienna, it was I who went there to fetch documents from Kovanda. On these occasions I learnt many things which afterwards stood me in good stead abroad. This continued after Professor Masaryk had finally gone abroad. The danger which threatened Kovanda caused him to find employment elsewhere in the second year of the war. But what he had done gave us a unique insight into the purposes and political methods of the Viennese Government, of Stürgkh, Heinold, and Thun, and was of the utmost service to us in our work.

I also acted as substitute for Professor Masaryk in the office of *Naše Doba*[2] before his departure abroad. When Machar obtained new documents from Kovanda at Vienna, he sent a postcard saying that he had a manuscript for *Naše Doba*, and I at once went to Vienna. Later on, when my time was more taken up by work in the "Maffia," Jan Hájek, also on the staff of *Čas*, would go to Vienna. The meetings, discussions, visits to Vienna, and attempts at contact with abroad were known not only to Dr. Herben, Dušek, and Hájek, but to the whole staff of *Čas*—Kunte, Šašek, Fischer, Cvetiša, later also Hajšman— although they did not take any direct part in the proceedings. On November 26th Cyril Dušek was arrested and then released, and for that reason was unable to attend the last and most

---

[1] J. S. Machar (b. 1864), poet and author, who at the outbreak of the war was living at Vienna. He exerted great influence on public opinion by his literary activity and, in particular, by his articles in *Čas*, where he co-operated with Professor Masaryk. After the war he spent some time as General Inspector of the Czechoslovak Army, but has now retired from this post and has resumed his work as a writer.

[2] *Naše Doba*, a monthly review, founded in 1893 and issued by the publishing firm of Laichter. Its first editor was Professor Masaryk.

important meeting at Dr. Bouček's. Drtina[1] was on leave from the University, writing his *Introduction to Philosophy* at Hněvšín.[2] I had enlisted Hájek's services at a very early date.

There were several meetings at Dr. Bouček's. The earliest were of an informative character with regard to the general situation. Their tendency was, of course, anti-Austrian, but for the time being they were without any expressly revolutionary or conspiratorial plans. As time went on there were more and more discussions on the possible results of the war, the aims of our policy, and the course of action we should undertake. With the exception of Professor Masaryk all those present, like our public as a whole, were so convinced of the weakness of Austria-Hungary that although they viewed Russia with critical eyes they were convinced that she would gain an easy and fairly rapid victory. The first Russian defeats, however, affected Professor Masaryk more deeply than all the others.

In November Professor Masaryk was already presenting his plans clearly and without reserve. Whatever happened, we must carry on an active opposition to the Government, otherwise we should obtain nothing from Vienna even if Austria were not victorious. And if Austria were to lose we also should have to be called to account. The various political possibilities were discussed. Masaryk admitted the possibility of defeat, but this was not to be regarded as a reason for adopting a passive attitude. For political and moral reasons, active opposition to the Government must be carried on, whatever the outcome of events. We also discussed our possible independence, the frontiers of the State, measures to be adopted at home, the need for work abroad. Masaryk finally announced his decision to go abroad and work there.

In the meanwhile I was travelling frequently to Vienna and, before long, to Germany as well. On his second journey to Holland Professor Masaryk had arranged for Dr. Seton Watson to send us the English papers (*Times* and *Morning Post*) to the Central Post Office at Dresden, as a number of foreign newspapers were allowed in Germany. Then from time to time,

---

[1] František Drtina (1861–1925), University professor and author of various books dealing mainly with the history of philosophy. He was one of the leaders of the Realist Party, which for some time he represented as a deputy in the Reichsrat. During the war he edited *Naše Doba*.

[2] Hněvšín, a village in Central Bohemia, the birthplace of Drtina.

always on Saturdays, I proceeded to Dresden and smuggled the papers across the frontier. In addition I arranged with the Czech waiters in the café opposite the railway station at Dresden to keep for me the Italian, Rumanian, and Dutch newspapers which were circulated in Germany either illicitly or with official permission. In this way I used to bring quite regularly to the office of *Čas* a considerable supply of news, which all of us in the office drew upon until my next excursion. The news thus obtained was utilized, of course, for journalistic purposes, but was also circulated privately. In this way, in the autumn and winter of 1914 and the spring of 1915, in the face of considerable obstacles and dangers, I accomplished a number of journeys, in the course of which I succeeded in smuggling over supplies of newspapers, sometimes also of books and pamphlets.

(b) ATTEMPTS AT CO-OPERATION WITH THE SOCIALISTS

7

In the October and November of 1914 I began more decisively to touch on these questions in socialistic circles. What exasperated me was the policy of the Social Democratic Party (with which I was closely connected), by reason of its intolerable opportunism, the absolutely inexplicable abandonment of its principles, and its attempt to justify its attitude by means of Marxist phrases. In the documents obtained from Kovanda and Machar we had found evidence of how this policy was approved by Vienna, of how the Social Democrats were compromising us in the eyes of history, and of how bad an example it was giving to those of our people who were not carrying out their national revolutionary duty.

I endeavoured to explain the matter to some of the leading elements in the party. What I said was noted rather with satisfaction, for from the secret Government documents it was evident that the party would be protected against persecution, if matters were carried to that length.

As a regular contributor to the literary section of *Právo Lidu*, I began my discussions and arguments with F. V. Krejčí.[1]

---

[1] F. V. Krejčí (b. 1867), a prominent Czech critic who was associated with the Progressive movement. He has contributed to the literary review *Rozhledy* (*Survey*), and then to *Právo Lidu*. Later on he wrote novels and plays.

Krejčí realized how matters stood, but he himself was unable to take any decisive step. I then began to talk to Dr. Soukup [1] and later on with Šmeral. Dr. Soukup hesitated. His hesitation, I think, was partly the outcome of his journey to Switzerland, during which he had talked to various people, including Jean Longuet, who throughout the war was a defeatist and wished to bring it rapidly to an end. These people naturally impressed Dr. Soukup that the Allies had not the remotest interest in our cause. Dr. Soukup accordingly returned in a pessimistic frame of mind, and until the spring of 1915, when I induced him to attend the meetings of the "Maffia," his attitude, out of regard for his party, was on the whole non-committal.

My experiences with Dr. Šmeral were less satisfactory. I had told F. V. Krejčí, who knew my views about the war, much of what I was doing. I made it clear to him in his capacity as a Socialist that we must aim at opposition to the Government, not only in a national, but also in a social respect. I added that it would be immoral for us to support Austria in any way, even by a passive attitude, and I showed that the point at issue was a struggle against the absolutism of Berlin, Vienna, and Budapest. I told him that the Socialist Party was simply failing to carry out its duties if it remained passive, and that it would be committing a crime were it to persist in its present course of action. Finally, I emphasized the fact that the end of the war, if it were not accompanied by the complete military defeat and political downfall of Austria-Hungary, must bring about a social upheaval and that we must at once prepare for these social struggles by subversive activities. It was the duty of the Czech Social Democrats to take their place at the head of all these activities.

As I have said, F. V. Krejčí readily admitted all this and was in full sympathy with the matter, but he had no clear idea of how to proceed with it in the party. Finally he suggested that we should both meet Dr. Soukup and Šmeral in the office of

---

After the war he was a member of the revolutionary National Assembly, and acted as envoy of the Czechoslovak Government to the Czechoslovak army in Siberia.

[1] Dr. F. Soukup (b. 1871), a Prague lawyer, one of the leaders of the Social Democratic Party. Took part in the Progressive movement before the war, and was a deputy in the Reichsrat. He was a member of the "Maffia," and after the war was Minister of Justice in the first Czechoslovak Government. He now represents his party in the Czechoslovak Senate.

account of his discussions with Dr. Hajn,[1] Švehla,[2] and others. He again expounded to me his view of the whole international situation and indicated how we should proceed in the case of various eventualities. He gave me the addresses of persons abroad with whom he was in touch (Mr. Wickham Steed, Dr. Seton Watson, Captain Voska, Ernest Brain, who was *The Times* correspondent in Holland, Professor Milyukov, and Professor Denis). He explained to me what he thought would be our future relationships with Germany, Russia, the Magyars, the Jugoslavs, and Poland. He examined in detail the difficulties which would be encountered in any attempt to unite the Jugoslavs, and he pointed out that we must try to reconcile the Jugoslavs and the Italians to prevent Austria-Hungary deriving any advantage from their dissension. Even at that time he mentioned the possibility of a corridor, and he pointed out the economic and financial problems which would emerge at the beginning of our independence. He also indicated the functions that should be exercised by the National Committee on the collapse of Austria, and expressed his wish for the formation of Sokol legions at home. Finally, he went closely into the question of the arrival of the Russians and of what steps our people ought to take, should this occur.

Professor Masaryk discussed all these matters in considerable detail. For example, he dictated to me the contents of a manifesto to be published in *Čas* if the Russians came. This was moderate and cautious in tone. He proposed a method for arranging the administration in Prague and Brno (he proposed to unite Moravia and Silesia). He also suggested how the mistakes of the Russians could be obviated and what precautions should be taken in case the Russians were driven back again by the Germans. In short, he had a complete political programme for the future in which he had provided for all possible contingencies.

I took down shorthand notes of all these details, as at all

[1] Dr. Antonín Hajn (b. 1868), one of the leaders of the Progressive movement, and then a leader of the Radical Progressive Party (State Rights). For some time he was a deputy in the Reichsrat. He was also editor of the party organ *Samostatnost* (*Independence*), which was founded in 1897. It appeared from 1911 as a daily, and was suspended in 1914. During the war he joined the National Democratic Party, of which he is now a deputy.

[2] Antonín Švehla (b. 1873), a prominent member of the Agrarian Party, of which he became the leader when the Czechoslovak Republic was established. He was Minister of the Interior in the first Czechoslovak Government, and is now Prime Minister.

costs I wanted to keep a record of them for every eventuality. And so, later on, when in danger of being searched, I destroyed many documents, but saved these jottings. Finally, when in September 1915 I went abroad, I put them, together with other notes on discussions with Professor Masaryk in Switzerland, on meetings of the "Maffia," and a number of messages sent by Masaryk to Prague, into a bottle which I buried in a garden in the country place where I was spending my holidays.(5)

We then decided how we were to keep in touch with each other after Masaryk's departure. We first of all agreed upon code-words for telegraphic communications. We arranged whole sentences which were to mean that such and such a person was in prison, that *Čas* was suspended, that there was danger either of the betrayal or arrest of Masaryk, that further persecutions were being prepared, and so on, as the case might be. Our relations with Kovanda made it possible for us to learn of these things in time. We also discussed, at least in rough outlines, how we were to keep in touch should Professor Masaryk not return.

Professor Masaryk left Prague on December 18, 1914. It was arranged that he would return about February 1st by way of Geneva, where he would receive telegraphic information as to whether he could do so safely or not. Should he not return I was to act as a link between him and the politicians with whom he was co-operating at Prague.

These details were arranged shortly before our last meeting at Dr. Bouček's in the first week of December 1914. At this meeting Professor Masaryk described his plans and his intention of returning once more. But he also sketched out what he intended to do if he should be prevented from coming back to Prague. He announced to his friends that for this eventuality he had authorized me to direct the work and to keep in touch with him.

He brought to this meeting a number of documents which had just arrived from Vienna, and he spoke about his last interview with Thun. He again expressed his doubts about the Russians and ended up by giving his conception of what our future State would be like. With regard to the form of the State he was decidedly in favour of a republic and regarded a kingdom as a necessary evil. The Russian dynasty was referred to in this connection, but Professor Masaryk insisted that he would give the preference to some Western dynasty (he mentioned the Duke of Connaught) in order that we might be able more easily to introduce a parliamentary system on the Western model. The frontiers were also discussed, and with regard to them we took into account the racially mixed areas and Slovakia. Masaryk expressed the view that if Austria-Hungary were defeated we should have a Czech national state. If Germany were also crushed we should obtain a state with historical frontiers and including Slovakia.

III

ORIGIN AND ORGANIZATION OF THE "MAFFIA"

(a) My First Journey to Switzerland

9

A FEW days later Professor Masaryk left for Italy via Vienna. I continued my journeys to Vienna and Dresden, collecting material, working in the office of Čas, supplying my friends privately with information about events, and obtaining money for further work.

We received scanty news about Professor Masaryk's stay in Italy. There were only a few messages on postcards sent to members of his family. The Austrian authorities in Rome, however, were following his activities and sent full statements about him. In particular, they had ascertained that he was in touch with the Jugoslavs, and informed Vienna about his seditious activities with Supilo and Trumbić. We received news about this from Machar and Kovanda in Vienna and we were much disturbed by it. At last we shared the view of Dr. Šámal that it would be better for Masaryk not to return. Professor Masaryk left Rome for Switzerland and on January 20, 1915, a student named Lavička, reached Prague with messages and inquiries from him as to whether he should return. I sent Lavička back with the reply that he should not, as Baron Macchio, the Austrian Ambassador in Rome, had been reporting very unfavourably on his movements. I also sent him a message to the effect that in view of the changed situation I proposed coming to Switzerland during the half-yearly university vacation at the beginning of February to make arrangements about further action.

After Lavička had left, I suddenly received a postcard from Machar asking me to come to Vienna at once as he had an important manuscript for Naše Doba. When I saw Machar he gave me the text of a telegram from the Austro-Hungarian Embassy in Rome, signed by Baron Macchio. This telegram contained the following passage: "Dragisir, mentioned in my telegrams, informs me that Professor Masaryk intends to

return to Bohemia within the next few days." The telegram
had been sent just before Masaryk's departure from Rome
and we had received it rather late.(6) In conjunction with
former reports which had arrived from Vienna we, together
with Machar and later also with our friends in Prague, inferred
from the telegram that matters were really serious. I therefore immediately acted as had been agreed. I sent a code
telegram to Geneva announcing that the situation was very
dangerous and that it was impossible for him to return.
Fearing, however, that something might happen to the telegram, and being uncertain whether Lavička had already
reached Masaryk with our message, I was alarmed at the
thought that Professor Masaryk might cross the frontier and
be arrested. I therefore decided at the last moment that at
all costs I myself would cross the frontier to warn him personally
and induce him to remain in Switzerland.

I had a passport dating from August 1914. In the meanwhile, however, passport regulations had become more stringent
and my passport was no longer valid because it contained no
photograph. Moreover, I had been called up for the second
levy and therefore had no military permission for a journey
abroad. For these reasons, on the day of my return from
Vienna, I obtained an identity book through an old school
friend who was at the Vinohrady police headquarters. With
this and my old passport I started off for Zurich via Vienna.
After a double inspection in Tyrol and numerous difficulties
on the frontiers, I reached Buchs just at the time when
Professor Masaryk, in accordance with the pre-arranged plan,
was to have left Geneva.

10

We met at Zurich at the beginning of 1915 at the Hôtel
Victoria. Professor Masaryk had been accompanied there by
Vsevolod Svatkovsky, a Russian journalist, who afterwards
rendered valuable services to our cause in the Government
circles at Petrograd and in diplomatic Russian circles in Western
Europe. Before the war he had spent a long time as a journalist
in Vienna. He knew Professor Masaryk, Dr. Kramář,[1] and other

[1] Dr. Karel Kramář (b. 1860), a prominent Czech politician, who, before
the war, represented the Young Czech Party in the Reichsrat at Vienna.
During the war he was sentenced to death by Austria, but was afterwards
amnestied. He was the first Czechoslovak Prime Minister, and is now the
leader of the National Democratic Party.

Czech politicians; he had studied Polish and Jugoslav politics, and he was familiar with affairs in Vienna. During the war he became chief Russian correspondent at Berne, Paris, and Rome, sending his reports direct to Petrograd. He was also in touch with military men. He at once began to co-operate with Professor Masaryk in Switzerland, and he had come to Zurich partly to hear my reports and impressions, partly also to get into closer touch with a number of our people there. He had his agents at Vienna and in Bohemia, and he was anxious, with my help, to improve and extend the organization of these links.

I informed Professor Masaryk of what had happened at Prague and why the situation made it impossible for him to return. It was with reluctance that he abandoned the idea of paying a final visit to Prague. He did not consider that the ground had been adequately prepared for a well-organized co-operation between our people at home and abroad. It accordingly became necessary to draw up a further plan for keeping in touch with Prague.

In the course of his conversation with Svatkovsky and myself Professor Masaryk announced, first of all, that he had decided to remain abroad throughout the war and to begin a resolute struggle against Austria, with a full acceptance of the personal and political consequences to himself which this would involve. What he aimed at was to organize the first modern group of Czech political *émigrés* who, in concert with the politicians at home, would take open and responsible action against Austria-Hungary. This was what I was to announce to all our friends and to the political circles with whom Professor Masaryk had been dealing before his departure from Prague. I was also to obtain either their tacit or open consent.

Masaryk further indicated to me the somewhat unfavourable impressions he had formed on his last journey to Rome. Austro-Hungarian affairs were imperfectly understood; the Allies took but little interest in our cause, and if we desired to gain something for our nation during the war we ourselves must get to work and draw attention to our claims.

Much would have to be done, however, to make the existence of the political *émigrés* possible. Above all, we needed money. Professor Masaryk therefore asked me again to arrange financial resources. He mentioned Dr. Scheiner and the Sokol [1]

---

[1] Sokol: The Sokols are an organization which was founded (primarily as a gymnastic society) by Miroslav Tyrš, assisted by Jindřich Fügner, in 1862.

funds, and I once more promised that I myself would also send money. I was particularly to emphasize the fact in Prague that the political *émigrés* of other nations, notably the Poles, were well off, while ours would be faced with considerable difficulties. Professor Masaryk intended to apply to acquaintances in America, but he insisted that some serious step in this respect must be taken at home, for without money no political action could be carried on abroad.

Another point was the selection of people and methods of work. Masaryk asked me to lay stress upon the need for somebody else among our politicians to leave home, however difficult this might be, in order that our political *émigrés* could acquire more significance by reason of their numbers. He pointed out how many Jugoslav *émigrés* there were. In addition we should need political workers and journalists because our colonies abroad did not contain many suitable persons for this purpose, and even those who were available were imperfectly acquainted with our conditions at home.

Finally, he agreed with Svatkovsky to send me with a message to Dr. Kramář. Svatkovsky had previously been indirectly in touch with the entourage of Dr. Kramář, whose political tendencies he had shared at the beginning of the war. It had been his endeavour to bring our affairs into a purely Russian sphere of influence, and he was anxious for Russian troops to reach Prague and attend to our interests there. At the same time, however, he was familiar with the conditions in Petrograd and he regarded them with the more critical eye of a Western European observer. He agreed with many of Masaryk's criticisms and misgivings, and during this first conversation he quite openly expressed to me his own fears. In particular, even at that time what he demanded from our people, with their Slavonic and Russian sympathies, was to be energetic, hardworking, venturesome, and unselfish, for he did not suppose that the victory of Russia would be an easy and simple matter. Moreover, he was aware of the alarm in Western Europe with regard to the expansion of Russia, and he was therefore cautious about all those political plans in which Russia was involved.

Since then it has developed into a national movement, with a membership of over 350,000. The Sokol funds, here referred to, consist of the subscriptions of the members, which are used for the purpose of establishing gymnasiums, libraries, and other centres of physical and intellectual culture.

And so I was sent to Dr. Kramář by Professor Masaryk and Svatkovsky in order that I might tell him of their impressions and deliver their messages. Svatkovsky asked me in particular to tell Dr. Kramář from him that something really must be done against Austria, and both expressed the view that it would be best if Dr. Kramář were to leave home and engage upon work abroad.

The last subject of our discussion was the question of how Professor Masaryk was to keep in permanent touch with our people at home. He told me to form a secret committee from among our political workers. In the manner of the Russian revolutionary methods, such a committee would have numerous ramifications at home; it would illicitly keep up communication with abroad and would be permanently in touch with official Czech and Viennese politics. From behind the scenes it would exert an influence on the conduct of policy at home and would keep the organized political émigrés informed about what was happening there. He also mentioned to me that it would be necessary to distribute this organization over the rural districts, to have a secret printing-press, and devoted helpers prepared at once to replace any of the members who might be arrested.

The share which Professor Masaryk entrusted to me was to maintain the connections with abroad and thus to co-ordinate what was being done at home. This would mean being in touch with the members of the Committee, collecting material and dispatching it abroad with the help of couriers. From time to time I should also attempt to make similar journeys myself. Masaryk urged the need of being always prepared for arrest and of having a substitute in case this should happen, because the connection with Prague must never be interrupted. We arranged with Svatkovsky a telegraphic code, a scheme for the sending of couriers, and the type of news, especially that of a military character, in which he was particularly interested. He promised me that at the beginning he would place some of his own couriers at our disposal.

(b) FIRST MEETING OF THE "MAFFIA"

II

When this had been accomplished I returned to Prague. At that time the atmosphere in Bohemia was tense. The frontiers were almost entirely closed and the defeats in Serbia and on the Russian front had produced an uneasiness which we all still remember. It was important for me to obtain as much interesting political and military news as possible, and I therefore made notes of what Masaryk and Svatkovsky had told me, especially about conditions in the seats of war and the action of our troops in Russia and France. I also bought a large number of military and political books which it would be possible to use at home for propagandist purposes. On my way back, I hid my written notes under the seat of the railway carriage in which I made the journey direct from Zurich to Vienna, and I put the parcel of books in the lavatory among the belongings of the railway employees. In this way I managed to pass successfully through two inspections. My passport had been taken away from me after an unpleasant scene at the Austrian Consulate in Zurich and had been replaced by a new one which entitled me only to return to Prague and would then be no longer valid.

I reached Prague in the middle of February and at once began to carry out our plans. I first delivered all the messages to Dr. Scheiner and Dr. Šámal, the latter of whom agreed to speak to Dr. Kramář and arrange for me to meet him. This meeting took place shortly after my return at Dr. Šámal's residence, where from that time onwards all the chief meetings of the "Maffia" were held.

It was my first meeting with Dr. Kramář, and the impression it left upon me was an agreeable one. Dr. Kramář received me in that cordial manner which is typical of him, and when I gave him an account of affairs in Switzerland and had delivered the messages from there he expressed complete agreement with Masaryk's undertaking.

From a political and military point of view the time was fairly favourable. The course of events on the Serbian and Russian fronts looked black for Vienna and Budapest. In Serbia, after the loss of Belgrade, Austria was unable to take any further action at all, while in Galicia the Russians were approaching Cracow. As Dr. Kramář was absolutely certain of a victory for Russia, Svatkovsky's recommendation, which I had brought with me, gained me his complete confidence. He agreed with the duties I had undertaken and expressed confidence in the course of action proposed by Dr. Šámal. We were to remain in constant personal touch, and whenever necessary we were to meet at Dr. Šámal's.

There were a few matters of principle or opinion in which I noticed that Dr. Kramář showed a marked disagreement with Masaryk. He indicated to me his absolute confidence in the part which Russia would play and the success which she would achieve in the struggle for our independence. He also told me what he thought about the political international tendencies of the future independent State, and of the close constitutional and political relationship between our State and Russia. He also said that it would be Russia who would decide the whole matter of the war for us, and that it would therefore be necessary for him to be at Prague and to direct matters in a fitting manner at the moment when the Russians reached us. He therefore hinted at this very first meeting that while it was a good thing for Masaryk to be abroad, his own place was not abroad but at home.

This attitude bewildered me. I began to raise objections, mentioning what Masaryk had told me and what Svatkovsky had confirmed. I pointed out to him the guarded attitude of Paris and London towards Russia, whose expansion was the cause of alarm, and I showed that we must therefore be cautious in our dealings with Western Europe. I repeated Masaryk's doubts about the relationship of Russia to us and the Jugoslavs, and also Svatkovsky's criticisms of the unprepared and backward state of affairs in Petrograd. Dr. Kramář disposed of my fears very briefly, expressing the view that when the time came, his personal intervention with Izvolsky on the subject of our cause would put matters right.

I saw that the divergence of views could not be eliminated in the case of Dr. Kramář by any further discussion, and I therefore deferred to his authority. It was enough for me that Dr. Kramář had heard the whole message, had given his consent to our work, had accepted the scheme of organization, had expressed a desire to keep in touch with us, and had agreed that we should hold further meetings as soon as fresh news came from Switzerland, or in case it were necessary to make any important resolutions. He also expressed his agreement with the suggestion that another one of our politicians should proceed abroad. I at once visited Dr. Scheiner and informed him of the main points in my conversation with Dr. Kramář. I also arranged with him and Dr. Šámal the final form which our organization and activities should take.

Dr. Scheiner then recommended me also to Dr. Rašín,[1] with whom I at once had a meeting at the offices of *Národní Listy*.[2] Through the Sokol organization Dr. Scheiner had arranged copious supply of military news, and he wanted to organize my dealings with Dr. Rašín so that the information which each of us obtained for transmission abroad could be mutually supplemented. We at once got on admirably with Dr. Rašín. He gave me a cordial reception in his editorial office and we had no difficulty in arranging a detailed and systematic collaboration. This work brought out all his courage, energy, and determination, and I have the most pleasant memories of our friendly relations which continued until the time of his imprisonment.

From now onwards began a systematic communication between these various centres for a mutual supply of information, and this led to the first regular meetings of the secret organization known as the "Maffia."

12

The first meeting of the new organization took place at the beginning of March 1915 at Dr. Šámal's, those present comprising Dr. Kramář, Dr. Rašín, Dr. Scheiner, and myself. This first meeting was taken up by a recapitulation of the news from Switzerland, by a consideration of ways and means for obtaining and dispatching news, and by a discussion on the military and political situation. I also communicated further news about the situation at home which I had obtained recently from documents at Vienna. We also considered the following three important questions :

(*a*) Our army in Russia and the lack of prominent people there with adequate authority. Further, Masaryk's proposal that Dr. Scheiner, as head of the Sokol movement, should escape to Russia for the purpose of directing the organization of our military affairs.

[1] Dr. Alois Rašin (1867–1923) was associated with the Progressive movement, and from 1907 was one of the leading members of the Party of Liberal Thought. During the war he, together with Dr. Kramář, was imprisoned and sentenced to death, but later received an amnesty. He was the first Czechoslovak Minister of Finance, and it was due to his skilful handling of the currency question that the economic position of Czechoslovakia was stabilized at a very early date.

[2] *Národní Listy*, one of the oldest Czech daily papers. It was founded in 1860 and was originally the organ of the Party of Liberal Thought. Since the establishment of the Czechoslovak Republic it has been the organ of the National Democrats.

(b) Our political *émigrés* in general and which one of our politicians should join them. It was clear to all that someone must join Masaryk. At the same time Dr. Scheiner and myself emphasized the financial side of things, and Dr. Scheiner was authorized to find some way of releasing the Sokol funds, which for fear of confiscation had been placed under strict control and could be issued only with the consent of persons whom we could not initiate into our plan.

(c) The extending of our circle of helpers and the admission of more representatives of Czech political parties to our organization, which would thus include all the trustworthy political elements at home and at the same time form a proper link with our revolutionary movement abroad. It was agreed that we must increase our numbers, but that extreme caution must be adopted in our choice of parties and persons. Thus, Dr. Kramář and Dr. Rašín adopted a guarded attitude towards the radical Progressives and the national Socialists, while as regards the Social Democrats there were many differences of opinion. It was, however, agreed—at the very first meeting, if I remember rightly—that we should take the Social Democrats, in the person of Dr. Soukup, into our confidence and invite their co-operation.

We were certain that the radical parties would agree to any revolutionary undertaking, but there remained the Agrarian, the Old Czech, and the Clerical Parties for us to consider. I think that several of those present said that the attitude of the Agrarian Party in general was guarded, the impression prevailing there that Austria-Hungary would win the war and that any revolutionary undertaking would be foolhardy. It was therefore proposed that for the time being we should not invite anybody from the Agrarian Party to collaborate with us direct; but the wish was expressed that Švehla should at least be informed in general terms about what we were undertaking abroad, in order that at any decisive moment the party should not take any action against us. With regard to the Old Czechs, it was decided that for the time being no representative of theirs should be asked to join us, while the Clerical Party were ruled out *a priori* on account of the markedly pro-Austrian character of their policy. On this we were unanimous.

Dr. Scheiner's position amongst us was that of a representative of the Sokol movement. My function was that of a link with abroad, and I also acted as a kind of unappointed secretary in whose hands the home and foreign news was concentrated and who, in agreement with Dr. Šámal, was to summon meetings when news was received from abroad or if anything important happened at home. I was also to keep in practical touch with our workers abroad.

During the following week we succeeded directly or indirectly in inducing the Social Democrats and radical Progressives to share our activities. I myself, somewhat contrary to the wishes of Dr. Kramář and Rašín, entered into touch with the leading radicals, such as Dr. Hajn and Viktor Dyk.[1]

(c) Conspiratorial Activity of the "Maffia." The Financing of our Revolutionary Plans

13

The whole organization of the "Maffia" thus began to acquire firmer outlines. As I have said, we used to meet at Dr. Šámal's whenever I received important news, either home or foreign, or when any request was received from Masaryk. I myself was in touch with Vienna, with various circles in Prague, and with the police.(7) Dr. Scheiner had extensive connections with the Sokols, and with military circles, and so had Dr. Šámal. Dr. Rašín knew a large number of people in politics and business. He used to obtain very good information from official circles, especially in connection with the railways, and sometimes he brought the complete text of secret instructions. From these individual groups in which—as was natural and proper—the members of the political "Maffia" did not generally know who the other collaborators were, the whole of our revolutionary organization in its final form was constituted.

Since my return from Zurich I had been in a state of continual tension. Not wishing to arouse suspicion, I continued my teaching work at the Commercial Academy and my lectures at the University. I paid frequent visits to Dr. Scheiner at his residence, and during the spring of 1915 we used to meet every morning in the Rieger Park, where we went for walks, and on one of these morning strolls we held a complete regular meeting of the

---

[1] Viktor Dyk (b. 1877), a Czech poet and author, who, before the war, was associated with the State Rights Progressive Party. During the war he was imprisoned for his anti-Austrian activities and now represents the National Democrats in the Czechoslovak National Assembly.

"Maffia." I used to visit Dr. Rašín regularly and often in the office of *Národní Listy* or at his home, and was in continuous daily touch with Dr. Šámal. I met Dr. Kramář at our meetings, and on two occasions I went to see him at his villa. Sometimes I used to accompany him from the meetings of the "Maffia," and we then had interesting political discussions which plainly showed me what his political tendencies and aims would be in the future, and how great the divergencies were between his views and those of Professor Masaryk and myself.

After I had collected material every day from various sources I would arrange it at home, and then, with the help of Hájek, Werstadt, and my wife, dispatched it regularly to Switzerland. This was done in various ways, and it was done frequently, sometimes every day. Professor Masaryk began to send couriers to me from Switzerland as early as January 1915. The first of these, as I have already mentioned, was the student Lavička and another was L. V. Fáček, who, for the purposes of his revolutionary activity, assumed the name of Strejček. It was he who supplied me with a cipher code for correspondence and a number of addresses in Switzerland to which letters and couriers could be sent. He also devised a set of fictitious names for those concerned in the conspiracy. Thus Professor Masaryk was called Hradecký; Svatkovsky was Fürst; Dr. Scheiner—Dr. Soukal; Dr. Šámal—Trkal; Dr. Kramář—Holec; Dr. Rašín—Schiel, later Ritter; Hájek—Král. I was known as Spolný, and later, on my numerous journeys, I assumed the names of Bělský, Berger, Novotný, König, and Šícha. It was under the latter name that I managed to escape the frontier, and in Holland I was known as Leblanc.

I used to send news regularly by post to Switzerland to the addresses of our fellow-countrymen who had settled there, most of whom were artisans. Various devices were adopted for this purpose. I prepared postcards in the following way: I would open them out into two halves, each of the same size, and insert the cipher message between them. I then had them joined together by a bookbinder so that no trace of the operation was left and the suspicions of the censor were not aroused. At other times I employed the same device with books, which formed our most frequent means of communication. I inserted long reports into the covers or the backs of books and sometimes I made word for word copies of documents obtained by Machar and Kovanda at Vienna. These reports were sent to Switzerland, and it sometimes happened that details of the proceedings in the Ministerial Council at Vienna appeared four or five days afterwards in the Allied Press. On other occasions items from Vienna were published in *La Nation Tchèque* and, as we ascertained, they infuriated the Government and police circles at Vienna. For they made it clear how rapid the communication was between Vienna, Prague, and Switzerland, and they accordingly demonstrated the efficiency of our organization.

For a long time, as arranged with Svatkovsky, I had ample opportunities for sending specially worded telegrams. It was not until the declaration of war by Italy that this had to be stopped, because most of these telegrams were sent to Rome. From May 1915 onwards all postal communication became increasingly difficult because persons sending letters abroad had to state their identity at the post office or at least leave an address for the reply. I therefore spent a great deal of time going from one Prague post office to another and giving sham addresses. I was prepared to be arrested in the event of any serious hitch.

This work made it necessary to be always on the alert. It also involved a good deal of travelling and the expenditure of much money. One of the most wearisome things we had to do was to codify or decipher messages. As time went on I obtained helpers for this, particularly Jan Hájek, my wife, and Miss Olič. Now and then I had occasional helpers or others who had joined the movement by chance. Thus, before my departure, I took Werstadt and Dr. Butter into my confidence, and they continued the work after I had left. It was about this time that we attempted to send messages through the advertisement columns of the Prague daily papers, mostly in the *Národní Politika* and *Prager Tagblatt*, but this scheme did not prove very successful. In the second phase of our activities it became necessary to limit ourselves to the use of couriers, for by this time our postal communications were likely to be discovered.(8) Moreover, the Austrian Government had taken to holding up letters intentionally for weeks at a time and this rendered information less valuable.

Long and interesting chapters could be devoted to an account of our couriers, but I will limit myself to mentioning a few of the most noteworthy of them. There was, for example, L. V. Fáček, to whom I have already referred. For a long time he travelled regularly between Prague and Switzerland, facing considerable risks. Like the other couriers he carried messages inside books, in the handles of bags and trunks, in pencils and fountain-pens, and also inside keys, which were specially made for this purpose. He brought back messages and, later on, large supplies of *La Nation Tchèque* and *Československa Samostatnost* in small trunks with hollow sides and in similar articles. I should here point out that on the other side of the frontier we had a kind of revolutionary workshop with a paid staff who assisted us in a systematic manner. There were some interesting incidents in connection with the courier Beneš, who went under the name of Frič. He was an enthusiastic Czech patriot, seventy years of age, who had served as a volunteer in the Franco-Prussian War. By a misunderstanding he had been sent in the first week of June with a message to Dr. Rašín. This message was hidden in a short English pipe, but Dr. Rašín, not having been informed beforehand that the courier was coming, was alarmed. He thought that it was a trick on the part of the Austrian police and in the presence of the courier he threw the pipe into the fire.(9) Old Beneš, who himself was very much scared, went away without leaving any address and thinking that he had been discovered. With the help of Hájek and Hajšman, however, who obtained the details from Dr. Rašín, he was run to earth in Prague and invited to a meeting. Hajšman discovered him and, in accordance with a pre-arranged plan, brought him to Václav Square, where he handed him over to Hájek. The latter informed him that he was to meet Spolný and took him to Charles Square, round by the New Town prison. These proceedings struck old Beneš as being suspicious. He knew the name of Dr. Beneš, but he did not know that the name which he assumed as a revolutionary was Spolný. He told Hájek that he knew Charles Square and also that there was a prison in the neighbourhood. Then, being suddenly filled with suspicion that he was being taken to prison, he refused to go and meet Spolný. Finally, after an animated scene, Hájek succeeded in inducing Beneš to accompany him. At Žitná Street, Hájek passed old Beneš on to me. He was still full of mistrust and was totally unable to make out what we were up to. We acted in this way because we feared that Beneš might be followed by the police. I told him my name. Old Beneš then perceived that after his queer adventure he had found the man he was searching for and that he could fulfil that patriotic task which Masaryk had entrusted to him. With tears in his eyes he assured me how happy he was to see me and to know that Benešes never betray the nation. And then by word of mouth he told me what little he knew. He also received messages for Dr. Sychrava,[1] which were placed in pencils and between the covers of a book. The message which he had brought with him had been of great importance, for it consisted of a definite draft for a public proclamation of our movement abroad against Austria, but, of course, as I have described above, we did not receive it.

I mention this as typical of the methods we had to employ and the troubles we encountered during our surreptitious activities. Many more such interesting episodes could be described if space permitted.

14

At the meetings of the "Maffia," which were arranged at regular intervals from February to the end of July 1915—that being a period during which I myself attended them—a number of important questions were discussed in addition to those already mentioned. The most important concerned the supply of money for our movement at home and abroad, the manifesto by which Professor Masaryk was to inaugurate his open action against Austria, and the departure of Dr. Kramář and Dr. Scheiner for the organization of troops.

The negotiations for financial support do not make an edifying story. For various reasons our revolutionary movement had not been able to obtain a timely and adequate supply of money. When Professor Masaryk went away, the money he had with him was, I believe, partly his own and partly some of what I had handed over to him before his departure. Besides that, Dr. Scheiner had contributed a sum of 10,000 crowns towards his journey. The circumstances, however, had compelled him to remain abroad without any considerable preparations, and he was without money for that purpose. He also had constant anxieties about his family

---

[1] Dr. L. Sychrava (b. 1886), barrister and journalist. At the beginning of the war he went abroad as the representative of the younger section of the State Rights Progressive Party, and collaborated with Professor Masaryk and Dr. Beneš. He was the first diplomatic representative of the Czechoslovak Government in Paris. After the war he become editor-in-chief of the legionaries' daily paper, *Národní Osvobození* (*National Liberation*).

which had remained at home. Before Professor Masaryk's departure, Dr. Scheiner was the only person who showed a genuine interest in, and a proper understanding of, the money problem. Unfortunately, the free use of the Sokol funds had been restricted, and so that source failed us. During my first and second journeys to Switzerland, Professor Masaryk continually laid stress upon this, for it was clear that without money we should accomplish nothing. Professor Masaryk himself hoped to obtain funds from his personal friends in America. He had received some support from Mr. Crane, and then he had written direct from Italy and Switzerland to his friends among the Czechs in America. Moreover, Dr. Scheiner had told him to apply to the banker Štěpina on behalf of the Sokol organization.

At home little could be obtained beyond that already mentioned. Dr. Šámal, with the support of Dr. Scheiner, managed to secure a few more thousand crowns in the spring of 1915, and then a few more thousands shortly before I finally went abroad. In each of his messages Professor Masaryk informed us how the movement would have to develop, how much money he would need, how much he would require for the current and the following year. For example, at the outset he computed that about 10,000 francs annually would be necessary for *La Nation Tchèque* (it was not nearly enough), and that he would need a few more thousands for the publication of his memorandum for the Allies. Whatever the reasons for these difficulties of ours, I was disappointed and exasperated.

In the spring of 1915 I twice sent Professor Masaryk sums of money from my own resources which I had at my disposal and which I was able to spare from my loan. I myself needed funds for my journeys to Vienna and Germany, for the equipment of couriers and for the supply of material. As I have said, the only person who contributed anything substantial towards these requirements was Dr. Šámal.

As a matter of interest I will add in what manner those two money consignments were dispatched to Professor Masaryk in Switzerland in 1915. It was at a time when we had to be extremely careful, as Professor Masaryk's movements were being watched. In his message Professor Masaryk had again asked for money. As there was nothing else that I could do, I decided to adopt a method which would arouse the least suspicion. And so the first instalment of about

3,000 crowns for the Czechoslovak revolutionary movement
was sent through the agency of an Austro-Hungarian Government department—the Austro-Hungarian Post Office Savings
Bank. The money reached Professor Masaryk safely, and the
receipt of it was acknowledged on an open postcard, which was
sent to me.

I have already mentioned that these obstacles irritated me
very much and I made no secret of this to a number of my
friends. Finally, I decided to collect money for the movement
in a somewhat wider circle, including members of the Progressive Party and a number of party colleagues and friends
of Masaryk. I very soon dropped this idea, for at the very
first attempt I saw how useless it was. I applied to two prominent party men, both of whom were known to be extremely
well off. One of them, after a long conversation, slipped
100 crowns into my hand one evening, and the second, a few
days later, while we were in a café together, discoursed to me
at great length about his upright conscience and his views of
these matters, whereupon he gave me nothing. The total
amount which I received from Dr. Šámal and Dr. Scheiner
for the movement was 11,000 crowns, the greater part of
which was obtained, if I am not mistaken, by a collection
among a small circle of their friends. During my second visit
to Switzerland I related these experiences to Professor Masaryk
and those who were working with him. He expressed his disappointment very outspokenly. One meeting of the "Maffia"
in March 1915 was taken up with money matters. There was
some discussion about certain funds from Russia, of which I
had no clear knowledge, and were supposed to have been
deposited at the Bohemia Bank in Prague. It was suggested
that we might be able to use them. The debate on that occasion
was only of a general character and it was proposed that the
matter should be looked into. Whether anything was done
about it later on, I do not know, but as far as I was concerned
this discussion led to no further supply of funds for our movement abroad.

It thus came about that during my second journey to
Switzerland Professor Masaryk indicated to me that the only
people who could save us were the Czechoslovaks in America.
Somebody would have to be sent there to collect money
among our friends. I mentioned my brother, Vojta Beneš,
and Professor Masaryk agreed, his only stipulation being that

the matter should be arranged with the co-operation of Dr. Scheiner, who must provide my brother with credentials. He added that as my brother had already been in America and had a number of friends there, it would be a good thing if he went with an express invitation from Bohemia since this would give him from the very beginning a definite political authority among our fellow-countrymen.

I therefore began to negotiate with Dr. Scheiner about sending my brother to America, partly for the purpose of organizing our colony there for a political campaign, partly for securing regular financial support which would enable us to maintain our revolutionary movement throughout the war. I then reported the matter at a meeting of the "Maffia" and obtained the consent of the members. My brother was already acquainted with America, having done a year's educational work there before the war. He accordingly talked things over with Deputy Habrman,[1] and after discussing the matter with Dr. Scheiner and Dr. Šámal he informed E. Voska that he was coming.

Various steps were taken to obtain a passport for Vojta Beneš and all his family to go to America. The authorities gave their permission probably in view of the purpose of his journey, for he stated that he intended to investigate the manufacture of artificial limbs for disabled soldiers. He managed to get away from Austria in the middle of July 1915 and safely reached his destination, where he at once began with much success to carry out the duties which had been entrusted to him by the "Maffia" and by Masaryk. With the help of other American friends and fellow-workers, he achieved important results which rendered possible the essential details of our political and diplomatic action in Europe.

Towards the end of 1915 Professor Masaryk received the first funds from the American collections, so that he was able to let me keep about 20,000 francs which I had brought with me when I escaped from home. This enabled me to live from my own resources and remain independent in a financial sense.

It will be seen that my experiences of money matters were

[1] Gustav Habrman (b. 1864), a prominent member of the Social Democratic Party, the Radical wing of which he directed during the war. On two occasions he has occupied Ministerial posts in the Czechoslovak Government.

not encouraging. I have often asked myself why this was. From the conversations on the financial question which I had with the persons concerned, I drew one conclusion: the determining factor was not so much the financial sacrifice involved but, in the majority of cases, the fear of being discovered by the police. But often this made me think how prone our people were at their meetings to shout: "To the last man and the last farthing," and when the decisive moment came how difficult it was to discover those who had the courage of their convictions.

MY SECOND JOURNEY TO SWITZERLAND. THE
LAST MEETING OF THE "MAFFIA." MY ESCAPE
ABROAD

(*a*) MASARYK'S MESSAGES TO OUR POLITICIANS

15

IN the second half of March Professor Masaryk asked me in
one of his messages to come to Switzerland. He said that there
must be a closer agreement between Prague and abroad, and
that messages and reports in cipher were inadequate as a
means of communication. I therefore took advantage of the
Easter holidays and started off for Switzerland. This time I
had great difficulties in getting a passport. I was rather
favoured through being in touch with Counsellor Olič and by
the fact that I was living in his house. I told the authorities
that the reasons for my journey were of a scholastic character.

At the same time I had begun to lecture at the University
on the philosophy of war. In *Naše Doba* I reviewed a whole
batch of war books, both native and foreign, and Viktor Dyk,
the editor of *Lumír,* published in that periodical in essay form
one of my university lectures in which I had quite openly
declared that our nation must engage in a revolution.
This escaped the notice of the police, so when the Chief
Commissioner of Police sent for me to ask the reasons for my
journey, I told him that I had an academic interest in these
questions, and he gave me a passport with his own hands.

I spent about a week with Professor Masaryk at Geneva and
overstayed my leave. On my return I apologized to Dr.
Řežábek, the head of the Commercial Academy, for arriving
after the commencement of the term, and I told him quite
frankly what the reason was. Dr. Řežábek had previously
surmised what I was about and heard with the utmost satisfaction what was going on abroad and what Professor Masaryk
was doing.

In many respects this second visit to Switzerland was of
greater political importance both to Professor Masaryk and to

us in Prague. It was on this journey that I first had a personal
meeting with Dr. Sychrava. We first of all went carefully into
the question of organizing our connections and our courier
service, and we again considered the financial side of our
meeting.

Professor Masaryk gave me precise estimates of his requirements and indicated what plans, notably as regards organization, propaganda, and publicity, he wished to carry out by
the end of the year, and approximately how much money he
would require for them.

In connection with this, Professor Masaryk described to me
the position of our colonists and the trouble which even then
their affairs caused him. He also mentioned the directives
which he had traced for their activities and finally referred to
the publications he intended to start. He wanted to begin by
issuing a Czech newspaper for our people abroad which would
be edited by Dr. Sychrava. His next concern was to found and
publish a political paper in French for the Allied public. For
the latter project, he had already come to an agreement with
Professor Denis, who had undertaken to edit the new review
and to supervise all the work connected with it. When I
reached Geneva the preliminary arrangements were so advanced
that it was possible to start publishing the paper as a fort-
nightly on the 1st of May under the title of *La Nation Tchèque*.

As I had a large supply of information derived from the
Viennese documents which Machar had passed on to me, I
prepared articles and reports on our affairs at home for the
early numbers, and Denis at once printed them in the first and
second issues.

Systematic and regular contributions from Prague to *La
Nation Tchèque* were then secured, chiefly by means of couriers.
I used to obtain articles from a number of writers in Prague
(Professor Kaloušek, for example, discussed our economic
situation and the financial problems of Austria-Hungary),
while at the same time I myself wrote articles and sent them
to Geneva. I mention this to show that, on the whole, Sychrava's
organization at Geneva and ours at Prague worked well.

A further important question which Professor Masaryk had
submitted to me at Prague for discussion was that of his open
opposition to Austria-Hungary. At that time Professor Masaryk
was already rather impatient about this matter. He wanted
new helpers, journalists, and politicians, to come to him from

Prague, but none came. He wanted to come out into the open as soon as possible, particularly at the time of the Austro-Hungarian reverses in Serbia and on the Eastern Front, but the people at home asked him to wait because there was a fear of persecution by the Austrian Government. He was thus compelled to bide his time while political and military events ensued in rapid succession. Seeing how little was known about our cause in the Allied countries, he could not help fearing that we were losing valuable time. It would not be possible to start a real movement for independence until open action had been taken by our responsible political representatives. In the meanwhile, there were disputes among the members of our colonies abroad, and there was a lack of leaders, particularly for managing affairs in Russia.

Professor Masaryk therefore asked me to emphasize in Prague how urgent it was to take public action at all costs. Nobody would give us something for nothing, and it would be a great political error to rely only on the Allies and especially on Russia. He also again urged the necessity of sending journalists and other political helpers abroad. To this he added his fears with regard to Russia and a rather strong criticism of the Allied policy, which was either ignorant of the German plans for Central Europe or else was making very inadequate preparations to deal with them. He drew special attention to the fact that Italy's entrance into the war was under consideration and that concessions were being negotiated for her to the detriment of the Jugoslavs, who were not united among themselves. At the same time he gave me messages from the Jugoslavs residing abroad and also his own messages for the Jugoslavs in our country, especially for Deputy Lukinić and Dr. Lorković. The latter came to Prague shortly afterwards to see me and other persons, and he then received the message.

Svatkovsky also spoke to me in serious and emphatic terms. He asked me point-blank to tell Dr. Kramář again from him that the Russians were dissatisfied with us, that we must do something at home, that we must set about things in a more resolute manner, that Dr. Kramář ought to escape from Prague and go to Russia. Svatkovsky, like Professor Masaryk, was dubious about the conditions in Russia. He feared for the success of the offensive against Cracow, and in particular he saw that Petrograd was either completely ignorant of the Austro-Hungarian problem or else was disinclined to go more closely into it. He mentioned also the experiences of Dr. Scheiner, who, as early as February 1914, had visited Petrograd, where he had discussed with Sazanov and other leading politicians Russia's attitude to the Czech question in case of war. Dr. Scheiner's account of this showed that Russia took a very unfavourable view of our cause. This was now complicated by the disputes between the Allies and the Jugoslavs with regard to the unification of the latter. At that particular moment these disputes were at their height, and in Russia there was a decided tendency to favour the annexation of Dalmatia by Italy and the unification of the remaining orthodox Jugoslavs with Serbia, the rest of them to be handed over to a diminished Austria-Hungary.

Svatkovsky was in touch with the Poles, the Jugoslavs, the Italians, and us. He was also in touch with Russian and Allied official circles, and on various occasions he confirmed the truth of the above details which he now mentioned to me once more. In particular he told me that Italy would certainly enter the war in about six weeks' time. I conveyed this valuable piece of news, which was to encourage all our people to further opposition and activity, to Prague and also to Vienna for Machar.

Professor Masaryk also gave me the text of his proposed manifesto with which he intended to inaugurate his struggle against Vienna and Budapest. He said that he wanted us to go through it at a meeting of the "Maffia," and by the next courier we should let him have our approval of it or else propose any changes which we might think necessary. In this connection he emphasized the following points :

(a) At all costs our action must be taken openly and it must be of a revolutionary character. Otherwise we should not derive from the war any kind of political success for our national cause.

(b) He wanted to take action in agreement with the politicians at home, and only when they had given him their express consent. This was important because our movement abroad must under no circumstances be disavowed by the politicians at home.

(c) In no case did he ever want our responsible political circles to be misled into disavowing our action abroad. Silence would answer the purpose in such a case.(10)

This was a demand which he repeated in all his messages and also verbally by the couriers. Later on we all emphasized it still more in all the messages we sent home in the years 1917 and 1918 when both at home and abroad an actual policy had been started.

(d) If Masaryk did not obtain the consent of the people at home, he would wait for some time, but in the end he would take action on his own account.

Finally, he asked me to let his friends know that at the end of April he was going to Paris and London. His purpose was to get into touch with Delcassé, Grey, and the Russian Ambassadors in Western Europe. He promised to send by courier a detailed account of the result of his journey.

16

These were the results of our discussion which I took back with me to Prague. I made a short stop at Zurich to meet Dr. Sychrava. He had left for Switzerland in September 1914 with the express intention of furthering our political aims, after conferring with his friends in radical Progressive circles. I knew Dr. Sychrava from my schooldays and we had met also at the beginning of the war. Through Svatkovsky and Masaryk we had begun to work together between Switzerland and Prague in January 1915.

The success of our work was due largely to Dr. Sychrava. It was he who for a long time managed our underground connection with Prague, and throughout the war he directed our foreign paper, the Československá Samostatnost. A considerable part of the work in connection with our general propaganda also devolved upon him, and he also helped to organize our movement. He was one of the first who, to his own detriment, threw himself into the struggle. Everything he did revealed his integrity, his devotion to our cause, his unselfishness and his modesty. He was one of those few people who were well acquainted with the conditions at home, with a sound political instinct and a well-balanced judgment. In short, he was one of those who realized that the decisive hour in our national history had come and were able at such a juncture to eschew all compromise throughout consistent in their policy.

It was with him that I arranged all the details relating to

the further organization of our courier service and the general technique of our secret activities. At his apartment in the Kreutzstrasse at Zurich I made all arrangements for my last return journey. I slipped my notes into the heels of my boots and sewed others into my clothes with the ones which had already been sewn into my coat-collar at Geneva by Olga Masaryk. I then bought a number of books on the war and started off for home.

At that time journeys to and from foreign countries involved considerable risks. The first thorough examination took place at Buchs and the second at Feldkirch. Besides that, however, all along the Tyrolese line military and police patrols were continually passing through the railway carriages and examining the travellers. I simply left matters to chance.

Beyond Arlberg one of these examinations took place in my compartment. I had several questionable books, and in order to hide this fact I had also bought German anti-Entente books as well as German and Austro-Hungarian propagandist literature. Having twice escaped detection and seeing that the decisive moment had again arrived, I decided to tempt fate for the third time. I made a parcel of all my books and on the top of it I put a copy of *Simplicissimus* and the *Internationale Wochenschrift*, together with a few German books. When the officials who were carrying out the inspection arrived and asked me what I had, I showed them the parcel and told them to look for themselves. One of the officials lifted up the copy of *Simplicissimus*, looked at the title of the two German books, examined one of them to see whether it contained any loose papers, and then passed on.

But I had no further desire thus to tempt fate. I therefore packed the books up, waited for a favourable moment, and put them into the next carriage into the lavatory with the railwaymen's belongings. They remained there during the new examination which took place before Salzburg, and when we had entered Austria I took the bundle out again. These and similar moments, many of which fell to my lot during the war, strengthened my nerves and helped me to cultivate presence of mind.

I stayed for one day in Vienna as I wanted to inform Machar, the chief representative of the "Maffia" there, about the general situation, the entry of Italy into the war, and Masaryk's views. I also had a message from Masaryk to deliver to Hlaváč, the correspondent of *Čas* in Vienna. Hlaváč did not agree with Masaryk's revolutionary policy. From time to time he used to come to Prague, where I had met him at the office of *Čas*. He had told me what was going on in Vienna and had proved to his own satisfaction why Germany and Austria would win and why Masaryk and all of us in Prague were mistaken in our attitude.

Masaryk had asked me to visit Hlaváč in Vienna and give him some account of the motives of Masaryk's action. I was also to obtain fresh information from the official circles there.

I carried out both these commissions. I spent a full three hours walking with Hlaváč round the Imperial Castle, explaining to him why every Czech worthy of the name must identify himself with the revolutionary movement. Nevertheless, I did not convince him. He had recently returned from Italy and refused to believe that it would enter the war against Austria-Hungary.

As soon as I reached Prague I visited Dr. Šámal and Dr. Scheiner and asked for a meeting of the "Maffia" to be arranged. I also paid a visit to Dr. Kramář and delivered to him the messages from Masaryk and Svatkovsky. He was very much startled by what Svatkovsky said and he agreed that our task must be approached more resolutely. The Russian reverses at Gorlice and in the Carpathians, which occurred a very short time after that, depressed him very much, but at the same time they strengthened his determination. He again agreed that our action must be taken openly and also that somebody must join Masaryk. On the other hand, he did not abandon his fundamental point of view and his opinion of events in general. He still believed in the victory of Russia and, in fact, he thought that it would come during the war when Vienna would apply to him to save Austria from a catastrophe.(11) I again realized how impossible it was to reconcile the two sets of ideas. Nevertheless, on this occasion Dr. Kramář's views had been sufficiently shaken to make him wonder whether, after all, he ought not to go abroad. In view of the fact that I had discussed this matter with the other members of the "Maffia," particularly with Dr. Rašín, from this moment onwards it became of urgent interest and was the chief subject to be considered at the very next meeting of the "Maffia" at which I gave a report on my journey to Switzerland.

Dr. Rašín approved of the plan by which Dr. Kramář was

to proceed abroad. In fact, he discussed with Dr. Šámal, Dr. Scheiner, and myself what steps were to be taken to persuade Dr. Kramář to go, and to arrange for his departure. My impression is that Dr. Rašín had already surmised the danger which then threatened Dr. Kramář and himself, and that was one of the reasons why he wanted him to leave the country. What still remained to be settled, however, was how the property of Dr. Rašín and Dr. Kramář was to be protected and what form their departure was to take. That is to say, whether they were to go secretly or with the consent of the authorities. All these points were discussed at the meeting to which I have referred, when Dr. Kramář had already given his provisional consent. He then attempted to obtain a passport for abroad, but this was refused him.

At that meeting of the "Maffia" I gave a detailed account of my journey, and communicated all of Masaryk's wishes. The question as to what steps should be taken was immediately gone into. Masaryk's manifesto was read and accepted. Dr. Hajn was the only one who suggested a number of modifications and additions, more formal than fundamental in character, and I sent these suggestions to Masaryk who agreed to adopt them. We passed a resolution to the effect that Masaryk should take no action until he received express instructions from Prague, as the members of the "Maffia" were of the opinion that the proper moment must be chosen according to the progress of events at home, when the political circles concerned were adequately prepared. Possibly, also, when somebody else had been sent abroad.

It was accordingly decided that, in any case, somebody must soon join Masaryk. I believe that Dr. Scheiner came to this meeting with the proposal that Dürich [1] should be sent. For some time he had been discussing with him the question of joining our movement and Dürich had finally consented. Everybody agreed that Dürich should be entrusted with this mission because, apart from anything else, he was a member of the Agrarian Party and would therefore discuss the matter with Švehla, who was its chairman. This would mean that we should have the powerful Agrarian Party on our side. It was accordingly resolved that Dr. Kramář should discuss the political aspect of the matter with Dürich, and

[1] Josef Dürich (1847–1927), deputy of the Czech Agrarian Party. During the war he was active abroad, mainly in Russia.

that all other arrangements with him should be made by Dr. Šámal and Dr. Scheiner. Dr. Kramář carried out these arrangements, but the instructions which he gave Dürich were in accordance with his own personal views of Russian affairs.

As Dürich already had some experience of Slavonic affairs and could speak Russian and French, we readily approved of him as being suitable for the mission proposed, especially if it involved work in Russia. He left Prague and went first to Vienna, from where, on May 9, 1915, he reached Zurich. Here he was awaited by Dr. Sychrava.

As far as I remember, it was during the discussions on Dürich's mission and on our troops in Russia that the "Maffia" started its first debate on the Russian and Slavonic bearings of our policy.(12)

There was one detail in the discussion which caused me much concern. In the opinion of Dr. Kramář and, at that time, of Dr. Rašín, the future relations of our State to Russia would be so close that our soldiers would be able to perform their military service in some Russian garrison, while Russian soldiers would come to Bohemia for a similar purpose. I tried to imagine our troops joining the army in Siberia and I felt many misgivings. I therefore opposed the idea and, being the youngest member of the "Maffia" and a non-politician at that, I expressed my reservations in a very moderate and cautious manner. Finally, we agreed that at the moment there was no urgent necessity for the "Maffia" to discuss these points and that we should see later what could be done.

We left this meeting of the "Maffia" after having taken a number of decisions, all extremely important. We had agreed upon the wording of Masaryk's proclamation; we had given our consent to his plan of taking open action at a date to be fixed; we had detailed Dürich for work abroad. We had also seriously considered the departure of Dr. Kramář and the question of sending journalists to co-operate with Masaryk. I at once transmitted the results of this meeting to Switzerland.

17

At that time I began to make a closer search for more political and journalistic helpers who would escape to Switzerland. I must admit that in this, just as in the money question, I met with a number of disappointments. I spent a long time looking for suitable persons. The men I wanted would have to

speak at least French and possibly English; they would have
to be sufficiently well versed in politics to be able to carry
on propagandist and journalistic work; they would have to be
sufficiently courageous to get across the frontier, illegally if
necessary; and they would have to be prepared—especially at
a time when we lacked money and I could make no promises
to anyone in this respect—to lead the hard life of a political
émigré who might never be able to return home.

To add to our difficulties it was no longer possible to obtain
passports, and any attempt of leaving the country illegally
meant running extreme risks. I therefore set about discovering
ways of obtaining passports and in this I met with a certain
amount of success. Hájek confided in some of his friends,
notably F. Vodsed'álek and Dr. Butter, who managed to obtain
a number of empty passports from the local passport office.
I also managed to buy old Austrian or foreign passports
(chiefly Bulgarian) from various sources.

From this material I now began to manufacture new passports and to provide *visas*. Thus, in May 1915, I was able to
arrange the departure of Plesinger, now our Minister in
Copenhagen, whom I furnished with a pass and *visa* in the
name of Božinov. He proceeded to Switzerland, where he
began to work in our cause.

Shortly after the arrest of Dr. Kramář and Dr. Rašín I began
to confer with the members of the "Maffia" on ways and means
of assisting Dr. Borský to escape. I sent his photograph to
Dr. Sychrava, as in Switzerland it would possibly be easier to
obtain a passport. When Dr. Borský had to join the army
and came home in the summer on leave, I offered him a passport which had just been made out in the name of Miroslav
Šícha, a commercial traveller. I obtained the necessary
military documents from the Prague magistrature. I ventured
to fetch the Swiss *visa* from the Consulate myself and I
obtained the German *visa* by removing it from the passport
of the real Miroslav Šícha. Dr. Borský declined the passport
because he did not think it safe enough. If he had been caught
on the frontier he would at once have been shot as a deserter
from the army. A few weeks later I put my own photograph
into this passport and used it myself, escaping from Austria
under the assumed identity of Miroslav Šícha, a traveller in
optical instruments.

(b) An Agitated Meeting of the "Maffia." The Arrest
of Kramář, Scheiner, and Rašín

18

On April 15, 1915, Masaryk left for Paris and London. On
May 1st the first number of *La Nation Tchèque* appeared, and
about the same time more detailed news reached Switzerland
with regard to our Russian enterprise, known as the "Družina,"
(Brigade) and the general activities of our colonists in Russia.
Masaryk had still not abandoned the plan of sending Dr. Scheiner
to organize our troops in Russia. It was Fáček who brought this
news to me from Dr. Sychrava, He arrived with a large trunk
about May 17, 1915. This was the first consignment of the new
variety. The trunk, which was an admirable piece of work
with hollow sides, contained twenty numbers of *La Nation
Tchèque*, four copies of Masaryk's memorandum entitled
Independent Bohemia, and a long report from Dr. Sychrava
on the position of our troops in Russia. In particular, Dr.
Sychrava mentioned that the organization of these troops was
making progress, that Nikolay Nikolayevitch, the Commander-
in-Chief, had sanctioned the formation of our army from among
the prisoners of war, the number of men being about twenty
thousand. He added that preparations were in full swing and
that it was urgent for Dr. Scheiner to go there. I should mention,
however, that these reports, in the form in which they reached
Dr. Sychrava, were not in accordance with the actual state of
affairs in Russia. As regards Dr. Scheiner, we had spent a
considerable time in planning his escape. It had been
arranged that he was to proceed to Holland on banking
business, but this fell through because he was unable to obtain
a passport.

The news from Dr. Sychrava, as well as the first printed
documents relating to our revolutionary movement, deeply
impressed me. I asked Dr. Šámal to summon a meeting of the
"Maffia" at his house, and I arrived there with the whole collection of trophies on the evening of May 20, 1915. During
my second journey to Switzerland I had also managed to
smuggle Denis's book, *La Guerre*, across the frontier, which I
had then passed round among a number of people in Prague.
I brought this also with me to the meeting to show the progress
that was being made by our cause.

At this meeting, which was attended by Dr. Kramář, Dr. Rašín, Dr. Scheiner, Dr. Hajn, Dr. Šámal, and myself, I gave a report on recent events, submitted the original copy of Dr. Sychrava's statement, and distributed several numbers of *La Nation Tchèque*. Dr. Kramář slipped his copy into his breast-pocket. We were cheerfully discussing the military events in Russia when suddenly Dr. Scheiner was called to the telephone. It was a message from the Sokols, if I remember rightly, to say that soldiers were making a search at Dr. Scheiner's.

It was a critical moment. If the police knew where Dr. Scheiner was they would be able to catch us all at one swoop and seize our documents as well. Dr. Kramář, Dr. Rašín, and Hajn left hastily. Dr. Šámal quickly removed and destroyed the documents which I had brought with me, except Denis's book, and then the three of us held a brief conference. I urged Dr. Scheiner to try to escape. Šámal quickly collected all the money he had in the house, and Scheiner, after a moment's reflection, announced that he would get away.

We took leave of each other. I went for a short while into a café to calm my agitation. I telephoned to Dušek at the office of *Čas* and asked him whether he had any news. I arranged to meet him at nine o'clock the following morning in the Parliament Café as I wanted to tell him what had happened. I then went to have a peep at Dr. Scheiner's. I walked up and down until one o'clock in the morning in Václav Square opposite his house and behind the lighted windows I saw vague forms moving from room to room. The soldiers were making a thorough search. When Scheiner reached home in the early hours of the morning he was arrested and taken to Vienna the the next day.

Kramář had looked in at the office of *Národní Listy* and then proceeded to his villa. Just as he was about to enter he was arrested. Among other things the copy of *La Nation Tchèque*, which I had given him a short time previously, was taken away from him and proved to be incriminating evidence against him.

When I met Dušek the next morning, as we had arranged, I told him what had happened at Šámal's and then, much to my surprise, he told me what had happened to Kramář.

At first I felt sure that the whole of our conspiracy had been discovered and that we were all done for. I therefore at once made some rapid decisions. Before leaving the café I wrote to my family to say that I was leaving the country immediately. I indicated arrangements with regard to various family matters which my wife was to attend to. I then went to Hájek and gave him the letter, informing him what had happened, what my intentions were, and what he was to do to keep things going.

I then went to have a look at my house to see whether the soldiers or the police were there, or whether any conspicuous sign had been put in the windows, according to the arrangement with my wife. I spent a whole morning watching and waiting, but as I saw nothing suspicious I ventured to go in about midday. I quickly cleared the house of all dangerous papers and waited to see what would happen. I was reassured by the fact that there were no signs of the police, and this gave me breathing-space.

In this situation the chief thing was to find out at once how far the two arrests were connected with our activities. This could be ascertained either from the police or from Machar in Vienna, but in any case it must be done quickly. I arranged with Dušek for him to try to find something out from Dr. Klíma, with whom he was regularly in touch. From his conversation with Klíma, Dušek gathered that what had happened had no bearing on the "Maffia." The whole thing soon became quite clear when we obtained news from Vienna, partly from political circles, partly from Heinold's documents. Among the latter was a report to the Archduke Friedrich, which showed us that the arrest of Kramář and Scheiner had been carried out as the result of orders from the military authorities, and was not in any way connected with the doings of the "Maffia."

From that time onwards I was in practically daily touch with Dr. Rašín. After the removal of Scheiner it was from him that I obtained most of my information, apart from what I received from my own private sources. I have the most pleasant memories of my dealings with him and of the work we did together in the "Maffia." He was hard-working, courageous, undaunted, loyal, and devoted. We had no difficulty in agreeing as to the direction which Masaryk's policy should take.

It was not long before Dr. Rašín quietly informed me that he was under the observation of the police and that he would be arrested shortly. One day, in the early part of July, I called on him as usual and towards noon accompanied him to the office of *Národní Listy*. He told me that he was expecting his arrest very soon and that perhaps it would take place on the very next day. Three days later, on July 12, 1915, he was arrested and taken to Vienna.

(c) My Escape

19

The first period of the activity of the "Maffia," which was perhaps the most important as far as our movement abroad was concerned, may be regarded as culminating with the arrest of these three members. I had arranged with Rašín what was to be done after the arrest of Kramář and Scheiner, and we had previously decided by an agreement with Šámal and Scheiner how things were to proceed in the case of Scheiner's arrest, which we were expecting. For this eventuality Scheiner had indicated that V. Štěpánek was to replace him as a representative of the Sokol organization. Šámal, therefore, at once took steps for Štěpánek to be informed so that he could take part in the further work of the "Maffia."

After the arrest of Kramář and Scheiner we had several further important meetings of the "Maffia" at which I communicated the reports received from Geneva after Masaryk's return from Paris and London in May 1915, together with his requests that somebody should join him and that he should receive permission to take open action.

Masaryk's message, after his return from Paris and London, was worded in more emphatic terms than before. He said that it would be a mistake to wait for the Russians. They had no political plan, there was disorder and obvious treachery in their army, chaos in their administration, and they were completely indifferent to our cause. Count Benckendorff, the Russian Ambassador in London, whom Masaryk visited, had never seen a racial map of Austria-Hungary before Masaryk showed him one. Such was the ignorance of those in high places. It was clear that the war would be a long one, decisive action was necessary, and we must come out into the open. Masaryk further stated that he had discussed matters with the entourage of Delcassé and Grey and had handed them his memoranda, but that he had not spoken with the Ministers themselves.

On that occasion Dr. Sychrava gave me, in addition to Masaryk's concise report, a very detailed account of Masaryk's journey, and of what Masaryk had told him and Svatkovsky at Geneva. On the whole it was a great disappointment. The Allies were ill-informed about Austria-Hungary, they scarcely knew anything about us at all and therefore had no definite intention with regard to our cause. The policy of Russia was appalling, and the reports of what had been said by Izvolsky, Delcassé, Trumbić, and Vesnić about their plans with Dalmatia and the Catholic Jugoslavs made him despair. At that juncture I refrained from telling the "Maffia" the whole truth because I did not want to discourage the members from continuing their work.

In the meanwhile, Dürich had left for Switzerland, and I was making vain attempts to arrange for journalists to be sent abroad. At Masaryk's urgent request I removed a number of books from his library, together with his notes on politics and other matters, partly in order to send them to him and partly to save them from being seized by the police whenever he might take action openly. I had them transferred to the cellar of my house where, however, after my escape they were discovered and confiscated. It was on this occasion that Dr. Alice Masaryk, with whose knowledge and assistance the protection of the books had been undertaken, was arrested.

After Dürich had gone, the "Maffia" dealt with the question of sending Soukup, Habrman, Borský, and Dyk abroad. None of them, however, managed to escape. In July and August 1915 Masaryk was extremely impatient because nothing had yet been settled about the arrival of further helpers or the definite consent to his open action. At a meeting of the "Maffia" in the second half of August it was decided that at least one of the above-mentioned persons should leave the country, but that open action should be delayed just a little longer until the necessary political preparations for this purpose had been completed at home. As I have said, however, nobody succeeded in getting away, and it was I myself who brought Masaryk the consent to his taking open action, when two weeks later I escaped to Switzerland. Rašín's arrest occasioned us some anxious moments, for there were a number of symptoms which indicated that more arrests were going to be made. We again went through our belongings and removed or destroyed all documents, messages, keys to ciphers, lists of names, addresses, etc. From that time onwards I always used to return home from my walks and meetings very cautiously. I was always ready to get away should I discover, from the signs arranged with my wife, that the police had taken proceedings or that they were waiting for me in my house.

From the end of June warnings had arrived almost every day, and ever since we had managed to send my brother to America I realized the necessity either of escaping or of preparing for prison. I therefore made the last essential arrangements for maintaining connections with Prague. At the beginning of August the police in Prague and Vienna had received the first news of the arrival of Vojta Beneš in America and of his activity there. The *gendarmerie* were at once informed and I was placed directly under police supervision. On the same day that these police instructions were issued, a report on them was supplied to me by Sergeant Hájek, a brother of Jan Hájek, who had regularly taken part in our movement from the spring of 1915 and had brought me valuable political and police news. A few days later, through Sergeant Šulc, a brother-in-law of Vojta Beneš, I was able to have a glimpse at the *gendarmerie* instructions concerning myself.

It was high time to get away. I explained the situation to Šámal, Dušek, and other friends of mine who had been helping me in my work. Then I once more spoke to the remaining members of the "Maffia" with regard to Masaryk's open action, as I wanted to take him a definite reply authorizing an open declaration of war on Austria. The consent to this was given, and Masaryk was left an entirely free hand in choosing the day for availing himself of it. Having made all arrangements with Šámal, Bělohrádek, and Hájek for continuing our work and keeping in touch with us abroad, I completed my final preparations to escape. On the advice of a number of friends I intended to make my way across Hungary, Transylvania, and Rumania to Russia. On the Rumanian frontier I was to be assisted by a certain Transylvanian priest, who was said to have already helped several of our people to escape.

At the end of August I left our summer quarters for Prague with the intention of making for Hungary. At the last moment, however, I changed my plan, as I regarded the journey by way of Rumania as unsafe. Having discovered that Dr. Amerling, an old fellow-student of mine, was the medical officer to the military garrison at Asch, I decided to go there and ask him to get me across the frontier under the protection of a military uniform. I did not want to submit my passport to the Austrian authorities as I feared detection and judged that it would be much less likely for a false Austrian passport to be discovered by the German authorities. This assumption proved to be correct.

I proceeded to Asch shortly before my final departure and arranged everything with Dr. Amerling. I selected a spot in the neighbourhood for crossing the frontier, fixed the day of my escape, and on that day, September 1, 1915, I arrived. Dr. Amerling carried out his promise and after some difficulty managed to get me across into Bavaria on the road to Hof, whence I took the train to Munich. From there I had an hour's journey to the Lake of Constance in the early morning between September 2nd and 3rd. On my arrival there I at once had to undergo an examination by German soldiers, which lasted for several hours and caused me great anxiety. Finally, at about five o'clock in the morning, I was allowed to go on board the steamer, which left for Rohrschach in Switzerland, and at six o'clock in the morning on September 3rd I set foot on Swiss soil. From St. Gallen I sent my wife a pre-arranged telegram to let her know that I was saved. Towards seven o'clock in the evening I was at Geneva, where Masaryk was waiting for me.

I had slipped away from home with only a small handbag, which my wife had hidden under her cape when she had accompanied me to the railway station at our summer quarters. I had promised her that I would return within two years at the most, and I told her to be prepared for hard times, as she would be harassed, cross-examined, and perhaps even imprisoned by the police. I advised her what attitude she was to adopt and what answers she was to give. Should things become unbearable she was to repudiate me. We were ready for whatever might befall. Every great and righteous cause demands sacrifices and they must be made resolutely, without sentimentality. And every sacrifice thus made will cost one's opponents very dear. Such were my feelings when I took my seat in the train bound for Cheb and bade farewell to those who were dear to me.

It was not long before my wife and the others who were implicated in the plot were arrested and imprisoned in Vienna, as we had expected. In accordance with the pre-arranged code,

I learned this in Paris a few weeks later from an advertisement in the *Národní Politika*. It was not until January 1, 1919, however, when my wife came to Paris, that I heard about the details of the court proceedings and the imprisonment which, I may mention in passing, rendered valuable services to the propagation of our cause.

(d) OUR SECRET COMMUNICATIONS WITH PRAGUE

20

It was after nine o'clock in the evening when, amid a heavy downpour of rain, I met Masaryk in the restaurant Des Eaux Vives. After I had given him the first messages from Prague, he asked me: "Who is going to take your place in the "Maffia," and who will look after the communication between Prague and Switzerland?" When I explained to him how I had left Prague at a moment's notice after the arrest of the members of the "Maffia," and indicated what Šámal, Dušek, Hájek, and the others would probably be able to do, Masaryk replied: "I don't think that will be enough. In my opinion you will have to go back again to make more satisfactory arrangements about keeping in touch with us before you can leave once and for all."

I said that I would go back if Masaryk wanted, but I added that my brother was in America, that his activities there were already known to the police, who were now after me, as I had ascertained from the *gendarmerie* reports, so that if I went back I should merely land myself in prison.

On the next day in the afternoon Masaryk came with a new plan: "I will go and settle down in London, you will remain in Paris, and Dr. Sychrava will continue to work in Switzerland."

This plan was at once carried out. We summoned Dürich from Lucerne and I informed him about events in Bohemia. It was arranged that he should wait in Switzerland until the time was ripe for his journey to Russia. We then at once began to make preparations for moving to London and Paris.

About September 10th I visited Dr. Sychrava at Zurich to arrange for the maintenance of our communications with Prague. Accompanied by three other Czechs, Baráček, Plesinger-Božinov, and Kyjovský, who were then in Switzerland, we went for an excursion to Küssnacht, where we decided on all the measures which were to be adopted for this purpose.

I reported the latest events at home, especially the meetings of the "Maffia," and I suggested what course our further work might take. The news that Dr. Soukup was taking part in our movement as a representative of the Social Democrats caused great satisfaction. It was suggested that we could now send couriers direct to Dr. Soukup, and Mme. Linhart was sent to Prague with a message for him. Unfortunately she was caught and this led to the arrest of a large number of persons, including Mme. Linhart herself, Hájek and his wife, Cyril Dušek, Miss Sychrava, Miss Olič, Dr. Alice Masaryk, and my wife. This was the first time our plans had been discovered since we had started our movement. (The second and last discovery occurred on October 21, 1918, when the authorities in Vienna had neither the time nor the opportunity to attend to persecutions.)

Bit by bit we learned about these wholesale arrests. We obtained the first news on November 19, 1915, in the form of vague newspaper reports sent by way of Switzerland in accordance with our pre-arranged code. I learned more about it on November 23rd during my visit to London when Masaryk received a letter from Dr. B. Štěpánek containing a detailed account of the whole affair. Dr. Štěpánek, whose letter had been sent from Amsterdam, informed us at the same time that he was returning to Holland at Christmas and that he would like to meet someone there for an interchange of news.

In giving an account of our secret communications I must avoid anticipating events. In order, however, not to have to return to the "Maffia," I will at once give as much of its subsequent history as concerns myself, and falls within the scope of the present work.

The proposed meeting with Dr. Štěpánek took place on Christmas Day, 1915, at the Hôtel Krasnopolski, at Amsterdam. We spent the day together and exchanged views. For us who were living abroad this was of great value, as after the arrests in Prague our communications via Switzerland had to stop for some time, and my meeting with Dr. Štěpánek represented the opening of a new set of communications. These he promised to maintain by way of Holland, and indicated that I might expect further news either on the arrival of the Czech Quartet or during the visit of the author, Jaroslav Kvapil. The latter did actually bring us news on several occasions.

In the course of the year 1916 we had only occasional communications by way of Switzerland. They were never entirely suspended, but the dispatch of couriers from Switzerland gradually became more and more difficult, for on the one hand nearly all our people had become compromised by their anti-Austrian activities, and on the other hand the attention of the Austrian police was concentrated mainly upon Switzerland. Nevertheless, from time to time, we managed to obtain a courier who reached Dr. Šámal, Bělohrádek, or some other of our acquaintances.

21

From the end of 1916 a new phase began in the history of the "Maffia." Our contact with Prague was maintained, as I have mentioned, by occasional communications via Switzerland, Holland, or America. The latter route, which was organized by Captain Voska, was particularly difficult and expensive, but we obtained important results from it.(13) As far as our work abroad was concerned, it was now restricted almost entirely to political messages, to reports on our progress, and on the prospects of our success, together with indications to our politicians as to what action we considered desirable at home. At the same time Šámal, Štěpánek, Hajšman, Jaroslav Kvapil, and others were sending us news of what was happening at home. A detailed account of this phase of the "Maffia" will perhaps be given by those who took part in it. Altogether, many interesting particulars of the whole activity of the "Maffia" still remains to be told.

The importance of the "Maffia" in our struggle for liberation may be summed up as follows :

1. It enabled us to establish our first revolutionary organization abroad, while systematically keeping in touch with the responsible politicians at home throughout the war. This, together with the fact that it helped us to obtain the permission of the responsible political circles in Prague for taking open action in due course and for continuing our work against Austria-Hungary, established our credentials with the Allies, and thus enabled us from the beginning of our movement until the end of the war to act on behalf of our political parties and our nation.

2. At critical moments it enabled us either to send our news home or to interpret authentically in the Allied countries, on the basis of news received from our friends in Prague, the

trend of events at home. This gave us an opportunity of exerting a considerable influence upon the development of political affairs both at home and in the Allied countries.

3. From its very beginnings the "Maffia" sent abroad valuable reports on political, economic, and military affairs in Austria-Hungary, which often proved of service to the Allies in military operations, in political action, and in economic or financial measures. This served our cause by enabling us to gain the sympathies of various Allied official circles, and thus the "Maffia" had a great practical significance.

There has never been a revolution without espionage and conspiracy. It was a good thing that our revolution possessed this aspect also. And even if our "Maffia" was not perfect in every detail, it shows at any rate that the whole of our revolutionary movement was an effective improvisation emanating from the soul of the Czech people and directed by individuals who had contrived to be at their places in good time, ready at any moment to sacrifice everything.

PARIS AND LONDON AS CENTRES OF OUR REVOLUTIONARY MOVEMENT

(a) My Beginnings in Paris

22

I HAD brought with me from Prague, besides important news on the whole situation, a fundamental decision arrived at by our political circles, who were represented directly or indirectly in the "Maffia," that Masaryk and Dürich could take open action against Austria in a public manifesto, the wording of which had already been agreed upon in Prague, and thus begin officially, on behalf of the Czech nation, definite resistance to the Habsburg Empire. Accordingly, at a conference in Geneva on September 4th, it was decided that on about September 15th I should meet Masaryk in Paris, where our open action against Austria-Hungary would be prepared with the agreement and co-operation of Professor Denis and our fellow-countrymen from France, England, Russia, and America.

I left on September 16th for Paris, where I spent a little less than two weeks, completing, as had been arranged, the first preparations for systematic political activity on French soil. Masaryk, who left at the end of September for a prolonged stay in London, introduced me to Professor Denis and instructed the Czech colony in Paris to co-operate with me. He also asked me to visit on his behalf, as soon as possible, our volunteers at Lyons (which I immediately did), and entrusted to me the management of our propagandist and political activities in Paris and France generally.

My beginnings in Paris were difficult. I took up my quarters in the Rue Léopold Robert in a small room on the fifth floor, for which I paid 120 francs a month. The few acquaintances which I had made in France during my first and second stay there (1905–8 and 1911) had either forgotten me or else had disappeared in consequence of the war. I was not in touch with official circles, and in accordance with the principles which we practised throughout the war I made no attempt to secure an entry into those circles at this early stage of our affairs; for we did not want to start any negotiations until our position was sufficiently strong.

There were two courses left for me to adopt:

(a) I could avail myself of the professors at the Sorbonne with whom I was to some extent acquainted from my previous stay in Paris. These included particularly E. Denis, A. Meillet, E. Durkheim, C. Bouglé, under whom I had studied, and also L. Eisenmann, who had been a professor at Dijon while I was studying there, and who, as the author of an important book on Austria-Hungary, had taken an interest in the thesis which I had written on the same subject. Through Masaryk and Denis I now entered into direct touch with him.

(b) I could approach the French Socialists, as since 1907 I had been a contributor to such Socialist periodicals as *La Revue Socialiste, Le Movement Socialiste*, etc., and was acquainted with their editors and with such leading men as Albert Thomas, Lagardelle, etc.

These, then, were the circles in which I began my work. Professor Eisenmann, as an expert on Austro-Hungarian questions, had been assigned to the Information Department of the French War Ministry. I had arrived from Austria with a quantity of fresh news and documentary material. He had been carefully following the Austro-Hungarian newspapers, and often needed a commentary on the events from one who had witnessed them at close quarters. Thus, in the very first month of my stay in Paris, I established an important contact with the War Ministry.

It was on September 30, 1915, that I first discussed with Professor Eisenmann what form our co-operation should take. It was agreed, in particular, that as the opportunity arose I should supply him with news and comments for the War Ministry. Immediately after that, on October 2nd, Eisenmann introduced me to officials of the War Ministry, where it was decided notably that counter-action against Austria-Hungary should be taken in Switzerland, and that assistance in this project should be given by our organization and Dr. Sychrava. I also at once received permission from the Ministry to arrange for newspapers to be sent to me through official channels from Austria and Germany, as well as books and reports from Dr. Sychrava in Switzerland. In this way I was enabled to establish rapidly the contact with Prague which was so necessary for our work in Paris.

My former relations with Albert Thomas made it possible for me at an early date—on October 16th—to get into touch with Professor Roques, his personal secretary at the Ministry of Munitions. At about the same time the members of the "Rovnost" (Equality), a Czech Socialist society in Paris, asked me to give a public lecture for the French Socialist organizations. I agreed; but I wanted a Frenchman also to speak at the same meeting, and I applied to Paul Louis, a Socialist and journalist whom I had known previously as the author of a history of the Labour movement in France. At that time Paul Louis was one of the foreign editors of the *Petit Parisien*. The lecture was held, and Paul Louis spoke ably on Austria and against Austria. In this way we gained fresh ground.

Paul Louis, who had been surprised by what I reported about the situation in Austria-Hungary, was anxious for me to speak to somebody in the Foreign Ministry. He referred me to M. l'Hermit, an acquaintance of his and then an influential official, who received me on November 16th and discussed Austro-Hungarian affairs with me. This did not immediately lead to any appreciable result, but, considering that I was an unknown foreigner, it was an important beginning, since it opened up a channel which, by systematic work and further connections, became more and more extensive and gradually led to definite political results.

It was about the same time that I met Auguste Gauvain, one of those men who, during the war, rendered valuable services to our cause in France. At the end of September 1915 I had become acquainted with the journalist P. Quirielle, through the painter L. Strimpl, who is now our Minister in Belgium, and Quirielle introduced me to Gauvain on November 10th, shortly before we took open action against Austria-Hungary. I was anxious for Gauvain on this occasion to write something about our cause.

Gauvain, the foreign editor of the *Journal des Débats*, was one of those French journalists who, from the very beginning of the war, thoroughly realized its significance and meaning. He was well acquainted with Austro-Hungarian politics, and it was no drawback to him that he was on the staff of a Conservative paper with Catholic tendencies. From the beginning to the end his attitude towards Vienna and Budapest was unrelenting, for he realized that they were the factors who were responsible for the outbreak of the war. Gauvain is also one of those few journalists of world-wide reputation who have had the courage to republish unchanged in book form their daily articles on the foreign situation during the war, the events of which he was able to comment upon with a rare insight. From the first moment he became our friend. On the occasion of my first visit he promised me that he would write a leading article on our movement, and even at that early date he succeeded in forming a correct estimate of the Czech problem. It was he, I believe, who alone of all French and, in fact, Allied journalists, supplied a serious and detailed report of our first official action. From that time onwards I was in constant touch with the editorial staff of the *Journal des Débats*, which became the most important journalistic pivot for our war-time policy in France.

Such were the relationships with which I began my work in Paris, and I made every effort to extend them systematically. The friends I gained in this manner helped devotedly to extend the scope of our influence. And when Štefánik joined us he brought with him a number of politicians and, later, representatives of military circles.

Knowing the situation in Prague and in our political circles generally, and remembering my experiences with the "Maffia," I proposed, after having discussed the matter with Masaryk, to supply my friends in Prague as regularly as possible with reports on the military and political situation in the Allied countries. I had seen when I was still in Prague what valuable services were rendered to us by even the smallest piece of news, and how great an encouragement it was to all of us when we obtained authentic information as to what was or was not true in the Austrian and German versions of current events.

At the same time, however, I was fully aware how fantastic and exaggerated certain of the reports were which emanated from our uncritical enthusiasts at home, who imagined that the military side of the war was already won, and that on the political side everything had long since been decided in our favour.

Accordingly, almost immediately after my arrival in Switzerland and Paris as soon as I had taken stock of the situation, I sent a report on it to Prague. I spoke with M. Bibikov, the Russian Ambassador at Berne (he was married to a Czech lady), with Svatkovsky and with all my new friends in Paris ; I read the newspapers, I observed the people and the conditions, and then compared everything with Masaryk's reports. The general view of the situation which I thus acquired was sent to Prague in the middle of October 1915. My report was couched in hopeful terms, but it contained a warning against our passive attitude. I drew attention to the fact that certain Allied circles were disappointed at our lack of activity at home, and that, as scarcely anything was known about the Czech cause, it was particularly important for more politicians of standing to join us.

To-day I regard this and all my following reports as documents which give quite a good idea of the general progress of our movement, our aims, our struggles and fears, our hopes, successes, and the gratification which they caused us.(14)

(b) Our First Open Action

23

Having settled in Paris I began, as I had agreed upon with Masaryk, to prepare for open action in which our colonists and *émigrés* were to take part. It was necessary to discuss this with our colonists in Paris, London, America, and Russia, and these discussions were not easy. Our colonies were not yet firmly organized, and there were differences of opinion as to the persons who should sign the manifesto. I myself did not sign it, since I desired to remain in the background for some time, out of consideration for my wife and friends. Moreover, my position among our people abroad was not yet sufficiently prominent. Then, too, seeing the differences which had arisen with regard to the persons who should sign the manifesto, I thought it would be better if I set our colonists an example of political reserve. I first arranged the matter with our colony in Paris, and as Dr. Sychrava had already discussed the subject with our people in Russia and America, on September 30, 1915, at Masaryk's request, I again went to Geneva to obtain Dürich's consent also.

There a course of action was agreed upon with Dr. Sychrava, and an arrangement was made also with Svatkovsky with regard to sending reports on our affairs to Russia. I then proceeded to Lausanne where Dürich gave me permission to take action, and on October 2nd I returned to Paris. I sent a report on these arrangements to Masaryk, who was making all preparations in London, and we reached an agreement by telegram with Masaryk and our unions in America and Russia concerning the signature of the manifesto. Finally, I went into the whole matter with Professor Denis on October 9, 1915. The reason for this was that Professor Denis considered the wording of the manifesto, as agreed upon in Prague, to be unsuitable for the French public. It was, he said, too dry and historical in tone, and he suggested changes. With Masaryk's consent he then revised our wording for the French public.

It was then for the first time that the problem of organizing our movement abroad became an urgent one. What had to be considered was the relationship of Masaryk and those of us who had arrived from Prague, towards our colonists abroad. Another important point was the extent to which our colonists were to take part in our work. As early as March 1915 Masaryk had drawn up a scheme for the activity of the colonists, which he had submitted to them. In it he had indicated what their status and duties should be in the work of liberation. The question was a delicate one in its personal aspect, chiefly because of the status, the interests, and the aims of some of the leading personalities among the colonists. It was clear that for managing our national and political movement we needed a firmly established central organization which would be permanently representative of our movement, and by its composition would form a serious body worthy of the confidence of our own people and especially of Allied political circles.

In September 1915 these matters were not sufficiently advanced for the purposes of a definite organization. A kind of *ad hoc* political body was therefore set up, and it exhibited all the marks of a provisional arrangement. At that time our colonists had no definite organization either in Paris or London, America or Russia. Altogether, from a political point of view, we saw how unprepared our colonists were; and so we created spontaneously a "Czechoslovak Foreign Committee," whose function was chiefly to provide signatures for our manifesto, and thus to exhibit unity among all who were concerned in our struggle for liberation and who at that time were able to speak freely. There were various difficulties and disputes with regard to the persons who were to sign the manifesto on behalf of the colonies and the regional associations, but an agreement was finally reached. The definite organization was postponed until such a time as the development of events should throw a clearer light on the situation and our requirements.

And so we took open action and declared war officially upon the Habsburg Empire on Sunday, November 14, 1915, when the proclamation of the Czechoslovak Foreign Committee was published in Switzerland, France, Russia, and the United States.

In this proclamation the Foreign Committee emphasized the fact that the Czechoslovak nation was entering upon hostilities, irrespective of their result, at a moment when Russia was retreating and Serbia was crushed. It associated itself with the Slavonic nations and the Allies, and proclaimed a life and death struggle against the Empire which was responsible for the war and had already lost its independence, having become a mere implement in the German war policy of an advance towards the East. The manifesto further described the struggle of the Czechoslovak nation against Vienna and Budapest before the war, and drew attention to the regime of persecution against us in Austria-Hungary during the war. It emphasized our historical right to a State of our own, and referred to the fact that the whole nation was resolved to gain its independence by its combative efforts in the war. The cause of Vienna and Budapest was proclaimed to be already a lost one, the downfall of the Habsburg Empire and the formation of an independent Czechoslovak State certain and inevitable.

The publication of the manifesto formed the beginning of our official opposition to Austria-Hungary. It was a step of historic importance, although the immediate effect was not considerable. It was the first decisive measure, open and deliberate, undertaken in agreement with the politicians at home and therefore fraught with responsibility to the nation and its future. There could now be no turning back. With this step began the phase of our organized activity abroad. That problem occupied us entirely for some time.

As in the case of all work, especially that of a political and revolutionary character, the problem of method and organization has a decisive effect upon the results achieved. What therefore concerned us mostly was how to organize, in a unified and well-knit movement, the co-operation of the colonies with those in charge of our policy; how to keep in touch with Prague; how to organize our propaganda and pass gradually from propaganda to politics while creating the executive bodies and financial resources necessary for this process. We were also faced with the task of finding competent workers and linking up the whole of our movement in the various Allied States. Finally, the question also arose as to how we were to organize our activity with regard to prisoners of war and fighting forces.

The solution of these problems could not be postponed for long. We were also urged forward by the Czechoslovaks in America, to whom our action then meant a great deal, since there our people were concentrated in serried masses. Moreover, in America, which at that time was still neutral, our action was to have the effect of inciting our people to open warfare against Austria-Hungary, and to clear up the situation among our *émigrés* who, from a political point of view, were unsettled in their tendencies.

Masaryk asked me to come to London to discuss these matters. It was at the time when the first envoy, Mme. Tvrzická, had just arrived from our fellow-countrymen in America. She had brought news about the situation there, and on behalf of our friends had asked Masaryk for the information and guidance needed by the Czech and Slovak colony.

I started for London on November 21, 1915. At the outset we discussed matters of organization, and then reported to Mme. Tvrzická on our plans and requirements, as well as on the military and political situation in Europe. We decided upon the next step which we should take in England and France immediately after our manifesto was issued. The final decisions on the form which our organization should take were not made until February 1916 when Masaryk visited Paris and Štefánik joined our movement.

During my stay in London Masaryk received a letter from Dr. B. Štěpánek in Holland announcing, as I have previously mentioned, the arrest of several members of our family and of our secret organization in Prague. Masaryk therefore asked me to go immediately to Switzerland to find out exactly what had happened, and what effect it would have upon our communication with the people at home. I was to reorganize with Dr. Sychrava the whole of our arrangements for keeping in touch with Prague, and I was to inform Dürich about the situation in Paris and London.

I returned to Paris on December 6th, and on December 9th I left for Geneva, from where I proceeded to Lausanne for the purpose of visiting Dürich. At Geneva I settled the question of how we were to establish touch with the people at home, and on December 12th returned to Paris, where I set about organizing my personal work. I secured A. Kudrnáč, the chairman of the Social Democratic society "Rovnost" in Paris, as my secretary, and in my small room I set up my first provisional propaganda office, in which the chief item of its scanty equipment was a typewriter.

(c) ŠTEFÁNIK JOINS THE REVOLUTIONARY MOVEMENT. MASARYK AT PARIS IN FEBRUARY 1916

24

On December 13, 1915, the day after my arrival from Geneva, I met Dr. Milan Štefánik [1] for the first time during the war. Two days later we again met to discuss plans for our further co-operation and the general directives of our political activity in France. I have given a detailed account of Štefánik elsewhere, notably in a speech which I made when laying a foundation-stone for his mausoleum. Here I will mention only the leading facts of our co-operation in accordance with the actual development of events. We became loyal and devoted friends and fellow-workers. There were many points upon which I did not agree with Štefánik, just as he, on his part, did not agree with me in everything, but this never hindered us in our common task. We had only one dispute, but that was not until the Peace Conference, and it was settled in a friendly manner.

Dr. Milan Štefánik, who was then a lieutenant in the flying corps, had returned to Paris from the Serbian front on December 6, 1915. He had called on Masaryk at an earlier date, as soon as he had heard of his residence abroad. He had then gone off on active service, after which nothing was heard of him until he now reappeared in Paris. My first meeting with him in Paris had been exactly ten years earlier, in 1905; now we saw each other again under new and strange conditions. Štefánik

[1] Milan Rastislav Štefánik (1880–1919), a Slovak who, at the outbreak of the war, was director of the observatory at Meudon. He entered the French Army as a volunteer, and served as an aviator. Later he became a member of the Czechoslovak National Council and Minister of War. He performed several military and political missions in Russia, the United States, and Siberia. His death was caused by an aeroplane accident which took place while he was on his way to Czechoslovakia.

told me what he thought of the situation, what he had been doing in the army, and what we could now undertake in common. The plans which he unfolded to me were extensive. He indicated the possibility of powerful political connections in France and outlined a scheme for our journalistic and political co-operation. Finally, he asked me also to go to London again, to submit the whole scheme to Masaryk. I was to induce him to come to Paris to negotiate with the French Government, as the opportunity might arise.

I was in agreement with the idea of going to London, especially as Masaryk had just telegraphically informed me of a request from our fellow-countrymen in Holland for someone to proceed there. I therefore left for London on December 22nd, and on the same evening I had a long conversation with Masaryk in the hotel about our common work with Štefánik, about news from home, and the journey to Holland, where a new branch of our organization was to be established.(15)

Masaryk received Štefánik's plans with reserve, but on the whole he was in agreement with them. He asked us to make preparations for his arrival in Paris and to let him know when everything was ready.

From January 12th to the 28th, the latter being the date of Masaryk's arrival, we were kept extremely busy in Paris. Štefánik had been operated on for stomach trouble, and was in the hospital. I therefore acted on his behalf and prepared quite an extensive journalistic campaign with the *Matin*. Further, in accordance with the proposal made by Denis, I discussed the question of a special series of lectures on Slavonic affairs to be held at the Sorbonne. Masaryk was to give a lecture on the position of the Slavs in the world, and I was to give one on the Czechoslovak problem. An arrangement was also made with Senator Louis Martin for the Government to be approached on our behalf. Finally, all the rest of our friends were informed of Masaryk's forthcoming arrival, and preparations were made for a press campaign.

25

Masaryk arrived in Paris on January 28, 1916. On February 1st he visited the Russian Ambassador, Izvolsky, and explained to him our plans and activities. Štefánik, who had now more or less recovered, applied through Deputy Lemery and Mme. de Jouvenel for Masaryk to be officially received by Briand, and this was managed without difficulty on Friday, February 4th. In addition to this audience with Briand, Masaryk had important political conversations with Deschanel and with G. Leygues, the chairman of the foreign committee of the Chamber of Deputies.

Masaryk explained to Briand our whole thesis. He pointed out the significance of the Pan-German Berlin-Bagdad scheme, and showed that it was Austria-Hungary which made the aggression of Germany possible and promoted the Pan-German aim. It was therefore necessary to limit Germany to her own resources by the destruction of Austria-Hungary and the creation of new independent States which, by their very existence, would be the natural aids of France against German expansion eastwards. This involved the organization of the whole of Central Europe, the regions situated between France and Russia, and between Finland and Greece. Their reorganization for the advantage of France and of European peace would mean the granting of independence to the small nations in Central Europe and particularly the destruction of Austria-Hungary. Such was the programme of the war, which was a war against Pan-Germanism, against the violent absolutism of the Central European States, and for European democracy and the freedom of the oppressed. These aims were in accordance not only with the interests of France, but also with her lofty traditions.

Briand understood. He agreed that an official *communiqué* should be published concerning his discussions with Masaryk and that this *communiqué* was to inform the world that France was giving her official support to our movement. This meant that the leading French political circles which hitherto, from our point of view, had been wavering with regard to Austria-Hungary, would support our political ideas and our programme.(16)

As a result of propagandist and press activities on the part of ourselves and our various friends in political, academic, and journalistic circles in France and England, this notion gradually became so widespread that at the end of 1916 its essential points were incorporated into a number of official inter-Allied proclamations (e.g. the Allied Note of December 30, 1916, replying to the Austro-Hungarian proposal for peace negotiations), and also into the famous Allied Note to President Wilson on January 10, 1917. In this respect it may be said without exaggeration that Masaryk, by plainly expounding our demands, had shown how the Allied war-aims against the Central Powers should be defined and submitted as a programme to official circles and to the public. President Wilson expressed what in their essentials were the same or cognate ideas—they were in a more general form, as they were concerned with less concrete matters—in his famous messages during 1916 and 1917.

Masaryk's visit to Paris was an important political success. In London, too, he had done extremely well having, through the efforts of our friends, Mr. H. Wickham Steed and Dr. R. W. Seton Watson, been appointed professor at King's College. On October 19, 1915, he had delivered his inaugural lecture there, the subject being the part played by small nations during the war. The chairman on that occasion had been Lord Robert Cecil, and Mr. Asquith, who was then Prime Minister, had sent a message emphasizing the fact that the Allies were waging war for the protection of small nations. This official English support was now enhanced by official political support on the part of France. Our work thus acquired a starting-point and a basis for extended activity.

Masaryk's lecture in London, just as his lecture on the position of the Slavs in the world, arranged at the Sorbonne on February 22, 1916; his account of our aims which was given to Briand ; various manifestos which he produced in England on other occasions ; his memoranda submitted to the Allies and particularly his *New Europe*, which forms a complete synopsis of all these ideas and views ; further, our journalistic activity in *La Nation Tchèque* from May 1, 1915, onwards ; a number of official memoranda produced by the Secretariat of the National Council ; my lecture at the Sorbonne issued as a pamphlet in 1916 under the title *Destroy Austria-Hungary* ; and several other manifestos—all this formed the basis of our programme.

We soon produced an impression in Western Europe, not only because we were well informed politically, and supplied accurate diagnoses of Central Europe, but also because Masaryk was able to explain from the philosophy of history the significance of the World War, and how it should be regarded by Western Europe. Apart from Wilson's later arguments, this formed the only complete synthetic interpretation of the World War, its significance and meaning as a whole, and that is why our ideas had so much influence on all those who examined them in any detail. That, too, is why our movement produced considerable influence on current thought, since it everywhere succeeded in demonstrating the sound theoretical basis from which it was derived.

We formulated our proposals and schemes in various ways on various occasions, but always in a direct and graphic manner so that Western Europe, unacquainted with our trend of thought, and without sufficient practical knowledge of Central Europe, could immediately and easily understand our meaning. It was particularly important for us to devise an effective formulation of the problem, and thus to secure the interest of prominent people who had no time to listen to long explanations. Several of our propagandist publications, leaflets, maps, and memoranda were models of what propaganda should be, for they provided a graphic statement of our case, and at the same time were accurate as to the facts.

All this made Masaryk's stay in Paris a landmark in the history of our revolutionary movement.

(d) ESTABLISHMENT AND ORGANIZATION OF THE CZECHO-SLOVAK NATIONAL COUNCIL. CENTRALIZATION OF OUR REVOLUTIONARY MOVEMENT IN PARIS

26

From the very beginning Štefánik emphas:zed the necessity for rapidly organizing political headquarters. In particular he was afraid that there might be personal antagonisms, and in this way he wanted to avoid them. I myself was not satisfied with the casual and primitive form of the Foreign Committee. Moreover, there were factors in the political psychology then current which compelled us to settle the matter promptly. The Allies as a whole, including even the French, had no knowledge of us as a nation, or of our aims, plans, and ideals. They had no very high opinion of our colonists and émigrés. While acknowledging that the latter were in the main quite estimable people with excellent intentions, our Allied friends did not conceal from us their fears that it would be easy for enemy agents to conceal themselves among them.

As I have already stated, Masaryk in the spring of 1915 drew up a special circular in which he defined the duties of the colonists, and their relationship to the Czechoslovak political movement. He indicated quite clearly that the colonists would have to leave the management of their own political and military activities to the organizers who had just arrived from home, as only they would have real political prestige in the eyes of the Allied Governments. The colonists must limit themselves to activities of a local character concerning their internal organization.

We discussed these matters in the presence of Masaryk at Paris. We summoned also Dürich, Dr. Sychrava, and Plesinger-Božinov from Switzerland. It was finally agreed that in place of the "Czechoslovak Foreign Committee," a body which was too closely dependent upon conditions among our colonists, a new central organization would be established with headquarters in Paris. Paris was chosen for fairly obvious reasons. The chief military front was in France; Paris was, to a considerable extent, the political, diplomatic, and military centre of all the Allied countries, and accordingly it was to be expected that the war would be decided, for us also, in France and not on the Eastern Front in Russia.

After long consideration the new body was given the name of "Conseil National des Pays Tchèques." In this connection I may point out that Štefánik, himself a Slovak, advocated the term "des Pays Tchèques," since in view of the complete ignorance of Slavonic affairs in Western Europe he did not wish to complicate our demands by introducing the Slovak question. The coherence and permanence of this body was a corrective to the circumstance that the chief members of the National Council were scattered and without a fixed domicile. A permanent General Secretariat was thus located in Paris, forming the headquarters of the whole movement. This secretariat, with permanent executive functions, was devised as a means of impressing the unified and substantial character of our whole movement upon the Allied Governments and their public opinion. It was also intended as a rallying-point for the whole of our activities, both as regards the Allies and also our troops and colonists in France, England, Russia, America, Italy, Serbia, and the neutral States.

By acting as an intermediary for news, by communicating instructions, and concentrating the whole of our movement in Paris, the National Council and its secretariat later became a real practical link between our colonists, between our prisoners of war, who afterwards became our fighting forces, and also between our leading political personalities. Although we at first had not seen the full scope of these measures in all their consequences, the scheme proved to be a sound one. From the National Council and its secretariat was then developed a body which attained first-rate importance in our revolutionary activity.

The Czechoslovak National Council was thus constituted in February 1916. Its president was, of course, Masaryk, its vice-president Dürich, while Štefánik was the representative of the Slovaks, and I was the general secretary.

27

Our task was to include in our organization all the Allied and important neutral countries and to unite in a central body the resources of all our colonies, as well as the whole of our movement relating to prisoners of war and the troops.

We in Paris were well aware that we must, as rapidly and efficiently as possible, develop headquarters there which, both formally and practically, would deal with matters relating to our diplomatic policy, as well as the whole organization of our troops. We set up quite a substantial office, where I worked regularly in the general secretariat. We notified this officially to all our colonies, and began our work of concentration. As the moral authority of Masaryk had never been contested by anyone, we had no initial difficulties with regard to the fundamental acceptance of the authority of the General Secretariat. The express recognition of the leadership of Masaryk and the National Council reached us from the various representative bodies abroad, whether civil or military, only by a gradual process, but morally this leadership was recognized from the time when our first public action was taken.

What was chiefly necessary was that in the various countries uniform central organizations of our colonies should be established, and then that these bodies, each of which had jurisdiction only for the affairs of the respective colony, should subordinate themselves to the main authority of the National Council. In matters relating to volunteers for military service, the colonies were allowed a free hand, but those involving prisoners of war and the organization of an army, being questions with a wide political range, were from the very outset reserved for the National Council. This development was accomplished with comparative speed in France and England, even though a number of minor disputes regarding the political jurisdiction of the National Council continued for some time.

The situation was equally simple in Italy where, however, the number of our fellow-countrymen was small, and also in the neutral States, where we were glad of the assistance offered by our people, but we were unable to permit their direct intervention in our political and military affairs in the Allied countries.

In France we succeeded in uniting our people, to the number of about 2,000, in the central organization at Paris. This organization attended to the civil protection of its members and also to their economic support. It brought together about 700 Czechoslovak volunteers serving in the Foreign Legion, over whose interest it carefully watched until the time when they were transferred to our national army. Its work received support from a number of our friends, such as Denis, Gaye, Senator Louis Martin, Sansbœuf, Regamey, later on, Lebon, and others. From the time when the leading members of the colony succeeded in gaining for the Czechs and Slovaks a special civil status as for the Alsatians and Poles, the colony exercised what may be regarded as consular duties.

As elsewhere, in this colony too there were disputes and factions. Just as in England, America, and Russia the leaders overestimated their powers at the outset, and tried their hand at high politics. They proclaimed the dethronement of Franz Josef and the establishment of a Czechoslovak Republic, they intervened in Ministries, etc. This was natural enough in the situation as it was then. As our movement progressed, what we had to do was gradually, and without causing offence, to replace these improvised measures on the part of political amateurs (who, it should be added, had the best of intentions and did excellent work) by the organized activity of political representatives from Prague, who were really proficient at work of this sort. After the establishment of the National Council in Paris a certain tension accordingly arose, but it never resulted in open disputes, as from the very start the colony in Paris had acknowledged the authority and leadership of Masaryk. There was a certain opposition to the secretariat of the National Council and to myself at the early stages, before the secretariat could confront the colony with the results of its work. I avoided conflicts, allowing the colony to carry on its previous activities in matters concerning volunteers, money grants, and consular functions, and waiting for a suitable occasion to adjust precisely the reciprocal relationship. In those early days my situation was not always an easy one. But the more influence the National

Council acquired, the more the colony withdrew, automatically ceasing to take part in politics. Štefánik had no dealings with the colony at all.

From the moment when the National Council obtained recognition of the status of our army in France, its relations with the colony were almost completely accommodated. In the end there was a settled agreement with regard to co-operation, so that, especially from the spring of 1918, the colony supported with great devotion the activities of the National Council. In the summer of 1918, when preparations were being made to transfer our volunteers in France from the Foreign Legion into our army, the political side of our volunteer movement, and the agenda of a politico-consular character were entrusted to the National Council.

When a provisional Government was set up, the final stage of this development was reached. The colony resumed its function as a central union of compatriots, and all its requirements in relation to the French authorities were attended to by the offices of the National Council. In addition to the central colony in Paris, a Sokol society and the Social Democratic league, "Rovnost," were active as well, and a Franco-Czechoslovak Chamber of Commerce also was established.

(e) The National Council and our Revolutionary
Organizations in the Allied Countries

28

In England, at the very outbreak of the war, an organization of our fellow-countrymen was formed, which arranged for volunteers to join the British and Canadian Armies and attended also to the legal protection of our people who were exempted from internment as members of a nation friendly to the Allies. It also immediately got into touch with our colonies in the other Allied countries. From time to time, too, it ventured upon political work. After Masaryk's arrival it recognized his authority and acted upon his suggestions.

At the end of 1916 Masaryk established in London the Czech Press Bureau, which at his request placed itself under the direct control of the secretariat in Paris. Later on it almost entirely severed its connection with the colony, which began to limit its activities to matters involving legal or material assistance to our fellow-countrymen, especially those who had volunteered for military service. Political activities were handled exclusively by Masaryk, and after he left for Russia and America they were transferred to the secretariat in Paris, where I personally dealt with them. At this period our work received very generous help from Olga Masaryk.

From the spring of 1917 I extended the Press Bureau so as to make it a branch of the general propaganda department of the National Council. As the National Council in Paris increased its influence and sphere of its activities, the colony in London readily adapted itself to the new requirements. The office of the National Council gradually developed into a regular official department, which in the spring of 1918 became the direct exponent of the Government then coming into existence. After consultation with members of the colony, I supplied the London Press Bureau with new statutes in May 1918. The effect of this was to divide it into a propaganda and a consular section respectively. The former was entrusted to V. Nosek, who showed great proficiency in propaganda work, while the consular section was placed under the charge of Pochobradský, hitherto president of the colony. The office of the National Council became the headquarters of the secretariat in Paris, and when on October 14th an interim Government was established there, it automatically became a Legation. Excellent work was done in the colony for several years by Sykora, Kopecký, Professor Baudiš, Pochobradský, and others, the office of the National Council being carried on by Nosek and Aleš Brož. Matters connected with volunteers for the army were managed by Kopecký and Sykora.

The progress of our organization in Italy was analogous to our proceedings in France and England. On the declaration of war by Italy the greater part of our fellow-countrymen were interned, and it was only in course of time that various influences succeeded in liberating them. It was not long before a number of colonists and prisoners of war reported themselves to Masaryk and to us in Paris, offering to join the liberation movement or to enter the army. When the prisoners of war began to increase in numbers, they organized themselves in their camps, and later on placed themselves at the disposal of the National Council. I shall say more about this later.

In January 1917 I proceeded to Italy and set up a Press Bureau in Rome as a branch of the Paris secretariat of the National Council. This office in Rome kept closely in touch with us in Paris and acted in accordance with our suggestions. This was particularly the case during the second phase of our movement, when we were concerned not with mere propaganda, but with an actual policy in co-operation with Italy. During my second visit to Rome in September and October 1917, seeing that it was necessary to give our organization a wider scope, I established an office of the National Council with a more extensive sphere of influence. Its work was of a twofold character, being connected partly with the prisoners of war and partly with propaganda. A number of devoted workers were released from the camps for the former purpose, while the political and diplomatic work—in view of the delicacy of the situation in Italy—was, by a common agreement, just as in London, reserved for the members of the National Council and the secretariat in Paris. What we, especially Štefánik and myself, feared was that the influence of the serious Italian differences with the Jugoslavs, by which we also were affected, might be detrimental to our policy, and that things might happen which, not fitting in with our political plan and our tactics as a whole, might do harm to our national movement.

Our organization in Italy produced excellent results. Just as in London, our office there was recognized as a branch of the National Council, so that at the moment when a provisional Government was set up, it automatically became a Legation, of which Dr. Borský took charge in November 1918.

In Switzerland we had our permanent centres of activity, partly for maintaining communication with Prague, partly for propaganda, and for combating German-Austrian-Magyar espionage. Our people in Switzerland were permanently in touch with us, but the arrangements in this respect were not too rigid on account of the dangerous character of the surroundings in Switzerland, where thousands of Austro-German agents were at large. From the end of 1917 a regular Press Bureau was established on an entirely reorganized basis, and it was directed by Dr. Osuský until the beginning of the Peace Conference.

29

In Russia, just as in France, the representatives of the individual associations endeavoured to get into touch with similar bodies in the other Allied States as soon as they had succeeded in organizing themselves on a firm basis. These attempts, however, met with little or no success until Masaryk came forward openly and was at once acknowledged by the vast majority of our people in Russia as their leader and the representative of the revolutionary movement. At first, chiefly for technical reasons, Masaryk's communications with the Czechs in Russia were infrequent (I believe that they began in January 1915 as soon as Masaryk left Rome for Geneva). Correspondence was difficult since it might reach the hands of the enemy, and travelling presented obstacles on account of passports and the other formalities which it involved. From the time when Masaryk's public action was first taken, and notably from the autumn of 1915, *Čechoslovák*, a periodical edited by Bohdan Pavlů, and issued by the League of Czechoslovak Associations in Russia, referred to him as a leader who was entitled to speak on behalf of the nation.

The first public manifesto of our centralized movement abroad, announcing the formation of a central revolutionary body under Masaryk's leadership (the proclamation of the Foreign Committee on November 14, 1915), was signed by B. Čermák and B. Pavlů as representatives of the Czechs living in Russia; but as it was not of a definitive character, it did not settle once and for all the question of the relation between the Czechoslovak organization in Russia and the Paris headquarters. What made it difficult to unite the whole movement with its Russian portion was partly the remoteness and the geographical isolation of the Czechoslovak colony in Russia, partly the special political conditions under which the Czechoslovak revolutionary movement had been obliged to work during the Tsarist regime. Moreover, a certain number of Russians and Czechs in Russia were prejudiced against Masaryk on account of his radical political opinions. And even among our colonists in Russia there were people who thought the Czechoslovak question should be solved by the Russians themselves in accordance with their interests.

These factors, as far as they could exert any influence upon the relations between the Czechoslovak revolutionary organization and the Paris headquarters, were not plainly manifested up to the summer of 1916, although the Russian Government, especially since Masaryk's audience with M. Briand in February, had begun to adopt a favourable attitude towards certain intrigues against him, and later prepared a scheme for a separatist National Council. Among the Czechoslovaks themselves these intrigues had no success from the very start.

In consequence of the reports which B. Pavlů brought from London in April 1916, the League of Czechoslovak Associations in Russia decided to reply to Masaryk's message to the Czechs and Slovaks in Russia by a telegram of greeting, referring to Masaryk as their leader, acknowledged by the will of the Czech and Slovak elements. Serious complications, however, arose when, at the beginning of June 1916, Dürich proceeded to Russia and was regarded by the Tsarist Government as a suitable person for placing in the foreground of the Czecho-slovak revolutionary movement to counterbalance the influence of Masaryk. Štefánik, who was sent to Russia after Dürich, endeavoured to dispose of these difficulties with the support of the Petrograd group of Czechs. He succeeded in arranging what is known as the Kiev memorandum of August 29, 1916, in which for the first time all the Czechoslovak groups in Russia recognized not only the authority of the Czechoslovak National Council with Masaryk at its head, but also its supremacy as an organization above the League situated at Kiev. Soon afterwards, however, under the influence of the Russian Government, the question of the relationship between the League and the National Council met with fresh complications. The Russian Foreign Office refused to acknowledge the Kiev memorandum, induced Dürich to repudiate it, and drew up conditions connecting the establishment of a Czechoslovak Army and the leadership of Dürich in Russia. It also began to promote the idea of a separatist National Council managed by Dürich. Under the influence of this situation, a cleavage began to develop among the Czechoslovaks in Russia. As a result, those in charge of the League, harassed by the opposition in Petrograd and the discontent among the organizations dealing with prisoners of war, endeavoured to strengthen their position by making concessions to the Russian Foreign Office and to Dürich. In the middle of November 1916 this cleavage was publicly manifested, and from that date onwards the administration of the League at Kiev openly identified itself with the principles advocated by the Russian Foreign Office and by Dürich, to the effect that ' the League could successfully negotiate only in complete agreement with the authorized and acknowledged representative of the nation, Deputy Dürich, who had placed himself at the head of our movement in Russia, just as Professor Masaryk had done in Western Europe."

This resolution led to violent internal warfare. The opposition in Petrograd, led by B. Pavlů, resolutely sided with the National Council and Masaryk, and started a vigorous campaign against the attempt to divide the Czechoslovak revolutionary movement into a Western and an Eastern group. It carried on an extensive agitation, but in spite of its energetic action and the numerous manifestos of agreement with its point of view, in spite of Štefánik's personal intervention with Pokrovsky, the Minister of Foreign Affairs, the Russian Government sanctioned Dürich's statutes for a separatist National Council, and, moreover, granted Dürich and his organization the financial resources for this struggle.

This led to the expulsion of Dürich from the Paris National Council, and a declaration by the opposition groups that they would never acknowledge his leadership. The revolution in March, which broke out a month after Dürich's statutes had been sanctioned by the Russian Government, immediately changed the situation. The new Russian Government repudiated Dürich and the League itself as well. Under these circumstances an application was made to Milyukov, the new Minister of Foreign Affairs, for the National Council, under Masaryk's leadership, to be acknowledged as the sole political representative body of the Czechs in Russia. At the same time B. Čermák, the former chairman of the League at Petrograd, was appointed plenipotentiary of the Czechoslovak National Council, and an attempt was made to constitute a branch of it in Russia.

For a short time the League at Kiev was successful in its endeavours, at least to the extent that Milyukov, fearing further blunders which might be caused by a fresh decision, postponed the question of a branch of the National Council until Masaryk's arrival in Russia, which had now been provisionally announced. The opposition in Petrograd thereupon took fresh steps against the League, and scored a decisive victory at a new congress comprising representatives of the Czechoslovak colonists, soldiers, and prisoners of war.

This congress, which opened at Kiev on May 6, 1917, unanimously adopted the following resolution:

The Czechoslovak National Council, with Professor Masaryk at its head, is the supreme organ of the Czechoslovak national political struggle, and it is therefore the duty of every Czech and Slovak to submit to its management.

This resolution definitely settled the question of the relationship between the revolutionary movement in Russia and the National Council. A branch of the latter body was established in Russia, its chairman being a member of the Paris organization who happened to be in Russia at that time.

30

As in all the other Allied countries, the Czechoslovak colony in the United States, comprising more than a million and a half persons, rose against Austria-Hungary at the very outbreak of the war. On the eve of the declaration of war against Serbia, a large Czech meeting of protest against the Habsburg Empire was held at Chicago, and a committee appointed to collect funds for the support of war victims in the Czech territories.

The Czechs in Omaha were the first to come forward with any constructive plans, and in the middle of August a practical revolutionary scheme was announced in Rosický's *Ameriká Osvěta* (*American Enlightenment*). Then, on August 18, 1914, on the initiative of R. J. Pšenka, J. Tvrzický, K. Vinklárek, and others, there had been a meeting between representatives of the American National Council, the Czech Press Bureau, and the above-mentioned committee, at which these bodies were amalgamated into a uniform organization known as "The Czech National Alliance." It was agreed that the programme of this body was to consist of propaganda for the Czech cause, collections on behalf of war victims, and finally, also, what was called political action. At the head of the National Alliance, the headquarters of which were in Chicago, was Dr. L. Fisher, whose place was taken later by Dr. Pecivál, while the movement in New York was directed by E. Voska, with the assistance of V. Sperakus, Koňas, V. Rejsek, Marek, and others.

From the manifesto of the new organization, which was published on the day after the inaugural meeting, we learned that the aim of the National Alliance was to inform the public in America and Europe about the just demands of the Czech nation for independence, and thus to prepare the ground for achieving it. This movement arose at the initiative of our fellow-countrymen in America. It got into touch with the leaders of our revolutionary movement abroad later on, after Voska had returned from Bohemia with the first news of the preparations which were being made by Masaryk and his friends. After the declaration of war, Voska was the first envoy from Masaryk to reach our friends in London and America.

The first task of the National Alliance after the outbreak of the war was to convince our fellow-countrymen in America that political action was necessary and opportune. This task was a difficult one, and it was complicated by the lack of unity among the Czechs in America.

The work of Tvrzický, Dr. Fisher, Šerpán, and others, caused the greater part of those in the liberal camp to join the revolutionary movement shortly after the National Alliance was established; but the minority of this group, under the leadership of Dr. Iška, remained hostile almost to the end towards liberation activities, and was reconciled only after it had been divulged that Dr. Iška's paper, *Vesmír* (*The Universe*), had been paid for by the Austro-Hungarian Embassy. The Socialists were divided into two groups. One part, led by J. Martínek and A. Novotný, editors of the *Americké Delnické Listy* (*American Labour News*), at once joined the movement, while the other part, associated with K. H. Beránek and Jelínek, editors of *Spravedlnost* (*Justice*), remained neutral. Immediately after the arrival of Vojta Beneš, however, and after the meeting at Sandusky in September 1915, the majority, including Josef Novák, branch secretary of the Socialist Party, joined the Czech National Alliance.

Great assistance was rendered to the movement by the Czechs in Cleveland who, in January 1916, under the able leadership of K. Bernreiter, devoted themselves to our cause and remained devoted to it until the end. Similar work was directed at Cedar Rapids by C. V. Svoboda and at Boston by Josef Kovář. The Czech Evangelical settlements associated themselves with the movement from the very outset. Their leaders were J. Zmrhal and Dr. Smetánka.

The Catholics were at first favourably disposed towards Austria-Hungary, but later, under the influence of events in Bohemia, they adopted an attitude of cautious neutrality, with a bias in favour of the Habsburg Empire. It was not until the spring of 1917, when the United States declared war on Germany, that under the influence of the Rev. O. Zlámal, of Cleveland, they gradually threw in their lot with the national liberation movement. In the end Vojta Beneš succeeded in inducing the central Catholic organization, the National League of Czech Catholics, founded on January 14, 1917, under the leadership of I. Kestl and F. Šindelář, to join the common cause.

In 1915 the Czech National League was joined by the Sokols and the National Mutual Aid Organization. About that time a regularly monthly levy on the members was introduced for the support of the political movement. The rivalry between Chicago and New York for the leadership was removed by an agreement at a meeting of the two organizations in Cleveland, when the Chicago organization was recognized as the headquarters. By the end of 1915 the organization of the Czech National League had been elaborated by lectures, journalistic work, and propagandist tours of Vojta Beneš, and this led to a great increase in the membership and in the financial resources. The Slovak League also took part in the work at a comparatively early date. As far back as October 22 and 23, 1915, it had sent members to a joint conference with the National League, and its representatives signed the manifesto of the Foreign Committee on November 14, 1915. The President of the Slovak League was Albert Mamatey, of Pittsburg, who rendered invaluable services, while Milan Getting was head of the Slovak Sokols. The leader of the Slovak Catholics was the Pennsylvanian priest, Murgáš, while the Slovak Evangelicals were represented by Bradáč. Of the Chicago group special reference should be made to the work of Andrej Schustek. Elsewhere I shall refer to the propagandist activity carried on by the National League in American political and journalistic circles. It was equally necessary to carry on propaganda work among our actual fellow-countrymen in America in order to enlist the sympathies of our colony there for the liberation movement of the National Council in Paris. For this purpose meetings and lectures were arranged, personal visits were made, pamphlets, leaflets, and copies of our Paris paper, *Československa Samostatnost*, were distributed, and so forth.

In 1916 a number of journalists (Pšenka, Dr. Vojan, Mach, Tvrzický, and Vinklárek) founded a weekly paper, *V Boj* (*Into Battle*), the aim of which was to counteract the activities of Dr. Iška and his paper *Vesmír*. Later on, the National League issued a monthly periodical *Poselství* (*The Message*), edited first by Vojta Beneš then by F. L. Musil. At the beginning of the war Zeman's *Válečná Tribuna* (*War Tribune*) appeared for some time. An effective and original method of propaganda, partly to promote recruiting, partly to stimulate the national consciousness among our fellow-countrymen, was supplied by the striking posters which the painter Preissig designed. Karel Horký's pamphlet, *Ted', anebo nikdy* (*Now or Never*), was issued and distributed by the hundred thousand, also in the prisoners-of-war camps.

In order not to have to return to the matter later, I will give an account of what was achieved by the Czechoslovaks in America in military matters. As early as 1916 a Canadian Brigade was organized from the first Czech volunteers. It was originally proposed to organize a whole Czech regiment in the Canadian Army, but this idea had to be given up on account of many insuperable obstacles (American neutrality, strict frontier surveillance, the impossibility of carrying on open agitation, etc.) The Canadian Brigade was first organized by Jaroslav Císař, with the help of Vinklárek, Votava, Tvrzický, Linhart, and others.

When the United States entered the war there was a swarm of Czech volunteers for the American Army, and accordingly the recruiting of volunteers for our own army in France, which had been arranged in the United States by Štefánik, met with a comparatively limited success. (The number of American volunteers in the Czechoslovak Army in France was about three thousand.) For several reasons the American Czechs preferred to join the American Army, while others were called up when conscription was introduced, so that there remained for the Czechoslovak Army only an insignificant fraction of the most enthusiastic of our fellow-countrymen, and those who were not American citizens. These military matters were directed by František Kopecký in New York.

The relations between our organizations in America and the Czechoslovak revolutionary headquarters in Paris developed smoothly. Our fellow-countrymen in America had already made the acquaintance of Masaryk during his trip there before the war, and their ideas had much in common with his. He was therefore acknowledged there from the very beginning, as the leading authority and head of the revolutionary movement, not only among the Czechs but very soon among the Slovaks as well. This process was either tacit, or revealed itself by occasional manifestos or by the subscriptions which were sent in from the Czech and Slovak organizations.

Thus there were no differences concerning the association with the European headquarters. Masaryk had communicated with his acquaintances in America immediately after his departure from Prague. Dr. Sychrava co-operated with the

American Press Bureau and with Tvrzický, while I myself, after the arrival of Vojta Beneš in the United States, was in regular communication with America, and later on, when I was General Secretary of the National Council, this became a systematic and official arrangement. The Czech and Slovak organizations in America identified themselves with the open action we took on November 14, 1915, and this attitude was confirmed by the beginning of a co-operation which was then automatically transferred to the National Council, and continued without difficulties or disputes of any kind until the proclamation of a provisional Government. Formal agreement as to joint action was reached by all our American organizations at the congress held in Chicago from February 9–12, 1918. Professor B. Šimek, of Iowa City, became president of the Joint National Committee of Czechs and Slovaks, with Vojta Beneš as secretary.

31

The National Council at Paris thus succeeded gradually in establishing communication with our fellow-countrymen throughout the world. They reported themselves from South America, especially Brazil and Argentine, then from South Africa, Australia, and China, and wherever possible they sent subscriptions. There were frequent cases in which our fellow-countrymen in these States spontaneously offered themselves for military service or sent contributions. As General Secretary I maintained a regular correspondence as far as possible with all organizations in the individual countries, thus linking our people with the central organization and strengthening its authority.

I kept up a correspondence with the League at Kiev, and quite regularly sent news to the National Alliance in America. Our communications with Switzerland and Holland were very active, and we were in close touch, both written and personal, with Italy and England. When we succeeded in starting our movement among the prisoners of war, and carrying out military plans on a large scale in France, Italy, and Russia (in addition to the recruiting scheme in America), our organization reached the highest point of its development as regards unity, discipline, and success. I need hardly add that I had kept in continual touch with Prague.

VI

THE PROPAGANDIST ACTIVITY OF OUR REVOLUTIONARY MOVEMENT

(a) THE ORGANIZATION OF OUR PROPAGANDA AND ITS CENTRES IN FRANCE

32

AFTER the publication of the manifesto on November 14, 1915, our work continued to be mainly propagandist, because, for the time being, this was the kind of work of which we stood most in need. Not only the public, but also official circles had so imperfect a knowledge of us that it was necessary to begin from the very A B C of the subject.

The official reception of Masaryk by Briand, however, the establishment and organization of our political headquarters and official national body in Paris, as well as the precise formulation of our programme, provided us with at least a hint of the direction which our further activities should take. The outward indication of this was only a gradual process. On the whole, we continued our work on the same lines as before, but nevertheless from political propagandists we were developing more and more into military organizers and, later on, into diplomats.

Our activity thus begins to assume the following aspects:

(a) Propaganda.
(b) Work connected with prisoners of war and troops.
(c) Political and diplomatic work.

It will perhaps give a clearer idea of our work if I deal with each of these separately.

The development of our movement from propaganda to politics, especially in France, took place in the first half of 1916. In the second half of that year there began an intensive and well-organized activity in connection with prisoners of war and troops generally. From August 1916 onwards I deliberately modified what I had hitherto been doing in my capacity as General Secretary of the National Council. I now more and more emphasized the official and responsible character of my activity, as a contrast to my previous work as a political *émigré* who had been free to undertake anything which he considered in the interests of his country. For all that, our propagandist work still continued to be one of the fundamental elements in our activity until the end of 1918. It was inseparable from the politico-diplomatic and military aspect of our movement.

Work in connection with the prisoners of war occupied the National Council most of all in 1917, the year when we made our general preparations for organizing our military resources. It was in 1918 that this organization reached its culminating point. In that year our troops were engaged in the Western and Eastern seats of war. It was also the year of our Siberian enterprise, and of our decisive political and diplomatic action, which resulted in our recognition and the proclamation of our Government and our independence.

Having established contact with a number of journalists, I supplied them with the news which I received from home by way of Switzerland, or obtained from our papers. The Viennese and Magyar papers with which I was supplied by Eisenmann and the French Ministry of War, my communications with Dr. Sychrava and, through his agency, with Prague, furnished me with so much information that every day I was able to satisfy the requirements of the French authorities, as well as of my journalist friends.

Thus, from October 1915 onwards, my work in connection with propaganda and news was fairly regular. On the one hand there was my systematic activity for *La Nation Tchèque*, on the other hand I was helping the French Ministry of War and several daily papers. At the same time I began to write for Czech papers in America to eke out my resources, for I was afraid that the long war would use up the small supply of money which I had brought with me.

In this way I gradually succeeded in penetrating into official circles and also into the world of journalism in France. My connection with a number of influential journalists (Gauvain; de Quirielle; de Nalèche, of the *Journal des Débats*; Duboscq, of the *Temps*; Bertrand, of *Paris Midi*; Bienaimé, of *La Victoire*; Chéradame, and others) enabled us bit by bit to bring our case before the public. At that period I was satisfied if we managed two or three times a week to get a few lines about our affairs into one of the papers I have mentioned. At first this was difficult, but as time went on we gained more confidence and influence, so that now and then we were able to publish whole articles or essays of considerable length.

I lived in the Rue Léopold Robert, on the left bank of the Seine, in student style, as I had done during my first residence in Paris ten years previously. I lunched and had supper for one and a half francs in a small restaurant in the same street. I prepared my own breakfast. When Masaryk was in Paris he often used to go there too, so that we could talk during the meal and decide upon our aims, plans, and further measures. I had no breathing-space, except for the time spent in the restaurant at lunch and supper. This went on throughout the war, except that later I obtained a somewhat better lodging, with somewhat better surroundings, on the premises occupied by the National Council in the Rue Bonaparte. But I never really had any intervals for rest, never any holidays or Sundays.

When Štefánik arrived in Paris in December, laborious propaganda of another kind was added. As I have mentioned, Štefánik had a number of acquaintances in Paris from former days. Prominent among these was the Parliamentary deputy de Monzie. As he was now a lieutenant in the Air Force, Štefánik, at the beginning of 1916, with de Monzie's help, established contact with a number of other persons, chiefly in society, such as Deputy Lemery, Mme. de Jouvenel, the Weiss family, and others. As a result of his military activity this circle became wider, just as my new acquaintances gradually introduced me to further connections.

Through being in touch with the circles which I have mentioned, Štefánik had an opportunity of spreading the news with which I supplied him every day from the Czech and Austrian newspapers. He was often asked for written statements, memoranda, comments, and articles on these subjects. I therefore used to visit Štefánik every morning at his lodging, and supply him regularly with material of this kind. Here we acted in a psychologically sound manner, for there were many people who would never read a newspaper article on a given subject, although they would study it eagerly if the information was given to them in the form of a confidential memorandum for their use only. And such people became the propagators of ideas and reports which they regarded as having been reserved solely for them. For whole months at a time

I would compile daily memoranda and informative articles in various guises, which Štefánik then placed in various quarters. This increased my work considerably, for my own connections with journalists and politicians were beginning to extend, and *La Nation Tchèque* also involved more and more work.

Our propagandist activity entered upon a new phase when Dr. Sychrava moved to Paris on April 18, 1916. He had had trouble with the Swiss Government on account of his political activities, and in the end, as the result of pressure on the part of the Austro-Hungarian Government, he had been compelled to leave Geneva. He had then settled for a short time at Annemasse, a French village on the Franco-Swiss frontier, where he continued to edit the *Československá Samostatnost*, and to communicate with Switzerland and Prague. The technical difficulties which this caused induced us to transfer the *Československá Samostatnost* to Paris. Thus arose a new centre of activity there in the form of an editorial office which demanded a new technical and propagandist organization.

In the first place we had to set up a printing office for the Czech paper. This was later extended so as to include the printing of our French publications, especially *La Nation Tchèque* and our second periodical *Le Monde Slave*, as well as all our pamphlets, books, maps, etc. This widened the scope of our propagandist activity. Dr. Sychrava began to work on the same lines and in conjunction with the same persons as I myself. When we had set up our more elaborate centre in the Rue Bonaparte for the National Council and its secretariat, for the editorial office of the *Československá Samostatnost* (later on for *La Nation Tchèque* as well), and also for the managing departments of our papers and publications, we were able to carry on our propaganda in surroundings, the more dignified character of which increased our chances of success. Our headquarters developed into a widespread and well-organized political undertaking, the strength and efficiency of which showed up very strikingly in comparison with similar undertakings on the part of other nations.

In June 1916 Štefan Osuský arrived in Paris from Chicago. I should like to say a few words here about his work. He had travelled by way of London, where he had met Masaryk. He had been sent from America by the Slovak organizations there in order to examine the situation in Europe and then, if the circumstances warranted it, to remain and co-operate with the National Council as a Slovak representative. He was accompanied by Gustav Košík, another Slovak delegate, who shortly afterwards proceeded to Russia and then returned to America.

Osuský, unlike Košík and others of his fellow-countrymen in America, soon gained an accurate idea of the situation in Europe, and realized what could and could not be done in a political respect. In spite of certain differences of opinion with regard to the co-operation between the Czechs and Slovaks and the organization of our whole movement, which we discovered at the very beginning, we worked together uninterruptedly and successfully. Osuský was capable, persevering and industrious. Being a Slovak, he devoted his attention mainly to Magyar affairs, and his knowledge of Magyar was of the utmost help to us in following events in Hungary during the war, and obtaining information which other people missed. He was able to proceed decisively and independently in important questions, and gained many acquaintances and friends. His abilities were soon recognized by those who were sharing his work.

Thus we gradually distributed the spheres of our activity and carried on systematic work for the ministries, for the Press, for our own papers, for a number of politicians, journalists, and various friends who needed special statements, memoranda, and commentaries on what was happening. We soon began to elaborate such memoranda, articles, and reports for London and Italy as well.

33

In order to give a general idea of our propaganda I should like to mention a few typical instances of the political propagandist work which we carried on in our Parisian surroundings. They throw an instructive light upon the democratic character of our work.

From the middle of 1916 to the end of 1918 I concentrated my propagandist activity on certain influential quarters in Paris. A part of the success of our propagandist work was due to the fact that we prepared material consisting of isolated news-items, reports, and whole articles for our journalistic and political friends, but ourselves remained in the background and allowed them to be the advocates of our claims, requirements, and ideas. If our demands were championed in England, France, and Italy by natives of those countries, this carried much more political weight under certain circumstances than if we ourselves had taken such action. Hence the political importance of what was done on our behalf by such people as Denis and Gauvain, Steed and Seton Watson, Milyukov, the people connected with the *Corriere della Sera*, etc., was considerable. One of the effective devices in politics is to know how to be at the right place in a discreet and unobtrusive manner.

The first of such spheres of our activity was around Professor Denis, and it comprised a number of professors from the Sorbonne, several of his personal friends, including some French Slavists and journalists. Among the members of this circle were, in addition to Denis himself, Meillet, Boyer, Haumant, Eisenmann, Moysset, Fournol, Gauvain, Robert de Caix, Victor Berard, and after a certain time Chéradame, Franklin-Bouillon, Albert Thomas. There were a number of other foreigners besides ourselves who frequented this circle. Thus, there were such Jugoslavs as Trumbić, Hinković,Vošnjak, Meštrovic, and De Giuli, while the Poles, who owing to the Russophil tendency of the whole group showed a certain reserve, were represented by Potocki. There were rarely any Russians, the most noteworthy being Maklakov, who was occasionally there from the end of 1917 onwards. After a certain time, especially in 1918, the Rumanians (Draghicescu, Florescu) made their appearance. Of the Czechs, the most frequent visitor beside myself was Dr. Sychrava.

Masaryk and myself, being professors, always sought to get into touch with scholars in France, Italy, England, and Russia, for reasons of principle, even when they were not politically influential, or took no direct share in practical politics. And although in diplomatic and political circles scholars and professors were often treated with caution and reserve, we always regarded them as skilful helpers, particularly for conveying definite and reliable knowledge about our affairs. This was the basis of what I may call our small-scale work, which began modestly enough, but which produced great results. The war awakened an interest in politics among all classes of the people, and it was therefore necessary to win their sympathies through all channels, and not merely to apply to ministers for an audience. Each of our academic fellow-workers had either influential political friends of his own, or else he himself was active as a writer and could introduce or recommend us to the more influential political circles.

All the members of Denis's circle were active either as writers or lecturers. Moreover, they were all closely in touch with various Slavonic questions—Russian, Polish, Jugoslav, or our own—and by disseminating information about these subjects publicly they also produced an indirect effect upon responsible circles. They took a direct share in our propagandist work by writing for *La Nation Tchèque*, and later on for our review *Le Monde Slave*. As university professors and scholars they helped to establish our credentials with the French public, especially at the start, by showing that our movement was a serious one, and that it would have to be taken into account as a political factor.

It is not possible to enumerate all that was done by the members of this French group. Here it will be enough to say that the most active of them was Professor E. Denis, who, by his propaganda and his moral influence, rendered great services to us in certain French circles. He joined us at the very beginning, before we had any central organization, and he remained our friend during the most critical period of our efforts.

After the outbreak of the Russian revolution this group endeavoured to found an association for studying and propagating Slavonic matters. This was successfully organized by E. Fournol. In 1917 and 1918 the association arranged a number of public debates which exerted an influence on public opinion, and gained many friends for the Slavonic cause and the oppressed nations of Austria-Hungary. It was this which, in the spring of 1918, gave rise to the idea of holding a congress of the oppressed nations in Rome in April 1918, and then another in Paris. The second congress, however, did not take place.

Another such centre, which in the spring of 1916 promoted our cause in the early stages of our work, was the special committee for foreign affairs connected with the French Senate and directed by Senator d'Aunay. This committee was specially interested in the oppressed nations of Austria-Hungary, and under its auspices lectures were held in the Senate on the Czechoslovak question. It was there that I got into touch with senatorial circles, and on several occasions spoke about our affairs. This was a further step towards strengthening our position in the political circles of Paris.

There were two other centres of a similar character, both of which were important from a political and propagandist point of view. These were the "Société de Sociologie" and the "Comité National d'Études." The former organization, at the head of which was the sociologist Professor Worms, was applying itself to the study of the war, and every fortnight held public meetings devoted to the various nations engaged in the war, their demands and aims forming the subject of discussion. All the Austro-Hungarian questions had been publicly examined in detail, and by this process further sections of the French public had been won over.

The "Comité National d'Études" was also influential. It is a society of prominent French intellectuals who meet every week to discuss some important problem in public life. The subject is first dealt with by an expert, a discussion is then held, and if any practical steps are considered necessary they are often taken by individual members who occupy an important position in public affairs. The lectures and discussions are issued in a limited edition as memoranda, and are placed at the disposal of persons in public and political life who are interested in the respective subjects. The Society carried out much admirable work, both during and after the war.

I regularly attended the meetings of the Society, and on several occasions I lectured there on Czechoslovak matters, and on the Austro-Hungarian problem in general. Those present on these occasions comprised such important and influential persons as Léon Bourgeois, Bergson, Appel (the rector of the Sorbonne), Professor Aulard, Gabriel Séailles, Professor Gide, Professor Bouglé, Albert Thomas, Professor Brunhes, Dubreuilh (the Socialist deputy), Professor Durkheim, Denis, Gauvain, Moysset, Eisenmann, as well as a number of senators, deputies, and journalists. The "Comité National d'Études" paid special attention to the problems of oppressed nations in the spring of 1918, and through its influential members intervened with the Government for the adoption of a point of view against Austria-Hungary. After the congress at Rome I lectured to the committee under the chairmanship of Léon Bourgeois, and this led to an intervention with the Government for promoting our recognition.

Besides these groups, there were three important organizations amongst which I made acquaintances. These were the Freemasons, the League for the Rights of Mankind and Citizenship, and finally the French Socialist Party. The latter party was a source of danger from 1917 because of the endeavours of certain of its influential members (notably Jean Longuet), who began to exert a strong pressure with a view to ending the war quickly. As regards the Freemasons, I established contact with them through the help of our fellow-countrymen in Paris, and with the support of the Jugoslav members of the Freemasons' Lodge there, I had an opportunity of lecturing to the Lodge on our affairs, and gained the sympathies of Free-masons in Paris.

I often attended the meetings of the well-known League for the Rights of Mankind and Citizenship, and on several occasions I gave lectures there on the Austro-Hungarian prob-lem. By its very character this was an excellent centre for our propaganda. By coming into contact with the members of the Socialist Party there, especially Albert Thomas, Dubreuilh, and Longuet, I endeavoured to counteract the tendencies unfavour-able to us, for at first, under the influence of the International, there were many in the Socialist Party who were emphatically opposed to the policy of destroying Austria-Hungary, which they regarded as involving an unnecessary prolongation of the war.

I add one remark in connection with the policy of the French Socialist Party. From the summer of 1917 a group of Socialists was formed in Paris, around Albert Thomas, to deal with the war aims of the belligerents. They endeavoured to lead the Allied Socialist parties towards a policy favourable to the oppressed nations and the destruction of the Habsburg Empire.

On his return from Russia, after the revolution there, Albert Thomas organized a special committee for the protection of oppressed nations, its members comprising Socialist represen-tatives of the Czechoslovaks, Poles, Rumanians, Jugoslavs, Ukrainians, Lithuanians, and the Italians from Austro-Hun-garian territories. After a certain time this committee carried out an important propaganda, taking part in a number of Socialist demonstrations, and exerting an influence upon the policy of the French Socialist Party and the English Labour Party. Together with Albert Thomas I had a share in this work throughout the period during which this committee existed. By this activity Albert Thomas rendered valuable services to our cause.

We used all these centres deliberately and systematically for our political purposes. From time to time I succeeded also in approaching a number of Catholic circles (e.g. Mgr. Baudrillart, and later on Mgr. Ceretti, now a Cardinal and an important political personage at the Vatican). I pursued my activities among them and they always granted me a benevolent hearing. Our propaganda met with considerable success in all these various circles. Those who took part in it were sincerely devoted to our cause. They all contributed an important share to our work, and in justice this should be emphasized.

(b) OUR PROPAGANDA IN THE OTHER ALLIED COUNTRIES

34

From what I saw of the situation as a whole, I should say that our propaganda in France was the most systematic and comprehensive. At the same time, a great deal was accomplished in England and Italy. As regards England, in addition to the important political and journalistic work carried on by Masaryk in the form of articles and interviews, a reference should be made to the Czech Press Bureau, already mentioned, which performed unobtrusive but thoroughly good services. The purposes of propaganda were admirably served by a well-appointed shop, the windows of which looked out on to Piccadilly Circus, and by means of maps, diagrams, statistics, pictures, and photographs gave the thousands of passers-by day by day a graphic idea of the Czechoslovaks and their aims.

Here I again find it necessary to emphasize the great services rendered in London to our cause by our faithful friends and fellow-workers, Mr. H. Wickham Steed, Mme. Rose, and Dr. R. W. Seton Watson. Mr. Steed's important position as Foreign Editor of *The Times* gave him access to all influential circles, and throughout the period of the war a large number of sympathizers met at his house for tea every Saturday afternoon. Here they conferred, debated, made plans and exchanged items of information. On these occasions I used to meet not only prominent Englishmen, but also Frenchmen, Italians, Japanese and Americans, Jugoslavs, Rumanians and Poles. It was here that I made the acquaintance of my present colleagues on the League of Nations—Avenol, Manthoux, and

Comert. Through them I was introduced to members of the French Embassy, such as de Fleuriau, and later to Paul Cambon himself. Steed was a devoted adviser and friend to our people. He has, and always will have, a place of honour in the history of our liberation.

The same applies to Dr. Seton Watson, who had done valuable work on behalf of the Slovaks before the war, and to this now added his extensive activities on our behalf during the war. In October 1916, after consulting with Masaryk and Steed, he founded the *New Europe*, a monthly review which championed our programme and, in fact, the programme for liberating all the oppressed nations of Central Europe. Seton Watson gathered round him a group of collaborators, such as A. F. Whyte, M.P., Sir Arthur Evans, the brothers Leeper, Sir Bernard Pares, R. F. Young, L. B. Namier, and others, who wrote on Central European matters. A number of others were associated with this work on our behalf, and of them I should refer in particular to the late H. M. Hyndman, with his paper *Justice*; the late Ronald Burrows, Principal of King's College; Lord Bryce; Dr. Harold Williams; Professor Sarolea, who at that time was editing the paper *Everyman*; the late Dr. Dillon; Mrs. Rosa Newmarch; and the Rev. Hunter Boyd. With the assistance of this group, and in co-operation with the Jugoslavs, Poles, Rumanians, Lithuanians, etc., public demonstrations and lectures were arranged.

Very valuable services were rendered to our cause later on by a new institution which came into existence at the initiative of Steed and Lord Northcliffe, and was located at Crewe House. This was a well-organized office for collecting detailed information about the political, economic, and military position of the Central Powers. This information was then used for propaganda, and for the assistance of both official and unofficial circles. Its work was carried on not only in England, but also in France, and from the spring of 1918 very widely in Italy as well. It operated by means of the distribution of pamphlets at the front among the Slav troops in the Austro-Hungarian armies. At first it was an institution for propaganda pure and simple, but under the influence of Northcliffe and Steed it became a powerful political factor, and played an important part in the movement for the destruction of Austria-Hungary. There is no doubt that in this respect it did much to change the orientation of British policy. I shall say more about this later on. Here I will only add that our Press Bureau and I myself actively co-operated with this institution, especially as regards its work in Italy.

Besides these various activities must be mentioned the wide contact established by Masaryk, more particularly in academic circles but also among journalists and writers.

It was not until 1917 and 1918 that our propaganda in Italy began to assume extensive proportions, when a Ministry of Propaganda was set up and directed by Deputy Commandini. The Minister himself, together with his secretary Gino Scarpa, paid close attention to Austrian affairs and keenly co-operated with us.

A favourable centre for us was established in the entourage of the Deputy Torre, who from the outset promoted our interests. He was gradually joined by a number of other workers, amongst whom I would mention particularly G. Amendola, a gifted and accomplished politician who was then one of the hopes of Italy and who later became Minister for the Colonies. This group comprised a number of contributors to the *Corriere della Sera*—Senator Albertini, Professor Borghese, Ugo Ojetti, Emanuele Campolunghi, and others. To these must be added a number of irredentists and nationalists of that period, some of whom, such as Dadone, were also in our army.

In the spring of 1918, before our army had come into existence, our propaganda made excellent progress. We were assisted by a number of Parliamentary deputies, such as Arca, Canepa, Calenga, Senators Ruffini and Scialoja, with whom the Congress of Oppressed Nations was arranged at Rome in April 1918. At that period the first suggestions were made for establishing the "Lega italo-czecoslovacca," which did much to spread a knowledge of our affairs in Italy and to cultivate cordial relations between the two peoples. Excellent work for the common cause was done especially by the Minister Lanza di Scalea, who afterwards served in our army. The co-operation of these sympathizers enabled us, notably after our army had come into being, to achieve much popularity in Italy, where our political aims and our military achievements were greatly appreciated.

Switzerland, of course, also came within the scope of our propaganda. Assistance was here given to our representatives by a number of friends of the Allied cause, of whom I should like to mention at least A. Bonnard, a contributor of many years' standing to the *Journal de Genève*, E. Chapuisat, A. François, and Maurice Muret, on the staff of the *Gazette de Lausanne*. The names of all these should be placed on record at a moment when, as a result of their support also, we have attained our national aims.

35

The propaganda for the Czechoslovak cause in Russia had many features in common with that which was carried on in the other Allied countries, but there were a number of details in which it was markedly divergent.

The leading members of the Czechoslovak organizations at Petrograd, Kiev, and Moscow endeavoured, at the very beginning, to draw the attention of the Russian public to the importance of the Czechoslovak question, partly by manifestos and meetings, partly by communications to the daily Press. To a certain extent their task was easier than elsewhere, for it was natural that the Czechoslovak question should be more familiar to the Russians than to the public in Western Europe. Thus, the papers often discussed it without external prompting. Matters were made somewhat easier also by the existence of enthusiastic sentiments for the Slavonic races, which was manifested notably in the Right Wing circles near the Government. This explains why, in the early months of the war, the Russian newspapers published articles demonstrating the vital necessity of dismembering Austria-Hungary and liberating the Slavonic nations.

The propaganda of the Czech cause was not overlooked by those who were managing the League at Kiev. Thanks to the personal relations which they possessed they succeeded in gaining a very useful medium in the newspaper *Kievlanin*, and also in a number of other papers at Moscow and Odessa. At the end of 1916 work on similar lines was started also by a number of former prisoners of war who were working for the League. Propagandist activities of the most varied kind (Sokol exercises, theatrical performances, lectures, etc.) were carried on also in the large camps for Czech prisoners of war at Tashkent, Tyumen, Bobruisk, and elsewhere.

The Russian revolution considerably modified the tendency

of Czech propaganda. After the short rule of the first interim
Government new people from Socialist circles took charge of
affairs. It was therefore necessary to begin the propaganda
of the Czechoslovak cause almost afresh. A special propaganda
commission was set up at the branch of the National Council,
and Masaryk himself attended to questions of propaganda
above all else. Immediately upon his arrival in Russia he
renewed contact with his acquaintances and began to extend
their circle. He succeeded in securing for the Czechoslovak
idea the Press organs of three political groups. These comprised
Ryetch and *Ruskiya vyedomosti*, the daily papers of the Cadet
Party; *Yedinstvo*, the organ of Plekhanov's group; and finally
Volya naroda, the organ of the Right Wing of the Russian
Revolutionary Socialists. Masaryk also lectured as the need
arose, and took part in what were known as concert meetings
which were then in vogue. At that time, too, numerous interviews which he granted to representatives of the Russian Press
were used for the purpose of informing the Russian public
about us.

At the end of the spring of 1917 Masaryk made an attempt
in Russia to bring out a paper on similar lines to the *New
Europe* in England. This attempt did not lead to any tangible
result. At Masaryk's initiative a group of Czech Social
Democrats in Moscow then issued a special memorandum for
the information of Socialist circles. The State Conference at
Moscow in 1917 was also used for propaganda purposes, and
on this occasion the Czechs in Russia were represented by
Dr. Girsa, who was also one of the speakers.

The Bolshevik Revolution naturally thrust the propaganda
of the Czechoslovak cause into the background. The Russian
public was too much occupied with its own affairs. Nevertheless,
as far as the disturbances in the early months of the revolution
permitted, the Soviet circles were kept informed about the
Czechoslovak programme. The Czechoslovak Army Corps,
on its journey from Russia to France, also endeavoured to
make the essentials of the Czechoslovak movement known
to the Russians by distributing leaflets in the localities through
which it passed.

The conflict between the Czechoslovak Army and the Soviet
Government naturally put an end to these efforts. The actual
achievement of our troops was of such a character that no
further propaganda of our cause was needed.

36

The propaganda of our aims and endeavours in the United States of America was somewhat different from that carried on elsewhere, chiefly because the United States did not enter the war until 1917, and the whole character of our propaganda at the beginning of the war thus had to be adapted to the conditions in a neutral country. Moreover, the American public, to whom European and, still more, Central European conditions were extremely remote, knew little about us. The methods, however, which were adopted for our propaganda in America were similar to those elsewhere. They included a supply of news to the Press, personal relationships, memoranda, deputations, public lectures, etc.

Leading members of the American colony in America, notably E. Voska, T. Čapek, K. Pergler, and J. Tvrzický, got into touch with Allied official representatives there, and also with a number of prominent American politicians and journalists. Thus Voska had an opportunity of making the acquaintance of Colonel House. It was Voska's counter-espionage work, too, which materially assisted our fellow-countrymen in their propaganda among American official circles. Voska, with the help of Consul Kopecký and others, drew the attention of the American authorities to the German and Austro-Hungarian diplomatic representatives' agents, who were systematically impeding the supply of foodstuffs and war material to the Allied Powers, and were provoking disorder and strikes in American factories. They even went so far as to arrange for a conflict between the United States and Mexico. It was through Voska's activity that the intrigues of Ambassador Dumba and of the German diplomats von Pappen and Boy-Ed were exposed.

In 1915 preparations were begun for carrying on a more extensive Press campaign. The *American Bi-monthly Review*, which was established in 1914 under the editorship of Professor Zmrhal for the purpose of informing the American public about our affairs, was soon discontinued; but a number of informative pamphlets, written by Dr. Smetánka, and Thomas Čapek's *Bohemia under Habsburg Rule*, the first extensive propagandist publication, were issued. We also succeeded in interesting a number of daily papers, notably those of Chicago, in our cause. From the end of 1916 this propagandist activity was intensified and began to exert a strong influence, particularly from the moment when the United States entered the war. Of the more important items of our activity during this period should be mentioned the manifesto of the Czech National Alliance at the American elections and the memorandum sent by the Czech Socialists in America to the Socialist parties throughout the world. Reference should also be made to the campaign against American pacifism, the culminating point of which was the open letter addressed by the National League to Miss Jane Addams.

In 1916 numerous lectures were delivered by Pergler, Professor Šimek, Šárka Hrbková, Dr. Smetánka, and others at universities and university clubs. At the beginning of the same year Meyer London, a member of Congress, was induced to bring forward a resolution calling upon the President to convene a conference of neutral nations on the subject of peace terms, and to include the principle of the self-determination of small nations among those terms. A public meeting of those interested in this matter was held on February 25 and 26, 1916, and K. Pergler, the representative of the National Alliance, took this opportunity of acquainting several prominent Americans with our cause. Similar action was taken by Pergler during the session of the legislative committees of the States of Texas, Nebraska, Iowa, Massachusetts, at the anniversary congress of the Alliance of Iowa State lawyers, and on other occasions. Special reference should here be made to Congressman Sabath, who did valuable work on our behalf.

Among the important steps taken in 1917 should be mentioned the activities in connection with the congress of small and oppressed nationalities, and the congress of the American Academy of Political and Social Sciences at Philadelphia. The speeches delivered on these occasions were nearly all issued in pamphlet form and then distributed among universities, libraries, members of Congress, and other prominent public men.

An important stage in the development of our propaganda was the foundation of the Slav Press Bureau, which formed the beginning of an organized and concentrated Press activity. The bulletins of this bureau were distributed among about five hundred daily American papers, which gradually began to print the reports contained in them. At the same time the Slav Press Bureau became a centre for all who wished to obtain information about Czechoslovakia and Central Europe.

Soon after America entered the war the effects of this propaganda began to manifest themselves. As early as May 1917 Senator Kenyon, of Iowa, brought forward a resolution in the Senate advocating the independence of the Czechoslovak nation.

Parallel with the activities of the Slav Press Bureau there was a continuance of the lectures held at various American clubs, organizations and universities during 1917 and later. Thus, the Czechoslovak question formed the subject of speeches at the Labour Congress in Minneapolis under the chairmanship of the late Samuel Gompers, and also at the conference on international relations. Tvrzický and Dr. Smetánka, too, founded *The Bohemian Review*, which was later known as *The Czechoslovak Review*, and continued to appear after the war.

This propaganda attained its maximum proportions after Masaryk's arrival in the United States. His visit to Chicago was, in itself, an important propagandist event. He was welcomed by an assembly of about one hundred thousand persons, and this attracted general attention. The undertakings which were planned, and the methods of work which were adopted at that period, have been recorded by Masaryk himself in his *Making of a State*.

I should here like to emphasize the fact that the greatest propaganda in the United States during 1918 consisted of the achievements of our Siberian Army, which, by reason of its romantic aspects, particularly appealed to the American Press.

VII

OUR REVOLUTIONARY MOVEMENT AMONG THE TROOPS AND PRISONERS OF WAR

(a) Beginnings of the Military Activity of the National Council. Our Military Work in Russia and France

37

The important decisions arrived at by the National Council during Masaryk's presence in Paris in February 1916 were concerned also with military matters.

At the outbreak of the war our colonies had everywhere begun to fulfil their military duties. Our colony in France, for example, had immediately arranged for several hundreds of our people to enter the Foreign Legion. In England the colony, directed by Sykora and Kopecký, proceeded in a similar manner, and the scope of its work there extended to our volunteer movement in Canada. The most important military movement, however, from a political point of view, at that time was the formation of our brigade in Russia. Altogether, what we accomplished in Russia in a military respect is of quite special significance, and I shall therefore refer in greater detail to these matters in my chapter on Russia. For the time being, I will mention only the essential facts. Our military activity in Italy, where there was no colony in the strict sense of the word, and where the National Council immediately took charge of things, will be dealt with specially in the chapter on Italy.

All this initiative, and all revolutionary work which the colonies spontaneously began, met with the warm approval and recognition of our political leaders at home and abroad. The "Maffia" had attended closely to it, and when Masaryk started his work abroad, he supported all such tendencies among our colonists. Before the organization of political headquarters in the National Council, his movement enhanced the good repute, and also the legal security, of our colonies in the Allied countries. At first it had no direct political consequences in Western Europe.

In Russia, where the number of our colonists was proportionately greater, and where the Russian military command soon made use of our brigade for special purposes, this movement acquired a political character, chiefly because it was thought that the Russian troops would advance rapidly into our territories. Besides this, before long, when our troops were surrendering wholesale on the Russian front, our colonists had to consider how they should deal with the problem of the prisoners of war. The disputes which arose on these matters in our Russian colony weakened the political effect of this important and meritorious work. Nevertheless, the first granting of the colours to our brigade at Kiev on September 28, 1914, as well as a number of deputations of our colonists to the Tsar and the Russian Government with regard to the organization of the brigade and the prisoners of war, at once imparted a definite political character and scope to the Czechoslovak military affairs in Russia.

Masaryk frequently intervened in these matters. Thus, in May 1915 he notified the "Maffia" at Prague of the organization of our troops in Russia as the most important item in our projected opposition to Austria-Hungary. He mentioned that a detachment of about twenty thousand prisoners of war was being prepared there, and that this was a matter which demanded the closest attention. For that reason, as I have previously stated, he wanted Dr. Scheiner to escape from Prague and devote himself to the organization of these military contingents in Russia.

The Russian colony, having acknowledged Masaryk's leadership, in spite of various contrary tendencies, referred to him in controversial matters concerning the troops and the prisoners of war, and on several occasions asked him to come to Russia as soon as possible. That is why, at our first deliberation in common in Geneva on September 3, 1915, we began by deciding that Dürich should prepare to proceed to Petrograd to attend chiefly to military matters.

During the negotiations at Paris in February 1916, concerning the organization of the National Council, these resolutions were again confirmed. Besides this, however, knowing as we did, the military activity of our colony, and seeing the increase of disputes on matters relating to the troops and the prisoners of war in Russia, as well as the increasing importance of the prisoners of war in the whole of our future military activity, we were compelled, when organizing the National Council, to elaborate a systematic and practical scheme for our military operations and organization.

I have already explained that it was not possible for us to allow the colonies by themselves to embark upon political activities, and this applied still more to our military movement, which we had to found upon a broad political basis and take under our control. The colonists themselves did not possess sufficient political discernment or moral authority for this purpose, as they depended too much upon the States in which they had taken up their residence. This was evident most of all in Russia, notably from the disputes which arose from our action in these matters. It was inevitable that there should have been, in any case, a difference of opinion between prisoners of war and colonists, and if it had not been settled by transferring the whole military movement to the broad basis of the policy directed by the National Council, it would have been a perpetual menace to the whole of our revolutionary movement.

At the moment when the National Council began its systematic work in matters relating to troops and prisoners of war, our brigade in Russia and our volunteers in France and England numbered slightly more than two thousand men. It was the task of the National Council to transform this movement into an enterprise of great political, diplomatic, and military scope. It would be wrong to underestimate the importance of the pioneer military work of our colonists in France, England, America, an. above all, in Russia. In the latter country the National Council exerted its influence upon the military undertakings, partly by Masaryk's intervention and more decisively by sending Dürich and Štefánik to Petrograd and Kiev respectively.

38

It was just after Masaryk's visit to Briand that Štefánik proceeded on his first journey to Italy. Masaryk remained in Paris, partly to discuss Slavonic affairs and the proposed series of lectures at the Sorbonne with Professor Denis and his friends, partly to elaborate with us a common plan for our political and military work. Dürich paid no great attention to these political matters, maintaining a certain reserve, and so, in the course of February, during numerous conversations with Masaryk almost every day after our evening meal, we made our own decisions as to military plans and the principles of our organization and action among the prisoners of war in Russia, Italy, Serbia, and France.

From the very beginning of our revolutionary work Masaryk had never for a moment lost sight of his proposal for a large army. In political terms he formulated this in February 1915 somewhat as follows:

> If we establish an army we shall acquire a new juridical status as regards Austria and the Allies. A further step might possibly consist of a formal declaration of war upon Austria-Hungary. This will create a political situation enabling us to attain at least our minimum demands when peace is negotiated. In any case, neither the Allies nor Vienna will be able to pass us by in silence if we have soldiers. The Allies and our people at home will have a compensatory means of attaining concessions to our national cause, even if it were to turn out badly. But without a decisive and military struggle we shall obtain nothing from anybody.

That was how our scheme was formulated before we had actually ventured to reckon with certainty upon complete success.

By its military activity the National Council became connected with one of the important factors in the whole war. France, then desperately defending herself for the second year against enormous pressure from Germany, was suffering great losses in man power, and was continually needing more and more soldiers for her front. Many difficult negotiations were being carried on in England and America by the French for the purpose of securing reinforcements. This question continued to occupy the Allies until the end of the war, and up to the last moment it had a decisive bearing upon our movement and the whole of our war policy.

Thus, in the spring of 1916 Russia agreed to send about 400,000 soldiers to the French front. This undertaking was carried out only to a very small extent, the actual number of Russians thus supplied being about 10,000, under the leadership of General Lokhvitsky. When it was ascertained what obstacles the dispatch of Russian troops would involve, the question was asked first by us, later also by French Government circles, whether it would not be possible to send to France, together with the Russian troops also, detachments of Czechoslovak prisoners of war from whom the national Czechoslovak Army in France could be organized. It was upon this that in February 1915 we based all our hopes and computations with regard to establishing large numbers of our contingents in France. It was accordingly arranged with Masaryk that the National Council would attend very carefully to questions concerning prisoners of war in the Allied countries as a whole, and that in particular it would not lose sight of the possibility of obtaining Czechoslovak prisoners of war from Russia for service in France. The intention was to inaugurate this scheme at the earliest opportunity, and if possible to adopt similar methods in Italy.

Within the next three months the journey of Dürich and Štefánik to Russia brought the scheme close to the stage where its gradual realization could have been started. Thus arose the idea which in its final consequences resulted two years later in our Siberian anabasis.

The proposal to transport at least a part of our prisoners of war from Russia to France was prompted by other important considerations.

The Russian reverses on the Eastern front were more and more shifting the centre of gravity of the war to the West. Masaryk's fears concerning Russia were being fulfilled to an ever more alarming extent, and we saw that the centre of our own movement was thus more decisively being fixed in Western Europe. This led to the natural conclusion that our problem would have to be settled in Paris, which was quickly developing into what was perhaps the most important Allied centre. It was clear that we should achieve success there if we had our own soldiers on the Western front, and it seemed to us then that we should obtain them most easily from Russia. The question of the Italian prisoners of war had at that time not yet been taken into account, and we still had very little news about our prisoners in Serbia. As a matter of fact, there were very few of them.

It was not our purpose to transport all our troops and prisoners of war from Russia to France. All we wanted was merely a part of the prisoners of war so as to have on the Western front in France, for all contingencies, thirty or forty thousand of our troops. Our alarm as to the turn which events might take in Russia confronted us with the question as to what would happen to our troops if they were all in Russia and a catastrophe were to occur there. In organizing the National Council, and in negotiating with the authorities, I myself saw clearly that our political significance in Paris would rise if we could manage to place a large number of military units on the French front. Being permanently settled in Paris and in Western Europe, I directed the whole activity of the National Council and of the secretariat consistently and unremittingly in accordance with this factor. In this matter I never changed my point of view or my tactics throughout the war.

Further events gradually tended to confirm us in this policy. The Franco-Russian agreement for the transport of Russian troops to the Western front soon broke down for political and technical reasons. It was evident that Russia was unable to keep her promise. General Lokhvitsky, who was in command of the Russian troops in France, was greatly upset at this, and so was General Count Ignatyev, the Russian military attaché in Paris. In the conversations which I had with them they made no secret of the fact. When we mentioned to them the scheme for transporting a part of our prisoners of war to France they both emphatically approved of it, and they took the view that our army might in some way be linked up with the Russian troops in France, so that close co-operation could develop between them, thus increasing their influence and strengthening their authority. These were the arguments which they brought to bear on me, on Dürich, and on the National Council in general.

Seeing this, I was not slow to take advantage of their personal interest to secure support for our movement, and I began, through them, to influence the Russian Ambassador in Paris and the authorities in Petrograd direct. I did this because I was afraid that the opposition of the leading people in Russia might spoil our plan. I did not anticipate any difficulties from the French, because I saw the continually increasing shortage of troops on the French front. Through our relations with official circles, Štefánik and I had already received the unequivocal answer that if the Russian Government gave its consent, France would promote the organization of the army in every possible way.

39

It was under these circumstances that in the spring of 1916 the question of Dürich's departure for Russia arose. On April 2nd Dürich informed me that he had received a message from Petrograd asking him to go there. On April 7th Masaryk telegraphed to me from London that it was time for Dürich to proceed to Russia and start work in Petrograd. Then, on April 12th, Dürich himself received a letter from M. Bibikov, the Russian Minister in Berne, who stated that, in accordance with a previous promise from Petrograd to inform Dürich of the moment regarded by the official circles there as suitable for his arrival, he could now start on his journey. Bibikov's letter was brought, I believe, by Svatkovsky from Berne to Paris.

On April 13, 1916, Dürich, Svatkovsky, and I met to discuss matters together, and to arrange a course of action for our work in Russia. At this meeting it was emphasized that the co-operation with Paris and London was to be thorough and continual. Approval was given to the plan, already agreed upon, of transporting a certain number of our prisoners of war to France in order that on the Western front also we might establish an army of some size in co-operation with Lokhvitsky, Ignatyev, and the Russian Embassy. Dürich and myself were to discuss this question further with them.

Finally Svatkovsky emphasized to Dürich one more matter which at that time was particularly important to us. He had often spoken with Masaryk and myself about affairs in Russia, and he was not at all satisfied with them. He, like ourselves, was afraid that events might take an unfavourable turn from within. He criticized the military unpreparedness, the political fickleness, and the internal disorder which threatened to produce an outburst. Moreover, he was dissatisfied with the politics of Petrograd in matters relating to the Poles, the Jugoslavs, and ourselves. He was well acquainted with these matters, and he did not conceal from us his opinion of what Petrograd was undertaking. He was also offended by the attitude of the Tsarist Government towards us. Among my notes on this meeting of ours I have a record of his exact words to Dürich: "Insist upon telling them in Petrograd quite plainly: In the West they have done everything for us that we wanted, but you in Russia have done nothing."

Dürich made preparations for his departure. First of all he paid a number of political visits to Briand, Berthelot, Lokhvitsky, Ignatyev, and to the Russian Embassy where he was received by Sebastopulo, the Ambassador's deputy. Unfortunately, he made a number of political blunders which did us considerable harm even in Paris, and from which (and, I may add, from a number of other symptoms) we saw that Dürich's political mission would probably end badly. After Dürich had visited Briand and Berthelot the people at the Ministry of Foreign Affairs told Štefánik quite plainly that they were unfavourably impressed, and the terms in which Sebastopulo expressed himself to me on the subject were even more emphatic.

This was a great blow to us and to the whole of our movement, which was then in its very promising initial stages. When General Lokhvitsky summoned me to him on June 16th to discuss once more the question of transporting troops from Russia to France, he said to me in the most direct manner: "Don't send Dürich to Russia. That's no job for him; he is incapable of it, and you won't do any good that way. Write and tell Masaryk to go to Russia himself while you negotiate here with the Embassy. Visit Protopopov and explain your whole business to him."(17)

To these blunders Dürich added a number of further new ones. He entangled himself in preposterous negotiations with the Czech colony in Paris, and particularly with certain of its members who compromised him in the eyes of the French Government. The persons whom he selected to work with him were quite unsuitable for such a political mission, and in private conversations the political views which he expressed on our relation to Russia, on our movement, and on Russia in general completely ran counter to our line of action in Paris.

This led to a disagreement with Štefánik and myself, which became acute at the beginning of June, when Štefánik decided to prevent Dürich's departure for Petrograd at all costs. I shared his view that under these circumstances Dürich ought not to go to Petrograd on behalf of the National Council. After a very heated scene with Štefánik, Dürich admitted his mistakes, and on June 14, 1916, he promised that in future he would adhere to our common line of action and avoid his previous blunders. He made it up with Štefánik, and at last again obtained his consent for the journey to Russia. I myself had no violent disagreements or scenes with Dürich, as I always endeavoured to persuade him in a friendly manner, but I persisted in opposing his journey to Russia because I did not believe that he was able to accomplish anything worth while, and I was afraid that a new and far-reaching complication would be added to the disagreements already existing in our colony.

Štefánik gave his consent to Dürich's journey, but with a new stipulation. He decided that he, too, would proceed to

Russia, partly because he was afraid that Dürich, in spite of the reconciliation and although he had repeatedly given his word, would not keep to the agreement and would work against Paris, partly also that under these circumstances our troops from Russia would certainly not reach France. I gave my consent to Štefánik's plan, although I was not entirely convinced.

40

On June 2, 1916, we began to make arrangements for Štefánik's journey to Russia. Officially, its purpose was to be indicated to the effect that Štefánik, being a French subject, was not going on behalf of the National Council, but in the interests of the French Government to study the conditions among the Czechoslovak prisoners of war in Russia, and to ascertain whether, and, if so, under what conditions, a definite part of them could be transported to France. He was also to negotiate immediately with the Government for sanction to carry out these plans. The mission was to be a French one, and, as I have said, it was the French Government and not the National Council which was to use its efforts to obtain this sanction. The arrangement had its advantages and also its disadvantages, the most dangerous of the latter being that Russia might possibly be aroused to jealousy against France on account of this initiative in Czechoslovak affairs.

Štefánik's proposal was as follows: I, as General Secretary of the National Council, was to secure Masaryk's consent, and Masaryk was to apply to Briand and the Russian Ambassadors in Rome and London, asking them to support this plan and to invite Štefánik to Russia.

I myself began to discuss the matter with Lokhvitsky and his officers Doroshevitch and Dalboshevsky, finally also with the Russian Ambassador in Paris. Masaryk gave his consent to Štefánik's journey, but he was not enthusiastic about it. He had no confidence that anything of real moment could be achieved in Russia at that time, nor did he regard the journey suggested by Štefánik as a feasible one. He therefore did not apply to Briand, Giers, or Benckendorff, and this gave Štefánik the impression that Masaryk was entirely opposed to this policy of his. At first he wanted to take extreme measures in consequence, and to sever his connection with us. I succeeded in pacifying him, and when Masaryk sent him a telegram of recommendation to Izvolsky, Štefánik was placated and resumed his work. On June 23rd he discussed the matter with Izvolsky and Sebastopulo, from whom he secured at least the promise that they would support him in his mission to Russia.

On the same day Dürich, with his escort, left for Russia. Before his departure I paid him another visit, and on behalf of the nation and of the whole of the revolutionary movement I again asked him either not to go at all, as we were not in complete agreement in this matter, or at least to remember that at all costs he must work in uniformity with us in Paris. But in particular I urged him not to take his escort, Crkal, and Lieutenant Štafl.(18) He tried to prove to me that I ought not to be opposed to his mission and his course of action, and that after Štefánik had given his sanction I should not insist upon my dissent. At the same time he declared that he took full responsibility before the nation for everything that he was doing and was about to do.(19)

Štefánik himself was unable to take the necessary steps for arranging his journey to Russia. He asked me, as General Secretary of the National Council, to attend to the whole matter, and to make the necessary arrangements both with the French and with the Russians. He was of the opinion that if the preparations were made by the Czechoslovak National Council, there would be a better chance to secure the consent of French and Russian official circles. His chief fear was that his journey to Russia might be regarded as his own personal undertaking, and he therefore asked for Masaryk's intervention also.

At that period Štefánik, seeing the departure of Dürich, and being alarmed as to what he might do in Russia, was in a state of feverish activity. He was impatient to know whether, as a French subject and a soldier, he would obtain sanction from the Government for his journey. He thought that if he were entrusted with the projected political mission it would be a great success for us, as the French Government would thus express its agreement, in principle, with the organization of our army in France, and at the same time would assist us to take the necessary steps in Russia. What he feared was that Dürich might have too long a start, and in the meanwhile would do harm in Russia.

On June 25, 1916, in accordance with my agreement with

Štefánik, I again went to the Russian Embassy and officially submitted the demand of the National Council to Legation Councillor Sebastopulo, the Ambassador Izvolsky not being present. I again received a promise of support and sanction in principle. A few days later, on June 30th, I proceeded officially as General Secretary to my first audience with M. de Margerie, then political director of the French Foreign Ministry and now French Ambassador in Berlin. Both Sebastopulo and de Margerie told me candidly that Dürich's journey was a political blunder, and that chiefly for that reason they agreed to Štefánik's journey, hoping that this would obviate at least any very serious mistakes and predicaments.

These were my first dealings with de Margerie and Berthelot who rendered us such extensive and important services in the later course of the war. What actually happened on that occasion was that the National Council had been officially recognized by the French Foreign Ministry, which for the first time negotiated with the National Council and with me as its Secretary, in a matter of such far-reaching political significance. This method of action was then always adhered to, and it was clear that our political position in France was becoming stronger every day.

In accordance with the decision of the Ministry, Štefánik at once discussed his mission with the Ministry of War. Even at that early date he conferred with Admiral Lacaze on the technical preparations which would be necessary to transport our troops via Vladivostok and Archangelsk to France. After his departure I continued the work very energetically, and from that time onwards we kept it continually in view. By a combination of circumstances it concluded with the famous Siberian anabasis.

41

At that time we in Paris established our first direct contact with our political and military fellow-workers in Russia. Hitherto we had been in touch with them only by correspondence. On March 16, 1916, B. Pavlů arrived in Paris from Russia. He had been sent by our people in Petrograd to give us an account of the situation in the East, and to view the state of affairs in the West, upon which he was then to report to Russia. In this way it was intended to strengthen the unity of the whole movement, as the uncertainty and the disagreements among our people in Russia demanded some authority which was to come from Masaryk and from Paris.

Pavlů had travelled via London, where he had discussed everything with Masaryk, and had then come to us in Paris. He had long been known to Štefánik, with whom he immediately reached an agreement. There had been certain differences of opinion between him and myself in Prague before the war, but now these were all cleared up and disposed of. Pavlů stayed in Paris for two weeks. First of all he initiated us thoroughly into the differences of opinion in the personal disputes which existed among our fellow-countrymen in Russia, and told us all there was to be told concerning their plans and ideas of our national revolution. He fully realized what was involved in the diversity of opinions about our position in Russia and in Western Europe, and he also quickly understood the political and military situation in Paris and London. He saw for himself how important Western Europe was with regard to Russia, and he also discovered our difficulties with Dürich. He agreed with us entirely, and approved of our plans in every respect. From that time onwards he was a loyal and unremitting advocate of the policy of the National Council, and of co-operation between our people in Russia and ourselves in Paris and London. He returned to Russia with messages to this effect on April 1, 1916.

The final preparations for Štefánik's departure to Russia had been completed. I discussed with him in detail the measures that would be necessary should our troops reach France, i.e. how they were to be organized, with which of the authorities the matter would have to be arranged, and what preparations should be made for the beginnings of the army. On July 26th Štefánik was invited once more to visit the French Supreme Command at Chantilly, where he received his final instructions from French quarters. At a new suggestion of mine the Ministry for Foreign Affairs at the same time sent an official communication to the Ministry of War and to Field-Marshal Joffre, instructing them to identify themselves with the policy which the French Government, by arranging Štefánik's mission, was inaugurating in Czech affairs and in its attitude to the National Council. The communication in question also instructed them to make every preparation which they might deem suitable for the transport of the Czechoslovak prisoners of war from Russia to France.

Two days later, on July 28, 1916, Štefánik left for Russia. From Paris he proceeded via Brest to Archangelsk. I accompanied him by train as far as Laval. Two days after that I went to London, as I wanted to give Masaryk an account of what we had been doing in Paris, and also to confer with him on our future work. It seemed reasonable to infer from recent events that the National Council was now entering upon a period of very important political and military activity. From the negotiations of the French authorities with the National Council and with myself as its secretary, I saw that they were beginning to assign to us a genuine political significance.

I remained in London two weeks. We discussed in detail all our problems, needs, and further plans. With Voska's help we sent an envoy, Miss Kvíčal, from London to Prague. She was returning from America to Austria, and at Masaryk's request the English authorities detained her and brought her to see us in London.(20) On August 10th I gave her a message which she learnt by heart and faithfully delivered to Dr. Šámal in Prague. The contents of this message give a very striking indication of the stage which our movement reached at that time, and also of our views, plans, hopes, and needs.

While in London with Masaryk I met Supilo and Milyukov. Supilo gave us a very frank account of his disputes with Pašić, of his experiences in Russia with Sazonov, of his discussions with Giers, and of his negotiations with the English authorities. He was impetuous and resolute, but he possessed also political instinct and sound intelligence. In London he was regarded favourably. He took an adverse view of Russia. He was convinced that Petrograd had consciously and deliberately betrayed the idea of Jugoslav unity by assenting to the London Pact with Italy, and by opposing the scheme for joining the Croats and Slovenes with the Serbs. Altogether he considered that Russia had no political policy of a Slav and anti-Austrian character. In my presence Masaryk discussed in detail with Milyukov the whole of our political plan for reorganizing Central Europe.(21) Milyukov agreed with it. He, too, criticized Russia severely. Masaryk and I paid a visit to Oxford, partly to interview English professors there—notably Dr. J. Holland Rose—partly also to have another meeting with Dmowski and Milyukov, who were then lecturing at Oxford on the problems of the war, with special reference to Russia and Italy.

Our visit to Oxford is associated with memories which I

recall with great emotion. It was at a time when the prospects of our success were precarious, and when we daily had to face the possibility of spending the rest of our lives abroad under conditions of great hardship. Professor Masaryk, too, had to contend with great anxieties about his family. Alice Masaryk, his daughter, had recently been imprisoned, and Mme. Masaryk, whose health was now seriously impaired, was living isolated at Prague. "When I take everything into account," said Masaryk to me on our way back to London, "I often consider whether I ought not to go home again. Of course, they would hang me, but at least I should see my wife once more ; and I am afraid that she will not live till the end of the war. It would cause a stir among our people at home and would certainly stiffen their opposition to Vienna."

I was deeply moved by these remarks, which caused me to reflect upon my own personal troubles. At that very moment my wife was in some Viennese prison, and the whole outlook was dark and uncertain. Nevertheless, I reminded myself that whether our undertaking ended in victory or defeat, what was now happening would one day be regarded as a great epoch in the history of our nation. Moreover, I had been brought closer to Professor Masaryk by what he had said to me, and I felt grateful to Providence for having allowed me to work with him at so great a task. Thus it was that I returned to Paris strengthened and encouraged for further work.

(b) The National Council and the Prisoners of War
in France

42

I returned to Paris on August 17th and at once set about my new and onerous tasks as arranged with Masaryk. The formation of an army in France was now to enter upon a stage of practical realization. It was now necessary to make preparations for receiving our prisoners of war from Russia, and also for systematically organizing those who were already in France. At the same time considerable activity had to be started in connection with our prisoners of war in Italy. After the marked success of the Press campaign in France in June, July, and August 1916, which had aimed at the destruction of Austria-Hungary and had taken advantage of Brusilov's offensive, as well as of the political persecutions and trials in Bohemia, we found a greater comprehension of our movement with regard to the prisoners of war and our military schemes.

From the moment when there appeared a justifiable hope that detachments of our prisoners of war were going to be transported from Russia, the question of our prisoners of war in the West acquired a new political significance. At that time there were in France about 4,000 Czech prisoners from Serbia who formed the remainder of about 25,000 of our people who had originally been captured there.(22) The greater part of these had, in company with the Serbian Army, undertaken that desperate retreat through Albania. For our troops this retreat had involved enormous suffering. While the Serbian Government had been concerned with saving the remnants of its army, it had regarded our prisoners merely as ballast who were depriving the Serbs of their food supplies, and so the Czech prisoners died of hunger and hardships by the wayside. The extent to which this catastrophe affected our people can be indicated roughly in figures. The total number who, in a pitiable condition, managed to reach the Albanian coast at Jadran and from there, with Italian help, the Island of Asinara, was about 11,000. There the treatment which they, as well as the Austrians, received was very bad. They contracted infectious diseases, such as typhus and dysentery, and again perished wholesale, their bodies being thrown into the sea.

As a result of intervention by the Serbian Government and by us, we managed to arrange for their transport to France. The number arriving there being, as I have mentioned, only about 4,000. And even there, at the beginning, they were wretchedly situated. This forms one of the instructive episodes in our history during the war. We were far from sharing the belief which prevailed in Viennese circles and amongst certain of our own people that the Allies were awaiting us with open arms. And if the official world of politics knew little about us at that time, the subordinate authorities were almost completely ignorant of us and treated our people accordingly. There were, of course, exceptions, but on the whole what our prisoners went through everywhere was in truth a calvary of suffering. This applies to Serbia, Russia, Italy, and France, particularly at the beginning. The Czechs who were prisoners of war in those countries could tell harrowing stories of their experiences. On Slavonic territory they were just as badly off as elsewhere. I am not complaining of this, but merely placing the fact on record. It will help to throw an accurate light upon our movement abroad. In the literature dealing with our struggle for independence there are detailed accounts of all these matters. I will therefore make no further reference to these hardships, disappointments, and struggles. I will add a few words on the subject from a political point of view.

When in September 1916 we began our systematic movement among the prisoners of war in France, and shortly afterwards in Italy, we could reckon with tens of thousands of such prisoners. In Russia their number certainly exceeded 50,000; in Italy there were more than 10,000 ; and in France about 4,000. We thus had the opportunity of forming an army containing tens of thousands. In Russia the movement among the prisoners was already in progress, while in the West the recent successes of the National Council had led us to expect equally rapid results.

The character of this movement was, of course, the same in all the Allied countries. It encountered the same difficulties and followed the same procedure. Accordingly, what I have to say about the organization of the prisoners in France will, in general outlines, apply to all the Allied countries.

This is a subject which most strikingly illustrates how ignorant the Allied Government and political circles were of conditions in Austria-Hungary. And although, in the course of time, they began to realize that preferential treatment should be given to our prisoners, and that it was possible even to use them for military and political purposes, we nevertheless for a very long time, and in many cases up to the end of the war, encountered complete lack of understanding on the part of subordinate officials and local authorities. It was a gigantic task to overcome all these obstacles. Our prisoners must have been endowed with superhuman patience to achieve what they did, without giving up hope or surrendering to complete despair.

In addition to this ignorance and lack of understanding, the mistrust and fear of spies which influenced the Allied authorities for so long, prevented us for a considerable time from achieving any noteworthy success. There were prejudices or principles of international law with which the Government circles opposed our endeavours with regard to the prisoners. Certain very authoritative quarters where conservatism, legitimism, and monarchism were rampant, harboured fear of our revolutionary tendencies. It was in Italy and Russia where these motives prevailed the longest. Advantage was taken of them in Russia also when, for political reasons, circles which were hostile to us desired to frustrate our purposes.

But there were obstacles on our side which proved difficult to cope with. Our prisoners had been still armed when they reached the Allied countries, and for that reason they had been treated as enemies. It was only in course of time that discrimination was shown towards them. In this respect matters were no better in France than in Russia or Serbia. And it was when they had been embittered by all these disappointments that we began our propagandist activity among them to show that the Allies really wanted to liberate us, and that we must therefore keep with them, even to the extent of being prepared for service at the front, a proceeding in which our prisoners would incur the risk of death on the gallows. Many of them found it difficult to understand at first, while in the case of others we met with direct opposition. It must be remembered that they were still under the control of Austro-Hungarian officers who terrorized them, or else they were exposed to the influence of their own fellow-countrymen who were either sceptics or opportunists. The obstacles which all these circumstances caused us were formidable. In fact, our movement among the prisoners of war produced results which were often miracles of patience and industry. Under the most difficult conditions in all the Allied countries we had to bring about a diametrical change in the official attitude towards our prisoners, and in the prison camps themselves we often had to win our people over with the utmost exertion, man by man. There were camps where the conditions were quite different, and where we found spontaneous enthusiasm, wholesale volunteering for active service. In these cases, however, disappointment and distress of a different character made themselves felt, for the men's initial enthusiasm was gradually crushed by their endless waiting to be released from the camp and drafted into the projected army.

The procedure was everywhere the same. We first asked for permission to send our publications to the camps, and to grant our people various privileges, such as clean linen, writing material, newspapers, books, etc. We then applied for our people to be separated from the prisoners of other nationalities, and placed under the charge of Czechoslovak officers. It was more difficult to arrange for the Slovaks to be placed with the

Czechs. Finally we secured permission to carry on recruiting propaganda.

43

After being transported from Asinara, our prisoners had been distributed over various camps throughout France, and we got into touch with them through the assistance of the French authorities. As early as spring 1916 the censorship of the prisoners of war and the military authorities had begun to apply to us, through Professor Eisenmann, for help in interpreting the prisoners' correspondence, in which they had found items of great value for estimating the moral, social, political, and military situation in Austria-Hungary. In this way we began to ascertain the places in which our people were located, as well as their number, the feeling amongst them, their sorrows, complaints, and wishes.

Having thus discovered where all our people were, we began to send them small sums of money, as well as newspapers, books, paper, linen, etc. Then, when the public work of the National Council, our propaganda, our relations with ministries, and finally the agreement connected with Štefánik's mission had strengthened our position, and we were enjoying sufficient confidence as a responsible political body, I gradually began on behalf of the National Council to undertake a definite political intervention in matters relating to the prisoners of war.

As we had few prisoners in France we had to proceed cautiously. The subordinate official bodies, being unacquainted with our aims or the foundations of our movement, and being unable at the outset to estimate the scope of the whole matter, might easily, for reasons connected with administration and organization, or owing to the personal interests of various local notables, have frustrated the whole movement, even though the central authorities were well disposed towards it. That was a frequent experience of ours, and that was why we had to proceed slowly. But at all costs we had to achieve success, as lack of success in France would have been a severe blow to the possibility of similar action in Italy.

Accordingly, on September 19, 1916, as our prisoners in France were under the jurisdiction of Serbia, I first applied to M. Vesnić, the Serbian Minister, asking him if he would induce the Serbian Government to let the National Council acquire authority over them. I also asked him to use his influence with the Serbian and French Governments in promoting our endeavour to organize the whole of our prisoners in France in an independent Czechoslovak Army. M. Vesnić promised his support, and gave us all the help he could.

The National Council then began to work on the same lines in French political circles. I have already mentioned that in the spring of 1916 I was introduced by Štefánik into the salon of Mme. de Jouvenel, where we used to meet with a number of politicians, journalists, deputies, and military men. In the same way I came into contact with other influential centres, such as the salons of Mme. Menard-Dorian and of the Baroness Lacaze, in which we began to find political support. From September 1916 onwards these circles exhibited a systematic interest in our problems, and furthered our movement in every possible manner.

On September 2nd M. Picard, a deputy who at that time was in quite close touch with M. Briand, promised me that he would intervene with the Government in the matter of our prisoners. At the same time I applied to a number of other friends, including General Valentin, of the Ministry of War, to whom I made a special written application on this subject. These interventions produced excellent results. The Ministry of War at once began to deal with the matter, and on September 21st it issued a telegraphic order to all prisoner-of-war camps that the Czechoslovaks were to be separated from the other Austro-Hungarian prisoners. They were also to receive more considerate treatment. This order, however, immediately encountered serious difficulties, which emanated from the Supreme Command at the front, and it also had to contend with obstacles of a bureaucratic nature in the various camps themselves. Moreover, there were delays in drawing up the details of the conditions under which the order of the Ministry was to be carried out.

I petitioned M. Briand, and thenceforth I discussed this question of the prisoners with the Government authorities only through official channels. The Foreign Ministry suggested that in order to negotiate on the subject of our demands enumerated in my application to the Prime Minister, I should get into direct touch with the central department in Paris which dealt with all matters relating to prisoners of war. The head of this department was Georges Cahen, with whom I reached an agreement as to all further procedure on October 18, 1916. I arranged the introduction of more favourable treatment to our prisoners, as well as our method of contact with them, the supply of periodicals, the carrying on of propaganda for a national army, and at least a partial concentration of them into exclusively Czechoslovak camps. The whole matter was then submitted to the Supreme Command at the front for approval. As from September 1916 I was able to obtain access to the headquarters at Chantilly, where there was a special section for matters relating to us under the charge of Colonel Billote, I applied direct to him both in writing and personally, and asked him for his assistance. Throughout these negotiations I received considerable help from the Ministry of War, on the one hand, from the information department, where Professor Eisenmann was also co-operating with us in this matter, and partly from the organizing department (Lieut.-Col. Cros) attached to the General Staff, where they were already reckoning with the possibility of organizing our army.

The actual work connected with the prisoners of war, which now became an actual fact as a result of the agreement reached with the authorities, proceeded very slowly. For weeks at a time it was necessary to carry on negotiations, and then intervene almost every day in order to overcome prejudices, bureaucratic inaction and pettiness, as well as political ignorance and failure to understand the point at issue.

The final result was excellent. Of the 4,000 prisoners from Serbia who were in France, nearly all passed into our national army in the course of the year 1918.

While this activity was developing, my negotiations with military circles in the Supreme Command at Chantilly were also making progress. Colonel Billote, who was in regular communication with the National Council, had concentrated at headquarters all details relating to us. He used to obtain reports from me and also from Štefánik in Russia, who sent documents dealing with our movement, with Dürich's activities, and with the progress which his own mission was making. Colonel Billote used to summon me regularly to headquarters, where I discussed everything with him from the point of view of the situation in France.(23)

At French headquarters the Serbian Government was represented by General Rašić, a charming Slav of the old-fashioned type. I entered into touch with him also, and arrived at an agreement on the subject of the prisoners as far as Serbia was concerned. My relations with General Rašić were nothing short of fraternal. He was a sincere friend to us, and promoted our cause among the French at headquarters. The progress of the work connected with our army in France led me to ask him whether the Serbian Government could not send us all our prisoners who were still on the Balkan Front, and also let us have all the Czechs and Slovaks who were serving in the Serbian Army. In particular, as I was afraid that we should not have enough capable officers in France, I asked him to induce the Serbian Government to release those of our officers who were serving with the Serbian Army.

The negotiations which these demands involved were protracted, and the plan was actually carried out just a year after the initial intervention. On October 31, 1917, when I again visited General Rašić, I received a notification that the Serbian Army had issued an order for our officers and men to be transported from the Balkan Front to our army in France.

This was the general framework of all my personal activities from the autumn of 1916, and also of those carried out under my management by the office of the National Council in matters relating to propaganda, prisoners of war, and political plans. This activity of ours, its character and its methods, became stabilized. Various persons engaged in it now had their definite function and degrees of authority. The organization was on a firm basis, communication with all our centres was more or less established, and the whole of our work proceeded on normal lines.

Such were the circumstances accompanying the approach of important events in international politics in which we also began to take our share, and in which the Czechoslovak movement became an important factor.

VIII

THE PEACE OFFENSIVE OF THE CENTRAL POWERS. THE ALLIED NOTE TO PRESIDENT WILSON, AND THE CZECHOSLOVAK QUESTION

(a) THE FIRST PEACE OVERTURES

44

FROM the end of September 1916 we passed through trying times in the National Council at Paris, in company with our French and Jugoslav friends. Military and political events assailed us with overwhelming weight, many of them of such a character that we had perforce to look on as passive spectators, a circumstance which served only to emphasize how critical they were from our point of view.

We greeted with enthusiasm the entry of Rumania into the war on August 27, 1916, for we regarded this as a further guarantee of victory. On behalf of the National Council I sent Prime Minister Bratianu a manifesto wishing success to the idea of the unification of the Rumanians, and the liberation of the oppressed nations in Austria-Hungary. From September the Allies were occupied with Balkan problems, especially the intrigues of King Constantine in Greece, which culminated with the revolution of Venizelos and the establishment of his government at Salonica. This somewhat strengthened the position of the Allies in the Balkans, especially when a French army, under General Sarrail, established itself at Salonica and the Serbs recaptured Monastir.

In spite, however, of these partial successes, matters soon became critical. The Rumanians, desiring chiefly to occupy Transylvania, were not expecting attacks from Bulgaria; and, moreover, not having sufficient support from the Allies, upon which they were relying, they were soon driven back on to their own territory after the first successes, and then thoroughly defeated by the Germans and Bulgarians. The Rumanian Government was obliged to migrate to Jassy, and at the beginning of December 1916 Bucharest was occupied by the Germans. The Russian offensive had been completely stopped.

The Central Powers had now occupied the whole of the Balkans as far as Monastir and Salonica, a great part of Rumania, Russian Poland, nearly the whole of Belgium, and nine French departments. The Italian Front remained unchanged. From a military point of view the Central Powers seemed to be victorious.

The Central Powers were nevertheless conscious that their internal situation was precarious. They also knew that there was war-weariness both among them and among the Allies. They therefore took advantage of their favourable military position for the purpose of attempting new politico-diplomatic manœuvres on a large scale. On November 5, 1916, they proclaimed the independence of Poland and the establishment of a Polish national army. The purpose of this was to bring the Poles and the new national army on to the side of the Central Powers, but actually it led to political results which were favourable both to the Poles and to ourselves. Germany and Austria-Hungary, being unable to agree about frontiers, constitution and regime, the head of the new State, or its incorporation either with Germany or Austria-Hungary in the near future, were obliged to leave these questions unsettled. They demanded only the establishment of an army which was to be subordinated to the military command of the Central Powers. They refused to add German and Austrian Polish territory to the new Poland.

The Allies naturally took advantage of this dilemma. After difficult negotiations, Russia decided upon the declaration of November 14th providing for the renewal of Poland as a State which was to remain in constitutional union with Russia. At the same time the necessity was emphasized for all territories inhabited by Poles, i.e. Russian, German, and Austro-Hungarian territory, to be united in a single State. Mr. Asquith and M. Briand associated themselves with this declaration on November 16th, and on the following day P. Boselli did the same on behalf of Italy.

We Czechoslovaks welcomed this step with great satisfaction. German-Austrian diplomacy had again played into our hands by compelling Russia and the Allies to make public commitments which brought our question also further into the foreground. If the Allies undertook to settle the thorny Polish question in this open manner, or even if they thus merely formulated the Polish problem, this could be only to our advantage, both as regards the duration of the war and also the further political consequences which we would derive from this contingency. What it really meant was that the problem of the integral character of Austria-Hungary, and thus the whole question of the reorganization of Central Europe, had again emerged. As far as we were concerned, any such tendency coming at that particular time was all to the good. Moreover, in consequence of this, the Poles were brought closer to the Allies, and began to have a serious interest in the struggle against the Habsburg Empire.

It seemed to us that the whole situation of Germany and Austria-Hungary was complicated by two diametrically opposing tendencies. On the one hand, there were those who favoured arrogance and intimidation, and on the other, there were the alarmists, whose endeavour it was, by means of intrigues and secret negotiations, to obtain peace with decisive promptness. This is what we instinctively felt, and from time to time we received proofs that such was the case. The undeniable military victories of the Central Powers at this juncture caused us some dismay, even though they did not deprive us of our hope and our optimism. We were convinced that Austria-Hungary would not be able to hold out, but we were misled by certain events, and also by the tactical measures of the Central Powers. We could interpret the Austro-German proclamation concerning Poland as a manifestation of power and self-confidence. A number of internal events in Austria and Hungary tended to produce the same impression. Thus, the projected unification of Cis-leithan territories in a single constitutional whole under the name of "Austria," with the exclusion of Galicia, the regulations concerning the use of the German language, Tisza's dictatorship in Hungary, the economic preparations and discussions on the subject of "Mittel-Europa"—all these things bewildered and alarmed us.

But the secret news from Prague which depicted the situation as being desperate, weakened the effect of these impressions, and often gave rise to the conjecture that the two Central Powers were not undertaking peace moves from a consciousness of power, but to strengthen themselves internally, and as a result of misgivings, if not actual alarm, as to the future.

These reflections and misgivings of ours were upset on October 21st by a regular bombshell. Friedrich Adler had killed Prime Minister Stürgkh with a revolver-shot. Koerber had become the first Prime Minister of "Austria" (not of the kingdom and provinces represented in the Reichsrat), had signed an agreement between Austria-Hungary and Germany concerning the re-establishment of Poland, and had prepared for a further internal development corresponding to the German wishes. In the latter process he had waged a severe struggle with Tisza on the subject of the Austro-Hungarian *Ausgleich*. At this juncture, however, there came a fresh piece of news which was fraught with great significance. On November 21st the Emperor Franz Josef had died, and had been succeeded by the Emperor Karl.

The period which now followed was a difficult one for us. The Emperor Karl did not have a bad reputation in the Allied countries. It was well known—and it was a matter which now began to much talked about again—that the Empress Zita was a Bourbon princess, and that she had two brothers in the Belgian Army. It was emphasized that the new Emperor was not responsible for the war, and that he would have no interest in prolonging it, and thus endangering his throne. In the meanwhile, on November 7th, Woodrow Wilson had again been elected President of the United States of America. His electoral campaign, in the course of which Roosevelt, an avowed partisan of the Allies, had carried on an agitation against him, had been followed in France with some alarm and even with exasperation. This was accentuated by the fact that soon afterwards the Viennese newspapers, notably the *Neue Freie Presse* and then those of Berlin, began to discuss "President Wilson's Peace Plan."

At the same time the Russian crisis quickly came to a head. On November 23rd Boris Stürmer handed in his resignation and was succeeded by Alexander Trepov. In Paris this news was received with relief, and the satisfaction at Stürmer's departure would have been complete but for the fact that Protopopov had remained Minister of the Interior. While this was going on, von Jagow had left the Wilhelmstrasse, and Zimmermann had become Minister of Foreign Affairs. The reasons for these events were not clear to us then. We knew only that Stürmer had withdrawn in consequence of the threatening attitude of the Duma, whose opposition he was unable to overcome, and that von Jagow's resignation was perhaps directly or indirectly connected with Bethmann-Hollweg's dispute with the General Staff, the Admiralty, and a part of the Reichstag on questions of war tactics, in particular those relating to unrestricted submarine warfare.

Our reflections on these events were disturbed by vague news that Russia, represented by Stürmer and Protopopov, were negotiating for a separate peace. We also heard reports about Rasputin and a forthcoming upheaval in Russia, about Court intrigues and the pro-German Tsarina, about dubious persons in and around the Government at Petrograd. We were somewhat reassured by Trepov's energetic pronouncement in the early days of September that Russia would not cease fighting until the Allies had gained a complete victory, and that there would be no negotiations for a premature or a separate peace.

Our confidence and peace of mind were increased when a few days later a Government crisis ensued in London. Asquith retired and was replaced by Lloyd George as Prime Minister. Lloyd George had the reputation of being an energetic and capable man. It was known that he wished to set up a small military committee in the Government for carrying on the war more smoothly, and that he was anxious for the formation of a united Allied front, political, diplomatic, and military.

It was under these circumstances that, a few days after the occupation of Bucharest by the Allied Powers, and three weeks after the accession of Emperor Karl, there came the culminating political event of the winter of 1916—the well-known peace overtures of the Central Powers on December 12, 1916.

45

The ideas which we had in Paris as to the origin of the peace note dispatched by the Central Powers were quite inaccurate. I am inclined to believe that even the Allies at that time were imperfectly acquainted with the underlying facts of the case.

It is certain that the note was not the result of any initiative on the part of Karl, as we in the National Council supposed, but that it was prepared some weeks before he came to the throne. It may be safely asserted that the actual instigator of the whole affair was Baron Burian.

While visiting the German headquarters in the middle of October 1916, Burian suggested to Bethmann-Hollweg that the Central Powers might prepare some peace overtures. He justified this on the ground of the general military and economic exhaustion. He also emphasized the prospect of appalling warfare in the spring of 1917 which, he urged, could not lead to any definite decision. Finally, he added that even if the attempt did not lead to success, it would not do any harm to the Central Powers, but on the contrary might prove a source of moral strength to them, and show the two States that they must fight to a victorious conclusion.

Burian's idea was that several weeks, if not months, of preparation would be necessary for the whole undertaking. Moreover, he wanted the Central Powers to define clearly what their peace conditions were. Bethmann-Hollweg agreed in principle with Burian, but stipulated that he must first obtain the Kaiser's consent. On October 28th he sent the Ambassador, von Stumm, to Vienna with the definite answer which he had promised, but it contained a proposal for a different procedure. The German Government accepted the scheme with such eagerness that they were anxious to carry it out as early as the first week of December. It was further their intention to publish within the course of the next two or three days the agreement on the independence of Russian Poland, which had been already prepared between the two Empires, to draw up a peace note with great speed, and to dispatch it to the Allied Powers, using neutral countries as an intermediary. Bethmann-Hollweg himself then wanted to make a special speech in the Reichstag during the same period, in which he would surprise the world with his peace offer. He was, however, resolutely opposed to Burian's suggestion that the peace conditions should be precisely defined. He laid stress on the fact that Germany could not state her conditions, for if she were to do so, matters would not reach the stage of concrete negotiations. It was, for example, not possible to say anything about Belgium, because German public opinion would not tolerate the demands of England, while England would not negotiate at all, if there were even only a remote indication of what were regarded as minimum demands by German official circles and public opinion.

This led to a dispute between Vienna and Berlin which lasted for several weeks. In the course of it the diplomats and politicians at Vienna formed a better estimate of the situation, gauged the international possibilities more accurately, and, on the whole, were on a higher level than the responsible circles at Berlin. This is an interesting and characteristic fact, and it is well that the world should know it.

The death of Franz Josef did not change the course of these

negotiations. It would seem that he, just as Karl later on, had no decisive voice in the matter at all. Karl, however, nevertheless intervened in the negotiations, although only at the last moment. When on November 5th the independence of Poland had been proclaimed, Berlin suddenly postponed the peace move. It turned out that this change was made as a result of pressure from the General Staff. Hindenburg and Ludendorff, regarding the matter only from a military point of view, had the intention of acting upon the Allies chiefly by a military thrust. They therefore proposed to start the peace overtures and to issue the proclamation of Polish independence simultaneously, as they considered that this manœuvre was in accordance with the psychology of the war and the tactics which it demanded—to deliver a blow with one hand and to offer peace with the other.

As in the meanwhile the campaign in Rumania was making good progress, the German military command regarded the fall of Bucharest as imminent. They therefore wanted the peace move to be postponed until after Bucharest had fallen. The authorities at Vienna were annoyed at this, and their estimate of the situation proved to be the more accurate. They were alarmed at the idea of proclaiming the independence of Poland simultaneously with an offer of peace, since they considered that the Allies would look upon such a step as provocative. They felt the same alarm with regard to any peace offer which might be made immediately after the fall of Bucharest. Accordingly Burian and Karl himself endeavoured to have the peace overture made before the fall of Bucharest.(24)

46

In the note which was sent on December 12, 1916, by the Central Powers to the chief neutral countries, i.e. the United States of America, Spain, Switzerland, and the Vatican, they suggested immediate peace negotiations, and announced that it would certainly be possible to regard as a basis for a lasting peace the concrete proposals which they would then submit. They emphasized the fact that the war had been forced upon them as a means for defending their existence against the hatred and treachery of enemies, and that the only purpose of their proposals would be to vindicate the honour and the free development of the nations comprised in the Central Powers.

The whole attempt was carried out on somewhat sensational lines, with much ostentation, and with a vast impetus derived from international propaganda. The aim of this was to produce the maximum of public excitement, and to create a strong impression throughout the world that the Central Powers were sincere in their endeavours for peace. A further aim was to derive the most favourable political and military results possible from the scheme, both at home and abroad.

On December 18th the representatives of the United States in Paris, London, Rome, and Petrograd handed the Allies the German and Austro-Hungarian peace offer. On the same day Baron Sonnino in the Parliament at Rome, just as Briand and Prokovsky had done, very decisively repudiated and rejected the whole of the peace manœuvre of the Central Powers. On December 19th Briand and Lloyd George again made speeches in their respective Parliaments declining the peace proposals, and some of the statements which they made became slogans which remained current for some time.

Briand, for example, designated the peace proposal as a new battle attack, and Lloyd George, speaking for the first time as Prime Minister, and emphasizing the need for Allied unity both in war aims and in the common action on the battle-fronts, energetically repudiated the manœuvre of the Central Powers. With the full weight of his authority he then pronounced the well-known formula: "Our war aim is complete territorial restoration, full compensation for property destroyed, effective guarantees against a repetition of a similar attack in the future."

The discussion on the Government proclamation had not yet ended, when a new and important item of news became public property. On Wednesday, December 20th, President Wilson's representatives in the belligerent countries had delivered a special note calling upon all the belligerent Powers to inform President Wilson of their war aims. President Wilson, speaking for the United States as the largest neutral country, emphasized the interest of the neutrals in a speedy conclusion of peace, and demanded that the States engaged in the war should, in some form or other, publicly inform the world what they desired to obtain by the war, in order that it might be clear "how far the world still is from the harbour of peace." President Wilson did not offer to act as intermediary, nor did he propose any peace negotiations. He merely wanted to sound both sides, and thus to gain both for them and for the neutrals the information necessary for clearing up the situation, and for making it possible, at the psychological moment, to start peace negotiations.

It was now that we in Paris felt most alarmed. We had already heard that both in Vienna and Berlin they were placing a certain amount of hope upon a peace intervention prepared by President Wilson. The papers had, at the same time, published reports to the effect that Mr. Gerard, the American Ambassador in Berlin, had been summoned to Washington for this purpose, and that Count Tarnowski, the new Austro-Hungarian Ambassador who had replaced Dumba at Washington after the latter had been withdrawn on account of his well-known intrigues against America, would be favourably received by Wilson.

47

Our uncertainty and alarm were increased when, during the period of excitement while preparations were being made for an answer to the peace overtures of the Central Powers and also to President Wilson's inquiry as to war aims, we received confidential reports with regard to projected secret peace negotiations, partly with Germany, partly with Austria-Hungary.

On December 20, 1916, Prince Brancaccio, head of the intelligence department of the Italian Military Mission in Paris, came to me with reports about peace negotiations between Germany, France, and Russia. Brancaccio was obviously perturbed. All similar reports about peace negotiations carried on without the direct participation or official knowledge of Italy gave the Italians the impression that their interests were going to be sacrificed. As far as I observed them, the Italians—whether they belonged to non-official political circles or whether they were in an official position—constantly had one idea in mind: they had entered the war, and in return for that were promised Trentino, Dalmatia, Trieste, and the Littoral. If the war were concluded before Austria-Hungary was compelled to grant these concessions, they would neither receive what was promised nor an adequate return for their share in the war. In this case it would be clear that they would have done better to have remained neutral (as Giolitti wished) and let Austria-Hungary and Germany reward them accordingly.

Throughout the war, especially in 1917, I had the impression that this was the argument which weighed in the minds of the Italians whenever peace negotiations were mentioned, and proved a decisive factor in the tactics they adopted. This impression was confirmed by Brancaccio's visit.

Brancaccio informed me that a few days before, a number of Dutch Socialists, under the leadership of Troelstra, had come to Paris, and by arrangement with the German Socialists they were endeavouring to bring about peace negotiations with France and Russia. Brancaccio was convinced that the offer was being made with the knowledge of the German Government, which in this way was exploiting its Socialists, while the latter were making use of the Socialists of a neutral country.

It was at this time, however, that our Russian friend Svatkovsky, whose reports concerned us far more closely, came to Paris. He first conferred with Izvolsky at the Russian Embassy, and then, on December 22nd, he had a meeting with me. Svatkovsky was uneasy and agitated. His attitude towards us was a hesitant one, and altogether I had never seen him in such a frame of mind during our conversations. My impression was that either he was embarrassed at not knowing how to inform us of certain matters, or else that he was concealing important developments from us, and for that reason felt rather ill at ease.

The general impression of my talk with Svatkovsky was disturbing. I saw that matters were more serious than I had supposed from my conversation with Brancaccio. From the reports of both our friends, I came to the conclusion that there really was a serious peace move being skilfully prepared or already under consideration in various quarters.

My tactics and, indeed, our tactics in general at Paris under such critical circumstances, were of a simple character. It was impossible for us in any direct manner to frustrate negotiations of such a kind and such a magnitude. So far we had not sufficient influence, nor even direct access to the authorities who were forming decisions on the subject. We were therefore left with indirect methods. At such moments we had recourse to a very energetic type of public agitation. We sounded the alarm among all our friends—politicians, writers, journalists—seeking to exercise an influence on the negotiating statesmen by stirring up public opinion.

Situations of this kind always constituted a sort of general crisis, even for the Allied Governments, and such crises could always be made use of for effective work with a fair chance of success. For if in such far-reaching negotiations the leading persons failed to secure what was expected of them, this generally resulted in a cleavage greater than existed before the negotiations began. There would ensue a movement in the contrary direction, and it was in such psychological situations that the best chance of achieving success was to be found. We therefore set to work with the utmost energy, realizing that even if we did not arrive at any direct success, we should at least have the satisfaction of knowing that we had done everything possible.

We therefore exerted all our efforts in Paris, London, and Rome towards starting a keen Press campaign. We supplied various quarters with detailed accounts of the situation at home, endeavouring in this way to counteract what was being done behind the scenes by the pro-Austrians, who at that time were very strong and dangerous. In addition, I myself attempted to enter into touch with official circles in Paris. Various official pronouncements (that of the King of England on December 22nd, the proclamations in the French Senate on December 23rd, the King of Rumania's speech from the throne, etc.) made it possible for us to take these steps. Nevertheless, we were painfully dubious about the result.

(b) The Allied Reply to the Central Powers. The Allied Note to President Wilson on January 10, 1917, and the Czechoslovaks

48

The Central Powers interpreted Wilson's initiative as their success. That at least is how it appeared to us when, on December 27th, we saw that they gladly availed themselves of the opportunity presented to them by Wilson, and on that day handed him their reply to his note of December 20th, referring to his "generous and lofty proposals."

This moment, however, represented a definite turning-point in the whole situation. The Central Powers evaded a precise reply to the question regarding war aims. They proposed a meeting of representatives of the two belligerent parties in some neutral place. As for an investigation into guarantees of future peace, this was a process which they wished to postpone until after the conclusion of hostilities. In other words, they confirmed the view that the whole of their peace offer was a manœuvre and an attempt to reach the stage of negotiations at all costs, since they supposed that there could then be no resumption of warfare.

The reply caused dissatisfaction at Washington. The Allies were therefore in a position to make good use of the obvious insincerity of their opponents, and to demonstrate convincingly the moral basis of the whole of this diplomatic move. At this juncture, however, reports reached Paris and London that Wilson's intentions had been different from what the Central Powers or Allied public opinion had at first supposed. It was said that he had waited for a considerable time before taking this step, and that it was only the Presidential elections which had induced him not to act earlier. The submarine warfare was too closely affecting the interests of America, whose situation had become so serious that there was now a danger of her being involved in the conflicts arising from the war. The purpose of Wilson's initiative at the moment when military circles in Germany were again threatening to start unlimited submarine warfare was chiefly to draw the attention of the American public to the dangerous position of the United States. The Press even reported a remark by Lansing to the effect that the United States were on the brink of war.

This immediately threw a different light upon the whole matter. The public disapproval which Wilson's move had evoked among the Allies gradually subsided. In its place the view gained currency that the diplomatic manœuvre of the Central Powers could be turned to their disadvantage, and that a moral and diplomatic victory against them could thus be gained in the eyes of the whole world.

In the Allied Note there are two points to be emphasized. Firstly, the Allies produced the proof that the war was caused by the Central Powers, and secondly, they indicated under what conditions it would be possible to start peace negotiations. They expressly declare that "Peace is not possible until a reparation of all infringed rights and liberties has been secured, together with a recognition of the principle of nationality and the free existence of small States."

After the various individual declarations on behalf of Belgium, Serbia, Poland, Rumania, the Jugoslavs, and the Czechoslovaks, this was the first collective proclamation containing anything like a categorical statement of the principles which were more and more gaining ground among the Allies. It was a proclamation due, largely in an indirect manner, to the activities of our various friends and ourselves. Although it had been drawn up with a view to Belgium and Serbia principally, the remaining countries not being expressly mentioned, it nevertheless showed what great progress had been made to the advantage of oppressed nations since February 1916, when Masaryk had explained to Briand our attitude towards the fundamentals of the Central European problem. I cannot precisely determine whether the wording of this reply was affected by our interventions and activities, which aimed at the adoption of a favourable point of view towards our cause in the note to President Wilson.

It was a source of considerable encouragement to us. We felt that the second projected reply of the Allies to President Wilson would give us an opportunity of achieving even more, and possibly even the maximum of what at that time could be secured.

49

The Allied reply certainly produced a very strong effect in the Allied, neutral, and enemy States. We immediately had evidence of this. The Press notices emanating from the countries of the Central Powers clearly showed that the peace manœuvre had failed, and that the official circles there were keenly disappointed and, indeed, depressed. Attempts were made to conceal this, partly by violent language accusing the Allies of being responsible for a further prolongation of the war, partly by open threats that before long something extremely unpleasant would occur.

The truth of the situation was still more plainly revealed in the solemn declarations of the two Emperors to their nations and armies, in which they shift the responsibility for the continuation of warfare to the Allies. They emphasize the great victories which they themselves have hitherto gained over a number of States, and announce that they will compel the Allies by force of arms to accept the terms which they refused when offered in an amicable manner. The Central Powers, seeing that the diplomatic manœuvre had come to grief, adopted a new tone, evidently to ward off depression from their public opinion and demoralization from their army. As far as the

Habsburg Empire and Karl were concerned, the situation was a tragic one. This was surmised by many people in Vienna; the anxieties and fears for the future had again increased, it being understood more clearly than ever before, that everything was at stake.

This was the international situation when the second Allied reply was prepared, in the form of their memorable note to President Wilson in which, for the first time, the Czechoslovaks received a solemn collective testimony from the Allies that their liberation was, and would be, an issue of the war.

(c) The Note to President Wilson and the Liberation of the Czechoslovaks

50

The Czechoslovak National Council, seeing that the situation was psychologically favourable, did everything possible at that time to ensure that the reply to President Wilson should contain a proper account of the Austro-Hungarian problem and of our national demands.

On December 27, 1916, at the French Foreign Ministry, I had my first conversation with Albert Kammerer, who had been detailed for service with Philip Berthelot, then head of the political section of the Foreign Ministry. I explained to him the situation in Austria, and mentioned what I then knew from confidential sources with regard to the political conditions and the state of the army. I also spoke of the attempts made by the Government, partly by threats, partly by promises, to destroy the opposition of the Austro-Hungarian nationalities. I specially laid stress on the necessity for strengthening this opposition by expressly mentioning the Czechs and their national demands, as well as the Slovaks. This latter point was one which I regarded as needing special emphasis.(25)

At my first interview with Kammerer he gave me an account of the situation which disconcerted me and very much chilled my optimism. He pointed out the feeling among the Allies as a whole, amongst whom the view prevailed that, although there would be a general statement in favour of the liberty of oppressed nations in Central Europe, it was not possible to enter into any detailed enumeration of the political problems concerning the individual nations in Austria-Hungary. In particular, the Allies shrank from giving any public promise to the Austro-

Hungarian nations that they would fight until the Empire had been completely broken up, since a situation might arise which would make it impossible for them to keep such a promise.

Kammerer then mentioned to me other considerations which had been very carefully thought out. Thus a number of influential factors were opposed to any decisive proclamation on the subject of Austria-Hungary, because it might seem merely absurd in view of the military situation at that time, and might produce the impression of being an empty threat in which the Allies themselves did not really believe. Other opponents of any decisive proclamation against the Habsburg Empire brought forward the further argument that it was impossible to promise us the break-up of the Empire, because many would interpret that as meaning an indefinite prolongation of the war. Moreover, as a matter of fact, the Allied Governments were not entitled to make such a commitment. They were unable to shut themselves off from any path—Kammerer said this to me quite frankly and honestly—which might lead to some other favourable solution.

On my part, I objected that France particularly could not desert us. I told Kammerer that the conditions in Austria were worse than was supposed, and that such a step would, on the contrary, hasten the end of the war. Before I left, Kammerer suggested that I should draw up a summary of my argument in a special memorandum which he would submit to Berthelot and Pichon.

Two days later, on December 29, 1916, I handed in my memorandum at the Quai d'Orsay. I depicted the political situation as I conceived it to be, judging from the newspapers and the special reports from the "Maffia," and I concluded as follows: "The Czechs form an element which, under present conditions, causes Austria-Hungary the greatest internal difficulties. If, in replying to Wilson, you recognize our political aims and plans, you will strengthen their opposition to Austria, which will thus be completely disorganized."

Kammerer took the memorandum. He now spoke in a somewhat more favourable tone, and promised to place the matter before his chiefs. He also informed me that I should be received by Berthelot in the near future. Shortly afterwards Berthelot received me, listened to my statement, and told me to have another discussion with Kammerer. My meeting with him produced no new result.

After experiencing these obstacles in official quarters, I was anxious to gain some other support which would produce influential results at the Ministry of Foreign Affairs. I therefore took new steps on the very same day. With the assistance of a friend of mine, Professor Moysset (an historian, a clear-minded and brilliant scholar), I managed to reach the chairman of the Foreign Committee, M. Leygues, later Prime Minister, as Moysset was his *chef de cabinet*. I asked him for his support, submitted a new memorandum on the situation to him, and explained what the effects would be if the Allied Note contained a declaration in our favour. Through my friend, E. Fournol, I met André Tardieu, then a leader-writer for *Le Temps*. I gave him an account of the whole history of our movement and asked him if he would write an article on it in his paper. Tardieu promised to do so, the article was published on January 3rd, and through the influence of *Le Temps* produced a considerable effect in political circles. From the Quai d'Orsay at my next negotiations there I learnt that the discussions on our demands had resulted in three plans and possibilities.

(a) It might be possible to insert into the note a declaration with regard to us.

(b) If this should be too difficult, it would be possible for Briand to make a Parliamentary declaration on the subject of the Czechs.

(c) Briand would be prepared to receive the secretary of the National Council at an official audience, and make the declaration to him. In such a case the audience would be arranged so as to obtain ample publicity.

I emphasized to Kammerer that the declaration must be inserted in the note because any other proceeding would be interpreted by our people at home as an indication that our position was a weak one. I supplied him with a formula which could be enclosed in the note and which would satisfy us. It could also be adapted to the general sentence on the liberation of the Austro-Hungarian nations which, he informed me, had already been prepared for the note and agreed upon among the Allies.

We then arranged for an article to appear in *Le Matin*, again emphasizing the necessity of supporting the opposition of the Austro-Hungarian nations, especially the Czechs and Slovaks I prepared the article and it appeared on the front page of the paper on January 3rd. On the same day I endeavoured to counteract the intention at the Quai d'Orsay of satisfying us otherwise than by the express mention of our aims in the note to Wilson. I visited Robert de Caix, a friend of Berthelot and an expert on colonial and Eastern European matters at the Quai d'Orsay. I asked him to let the Foreign Office have my reasons in favour of a direct mention of our aims in the note, and he expressed his willingness to intervene with Berthelot.

Finally, I applied for support to our friend August Gauvain. I wrote for the *Journal des Debats* an original letter from Austria, containing the latest news which we had received from Prague. The letter was published towards the end of December. In a leading article Gauvain referred to it, and demanded an unequivocal declaration of the Allies against Austria-Hungary and in favour of the oppressed nations. Other papers also took notice of it, and in this way exerted an influence on public opinion and Government circles.

On January 4th Kammerer invited me for a final interview. He informed me that, on principle, the Quai d'Orsay was resolved to do something for us, but that the form of action was still being considered. A decision would probably be reached at the Inter-Allied Conference then being held in Rome. So far, the Allies had agreed that the note should express in general terms the necessity for liberating the Austro-Hungarian Slavs, the Italians, the Rumanians. What made it difficult to mention the Czechs and Slovaks specifically was, that if this were done, it would be necessary to refer in a similar manner to the Jugo-slavs, a course against which the Italians were fundamentally opposed. France would, however, do what she could. I again, and for the last time, urged upon Kammerer how essential it was not to forget the Slovaks, and, as I have already mentioned, I suggested the formula to the effect that one of the Allied war aims was "the liberation of the Czechs united with Slovakia" or else "the liberation of the Czechoslovaks," leaving the Allies, of course, free to word it in accordance with the context.

On January 7th the Quai d'Orsay at last informed me that the Allies had accepted the French proposal, and that the liberation of the Czechoslovaks would be expressly mentioned in the note. The reference to the Czechoslovaks in the note had been accepted by the Allies as an amendment after the previous formula had already been sanctioned. This formula spoke of the establishment of an independent Poland with access to the sea, and of the liberation of the Austro-Hungarian Italians, Rumanians, and Slavs. It will be seen that even in the revised form the note contained no special reference to the Jugoslavs.

The wording of the note thus acquired an inexactitude and inconsistency which caused much surprise. This was a typical example of the political difficulties and disputes between the Italians and the Jugoslavs, which at that time proved troublesome to us and the rest of the Allies. The Jugoslavs made no attempt to conceal their disappointment after the publication of the note.

The account of the matter which I have given makes it clear that the negotiations between the Allies with regard to the contents of the note to President Wilson were the result of French initiative, and were concentrated in Paris. Masaryk was following them from London (Štefánik was now in Russia), and reported to me how matters were regarded there. Our success caused him a pleasant surprise.(26)

The significance of the Allied Note to President Wilson is sufficiently well known. For us who were working abroad it represented the first obvious diplomatic success of any magnitude. There were great rejoicings in our various headquarters abroad. We received telegrams and letters of congratulation from our Russian colony, our troops, our American colony, our compatriots in Italy, Switzerland, and elsewhere. It acted upon me as a stimulus and encouragement to continue our military movement.

ITALY AND CZECHOSLOVAKIA IN THE GREAT WAR.
THE ENTRY OF THE UNITED STATES INTO THE
WAR. RUSSIA AND OUR LIBERATION MOVE-
MENT. THE RUSSIAN REVOLUTION.

(*a*) ITALY AND THE CZECHOSLOVAK QUESTION

51

AFTER our success in connection with the Allied Note to
President Wilson, I decided that the time had come to pay a
visit to Italy. Our work at Paris with regard to political
matters and the prisoners of war was making satisfactory
progress. In London Masaryk's influence and authority had
advanced considerably, and our propaganda was spreading
ever further afield. In Russia, where Štefánik was at work,
the whole of our political and military movement was developing on hopeful lines. In America our colonists were unsparing
in their efforts. Only in Italy was our movement still at its
initial stage.

Masaryk himself had been in direct touch with Italy until
1915, and he had kept this up from London indirectly through
a number of his friends. Štefánik had stopped in Rome on his
way back from the Serbian front in the winter of 1915, and on
this occasion he had been received by a number of Court
functionaries, as well as by the French and Russian Ambassadors. Then, in the spring of 1916 he had been entrusted with
a mission in matters relating to the Jugoslavs. Both his visits
had been of considerable importance, leaving definite traces
in Rome. But there had been no attempt at organization.

In Italy not much was known about us, although in some
ways matters were more favourable there. The Italian public,
anti-Austrian and anti-Habsburg in feeling, entertained sympathies towards any movement directed against Austria. The
responsible statesmen were not a priori unfavourably disposed
towards us, even though their attitude on the whole was
reserved. Difficulties arose from the fact that the public

and the greater part of the politicians, were apt to mistake us for the Jugoslavs.

The Jugoslav movement had naturally been closely followed by the Italian Government and the Italian public. They turned their attention to us at a later date. Sonnino, when entering the war, was not thinking of the break-up of Austria-Hungary. The attention of official Italian circles was drawn to our movement, partly by the increasing number of our prisoners of war who, from the very outset, came forward as volunteers for our revolutionary activity, partly through the reports from the Italian Ambassadors and intelligence departments on our movement, principally in France, England, and Switzerland.

My first contact with official Italy had been at Paris in the summer of 1916. In connection with his visits to Italy, Štefánik had come into contact with the Italian military mission at Paris, at the head of which was Prince Brancaccio, and, as I have mentioned in the previous chapter, I supplied him with reports from Prague. Our movement in Switzerland and France began to receive closer attention from the ministry of Commandini, whose function in the Cabinet it was to keep a careful watch on all Austro-Hungarian propaganda against Italy and the Allies, and to follow the internal affairs of Austria-Hungary, more particularly those involving the Jugoslavs, but also, of course, the Czechoslovaks and Poles. Gino Scarpa, who was Commandini's secretary, visited Switzerland in 1916 and got into touch with our Bureau there. He then came to Paris and arranged to work in collaboration with me. He subsequently began to co-operate at Rome with Veselý, Brázda, and the rest of our workers there, and this was the beginning of our co-operation with official Italy.

Definite co-operation was established in the autumn of 1916. I sent Scarpa reports systematically on the internal conditions of the Habsburg Empire, either direct to the Ministry or through Veselý. The latter then began, with Scarpa's assistance, to place our reports in the leading daily papers in Rome. When the peace overtures of the Central Powers were imminent, we were, in fact, asked for help in the form of information. At the same time the wish was expressed that I should go to Rome, come into personal contact with the officials at the Ministry, arrange contact with Commandini, and establish an office at Rome analogous to our Paris headquarters. On

December 17, 1916, Veselý reported the opinion of the
Ministry that we were holding too much aloof from Italy;
that our movement at Rome should be established on a
footing equal to that in Paris and London, and that, above
all, we should not concern ourselves so much about Jugoslav
matters, since this would tend to alienate Italian sympathies
from us. I promised to go to Italy as soon as possible, and in
the following month I went.

52

Before his death San Giuliano, who was the Foreign Minister
of Italy at the outbreak of the war, was evidently inclined to
believe that the Triple Alliance was dead, and that Italy
would be obliged to enter the war in company with the Triple
Entente. This would mean the fall of Austria-Hungary and the
gain of considerable territories by Italy. There were, however,
two dangers which caused him concern. On the one hand he
was not certain whether the Triple Entente would continue to
oppose the Habsburg Empire until the end, and on the other
he feared the expansion of the Russians and the Slavs in general,
if they were victorious.

In spite of his defects and political blunders Baron Sonnino
was indisputably Italy's strong man during the war. He was
honest, consistent, and persevering, even to the point of
obstinacy. If he gave his word he kept it, but he did not
always properly understand the problems on which he made
decisions, and he kept too rigidly to his preconceived ideas.
The general design of his policy was simple. The majority of
the leading politicians in Italy must soon have realized that
an attitude of neutrality could not be indefinitely maintained.
The war had become a European war, and its influence on
Italy, both in a political and economic respect, was such that
the whole country was faced daily with difficult problems
arising from it. Neutrality would, in the end, have had worse
results for Italy than actual warfare. Sonnino did not think
that a permanent, or at least a prolonged, neutrality was
impracticable. He was in agreement with Salandra's later
formula concerning *sacro egoismo.*

On these lines Sonnino began to negotiate with Vienna on
the subject of the well-known concessions in return for continued neutrality in the war, and a disinterested attitude in

Balkan matters. He demanded the Trentino, Gorizia, Gradiscia, a number of islands, and also the proclamation of Trieste as a free city. There are politicians who hold the view that, if Vienna had accepted these terms, Sonnino would have demanded colonial concessions from the Triple Entente in return for his neutrality. If both negotiations had proved successful, he would have continued his policy of neutrality, reserving for himself, however, the opportunity of entering the war at any moment which he might consider most favourable to Italian interests.

But in spite of all Bülow's endeavours, Vienna remained firm. For concrete reasons, in addition to their prestige, the Austrian diplomats refused to make the slightest concession to their one-time enemy, and so Sonnino, not being able to sell neutrality for his country's profit, was obliged to sell his military power to the best advantage. He decided to repudiate the Triple Alliance and to conclude the well-known London Agreement with the Triple Entente. This was done on April 26, 1915, and on the basis of it Italy entered the war on May 24, 1915. By the terms of the London Agreement Italy was to receive Trient, Gorizia, Istria with Trieste, but without Fiume, and Dalmatia as far as Narenta.

When entering the world-conflict, official Italy, just like the rest of the Allies, had no definite political design. This is proved by the London Agreement itself. (I may add that the Allies were dissatisfied with this Agreement, the awkward consequences of which they realized as soon as they had signed it.) Sonnino, personally, was a Conservative and a legitimist, and he therefore could not have much understanding of, or propensity for, the traditions of Mazzini, which were democratic and national (in the sense of justice to nationalities). He thought of the war as being solely an Italian one, and the idea of destroying Austria-Hungary hardly entered his mind. Moreover, for many years he had been an advocate of the Triple Alliance policy, believing in the great strength of Germany. He was sceptical of a decisive victory, which could only destroy one side or the other. For that reason also he feared the strength of the Germans after the war, and allowed a considerable time to elapse before he declared war on them.

But his opinion and attitude with regard to the Jugoslav question constituted a source of trouble. For one thing, it was a subject about which he knew very little, as I discovered in the course of several conversations with him. Then, too, he was strongly influenced by the theories of the extreme Italian nationalists during 1915 and 1916. He, as well as the rest of the Allies, regarded the London Agreement as denoting the preservation of an Austria-Hungary reduced by the territories ceded to Italy, the establishment of a Greater Serbia with the Croats and Slovenes, the preservation of Montenegro, and later, after the entry of Rumania into the war, the incorporation of Transylvania and Bukovina with Rumania. He therefore consistently pursued a policy favouring the fulfilment of the London Agreement and opposed to the unification of the Jugoslavs. This accounts for his reserve upon all schemes involving the complete break-up of the Habsburg Empire. It explains why, in spite of his sincere good will towards us, he would never utter his final word on the subject of our cause, at least not until October 24, 1918, when he acknowledged our provisional Government.

In this respect his constant opponent in Orlando's Cabinet was Leonido Bissolati. Together with his immediate followers (Salvemini, Antonio da Viti de Marco, and others), Bissolati was perhaps the only man in Italy who, at the beginning of the war, realized with anything like clarity the significance of the war for Central Europe. As a Socialist he proceeded from democratic principles, identifying himself with the ideals which Mazzini had entertained with regard to the oppressed nations of Central Europe. He was in favour of Italian intervention on behalf of European democracy, as well as on behalf of the unification of the Italian people. He was therefore in favour of a peace based upon permanent factors. Bissolati was one of those few politicians and thinkers in Europe and America who, from the beginning of the war, in varying degrees, correctly gauged the scope of the ideas behind it. For this reason Bissolati was in favour of an agreement between Italy and the Serbs, as well as all the oppressed nations of Austria-Hungary, whom he always unreservedly supported in their endeavours during the war. In his opinion an agreement between Italy and the Serbs would have made it possible to conclude the war against the Habsburg Empire rapidly and victoriously. Such an agreement would also have ensured a long period of peace for Italy and Central Europe in the years immediately following the war.

Throughout the year 1917 Bissolati was helping to make these ideas familiar in Italy, and in 1918 he endeavoured to get them accepted by the Cabinet, by Orlando, and Sonnino. He thus contributed directly and indirectly to the success of our efforts in Italy, and finally, in September 1918, he caused the Italian Government to issue its proclamation in favour of the unification of the Jugoslavs, although he did not manage to overcome Sonnino's opposition to withdrawal from the London Agreement and to a new convention with the Jugoslavs.

I do not propose to discuss here further details of Italian policy and diplomacy during the war, the disputes on Greek questions and Albania, on Asia Minor, on the unified front, and what was known as the "Italian" War. Nor do I propose to refer to the struggles in Italy concerning the Jugoslavs. I will mention only what is essential for the understanding of the relations of Italy towards our cause. There is one important fact to add. Throughout the war Italy was, in a certain sense, isolated with regard to the other Allies. They regarded Germany as the chief opponent, while for Italy it was Vienna and Budapest who occupied that position. Up till April 1918 the rest of the Allies believed that it was possible to separate Austria-Hungary from Germany, and they would certainly have concluded peace with the Habsburg Empire if the opportunity had presented itself. Here was the fundamental divergence in the views and interests of both camps. In this respect we were closer to Italy than to the other Allies.

We regarded Italy as a decisive power, and it is my duty to state plainly that she rendered us extremely valuable services in the struggle against a premature or separate peace with Austria-Hungary. It was none other than Sonnino who, by his opinion and character, became the advocate of this policy directed against a premature peace with Vienna, and by this very fact he deserves our gratitude in bringing about the break-up of Austria-Hungary and the liberation of our people. I am glad to place this on record, even though it came about, not through any theoretical sympathies for us or other oppressed nations, but because our vital interests in this matter coincided with those of Italy during the war. It must, of course, be added that the efforts of our nation always had a sincere and friendly reception from the Italian public and from the Government.

(b) My First Journey to Rome. Negotiations in Rome and their Consequences

53

The Allied Note to President Wilson proclaimed a life-and-death struggle against Austria-Hungary. Of the greater Allies, Italy was more interested than any other in this question. In referring definitely to us, the note also emphasized the significance of our cause. I judged that under these new circumstances it would be all the easier in Italy to establish a satisfactory basis or organizing our political work, especially in connection with the prisoners of war. My idea was first to organize a political and propagandist bureau at Rome, and to connect it with our organization as a branch office of the National Council at Paris. It was further my intention, as a representative of the National Council, to enter into direct personal touch at Rome with those journalistic circles who were prejudiced against us because of their objection to the Jugoslavs, and I wanted to win over to our cause some influential persons in public life. It was also my aim to try to establish official contact with persons in the Government, to tell them about our military and political work in France and Russia, and to obtain for the National Council, as our official body, something like the position which we had secured in Paris.

With these purposes in view, for the first time in my life, I arrived in Rome on January 12, 1917. At one of the stations before Rome I bought the morning papers. The sensation of the day was the publication of the Allied Note to President Wilson. My arrival in Rome on this occasion was one of the incidents in the war which caused me a deep and lasting gratification.

But a journey to Rome just at this moment involved also serious risks, as far as our cause was concerned. The dispute on the subject of the Jugoslavs had just become acute, and the negotiations with regard to the wording of the Allied Note to Wilson had served only to intensify this dispute. The problem of the London Agreement was one of the topics of the day, the Press was full of articles against the Jugoslavs, demonstrating the Italian character of Dalmatia, the

unreliability of the Jugoslavs (Croats) in the struggle against
Austria-Hungary, they being accused of double-dealing with
Vienna, and so on.

Accordingly, the political aspect of my journey to Italy
presented considerable difficulties. The Government circles
were naturally guarded in their attitude, and a part of the
public was mistrustful. On the other hand there were certain
Italian circles who welcomed my visit as an opportunity for
them to try to use the Czechoslovaks as a counter-weight
against the Jugoslavs. They wanted to show that if the
Jugoslavs were tractable, and, as it was occasionally expressed,
as reliable as we were, Italy would act in the same manner
towards them as towards us. But this might have constituted
an argument against the claims of the Jugoslavs. The whole
month of my stay in Italy was spent in discussions along these
lines. All my explanations and endeavours to bring forward
the Czechoslovak question merely brought a reiterated statement of the Italian case against the Jugoslavs. There was
considerable ignorance of Jugoslav affairs, together with unjust suspicions of the Serbs, the Jugoslav Committee, Trumbić, Hinković, Supilo, etc. With certain of the nationalists
these suspicions were deliberately exaggerated. Chauvinism
was regarded by the majority quite sincerely as being right
and proper; it dominated the greater part of the Italian
public. The only reaction against this tendency proceeded
from the associates of Bissolati and Salvemini. But there
were judicious elements also in Liberal Parliamentary circles,
who were seeking a method of reasonable agreement with the
Jugoslavs, based upon fair compromise.

Perhaps I overestimated the extent to which this feeling in
Italy involved a danger to us also. My fear was that in the
end Italy, a country which should have been at the head of
the struggle for the destruction of the Habsburg monarchy,
might, through her objection to the Jugoslavs, choose the very
opposite policy. That was the question which I often asked myself, bearing in mind Sonnino's policy, the irritability of Italian
public opinion, and the prejudiced attitude of nationalist
circles towards the Jugoslavs. I then had quite a high opinion
of the influence exerted by Giolitti's group and politicians
such as Nitti, who, as late as the spring of 1918, did not
believe in the break-up of Austria-Hungary.

As Italy, both official and unofficial, was then openly

opposed to the unification of the Jugoslavs, I endeavoured to render the latter a service in as tactful and unobtrusive a manner as I could. I had several discussions, for example, with the leading members of the "Dante Alighieri" League (Zaccagnini, San Miniatelli, Scodnik, and others), to whom, while emphasizing my loyalty and sincerity towards Italy, I endeavoured to demonstrate the inaccuracy of their views.

The attitude which I then adopted towards Italy, both official and unofficial, was one to which I adhered throughout the war. I never concealed the bonds of friendship which united us inseparably with the Jugoslavs, but under all circumstances I continued to be loyal to Italian interests.

54

I began my political activities in Rome on January 13, 1917, by visiting my friend Erazim Piltz, who was a member of the Polish Committee. I hoped to obtain from him some account of affairs in Rome, before beginning my negotiations with official Italian circles and with the Allied ambassadors.

Piltz received me in a friendly manner, gave me the information I wanted regarding the situation in Italy, and at once told me about his last visit to the Vatican. He explained that the Vatican was in favour of the Poles, but wanted to save Austria. It appeared that Piltz had spoken to the Pope about us also, and he advised me strongly to get into touch with the Vatican circles and to gain their sympathies, as they were very powerful. He said that their attitude towards us was a reserved one, and that we were not in favour with them; but if a visit were paid to them, it would be possible at least to persuade them from working against us. I followed the advice which Piltz gave me.

It was Veselý who prepared Commandini for my visit, and Gino Scarpa introduced me to his Minister, with whom I had a detailed conversation on the affairs of Austria and ourselves. He was quite well acquainted with these questions, and was keenly interested in them. I gave him an account of the progress which our movement had made, as well as of our plans and aims, and of our work in Russia and France concerning the army and the prisoners of war. I asked for assistance from Italy, in particular, to enable us to get into touch with our prisoners of war and possibly also, in due course, to liberate them. Commandini agreed with my plans and views, and he promised me that he would do everything that was possible in Italy under the existing conditions. He and his ministry kept this promise, and in the course of the year 1917 helped us considerably.

Before approaching the Italian Ministry of Foreign Affairs, I visited the Russian and French Embassies. Both Giers and Barrère, as well as all their staffs, received me in a favourable manner. I have the most pleasant memories of these negotiations, more particularly since at that time I was a beginner in diplomatic matters, and at Rome I entered more fully than at Paris into what was then a new world to me.

I was received by Giers, the Russian Ambassador, on January 18th. I explained to him my ideas and also my plans of action in Italy. He recommended me to be cautious with the Italians, but otherwise he spoke of Italy in sympathetic terms, and agreed with my moderate tactics. With regard to the Jugoslavs, he criticized the radical tendencies of their policy. His view of the situation, as he communicated it to me, was as follows: the Italians went too far on the subject of the Jugoslavs, and they were wrong about Dalmatia. The advance of history, he said, could not be held back. Both the Jugoslavs and ourselves would win the day, Austria would collapse, and Russia would fight until the end.

He then promised me all possible assistance in Rome, referred in terms of commendation to Štefánik, who had visited him during his stay there, and he spoke of us and our aims with sympathy. He was sincere and straightforward. He had recently returned from Russia, and was quite well acquainted with the progress of our movement at Petrograd, Moscow, and Kiev. He told me frankly that the conditions prevailing among our people did not impress him favourably. There was a great deal of dissension among them, and the political movement contained elements whose integrity was dubious. Above all, there was not a single political personage who could exercise the necessary authority. I informed him that Masaryk was already making preparations to proceed to Petrograd, and this gave him real satisfaction.

I spent the following days discussing matters with Charles Loiseau, the French journalist, who was attached in an undefined manner to the French Embassy. He was concerned with ecclesiastical affairs, and was in close touch with Vatican circles. He and the Rumanian priest, Vladimir Ghika, introduced me to the Belgian priest, Monsignor Deploige, Professor of Christian sociology at Liège, who was working at the Vatican on behalf of Belgium. They also brought me into touch with Cardinal Bourne, who was then spending some time in Rome. With the help of these new acquaintances I supplied the Vatican with a detailed account of our affairs. All four—Loiseau, Ghika, Monsignor Deploige, and Cardinal Bourne—assured me that they would draw the attention of the appropriate persons at the Vatican to our conversations, and would hand over to the right quarters my notes on our aims and opinions which I had placed at their disposal. Loiseau himself, with whom I continued to maintain friendly relations from that time onwards, did so in a thoroughly conscientious manner and with the best of intentions, acting in this capacity as intermediary until the end of the war. I never ascertained definitely what the others did, but I was informed that they had made a report to the Vatican.

My statement for the Vatican presented the fundamentals of the Czech problem in terms of moderation. I particularly pointed out the unfortunate influence which the Austro-Hungarian State exerted on the Church, and the manner in which it was misused to our detriment. I showed how the Catholic Church there had been the instrument used by those in authority against the oppressed, and at the same time I indicated that we should be quite satisfied if the Vatican merely refrained from acting against our interests. If it were to oppose us in an active manner, and we were then to emerge victorious, this would prove detrimental to Catholicism amongst our people, all the more so since it was our intention to grant full liberty and rights to all religions and churches in our State and accordingly also to Catholicism, which had a strong position amongst us.

I have never discovered whether the Vatican took this into account during the war. At any rate, wherever it could, it rendered all possible assistance to Austria-Hungary as being the most Catholic of all the belligerent Powers. Loiseau used to tell me that the dominant forces in the Vatican had misgivings about our Hussitism, and that they were displeased because our troops in the Russian brigade had gone over to the orthodox Russian Church. He advised us to put a stop to this, as by so doing we should demonstrate our good will, and win over the Vatican to our side. I sent this information to our people in Russia.

On January 23rd Loiseau introduced me to Barrère, the French Ambassador. At that time he was one of the most influential personalities in Rome, partly because he had been ambassador there for nearly twenty years, and partly through the prestige of the country which he represented. Like Giers, he expressed approval of our moderate tactics and urged us to be cautious. When I told him that I wanted to ask the Italian Government to liberate our prisoners of war and allow them to be transferred to our national army in France, he informed me that the Jugoslavs had made a similar application, but that Italy had emphatically refused it. The conditions, however, in our case were different. There were difficulties, but it was not altogether out of the question that we, in contrast to the Jugoslavs, might have our request granted.

Barrère criticized Italy and the Italian policy which, he said, was sometimes short-sighted and selfish. Nevertheless, he manifested considerable sympathies for Italy, as well as admiration for her efforts during the war. He also commended Sonnino, although in a number of respects he condemned his line of policy. He referred approvingly to him as a strong man who, although he made mistakes, knew what he wanted and remained firm until the last, even although others gave way. He also spoke favourably of Giers, whom he described as an honest man with progressive ideas. Finally, he promised me his personal assistance, and asked us to keep in touch with him. He also gave me a number of practical hints as to how I should proceed when negotiating with official circles in Rome, especially as regards Demartino, the general secretary of the Consulta, and De Morciere, Sonnino's secretary. Throughout the war he helped me liberally and proved himself to be a sincere and devoted friend.

55

I obtained access to the Italian Foreign Ministry through the recommendation of Commandini and of my new acquaintances from the "Dante Alighieri" League. I was received for the first time on January 24th by Demartino, the general secretary.

Being a novice, and more particularly one who had come to ask a favour, I was considerably disconcerted by his bureaucratic reserve and the self-assurance of his manner as a diplomat. At the same time the general tendencies of official Italian policy at that period prompted me to be extremely guarded.

However, I expounded our cause, explaining why I had come to Italy, and what significance the Czech problem had in its bearings upon the struggle against Austria-Hungary. I pointed out that here our interests were identical with those of Italy, and that an independent Czechoslovakia would be an important factor in the affairs of Italy after the war. I added that we were anxious to organize our prisoners of war and to create a national army. For this purpose we were applying to Italy for assistance, just as we had already done in France. Finally, I made no secret of our relations with the Jugoslavs. We were quite sincere in acclaiming them as a kindred race, but we wanted them to arrive at an agreement with Italy on a basis involving reasonable compromise and action in common, for which purpose we wished to work on both sides.

Demartino acknowledged the importance of our affairs. Italy was investigating them and would continue to do so, but for the time being the most important question for her was the Italo-Jugoslav dispute. The Jugoslavs must bear in mind that Italy had an agreement with the Allies and, having regard to this, they must make concessions accordingly. He said that we should bring our influence to bear upon them in this sense. In Dalmatia the towns were, he stated, Italian, and the statistics produced as a result of the official Austrian census were inaccurate. Altogether, as far as culture was concerned, Dalmatia was really Italian. Moreover, the Italian claims were based upon considerations of strategy and national security. Apart from this, he agreed that the rest of the southern regions of the monarchy should be given to Serbia, or to whatever State might subsequently be formed there— either Greater Serbia or Croatia and Serbia. Demartino emphasized these concluding ideas, which indicated his reserve on the subject of national and State unification.

From this conversation I obtained a first-hand knowledge of the difficulties which Italian diplomacy was causing, and would continue to cause, as far as Jugoslav affairs were concerned. And although Demartino did not expressly mention the fact, it was clear to me that he was opposed to the unification of the Jugoslavs. I also had a definite feeling that he was expressing the view held by the Consulta and the exponents of Italian foreign policy in general.

As regards ourselves, however, he showed that he understood our aims quite well. He promised assistance and asked me to visit him again. He also sanctioned the establishment of a branch office of the National Council in Rome with which, as in France, the Government would be officially in touch. In the same way he gave his consent for our organization to establish contact with the prisoners of war. This latter question, he said, was one which the Italian Government was then carefully considering, and it would decide to what extent it could adopt the same procedure as the French Government. He recommended me while in Paris to keep in direct touch with the Italian Embassy and military mission there, making any applications to the Italian Government through them.

My interview with De Morciere was similar in character. He was more guarded on the subject of the Jugoslavs, but more amenable to my arguments in their favour. He was greatly impressed by what I told him about our military plans, and about what we were already doing in France and Russia. He was also interested in the possibility of organizing our prisoners of war in Italy. He promised his support and assured me that he would give Sonnino a detailed account of the matter.

Such were my official negotiations. All the promises or agreements which I thus obtained were, in due course, carried out with the loyal co-operation of the Italian authorities. And so the result of my negotiations was by no means unsatisfactory, although it was clear that in Italy our task would not be an easy one. It would depend mainly upon tactics and the manner in which events took shape. The Press and public opinion had shown comprehension, sympathies, and good will to the fullest extent. Official circles were well-disposed as regards procedure, but were guarded in their attitude towards the cause itself.

The events of the year 1917 in France, Russia, and Italy, as well as the political and military progress of our movement in the Allied States, as we shall see, led the Italian Government, in September of the same year, during my second visit to Rome, to take further decisive steps on the subject of our cause.

On January 25, 1917, I received a telegram from Masaryk

asking me to proceed from Rome direct to London. He wanted to discuss the political situation which had arisen after the last Allied Note to Wilson, and to decide what inferences could be drawn from it as far as our interests were concerned. He was also anxious to decide what action to take with regard to our affairs in Russia, where at that time the energies of Štefánik were being almost entirely exhausted by the dispute between Kiev and Petrograd, between Dürich and his opponents, who were on our side. Masaryk had some misgivings as to whether Štefánik's course of action was the right one. Then, too, I was to report to him on the situation in Italy and arrange the further organization of our work in Rome.

In the last week of January I concluded the whole of my negotiations. I had one more interview with Demartino, who again assured me that what had already been promised would be carried out. I also saw Barrère and Giers again, and settled the further co-operation between our office in Rome and the Paris headquarters of the National Council. On leaving Rome I travelled by way of Paris, where my stay was very short, to London, where I arrived on February 5th. After having discussed the above-mentioned points with Masaryk, I returned to Paris on February 13th.

(c) THE ENTRY OF THE UNITED STATES INTO THE WAR, AND OUR MOVEMENT

56

At Paris we eagerly waited to see what effect would be produced at Vienna and Berlin by the Allied reply of December 30th and the note to President Wilson. We were no less curious as to the reports which we should receive from Prague, and how our people there would react to our diplomatic success contained in the note to President Wilson. These are matters, however, to which I shall refer later.

The violent official reply of Germany and Austria-Hungary, stating that the Allied declaration denoted war until the final victory of the Central Powers, taken into conjunction with the confidential reports which we had previously received from Prague, led us to surmise that at Vienna a drama was being enacted which was overwhelming the responsible personalities there. For whenever any decisive action was taken against the Allies, the Austro-Hungarian leaders were either dragged into it by Berlin or else in many cases merely confronted with a *fait accompli*. The news which we received from the "Maffia" at this time confirmed these conjectures. They referred to the desperate situation in the Empire, the gratification in the Czech territories at the note to President Wilson, the dissension between Vienna and Berlin, as well as the conviction of everybody in Austria that the Central Powers could not win the war and that the end was rapidly approaching.

At that time we did not know that, after serious conflicts, the Chancellor had given way on the question of submarine warfare. That decision was reached on January 9, 1917, at a conference which was held at Pless and presided over by the Kaiser. This was done without consulting Austria-Hungary. When Czernin heard of the decision from his ambassador at Berlin, he opposed it. Holzendorf and Zimmermann therefore proceeded to Vienna for the purpose of convincing the Government there. On January 20th a conference was held, the Emperor Karl presiding. Holzendorf and Zimmermann advocated Germany's point of view, while Czernin and Tisza opposed the scheme for submarine warfare. The two sides failed to agree, but the Viennese Government did not venture to act in opposition to what Germany had decided, and therefore submitted. It is said that Czernin then advised the Emperor Karl to separate from Germany on account of this matter.

It would appear that Germany's decision, on the whole, did not produce any surprise or considerable excitement either among the Allies, the neutrals, or the Central Powers. It looked as if they had all guessed what was coming. And yet the decision was one which had a considerable, and perhaps even a critical, effect upon the result of the war. On February 3rd, by a solemn declaration in which he analysed the whole course of the dispute between the United States and Germany on the subject of submarine warfare, President Wilson broke off diplomatic relations with Germany, and handed Count Bernsdorf his passport. Those who had any close knowledge of political events realized that this meant the entry of the United States into the war.

In the meanwhile, Wilson had not declared war on Austria-Hungary. It appeared as if he wished to reserve for himself the possibility of adopting a more lenient attitude towards the Habsburg Empire, and that in this respect his point of view was fundamentally the same as that of France and England. This implied that Austria-Hungary would, if possible, separate from Germany, who could then be more easily defeated by military means. The Government at Vienna naturally took advantage of this for a long time, and until the spring of 1918 it caused us much anxiety.

Nevertheless the entry of the United States into the war was a new guarantee of victory for us. After the crisis brought about by the peace overtures in December and January, the Allies themselves accepted America's step as a great success. France was filled with enthusiasm, having now regained her confidence. Wilson immediately became the world's great moral authority. His preparations for warfare, which were being made on a vast scale, were discussed everywhere with complete hope and confidence. A military victory was now regarded as certain, even though it was realized that the American preparations would take a long time. As soon as the United States entered the war, public opinion in France was practically unanimous that the only thing to do was to hold out until America was ready.

This feeling was shared by us also. We were confident that the United States, partly because of their strength and prestige, partly in view of the principles consistently enunciated by President Wilson, would not relax their efforts until Germany at least had been forced to capitulate. I took this view also because it was obvious that the United States had no direct interest in the war, and thus, as they had no definite war aim of their own, the steps which they had taken had been prompted largely by Wilson's democratic convictions. He had rightly judged that the point at issue was not merely one of frontiers or States in Central Europe, but the great problem of reorganizing Europe and, indeed, to a certain extent, the whole world.

(d) THE PROGRESS OF THE RUSSIAN REVOLUTION, ITS
FOREIGN POLICY AND OUR MOVEMENT

57

Those associated with our movement in Western Europe welcomed the Russian revolution. I have already mentioned the difficulties which we encountered in Tsarist Russia, and our internal dissensions which developed from them. In consequence of the revolution all these obstacles disappeared. The satisfaction which this caused us, however, was soon mingled with a feeling of anxiety as to what course the revolution would take, and what effect it would exert upon the general military situation. At first I, just as Štefánik, who had witnessed the early days of the revolution before returning to Paris in the following April, had supposed that the revolution would reveal Russia's military strength in an unprecedented manner, but before long we realized that we should have to be satisfied if Russia managed merely to hold the front, and that in any case the war would be decided in the West.

The first actions of the new provisional Russian Government tended rather to justify our early hopes. On March 18th Masaryk sent Milyukov a telegram in which he emphasized our co-operation with Russia and the Slavs hitherto, and greeted the victory of the Russian revolution which was to bring Russia order and success in the war, besides uniting the Poles, Jugoslavs, and Czechoslovaks, whose independent States it would help to establish. Milyukov immediately acknowledged the receipt of this telegram, to which he replied as follows :

I agree entirely with your ideas as to the perspectives which a free Russia is opening to the family of civilized nations as regards the final re-shaping of Central and South-Eastern Europe.

At the same time the Russian Press Bureau distributed another proclamation by Milyukov made to the representatives of the Russian Press. In it the Russian Foreign Minister referred in detail to a scheme involving the dismemberment of Austria, and said:

The establishment of the Czechoslovak State will set a limit to the aggressive German plans towards the Slav countries. German Austria, as well as Hungary, must be kept within its ethnographical frontiers. The Italians will be united with Italy, the Rumanians with Rumania, and the Ukrainian territories will coalesce with our Ukraine. The natural problems propounded by history demand also the unification of all the Jugoslav regions.

Again, on March 18th, Milyukov distributed among the Russian diplomatic representatives in Allied and neutral countries a circular telegram which also gave us reason for satisfaction. In this telegram Milyukov showed the necessity for the revolution by drawing attention to all the harm which the old regime had done to Russia, and pointing out its criminal method of procedure even during the war. He indicated the war policy of the new Government in the following emphatic terms:

Revolutionary Russia will continue until a victorious end, unweariedly and unreservedly, in the struggle against the common enemy and its aggressive spirit which desires to achieve hegemony over Europe for the advantage of Prussian militarism.

The manifesto of Prince Lvov's provisional Government, which was issued just afterwards, emphasized and supplemented these principles. Under these circumstances we in Paris were at first not alarmed by the difficulties which arose after the abdication of the Tsar and the Grand Duke Michael, nor even by the reports about the arrival of the first Russian revolutionaries and anarchists from abroad with the consent and assistance of the German Government. But after March 20th the political circles in Paris and London began to change their opinion of events in Russia. Their misgivings arose when the Petrograd Soviet of workmen and soldiers, which had soon taken upon itself the function of a subsidiary Government, began to exercise an influence both on the political and military policy of the Government itself. In the last week of March 1917 the conflict between the two tendencies had reached its height.

At first it looked as if Prince Lvov's Government would emerge successfully from the contest. Its proclamation of March 30th that revolutionary Russia would resolve to establish an independent Poland, which was to include the Polish areas in Austria and Prussia, and that this independent State would be bound to Russia only by a military alliance, strengthened the authority of revolutionary Russia and its Government in all Western European States. In the middle of April the Allied Governments replied to Milyukov's manifesto, "emphasizing . . . their entire solidarity with the plans of the Russian Government concerning the restoration of Poland in its unbroken territorial unity." This was a source of fresh gratification to us. As I have already pointed out, we were so convinced of the indivisible connection between all Central European problems that we regarded every Polish success as a considerable advance for our own cause also. In the course of April and the first half of May, however, the Government was evidently making concessions to the Left Wing elements among the workmen and soldiers, whose council at Petrograd had been established on the same day as Prince Lvov's provisional Government. The moderate Socialist elements which it had contained at the beginning were gradually over-ruled by the Radicals under the leadership of Lenin and Trotsky. It had been the Government's intention to convene a constituent assembly only at the conclusion of the war, when it would proceed to deal with the distribution of the soil by a legislative process. This was skilfully used by the extremists as a means for inciting the masses against the Government. They took advantage of the fact that war-weariness had now permeated the entire population of Russia and, by holding out a prospect of immediate peace and distribution of the soil, they had no difficulty in winning the people over. They disposed of the commitments to the Allies by describing them as part of the imperialistic policy of the former Russian regime, which would involve the shedding of Russian blood for the benefit of English and French capitalists.

Under these circumstances our liberation movement could only intensify its efforts for concentrating all our work in Western Europe, endeavouring at the same time to preserve our army in Russia, which Masaryk had succeeded in organizing on Russian soil during the revolutionary period, when political, administrative, and military affairs were in a state of chaos. He had arrived in Russia on May 16, 1917, two days after Milyukov's resignation, which had been an unpleasant surprise for him. He had at once taken charge of the branch of the National Council, which had been established by the Congress in Kiev. He was fully recognized by the Russian revolutionary authorities and received everywhere by them with respect, but on account of the disorder prevailing in the ministries and military circles he was not always able to achieve his aims easily. He himself has given a detailed account of this in his *Making of a State*. Nevertheless, on October 9, 1917, his proposal for the formation of an independent Czechoslovak army corps was finally sanctioned by the Russian authorities.

As a result of the events which ensued in Russia after November 7th, it became urgent to transfer not merely a part, but the whole of our army to France, as this was the only way to save our troops. The establishment of an autonomous Czechoslovak army in France was made possible by a decree of the

French Government in December 1917, an account of which I shall give in the following chapter, and accordingly Masaryk was able on February 7, 1918, to proclaim the Czechoslovak army corps in Russia as a constituent part of this army. The Soviet Government at once recognized the international character of these troops, and accepted Masaryk's proclamation of February 7th without demur, likewise granting permission for our army to be removed to France.

THE FORMATION OF A CZECHOSLOVAK NATIONAL ARMY IN FRANCE. NEGOTIATIONS FOR A CZECHOSLOVAK ARMY IN ITALY

(a) Our Military Movement in the United States. The Mission of Štefánik and Franklin-Bouillon

58

After my return from Rome and my talk with Masaryk in London at the beginning of February 1917, I directed all the work of the National Council towards settling the problems connected with the prisoners of war and the organization of an army in France and Italy. The two great events of international politics—the Russian revolution and the entry of America into the war—provided us with a further incentive for carrying out these plans, since we now had additional ways and means of realizing them. I therefore worked in this direction at Paris and Rome during the months of March and April, waiting for Štefánik's return, and hoping that when Masaryk reached Petrograd our affairs in Russia would take a turn for the better.

In the first half of April 1917 I received a fresh message from Štefánik, in Petrograd, announcing that he would be in London after April 20th. I was anxious to take advantage of his presence there to hold a general meeting of the National Council, and discuss questions relating to Russia and ourselves in the light of the new international situation. I therefore started for London on April 25th, but failed to meet Štefánik. We must have passed each other in the Channel.

It turned out that Štefánik had reached London somewhat earlier than he had expected. He missed Masaryk, who had already started off for Russia, and by this time was waiting on board a vessel in the North of Scotland. Štefánik sent G. Košík, who was returning with him from Russia, to overtake Masaryk, and to ask him to come back to London to hear Štefánik's report. Masaryk did so, and having heard what Štefánik had to say, he introduced him to a number of politicians in London. Štefánik had then left for Paris, on the day that I arrived in London.

Masaryk's journey to Russia was thus postponed for a month, the delay being partly due to the fact that on his return to London he fell ill and had to remain in bed for two weeks. Upon the conclusions he had formed from Štefánik's report, he told me that the time had now come when he could most opportunely intervene in Russia. He had not been greatly disposed to go to Russia while the old regime was in power. While preparing for the journey, he felt misgivings that he would never return. He had heard reports of intrigues against his personal safety, and he had also felt uneasy about the possible danger from submarines. Then, too, there was the likelihood of treachery or unforeseen developments in Russia. He had therefore written his will (together with some political notes) in the form of a letter addressed to me. He had given it to his daughter Olga, with the message that I was to act as his executor if he did not return.

I was deeply touched by this episode which occurred when we had little time for personal feelings. I am not sentimental, but I sat for hours over that sealed letter in August 1917, and wondered what would happen to Masaryk and what would be the fate of our movement.

Štefánik had returned from Russia with a number of new plans. First in London, then in Paris, he had given an account of his experiences, and he wanted to make a similar report in Rome. He had a good opportunity for doing so, as Carlotti, the Italian Ambassador in Petrograd, had given him messages for his Roman friends. He therefore proceeded to Rome in May 1917 and spent about a month there.

His second plan, which he had evolved while in Russia, was to go to the United States. He had returned from Russia with scanty results in the military affairs on which he had been sent there by the French Government, but he had not lost hope that our military endeavours would finally meet with success. He saw that our work in connection with the prisoners of war in France was making considerable progress, and he still felt confident that it would be possible to transport a number of our prisoners of war from Russia. Indeed, he himself had already prepared the first contingent in Rumania for this purpose. What he therefore proposed to do in the United States was to assist in organizing the volunteer movement for our national army among the Czechs and Slovaks there. As a matter of fact, all of us in Paris felt confident that among the one and a half millions of our fellow-countrymen in America, we should find several thousand volunteers, and the reports from those who were working for us in America tended to confirm this view. Štefánik also thought that he would be able to win over the United States Government to our cause.

After discussing matters with Štefánik we adopted the same procedure as in the previous year when dealing with Štefánik's mission to Russia. On behalf of the National Council, I asked the French Government to entrust Štefánik with a mission involving negotiations with the American authorities for the purpose of obtaining the consent of the latter to the proposed volunteer movement on behalf of our army in France.

The consent of Ribot, as Foreign Minister, was again secured through the help of Berthelot, who even at that early period was a sincere friend to Štefánik and myself, and a supporter of all our undertakings. We secured the consent of the War Minister by means of direct interventions with M. Painlevé, the Minister of War, and through the help of Franklin-Bouillon. This was the first occasion on which I got into touch with Painlevé, and I maintained this personal contact until the end of the war. He was a sincere and devoted friend to us, and it is to him that we owe a settlement of the many questions relating to our army. Under his regime also a definite agreement was reached with regard to our army in France, although in a formal respect a number of documents were not actually signed until his successor, Clemenceau, came into power. Štefánik was also on good personal terms with Painlevé.

It would not, however, be quite correct to attribute the initiative in this matter to us alone. It was facilitated by the fact that the possibility of securing volunteers in America had already been brought to the notice of the French Government from other quarters. At this very moment M. Jusserand, the French Ambassador in the United States, and André Tardieu, the French High Commissioner there, were working in a similar way for the organization of the Polish Army in France. In this they were supported to a considerable extent both by the Government and the public opinion in the United States.

The Polish National Committee in Paris had, like ourselves,

been working very closely at the organization of a national army from 1916 onwards. The Poles did not have our opportunities in Russia, Italy, or even at first in France, and probably for reasons of their own they did not wish to ventilate the question of the prisoners of war to the extent that we had done. They therefore had recourse chiefly to the United States, where their activities were concerned solely with volunteers. Their organization in America was a strong one, partly because of the large number of Polish emigrants there, partly also because of the good feeling which had been shown towards them by the American Government and people ever since the beginning of the war, such as had not been shared in the same degree by other oppressed nations. The position of the Poles in America proved advantageous to us also, just as elsewhere they benefited by the more privileged status which we had secured.

The French Government, having first accepted the Polish scheme and then ours, began to give them practical effect. It was decided to send a special political mission for this purpose to America. This mission was to be headed by M. Franklin-Bouillon, and its aim was expressly stated thus: "To secure the consent of the United States Government for recruiting volunteers from the emigrants in America for the Slav national armies in France." This referred to the Polish and Czechoslovak armies.

The political importance of this mission was considerable. Franklin-Bouillon was a prominent statesman, and at that time was also a parliamentary deputy. The undertaking had been arranged at a moment when America's entry into the war had aroused general enthusiasm. Under these circumstances such a step on the part of France was a sign of further progress towards our goal.

At this time Franklin-Bouillon was actively engaged with the Inter-Allied Parliamentary Committee, the purpose of which was to seek for new paths of collaboration in the war, and thus to help towards a speedy victory. The secretary of the French group was E. Fournol, with whom I co-operated very closely.

From 1916 onwards, and more especially since the outbreak of the Russian revolution, this body had been paying very careful attention to Slavonic matters, and to the problems of Central Europe generally. It was, I believe, among the members of this body that the idea of Franklin-Bouillon's mission originated. We of the National Council assisted actively with the preliminary arrangements of the American mission. I myself discussed the matter with the Government on several occasions. I also supplied material necessary for carrying on the work among our colonists, and I conferred with the Poles on the course of action. Franklin-Bouillon sailed for America on August 10th. We benefited to no small extent, both in France and the United States, as the result of his mission.

The difficulties of recruiting troops in America at that time were not due merely to international politics. The United States Government had two considerable objections to our volunteer movement. In the first place, the Americans were afraid that if they permitted recruiting for national armies, this would prove detrimental to their own army, which was then in process of formation. Besides this, the United States were here faced by one of the most serious problems of their war-time policy. The war could and should serve to cement all American citizens, whatever their origin; the war could and should bring together and unify all the nationalities living in America; the war could and should serve to transform the heterogeneous emigrant elements into a real American nation. A movement such as ours tended rather to frustrate this process.

It was therefore necessary for Franklin-Bouillon, in stating a case for the Polish and Czechoslovak national movements, to keep their demands within limits acceptable to the United States.(27) Štefánik quickly adapted himself to these conditions. With the help of the French authorities he succeeded in obtaining the concession that those Czechoslovaks who were not liable for American military service would be allowed to volunteer for the Czechoslovak National Army. Our original estimates of the number of volunteers which we should obtain proved excessive ; between the end of 1917 and the summer of 1918, nevertheless, we managed to secure about 2,500 of our fellow-countrymen from America for service in France. When Štefánik left the United States at the beginning of November, he was able to bring the first eighty volunteers with him.

The mission of Franklin-Bouillon and Štefánik denoted a considerable advance in our work. In the United States it had a distinct effect, especially as propaganda. Štefánik himself was able to reach representatives of the Government, and draw

their attention to our endeavours. In this way he gained the
sympathies of several military men and notably of Roosevelt.
Towards President Wilson he maintained an attitude of
reserve, and he continued to do so, even to a greater extent,
at the Peace Conference. There was much in Wilson's democratic
ideas and his political tendencies with which Štefánik was
unable to agree. In this connection, I should recall the valuable
work accomplished by Štefánik in overcoming the difficulties of
organization among the Czech and Slovak colonists in America.
From the end of June I kept him informed in detail about the
progress of our military movement in France, and about my
negotiations with the French Government for the purpose of
obtaining official permission to constitute a Czechoslovak
Army of liberation. On July 17th I was able to notify him that
this had been secured, and on August 10, 1917, in a letter which
was taken by Franklin-Bouillon, I announced to the National
Alliance that the agreement between the National Council and
the French Government was complete.

This accelerated the success of the volunteer movement in
America, especially as in the meanwhile Masaryk had adjusted
our military organization in Russia, and our brigade, by distinguishing itself at Zborov on June 3rd, 1917, helped indirectly
to promote the success of our military schemes with the other
Allies.

(b) AGREEMENT WITH FRANCE ON THE SUBJECT OF OUR
ARMY. FRENCH POLICY AND ITS ATTITUDE TO AUSTRO-
HUNGARIAN PROBLEMS

59

After Štefánik's departure to America I embarked upon a
series of activities, the scope of which I made as wide as
possible. In this I was prompted by the success which our
movement had scored in organizing a strong army, more
especially in Western Europe. My tactics would have been the
same, so far as this was concerned, even if the Russian revolution had not occurred. What I had always feared was that the
Western Powers might object to any predominance of Russia
in matters affecting Austria-Hungary and ourselves, and my
work in the National Council at Paris was guided by the
principle of imparting a general European character to every-

thing we did, whether in politics or military affairs. It was my belief that this was the right basis upon which to build. Apart from this, I was always anxious lest Russia should exert too marked an influence upon our internal affairs. Even at that time, what I aimed at was a policy which was neither Eastern nor Western, but European and Czechoslovak. After the first symptoms of collapse in Russia, I further accentuated this line of policy.

Thus, all the centralizing military activity of the National Council was directed by four considerations:

(*a*) To transfer from Russia to France the greatest possible number of prisoners of war or other troops.

(*b*) To concentrate as rapidly as possible all the prisoners on French soil, together with the prisoners which it might be possible to obtain from the Serbian Government.

(*c*) To undertake an extensive volunteer movement in America.

(*d*) To make full use of the new and large resources which were provided by our numerous prisoners, who in the meanwhile had been collected in Italy.

From the end of June 1917 it was clear that we should establish our army in France. All that remained was to make it as large as possible. The concentration of our prisoners of war in France, in special Czechoslovak camps, and the recruiting activities among them which were carried on by the National Council, continued to make satisfactory progress during the spring of 1917. A similar concentration of prisoners was begun also in Italy. From Russia, Masaryk announced that at Petrograd, on June 13, 1917, with the consent of the Russian Government, he had signed an agreement with Albert Thomas, the French Minister of Munitions, by which at least 30,000 of our prisoners of war would be transferred to France, partly for military service, partly for munitions work. This was a further important step in our progress.

In the same communication Masaryk requested me to discuss the matter in detail with Albert Thomas, as soon as he returned, and to organize the arrangements for allotting the prisoners to their respective duties, either in the army or in factories. He also sent me the rough draft of a scheme for organizing our army in France on the same model as that adopted in Russia, and asked me to try to reach an agreement on the subject with the French authorities.

Hitherto we had obtained no binding agreement with France on the subject of an army. What we had was, in the first place, Briand's very important declaration to Masaryk, and then the mission of Štefánik and Franklin-Bouillon. There had also been discussions and negotiations between the National Council and the French Minister of Foreign Affairs, as well as Briand's sanction for our scheme in connection with the prisoners of war. But as I have indicated, none of these things involved any definite political commitments. After the signature of the agreement between Albert Thomas and Masaryk, what was wanted was a definite undertaking on the part of the French Government with regard to the formation of a Czechoslovak Army, and a clear statement of how such an army would be regarded by the French Government from a political and diplomatic point of view.

Thus on June 20, 1917, the National Council began to negotiate on the subject of an army with the French Ministries of War and Foreign Affairs respectively. These negotiations concluded with a decree which was issued on December 16, 1916, the signing of the statutes of our army on February 7, 1918, the decisive letter of Pichon on June 28, 1918, and finally the recognition of an independent Czechoslovak State on October 15, 1918.

60

The year 1917 and the beginning of 1918 formed a period of crises for France. The Russian revolution, resulting in the defection of her great Eastern ally, the military reverses in Nivelle's offensive, the unsatisfactory internal conditions, the war-weariness and spread of defeatism, the encyclical of Pope Benedict on the subject of peace, the proceedings of the Socialists at Stockholm, the defeat of Italy at Caporetta, the peace of Brest-Litovsk, the preparations for a resolute German offensive after the relief of the Eastern Front—all this aroused misgivings in Government circles as regards the French war aims set forth in the note to President Wilson.

In February 1917 there began a series of secret attempts to bring about a separate peace with Austria-Hungary. During 1917 and up to the early part of 1918 the French Government regarded itself as faced by these alternatives : either defeat, involving the loss of the position which France had hitherto occupied in Europe, the loss of her political and cultural influence, the loss of her colonial power, and perhaps ruin with even worse consequences; the possibility of arranging the separation of the Habsburg Empire from Germany, a course which could almost certainly lead to a military victory over Germany. This was the idea dominating the plan of the French military leaders.

It is not surprising that the French statesmen, thinking themselves confronted with these alternatives, should have chosen the one which seemed to them to be in conformity with the vital interests of France, and there is no doubt that they would have concluded peace with Vienna at that time. All the various Governments responsible for the destinies of France, from Briand to Clemenceau, as well as such brilliant leaders as Foch, were of the same opinion. They evidently considered that they should not fail at least to make an attempt, in order that they might not later be reproached with having unnecessarily caused the death of hundreds of thousands of French soldiers. I shall not discuss whether, in taking this view, they had formed a correct estimate of the situation of the Central Powers. The events themselves showed that they had not. I am here concerned only with the moral issues. It is my view that the French Government regarded its commitment in the note to President Wilson as a sincere programme of aims on a maximum scale, for the realization of which France would do everything in her power, short of sacrificing herself. I did not and I do not therefore regard the French negotiations for a separate peace with Austria-Hungary as a breach of faith. In this respect the attitude of Ribot, in particular, was exemplary, loyal, and honourable.

During 1917, therefore, France was apparently pursuing a twofold policy. She was granting us permission to organize the prisoners of war and to establish our own army, and at the same time she was prepared to conclude peace with the Habsburg Empire should the opportunity present itself. I cannot reproach her for this. France was waging a life-and-death struggle. Never, in my dealings with the French, had I expected them to assist us in securing an independent State at the price of their own ruin. I only wanted them to make it possible for us to exert all the powers at our disposal for achieving success. That was my attitude towards the commitments of France, and in adopting it I was prompted by the certainty that the forces of the oppressed nations, once they were released, would never let themselves be kept back. Then, too, I firmly believed that all the conjectures on the part of France and the other Allies as to the possibility of separating Austria-Hungary from Germany were erroneous, chiefly because, in the end, such an arrangement could not depend upon the will and strength of Vienna and Budapest. I knew that it was merely harmful to take into account the possibility of a separate peace, since it weakened the Allies in their intensity of purpose.

I was never in agreement with those opportunists amongst us who, fearing a premature or undecisive end of the war, or wishing to conceal their alarm and lack of decision, were always asking what guarantees the Allies would give us if we entered on a life-and-death struggle, and what reasons we had for believing that they would not end by deserting us or concluding a premature peace. I had not failed to take these possibilities into account, but I was in agreement with Masaryk's views; I regarded the struggle against Vienna and Budapest, first and foremost, as a fundamental moral question.

As far as the Allies were concerned, our only guarantee could be the success of our revolutionary activities. The Allies could desert us only if we ourselves were to desert beforehand. This meant a perpetual struggle, and the gradual establishment of our independence during the war by means of our own work and the sacrifice of our own blood. We simply had to thrust our cause into the main streams of world events, in the midst of which it would become too important a factor to be afterwards ignored.

(c) NEGOTIATIONS WITH THE FRENCH WAR MINISTRY AND THE MINISTRY OF FOREIGN AFFAIRS CONCERNING THE DECREE AND STATUTES OF OUR ARMY. POLITICAL SIGNIFICANCE OF THE AGREEMENT

61

The actual discussions with the various Ministries concerning the organization of our army caused me some difficulties. I had no military experience, and was aware of the political responsibility with which I was faced as a representative of the National Council. I received ample help from Dr.

Sychrava, but he, too, was without military experience. I therefore bought a number of books on military subjects, and made a rapid study of army organization, modern warfare, the new military aspects of the Great War, and various current military topics in general. We had a number of officers among our volunteers in the Foreign Legion, but they had no political training. They lacked judgment and had a marked bent for adventurous escapades. For this reason I dealt personally with all negotiations on army matters from the very outset.

In the French Ministry of War the Government had set up a special section to deal with "the organization of national armies," these being chiefly those of Poland and Czechoslovakia, although at a certain period Rumanian contingents from Transylvania were also involved. This department was under General Vidalon, and Lieutenant-Colonel Cros was in charge of it. Our affairs in the department were handled by Major Dresch. These were the military authorities with whom I conducted the chief technical negotiations in the War Ministry, while for negotiations on fundamental matters I was summoned direct to General Alby, Chief of the General Staff, and then also to M. Painlevé. During June and July I had several conversations with Painlevé on the subject of the army and our political affairs in general. I never encountered the slightest obstacle in my dealings with him. He discussed matters with me direct in a sincere and straightforward manner. He told me plainly what he considered to be possible, and what he thought could not be managed. Let me add that he always carried out what he promised me. With Briand and Clemenceau he deserves the greatest credit for our political triumph in France.

I handed to General Vidalon and Lieutenant-Colonel Cros the text of the proposals which had arrived from Petrograd. The Ministry itself had also received them from the French Mission in Russia. The negotiations on these proposals began, as I have said, on June 20, 1917, and were concluded on August 4, 1917. The outlined scheme for the organization of an army which had been sent from Russia was regarded as being of secondary importance. The French military authorities, whose mistrust of affairs in Russia was increasing from day to day, at the very beginning emphasized the fact that conditions in France were quite different, and that the organization of our army in Western Europe would have to be directed in accordance with them.

The Ministry of War and Ministry of Munitions, therefore, in agreement with myself, re-drafted the Russian proposals in their technical aspect. Their political bearings were discussed at the Quai d'Orsay with M. de Margerie and M. Laroche, who is now French Minister at Warsaw. The negotiations at the French Ministry of Munitions were carried on partly with Professor Roques, who was then working with M. Thomas, and partly with the economist, Professor Nogar, who was concerned with the problem of recruiting foreign munition workers in France. The point at issue was to establish the conditions under which our prisoners of war, who had not entered the army, would work in French munition factories as free citizens.

At the very first discussions with General Vidalon and then in greater detail later, the following problems were dealt with:

1. The relation of the Czechoslovak National Army to the French Government and Army, and also to the Czechoslovak National Council.

2. The question of the flag, the uniform, and various distinguishing marks to indicate the national character of the army.

3. The recruiting of Czechoslovak troops.

4. The appointment of officers.

5. The question as to the use of the Czech language for the purposes of command, and also on the administrative side.

6. The question of court-martial discipline.

7. The question of financing the army and payment of Czechoslovak troops in relation to that of French troops.

8. Conditions under which the army could be used at the front.

9. The question of prisoners of war, not in the army, but as volunteers for munition work.

10. The question of disabled and discharged soldiers.

The political and military importance of each of these problems is obvious. The first one was of a fundamental character, and from the manner of its settlement would depend the logical solution of the remainder. In this respect the difficulties in France were considerable, perhaps even greater than those in Russia, for at the beginning neither the Ministry of War nor the Ministry of Foreign Affairs had reckoned with any large measure of autonomy for the Czechoslovak Army.

Apart from this, at the time when I was discussing these matters, a precedent had been created with the Polish Army in France which was unfavourable to us. The Polish National Committee had accepted a proposal of the French Government to the effect that the organization of the Polish Army in France should be presided over by a special mixed "Commission militaire franco-polonaise," directed by a French General. It was to comprise officers of both nationalities, and would be the leading body for organizing and administering the Polish Army, while at the same time it was to form a connecting link between the French Government and the Polish Committee.

The Ministry of War suggested a similar organization to me. My attitude was one of decisive opposition to such a proposal, and Dr. Sychrava, who saw the political danger of the plan, was also against it. We objected to the existence of any intermediary between the National Council and our army. I demanded that the army should be entirely ours, and that its political administration should be fully allotted to us as representatives of a sovereign nation, but that the French Government should have the right of supervision so as to satisfy itself that things were being done in accordance with the preliminary agreement which it had made with the National Council. The Ministry of War was to have full control in all technical matters and details of pure organization, but that, in this respect, the consent of the National Council was necessary for any measures which might at all affect the fundamental politico-military questions.

In the end this principle was accepted. The Ministry of War reluctantly abandoned the idea of a mixed Franco-Czechoslovak commission, since in this way an analogy with the Polish Army would have been produced, and it was feared that all further negotiations with us would be more complicated. In reality it soon proved that the contrary was the case, and that the direct contact of the Government and the army with the National Council simplified matters. It was, of course, true that this made our army less dependent on the Ministry.

As I have said, the rest of the problems were, of necessity, settled logically in accordance with this first and governing principle. It was agreed that there should be a Czechoslovak flag and uniform with special Czechoslovak badges and a béret. The National Council reserved to itself the right and duty of submitting its proposals to the Ministry of War. Negotiations on the practical and technical side of these matters were long, and were still in progress when Štefánik returned from America. In negotiating on the wording of the agreement in July and August, I was concerned only with specifying the principles and our rights involved in these practical matters.

The main principles of the new military organization included, of course, the recognition on the part of France that the soldiers of this army must take an oath of allegiance to the Czechoslovak nation. The recruiting of troops was to be carried out by the National Council in France, Russia, America, Serbia, and Italy for the whole duration of the war. The implication of this was that this agreement with France contained a formulation of our whole politico-military scheme, as elaborated by us with reference to the current political events in Paris. The elaborated scheme of organization dealt with all details of recruiting, and provided for recruiting committees, their rights and duties. Recruiting could be carried out only in the name of the National Council, and the French authorities were to act merely as executive bodies.

The officers were to be appointed and promoted only by the National Council in agreement with the French Government, and Czechoslovaks were to have the preference. The language of command was to be the national language, but all important documents were to be bilingual. The head of the army was to be a French General, appointed after agreement with the National Council. As regards discipline, the French military legal code was to be adopted, and it was agreed to set up Czechoslovak courts-martial as soon as an adequate staff of Czechoslovak officers was available for this purpose.

In financial matters the principle agreed upon was that our troops should receive the same pay as the French, and that all expenditure should be recorded in special accounts, a settlement of which by the Czechoslovak nation could, if necessary, be stipulated during the peace negotiations.

As regards prisoners of war who were unfit for military service, and disabled soldiers, the National Council and the Ministry of Munitions were to arrange a special "Statut du travail pour les ouvriers tchécoslovaques en France." The negotiations concerning this were begun and concluded at the same time as those with regard to the army. The Czechoslovak workmen(28) were to be regarded as free citizens, and the National Council was to have the same consular rights with regard to them as were enjoyed by the Allied Governments towards their subjects in France.

Considering the circumstances existing at that time, it must be deemed a great success that the negotiations secured the autonomy of the army and the political supremacy of the National Council, which thus received express recognition by the French Government as a body representing the Czechoslovak nation. The same remark applies to the circumstance that our troops were permitted to take an oath of allegiance to the Czechoslovak nation. By these concessions France acknowledged our right to independence, and made it a constituent part of her war programme.

It was therefore my concern that this significant document should include an express statement to the effect that the army in process of formation, being composed of volunteers, was purely political in character, and that its aim was to achieve the independence of the nation. It was further my concern to guarantee this success in one form or another. From the outset my leading idea was to adopt a course of action which would obviate the possibility of our being set aside at the peace negotiations.

In negotiating on the subject of the army I therefore formulated the demand that a part of our future army, even though it might be used at the front, should, as far as possible, be preserved so as to be still in existence at the time of the peace negotiations. In this way it would help to promote the political demands of the Czechoslovak nation. What I feared was that our army would be destroyed after its first use at the front in such fighting as the Verdun struggle, and that thus our political significance as regards diplomatic negotiations would be lost.

No less serious was the question of the decree by which the army was to be constituted. It had been arranged that the decree should simply contain, in the abbreviated form of a few paragraphs, all the political principles agreed upon in the scheme for the organization of the army. The final wording, however, was not to be drawn up until after my return from Italy, whither I proposed to proceed in August for the purpose of discussing the question of our prisoners there, and the possibility of their transport to France.

In accordance with the request of the Ministry of Foreign Affairs, and with my consent as Secretary of the National Council, the publication of the decree was to take place at a time which, from a political point of view, was more favourable and opportune than July and August 1917. Another important factor in this respect was the circumstance that it was necessary to wait until some considerable number of our prisoners had been concentrated in France. These prisoners, who had been demoralized by their hardships in Serbia, at Asinara, and, at the beginning, in France as well, could not be regarded as the mainstay of our army, the nucleus of which would have to be derived from Russia, Italy, or America. In agreement with both Ministries we centred our hopes largely on my forth-coming visit to Italy, which had been projected as early as June 1917. In common with the French military authorities, we hoped that we should be able to win over several thousand prisoners of war in Italy, and transfer them to the French front. In July 1917 the number of prisoners at our disposal was too small to form our first military contingent.

We therefore agreed that the final text of the decree should be issued after my return from Rome. The publication of the decree was to confirm the existence of the army, and not merely to announce the preparations for it. Only in this way could the political and military significance of our whole undertaking be made duly prominent.

62

When all these questions had been fully discussed at the Ministry of War, the matter was transferred to the Ministry of Foreign Affairs. The military authorities, who had to cope with practical problems of warfare, little by little conceded my political demands. The task was far more difficult for me at the Ministry of Foreign Affairs, where de Margerie and Laroche had carefully considered all the juridical and political implications of the scheme for organizing a national army, as arranged between General Vidalon, Lieut.-Col. Cros, and myself. Accordingly, there now ensued a struggle to preserve the concessions which had been made to the National Council when the scheme had been discussed at the Ministry of War.

In the end the Ministry of Foreign Affairs withdrew all its original reservations with the exception of a few minor details.

In one matter the negotiations were remarkable. I had discussed the wording of the scheme with Laroche. In formulating the article on army expenditure I had asked for an explicit statement that the expenditure was to be recorded in special accounts, for which the Czechoslovak State would make itself responsible after the peace negotiations. The expression "Czechoslovak State" or "Czechoslovak Government" had so far never been used in connection with the scheme. Even when mentioning the autonomous army, the National Council as a representative of the Czechoslovak nation, the political character of the army and the Peace Conference, the French authorities avoided the use of any phrase which would at all form a commitment to the French Government at the future peace negotiations.

By making my specific demand, I endeavoured to clarify the discussions in this respect, but I met with steady opposition. At last Laroche said quite openly: "Do not make this demand of us now. It would mean inserting into the document, indirectly and surreptitiously, a far-reaching political commitment which can be made only in a ceremonious manner on a special occasion, and when the political situation might be opportune for such a course. This is not the case to-day. The recognition of the National Council, the autonomy of the army, the undertaking to preserve a portion of the army for the peace negotiations, so as to emphasize its political character, are far-reaching matters. I assure you quite frankly that we are willing and anxious to render you political assistance, and that when the proper moment comes we will give you a solemn assurance to that effect. But if we enter upon such a commitment we shall keep our word, and for that reason we cannot do so on this occasion and in this form."(29)

In consequence of this statement I withdrew my demand. These negotiations with Laroche took place at the Quai d'Orsay on August 4, 1917. On the same day the whole of the negotiations with the Ministry of Foreign Affairs were completed, and the wording of the agreement received the approval of both parties.

This was one of my happiest days throughout the course of our movement abroad. I attached great political importance to these negotiations, and in my mind's eye I saw the army in course of formation, the National Council as a Government, our share in the Peace Conference, and the establishment of our State. At that time, too, I was already convinced that even before the war was over the moment would come when we should be obliged to form a real national army abroad.

63

In accordance with what had been arranged between the Ministry of Foreign Affairs and ourselves, this agreement was to become a binding diplomatic document, signed by the head of the French Government on the one hand, and by the authorized representative of the National Council on the other. The actual signatures were to be affixed after the wording of the decree had been settled, and after my return from Italy. As we shall see, the signing did not actually take place until February 7, 1918, partly because the negotiations as to the wording of the decree were protracted, partly through the change of Government and the entry of Clemenceau as the new Prime Minister and Minister of War.

At all events, on February 7, 1918, this agreement was signed by Prime Minister Clemenceau on behalf of the French Government, and by me on behalf of the National Council, as the statute for the organization of the Czechoslovak Army in France. The wording differed only slightly from that which had been accepted on August 4, 1917, in the negotiations at the Quai d'Orsay, and during my subsequent conversations with the Ministry of War in the course of January 1918.

The satisfaction which I felt at the success thus attained was expressed immediately after the conclusion of the negotiations, which were carried on parallel with the negotiations concerning the dispatch of Franklin-Bouillon's mission to the United States, in the reports which I sent to our fellow-countrymen in Russia and America. I at once communicated the results of the negotiations to Masaryk in Russia by a brief telegram which was sent on August 4, 1917.

The French Government realized the importance of the agreement thus arrived at, and at once began to put it into effect. As early as August 8th the French Ministry of Foreign Affairs sent a telegram to Petrograd informing its Embassy there that the French Government had reached an agreement with the Czechoslovak National Council on all matters concerning the organization of the Czechoslovak National Army.

At the same time it forwarded the wording of the agreement to show the divergencies in the organization of our army in France and Russia respectively. The French Foreign Ministry intended this also as a confirmation of the arrangement which had been made with the Russian Government concerning the transfer of Czechoslovak prisoners to France, for the policy of the Quai d'Orsay and of the French military authorities as regards our army in August 1917 counted decisively upon the concentration of a substantial number of our troops from Russia, America, and Italy. The struggle to achieve these aims was continued in Paris until the summer of 1918.

For these reasons I arranged with the French Government for the dispatch of a special French Mission to Russia for the purposes of recruiting and organizing the transport of our prisoners and, in fact, for carrying out the Masaryk-Thomas agreement. This Mission, headed by Major Verger (who during his stay in Russia did admirable work in the interests of our troops, and made it possible for at least the first contingent of them, under Captain Husák, to be transferred to France), started for Russia in the first half of August 1917.

Simultaneously with the negotiations for a politico-military agreement, the agreement with the Ministry of Munitions concerning our workmen, to which I have already referred, was reached in the course of July. The negotiations with Professor Nogar concluded on July 30, 1917, and on August 4th Albert Thomas sent me a note in which, on behalf of the Government, he gave his consent to the scheme drawn up by Professor Nogar and myself. In itself, this document has no special military significance, but judged in connection with the rest of the negotiations it denotes the logical solution of the problem concerning our civilians in France, who were gradually granted the status of subjects belonging to an independent country.

The conclusion of these tasks marks a definite landmark in the progress of the National Council in France. A further step towards the development of our political and military organization could now consist only of a proclamation incorporating our agreements, and of a binding character in an international respect. Such a proclamation would then lead to the establishment of the Czechoslavak Government, and to its international recognition by France and the Allies.

An undoubted success was attained by our systematic

policy in France, which consisted of proceeding gradually, step by step, of allowing things to take their course and come to a head through the influence of persistent but unobtrusive work, and of gathering together a variety of helpers to co-operate in pursuit of our common aims. We were also careful not to embarrass France by far-reaching and premature demands, declarations, formulations of schemes, or official visits and audiences.

(d) Negotiations with the Italian Government and our Army. My Second Visit to Rome

64

I now turned my whole attention towards winning the Italian Government over to our military plans. I had been arranging ways and means for doing this throughout the period of the negotiations with the French Government. What I proposed to do was not to proceed to Rome until I had made a provisional arrangement with Italian circles, and until the scheme had been prepared from Paris in some detail.

Since my first visit to Italy, I had been in constant touch, on the one hand, with the Italian Ambassador in Paris, but most of all with the Italian Military Mission. At the time when I first established relations with the Embassy, it was under the charge of T. Tittoni, the supreme President of the Senate, a distinguished politician and a diplomat of a broad outlook who had a thorough understanding of our affairs. He always received me willingly and gave me abundant help in my work. He continued to be a sincere friend to us later on when he became Minister of Foreign Affairs and President of the Senate. The military intelligence section throughout the war was presided over by Prince Brancaccio, a man of refinement, who was loyal and favourably disposed to us. He was a moderate nationalist, who gradually abandoned Sonnino's ideas as to the annexation of Dalmatia and the reduction of Austria, which by this scheme would retain the Croats, and under our influence he came round to the opinion that the monarchy must be destroyed and the Jugoslavs united. He was, however, mistrustful of the Jugoslavs until the very end. He rendered us useful service, in spite of the fact that his official position in Rome was not of the strongest.

As I have already indicated, I was a frequent visitor at the

Italian Embassy in Paris during 1917 and 1918. The first ambassador whom I met there was Tittoni, who, before my second visit to Rome, placed every facility at my disposal. The subsequent ambassadors were Salvago Raggi and Count Bonin Longare. From January 1918 onwards, the Italian Government, and various bodies connected with it, evinced great interest in all our political and military affairs. At the same time they carefully watched our relations with the Jugoslavs and the rest of the Allies, as they were anxious that amid the tangle of Austro-Hungarian questions our claims should not be settled to the detriment of Italian interests.

From February 1917 K. Veselý, who was in charge of our Press Bureau in Rome, and who was being supported from Paris, redoubled his efforts, partly in the Press, partly with Commandini's Ministry. With the assistance of G. Scarpa and his friends he prepared the foundation of a Czechoslovak-Italian Committee (Comitato italiano per l'independenza czecoslovacca). He also furnished news to the daily papers, and began to attend to the concentration of our prisoners, to whom he sent supplies of our printed matter. Besides this, Italian editions of our books and pamphlets were in preparation. At the beginning of June, arrangements were made for extending the activities of the Bureau in Rome. In the meanwhile, Plesinger-Božinov had arrived in Italy from Switzerland and visited several prisoners' camps, where he inspected the preparations for a volunteer movement. He then sent us a report on the situation, and he also negotiated with the Italian authorities, for whom he offered to draw up a special statement concerning the situation of the prisoners. This was done later after an agreement with us in Paris.

These activities gave an impetus to what was being undertaken in connection with our prisoners. Thus, the Italian Government began to make inquiries into what the prisoners had already done independently of us. The first considerable concentration of our prisoners took place at the beginning of 1917 at the camp of Santa Maria Capua Vetere, near Naples. Here, in January 1917, was started the organization of a Czech volunteer corps (later known as the Czechoslovak Volunteer Corps), which grew rapidly, so that by the following May it comprised more than 1,000 members. In April, Plesinger-Božinov visited the camp with messages from Paris, and from that time onwards our prisoners were in regular communication with the National Council. In May an attempt was made to secure the consent of the Italian Government for the use of the volunteer corps on the Salonika front, but this was unsuccessful.

The progress of the corps was then hindered for a short time because some of the prisoners were employed for agricultural work, and the remainder were transferred to Padula, south of Salerno. Matters improved, however, towards the autumn, and when I visited them in September 1917 I had every reason to be satisfied with their organization and with the extensive work—propagandist, educational, and political—which they were carrying on. On that occasion I arranged with them what further steps they should take and generally encouraged them to continue their preparations for establishing a national army. At that time there were more than 10,000 men in the camp, and the volunteer corps was beginning to increase enormously. In January 1918 its strength exceeded 5,000, while by the following April some 14,000 men had entered its ranks. They were all drafted into the army and saw active service.

Even then I realized that our volunteers in Italy, by their remarkable initiative and enthusiasm, were performing invaluable work. It was largely due to their efforts that we politicians were able at the opportune moment to achieve success in our negotiations for the official recognition of the army.

65

The work thus accomplished in Italy caused the Italians to modify their original attitude of reserve towards us. From June 1917 onwards Brancaccio, during his visits to me, repeatedly urged that I should not limit myself to negotiating with France, but that we ought to co-operate more with Italy. It was he, too, who suggested that I ought to proceed once more to Rome, and take some definite steps in connection with our prisoners.

On the occasion of the Inter-Allied Conference in the spring and summer of 1917 in London and Paris, when Brancaccio discussed matters personally with Sonnino, he assured me that the ground was prepared in Italy for successful action, and that from what he had heard he was sure that Sonnino, like the French and Russians, would liberate our prisoners, and perhaps even allow them to join our army in France.

The attitude of Brancaccio, who took a closer interest in our affairs than did the authorities in Rome, was connected, I think, with Italy's military and diplomatic situation at that time. In February 1917 began the notorious secret attempt of Prince Sixtus of Bourbon to bring about a separate peace with the Emperor Karl and Zita, and the Italians rightly feared that this attempt might result in saving Austria at their expense. They saw in us direct allies, and it was therefore in their interest that the Czech movement should not be too much under the influence of the other Allies, who were not so closely concerned about Austria as Italy was.

Another important factor in this respect was the Italian alarm that we, of our own accord, might reach an agreement with the Jugoslavs against Italy. I surmise that Brancaccio and certain other politicians of importance made representations in Rome that we were not to be neglected, but that we were to be granted at least enough to secure Italian influence on our political and military movement. At that time, when it was not clear to the Italians what would happen, and when Sonnino continued to be sceptical as to the fate of Austria-Hungary, this policy was obviously prudent from an Italian point of view.

Under these circumstances I therefore arranged matters so that the initiative for my visit to Rome should not come from us, but that I should be invited in at least an unofficial manner, and that I should receive assurances of at least a partial success in military affairs. After further preparations this was arranged.

On August 22, 1917, Brancaccio called upon me at the office of the National Council and brought a message from Sonnino, who was anxious for me to visit him, and who would see that some of our military schemes were realized. It was noteworthy that Brancaccio transmitted to me also a second message from Sonnino, who was anxious to know whether it was true that a definite agreement had been made between the Czechs and the Jugoslavs with regard to our access to the sea when the respective States were constituted. There was no such agreement, and I gave a plain answer accordingly.

I again impressed upon Brancaccio that after the agreement with the French Government on the subject of our army, I could not proceed to Rome and start negotiations with the Italian Government if they were to lead to nothing. If Sonnino could do nothing for us, if he was unable officially to recognize the National Council, and take some steps on behalf of our prisoners, it would certainly be better for me not to go to Rome just yet. I received a prompt and repeated assurance from Brancaccio that something could be managed.

(e) NEGOTIATIONS WITH SONNINO

66

Sonnino received me on the morning of September 6, 1917. At that time those who were advocating the destruction of Austria-Hungary and the unification of the Jugoslavs regarded him as the evil spirit of Italian and Allied policy. As I have suggested elsewhere, my own opinion of Sonnino was slightly different, although I perceived his faults and errors plainly enough.

Personally, I have the very best impressions of the whole of my intercourse with him. He spoke to me in a frank and pleasant manner, and this caused me a certain amount of surprise, as my Italian friends had always given me to understand that he would listen to everything but make no reply. He gave me the impression of being an honourable man, pleasant to negotiate with, and, in certain respects, politically capable. In the years 1917 and 1918, when the military and political position of the Italians was in a bad way, there is no doubt that the guiding spirit of his policy was to remain cool and resolute.

My interview with Sonnino left a lasting impression upon me. I explained to him the history of our movement, the point it had then reached, its connection with our policy at home, and also how it was situated in Russia, France, and England respectively. I also told him about the organization of the National Council. I then went on to point out what France had already done on our behalf, and I mentioned the purport of the agreement on the subject of our army which I had just concluded with the French authorities. At the same time, I handed him a lengthy memorandum containing all these particulars. I later submitted a copy of this memorandum to all influential members of the Government, and to the various politicians and authorities with whom I discussed our affairs on that occasion.

Together with my statement to Sonnino, I made the following demand:

(*a*) The Italian Government should officially recognize the National Council as the central body representing all Czechoslovak interests, and with this body all Czechoslovak questions (relating to the army and prisoners of war) should be discussed officially, exclusively, and directly.

(*b*) The Czechs and Slovaks should be recognized as a friendly nation, and that in consequence of this all Czechoslovak civilians interned on Italian territory should be released.

(*c*) The Italian Government should release all our troops who were anxious to join the Czechoslovak Army, and should consent to their transport to France, just as this had been agreed upon with regard to our prisoners in Russia.

Thus, at the beginning, I did not make any direct demand for the organization of a Czechoslovak Army in Italy. In the first place, the Italian Government had already refused a similar application on the part of the Serbs, and then Brancaccio himself had expressed to me his doubts whether it would be possible to establish our army in Italy without much delay. From what Brancaccio had told me, and also from the attitude which Sonnino had hitherto adopted, I inferred that our demand for the establishment of an army in Italy would be regarded by the Italians as excessive. Then, too, I was afraid that our movement in Western Europe might be split up. It seemed to us unnecessary to have two armies, and, in a technical respect, this would mean two sets of difficulties. Moreover, the French front had greater political and military importance than any other, and to collect only an insignificant number of troops there would mean military and political failure, resulting in a menace to the whole of our movement in France.

For these reasons I had arranged with the French Foreign Ministry, before my departure to Rome, that the main purpose of my discussions there would be to secure from the Italian Government the permission to liberate our prisoners of war in Italy, and to transfer them rapidly to France. Politically, it was most important for our movement to have a large military unit ready for action on the French front with the least possible delay.

67

I have already stated that Sonnino surprised me by the frankness of his attitude. He informed me that my statements were very convincing, that he was in complete agreement with our political aims, and that we could reckon upon his help. He added that Italy, of all the Allies, had the greatest interest in the realization of these aims, and had most in common with the Czechs in the struggle against Austria-Hungary.

On this subject Sonnino showed no reserve or hesitation. He did, however, openly express to me his fear that the Allied victory would not be decisive enough for us to secure all we desired.

He accordingly promised me the immediate fulfilment of my first two demands, which were purely political in character. The Italian Government would recognize the National Council, and would give its consent to the organization of a branch of that body, which would be subordinated to the secretariat at Paris, and would have official dealings with the Italian authorities in the settlement of all questions affecting our interests in Italy. He also agreed to our second demand concerning Czechoslovak civilians in Italy, and said that he would give me a recommendation to the Ministry of the Interior for a satisfactory settlement of this matter. He at once did so, and I thereupon applied to the Minister of the Interior—Orlando—who received me, and in quite a short time settled the principles involved by these questions. This was the first time that I had come into contact with Orlando. For the details of all the matters which we discussed, Sonnino referred me to his officials, Demartino and Manzoni, as well as to the Ministry of War.

On all military matters Sonnino expressed very decided reservations. Italy, being a direct neighbour of Austria-Hungary, must be particularly cautious in all matters relating to prisoners of war, and must, above all, adhere to the terms of the Hague Convention, so as to give Austria no ground for reprisals. For that reason, he said, Italy did not want to make use of the prisoners, and the question was whether she was able to liberate them at all. For the same reasons, of course, she could not sanction their transport to France. If Italy were to allow that, Austria-Hungary would begin to dispatch her thousands of Italian prisoners to the devastated Balkans, to Asia Minor, to Syria and Turkey, where they would perish wholesale. This would arouse so much opposition and ill-feeling among the Italian public that he could not, in the face of Parliament and public opinion, vindicate any transfer of our troops. Under such circumstances, the whole scheme would cause the Allies more trouble than it was worth.

One of the main reasons why he took this point of view—so Sonnino explained to me—was his regard for internal politics, and particularly his delicate position towards the followers of Gioliti, towards the Socialists, and also the extreme nationalists, who would seize every opportunity for defeating the Government then in power. The Government, therefore, must not, of its own accord, increase the difficulties it already had, by creating fresh difficulties. And if Austria were to apply such reprisals towards the Italian prisoners of war, it would certainly cause Italy fresh embarrassments as soon as the relatives of the prisoners heard about it.

The manner in which Sonnino laid his arguments before me convinced me immediately that Italy would not permit any wholesale transfer of our troops to France. From what he said, I also felt that in addition to the arguments which he brought forward, there were others, perhaps still stronger, which he did not mention. As a matter of fact, Sonnino himself told me what they were later on during the discussions with regard to the recognition of our independence. It seems that he had two further special reasons: He judged that Italy must preserve all her prisoners for the peace negotiations, in case Austria-Hungary should be saved, and then, too, he was unwilling in this form to assist France in extending her political influence upon our affairs.

I accordingly at once changed the plan, and asked Sonnino for permission to liberate the prisoners and establish our national army on Italian soil, as had been done in France. In particular, I gave him a detailed account of what had already been done in this respect by France, Russia, and the United States, all of whom, unlike Sonnino, had not taken into account any considerations of international law. Sonnino did not oppose these arguments, and after some hesitation he replied that he would look into the matter from a juridical point of view. He declared that he would be willing to grant the establishment of our army in Italy, if a convenient formula could be found for this purpose. In such a case it would be necessary to discuss the details with Demartino, the general secretary of his department, and also with General Montanari and Colonel Vacchelli, of the Ministry of War. He added that Demartino, after investigating the whole scheme from a legal and technical point of view, would, within a few days, let me have Sonnino's definite answer.

68

On September 7th Demartino received me at the Consulta for our first extensive interview. I repeated to him what I had already explained to Sonnino, and also placed at his disposal a memorandum on the Czechoslovak movement in the Allied countries.

In reply, Demartino first of all discussed with me the question of Captain Pučálka. The latter had come to France and Italy, as I heard, with a mission from certain Czechs and Serbs in Russia to establish a Czechoslovak-Serbian Army on the Balkan front from among the prisoners of war in Italy. His plans resulted from difficulties which had arisen in the organization of our army in Russia, and indicated the differences of opinion and the embarrassments existing among our fellow-countrymen there in their political and military activity. While passing through Italy, Captain Pučálka had called upon M. Giers, the Russian Ambassador, and had endeavoured to win him over to his scheme. At first he had obtained a certain measure of support, but when the Russian Ambassador became more closely acquainted with the situation he refused to assist Pučálka any further.

We, as well as the prisoners in various Italian camps, had been informed by Pučálka that he had a promise from the Italian Government to allow our prisoners to be liberated and transferred to the Balkan front. In view of our plans and negotiations in Paris, we on the National Council were, in principle, opposed to letting our troops join the Russian contingents at Salonika, quite apart from the fact that we were acquainted with the situation in Italy, and could therefore tell beforehand what attitude the Italian Government would adopt towards such a scheme. To ask Italy, at a time when the most desperate struggle was being waged with the Jugoslavs, and when the Russian front was breaking up, to surrender prisoners for active service on behalf of the Serbs and Russians in the Balkans, showed a complete ignorance of political methods. This proposal naturally did us much harm in Rome, and was certainly one of the reasons why the Italian Government objected to the transfer of Czechoslovak prisoners even to France.

Demartino declared in the most emphatic terms that he would have nothing to do with Dr. Pučálka, and that he had

not promised him a single soldier. He further stated that the
Ministry of War had expressed a similar view, and would not
allow our prisoners to proceed to the Balkans. A few days
later M. Giers also expressed the same opinion about Pučálka's
undertakings.

We thereupon discussed the demands which I had submitted to Sonnino. Demartino asked me to draw up my
arguments and requests in writing. In this way I should obtain
an official reply from the Government. At the same time he
informed me that after my visit Sonnino had decided upon
what point of view he would adopt towards the political
questions which I had submitted to him. He added that the
Government was disposed to grant political recognition to the
National Council, to enter into official contact with it openly,
and to accept whatever consequences that this would involve.
He also indicated that the Government would evidently be
opposed to sending our troops to France, but that negotiations could be arranged for organizing our army in Italy.

The text of the statement which I had submitted to Sonnino
on September 14, 1917, became the starting-point for detailed
discussions with both Ministries on political and military
affairs, and these discussions lasted until October 8, 1917.
During this visit to Rome I negotiated with Demartino on
five occasions altogether. I also had several discussions on the
same subjects with Manzoni. It was on September 14th that
Demartino gave me verbally the official reply of the Consulta to
my communication. It was affirmative in principle on all the
points concerned, but there were reservations as to the form of
organization which the army should assume. In informing me of
this, Demartino explained that the outstanding questions would
have to be settled by the Ministry of War, acting in agreement with the Consulta. He therefore recommended me to
discuss these practical matters with the Ministry of War
direct. This was no less interesting and no less important than
the negotiations with Sonnino and his Ministry.

(f) OUR FRIENDS IN ROME: GIERS, BARRÈRE, SIR RENNELL
RODD, SIR SAMUEL HOARE, BISSOLATI, COMMANDINI

69

Having concluded my personal negotiations with Sonnino
and Demartino, I informed Barrère, Giers, and also Sir Rennell

Rodd, the English Ambassador. Of these three the only one who was not satisfied with the results was Barrère. From Paris he had received instructions to support me in the scheme for transferring our prisoners to France. When I gave him an account of my first interview with Sonnino, he was indignant. He rightly regarded the attitude of the Italian Government as indicating opposition to the military and political anti-Austrian movement in France. He promised that he would tell Sonnino this, and advised me not to accept the Italian scheme, but to insist that our troops should be sent to France.(30) Seeing the situation in Rome, I did not agree with Barrère. Giers, on the other hand, declared that the results of the negotiations were a great success, and he added that, considering the Italian opposition towards the Jugoslavs and Sonnino's sceptical opinions as to the fate of Austria-Hungary, he had not expected that matters would turn out so favourably for us. He advised me to accept as a first step whatever concessions the Italian Government might now make. The general trend of affairs would then show what could be done later.

A similar opinion was expressed by Sir Rennell Rodd, to whom I was introduced by Sir Samuel Hoare, then head of the Military Mission in Rome. Sir Samuel Hoare had first occupied a similar post in Russia, where he had met Professor Masaryk, to whom, I believe, he had rendered assistance. We were staying in the same hotel in Rome, and so I made his acquaintance and we began to work together. Throughout the period of my stay in Rome, and also subsequently, I kept him supplied with information and memoranda on the progress of our movement and on the situation in Austria-Hungary. I kept in touch with him from that time onwards, and we continued a fruitful co-operation until the end of the war.

Sir Samuel Hoare rendered valuable services to our cause in Rome, and later on also in London. I kept him informed about everything that I was doing in Rome, and he passed this information on to his Ambassador there, from whom these details reached the Government circles in London. Through him, too, I make an attempt from Rome to secure the consent of the British Government to our military enterprise, and he it was who suggested that I should visit London for the purpose of taking the same measures there with regard to the recognition of the National Council as I had done in

Rome. He promised to prepare the ground in London to this end, and he kept his promise. Later on, when I actually visited London, he introduced me to Government circles, and notably to Lord Robert Cecil, who was then acting as deputy Foreign Secretary. When I sent telegraphic reports to Masaryk on the subject of my negotiations in Rome, it was Sir Samuel Hoare who forwarded them through English official channels.

Sir Rennell Rodd himself received me very cordially, and gave me his frank opinion about Italy. He also made a number of suggestions as to how I should proceed in negotiating with the Italians. He considered that the negotiations with Sonnino had resulted in a success, of which advantage ought immediately to be taken. He therefore advised us to give up the idea of transferring our troops to France, and to organize an army in Italy. Finally, he promised that he himself would help us with the Italian Government.

It was during this visit to Rome also that I first met Pašić. He had arrived from Paris and had put up at my hotel. In this way I had an opportunity of observing him throughout his stay. He received me on September 9th. He took a very guarded view of affairs, but he showed a thorough understanding of our cause. He considered, however, that the only chance of realizing the hopes of the Jugoslavs and ourselves lay in a military victory on the part of the Allies. Unlike the other Jugoslavs he spoke of Italy and Sonnino in moderate terms. He was very emphatically opposed to the Italian demands, but he looked at the whole situation in a very practical manner, and endeavoured to make an allowance for the conditions under which the Allies had promised territory to Italy. His attitude in the dispute, which was then occupying public attention, was cautious, reserved, and moderate.

I explained to him my plans in connection with Italy, and told him the results of my interviews with Sonnino. He strongly advised us to accept the Italian point of view, and to try to form an army in Italy. He expressed the opinion that in time this would be a good thing for the Jugoslavs as well, and that for Austria it would be a severer blow than if the army were only in France. He further asked me to arrange for the National Council in Paris to keep in direct touch with him, and to send him personally all documents and reports on the progress of our affairs with the Allies. I kept in touch with Pašić until the end of the war, and also during the Peace Conference in Paris. Throughout this time our relations were of the most loyal and friendly character.

While speaking of these political interviews and negotiations, I may mention the visit I paid to Bissolati on September 22nd, 1917. It is a real pleasure for me to recall this and my subsequent meetings with him. Bissolati, an independent Socialist, had been taken into the Cabinet to counteract partly the influence of Sonnino, who was too much opposed to the Jugoslavs, and partly the policy of the neutral-minded Socialists. It was also intended that by his popularity and his well-known optimism he should act favourably upon public opinion at a time of political and military depression. Being a minister without portfolio, he paid attention to a large number of things, notably Jugoslav questions, which included Austro-Hungarian affairs and, later on, ours also. As far as public opinion was concerned, Bissolati's name was identified with *jusqu'auboutisme*, a programme which involved the destruction of the Habsburg Empire. I was therefore anxious to gain his sympathies, and to induce him to intervene on our behalf during those decisive weeks.

I gave him an account of the history of our movement, and told him what we had already achieved in Russia and France. I then pointed out what I was aiming at in Italy. He was delighted, and promised to help. He asked for all the memoranda which I had given the others, and declared that he would immediately discuss matters with Sonnino, Giardino, Montanari, and other influential men, with a view to securing for us a complete fulfilment of our aims. He was as good as his word, and granted us the support thus promised.

In the course of the interview Bissolati referred to the importance which he attached to England. He was afraid that the British Government might want to preserve Austria-Hungary. This idea was clearly a sequel to all the negotiations for a separate peace with Austria-Hungary which had been begun by Sixtus of Bourbon, and carried on from February 1917 until the autumn of the same year. To-day I can see that Bissolati knew what was going on, and that his attitude was due to Lloyd George's proceedings in the Sixtus of Bourbon negotiations. Bissolati asked me with particular interest whether we expected that the National Council would be recognized also by England, for he said from an Italian point of view

212 MY WAR MEMOIRS

this was the most important factor. He then told me about his last meeting with Lloyd George. He had asked him his opinion, adding that, as he thought, England wanted to preserve the Habsburg Empire. According to him, Lloyd George had replied: "In this matter my opinion is the same as Gladstone's. Austria has already done so much harm in the world that it must be destroyed." I was gratified and encouraged by this interview.

(g) NEGOTIATIONS WITH THE MILITARY AUTHORITIES. THE LETTER FROM GENERAL GIARDINO, THE MINISTER OF WAR. OUR REPLY

70

At the Ministry of War the subject of our troops was being attended to by General Montanari (the Under-Secretary of State), Colonel Vacchelli, Lieutenant-Colonel Zanghieri, and Major Sogno. With them I continued all the difficult negotiations about prisoners of war and the organization of the future army, almost daily until October 9th. I found them most considerate and obliging in their personal dealings with me, but there was a sustained struggle over every concession, however slight. At the beginning and conclusion of the negotiations I had a conversation on our affairs with General Giardino. He himself had not been much concerned with these matters, and in everything except purely technical questions it was Sonnino and the Consulta who had the decisive word.

I negotiated on several occasions with General Spingardi, to whom I had been referred for the discussion of technical measures and details concerning the liberation of prisoners. While discussing matters with me, he exhibited a favourable attitude towards our requests. But in reality he hindered the whole of our movement, and was preventing the prisoners from being liberated. My experiences with him were remarkably similar to the difficulties which we encountered in Russia when dealing with the subject of prisoners. Two reasons were given for this action on his part. In the first place he did not favour the idea of liberating the prisoners for the purpose of forming an army, as this would restrict his sphere of influence, and on the other hand he was said to be an Austrophile, and therefore did not regard our movement with a favourable eye. At all events, the fact is that he stood in our way, and we had many unpleasant conflicts in our official dealings with him.

On Saturday, September 22nd, I concluded the main negotiations with the Ministry of War and the Ministry of Munitions, where a discussion took place as to the possibility of
utilizing as factory workers those prisoners who proved unfit
for military service. On behalf of Giardino, the Minister of
War, Colonel Zanghieri informed me that I could consider the
question of the Czechoslovak Army in Italy as settled. The
Ministry of War had, in this sense, given its definite answer to
the Ministry of Foreign Affairs, and now only the details were
being discussed. After my return from the prisoners' camps I
should receive a formal answer in writing, and the organization
of the army would then immediately begin.

Accordingly, I was fairly satisfied when, at the end of
September, I started off to spend a few days among our
prisoners. I visited several camps in the South of Italy,
especially those at Certosa di Padula, Sala Consilina, Citta
Ducale, and Pola. At Certosa di Padula, where more than ten
thousand of our people were located, my visit was quite a
ceremonial affair. My impressions on this occasion and on my
subsequent visits in the other camps are unforgettable
memories. I saw how the freedom of the nation was being
born, and the State was being formed. Our troops, who by
detachments had already been collected in a military organization for several months, were only waiting for the command
to proceed to the front. They were getting impatient, and
through being kept waiting they were beginning to be mistrustful and embittered. Having Zanghieri's assurance, I announced
the joyful news to them, and promised that they would soon be
set free. Unfortunately, this occurred rather later than I
myself had expected, and this was the same in the other camps.

The Italians were pleased with our prisoners, and they
received me with readiness and understanding. As time went
on, the local authorities showed a willing spirit. On my return
to Rome the Ministry confirmed to me the settlement of our
army question, but the actual formation of the army was
delayed for several months longer. The result was that after
my departure from the camps, it was not long before our
prisoners again became sceptical and despondent.

71

The note from the Ministry of War, which had been eagerly
awaited, reached me on October 4th in the form of a letter

from General Giardino to the Secretary of the National Council as a reply to my conversations in the respective Ministries and to my statement of October 14, 1917. My interviews with Zanghieri and Sogno immediately after my return from the prison camps, had caused me much concern, as both these officers began to formulate reservations which they had not mentioned at first. Nevertheless, I was hardly prepared for the disappointment which Giardino's reply caused me. I had not expected a complete success at the very outset. Even in France, where the conditions were more favourable, we had worked longer and harder to achieve success than we had done in Italy. I therefore regard the note as a sign that we were making progress, but considering the circumstances at the time I could scarcely describe it as adequate for our purpose.

In his communication Giardino, on behalf of the Italian Government, made the following concessions:

1. In accordance with our demand he would grant political recognition to the National Council as the supreme body representing our movement, and he would enter into official relations with it.

2. He would liberate our prisoners and place them under a kind of joint control by the National Council.

3. He would set up semi-military detachments which would not be used for service at the front, but would perform military service on the second line of defence.

4. These troops would wear special badges as Czech soldiers.

5. They would take an oath of allegiance to the Czechoslovak nation, and their attestations to this effect would be placed in the hands of the National Council.

6. From a juridical point of view they would be subject to the discipline of the prisoners and not of the army.

7. The Italian Government would comply with our wishes with regard to the internment of Czechoslovak nationals.

There were two fundamental matters which caused us extreme dissatisfaction. In the first place, it was proposed to form only semi-military or labour corps, and then, too, our troops, although liberated, would in a juridical respect retain the character of prisoners. Neither of these proposals was acceptable to us. Both of them exhibited Sonnino's fears and reservations, to which I have already referred, since the suggested compromise was the work of the Consulta. The Italian military authorities, even at that time, were prepared to go further than this, as they plainly showed in the course of conversation. At the Ministry of War and the Consulta they were anxious to convince me that these Czechoslovak contingents really represented a considerable advance, and that further progress would soon be made in the direction of an actual Czechoslovak Army. These statements were obviously prompted by the endeavour to show that the reservations were not due to hostility or to any tendency against our movement. In a word, Italy was still seeking a compromise involving something which might be or might not be an army according to requirements. The Italian authorities did not venture to say this plainly, as they were not certain whether the Czechoslovak cause, as an international question, would produce successful results. They were genuinely anxious to do something for us, but they were trying to improvise an arrangement which could be withdrawn if necessary.

I gave them full credit for their good will and, as I realized the circumstances, I continued to be patient. But Sonnino was in error; even the concessions which General Giardino had made in his letter were contrary to the usages of international law then in force, and this alone offended Sonnino's legitimistic instincts. In its essentials this concession was a considerable one, and among a number of fundamental matters it answered our purpose. The reservations which the Government had made were safety-valves of a formal character, which at the next approach of an explosion could be open to the utmost capacity. So much was clear; the whole scheme was merely an indication of the political weakness and indecision then prevailing in the Government, and of the uncertainty which marked the Italian aims and plans. For this reason I was sure of final success on the next occasion.

Before making any definite decision, I once more visited all our friends in Rome. I discussed matters first with Barrère, then with Giers, Sir Rennell Rodd, and Sir Samuel Hoare. I also consulted the Serbian Minister, Antonjević, who was a loyal friend and fellow-worker of ours. All these persons were familiar with the matter and had an interest in it. I valued their advice and assistance, both in Rome and with their respective Governments, and by discussing matters with them I was emphasizing the fact that we stood in the same relationship to all the Allies, and that the whole of our movement was uniform and pan-European in character. Incidentally, I may add, I acted similarly in Paris and London with regard to the Italian representatives there.

Barrère was very reluctant to reconcile himself to the situation. From Paris I received a message from Dr. Sychrava, whom I had informed about the progress of my negotiations in Rome, that Colonel Cros and Major Dresch, of the French War Ministry, were very disappointed, for they had counted on obtaining five or six thousand of our prisoners from Italy for the army in France, and had already made arrangements accordingly. Barrère had received similar reports from the Ministry of Foreign Affairs.

At the Secretariat of the National Council in Paris they felt the Italian refusal very keenly, for it had caused a slight setback to our plan for an army in France. The news which was coming from Russia was not particularly encouraging, and in the meantime nothing was being heard from Štefánik in America. As a result of the unsettled state of affairs in France, there were signs of demoralization among our first contingent of prisoners, who had been sent from Rumania by way of Russia. Dr. Sychrava impressed upon me the necessity of returning to Paris without delay, and of putting an end to this situation by an energetic recruiting campaign among our prisoners in France, so as to save the prestige of the National Council, and prevent the scheme of a national army from being discredited.

Nevertheless, ever Barrère advised me not to refuse Giardino's offer. He finally admitted that even this half-concession was a greater success than he had expected. Knowing Sonnino and his fears as to the outcome of the war, he would far sooner have expected him to grant a few thousand prisoners for the army in France. He, too, considered this as a far less binding step than was the sanction for a semi-military body, which must necessarily within a short time be transformed into an army. Hence he agreed with me that the offer should be accepted and the way left open for further negotiations. As the organization of our army in France made it urgent for me to return to Paris at once, Barrère suggested that I should come back to Rome in a few weeks when a final settlement would certainly be reached.

Giers and Sir Rennell Rodd, however, from the very beginning, considered the settlement offered in Giardino's communication as a far greater success than the dispatch of our troops to France would have been. They saw in this a change of front in the Italian policy which would be of considerable significance in its bearings upon the affairs of Austria-Hungary and the Jugoslavs. They therefore advised me strongly to accept the proposal, and to come back to Rome at an early date. In their view we could regard this proposal as a sign that our cause was victorious in Italy. The next step which must come soon, and which was a logical consequence of the present one, would be the formation of an independent Czechoslovak Army, and this would mean that Italy was publicly identifying herself with the policy of destroying the Habsburg Empire. This again, they said, would bring her into official agreement with the scheme for unifying the Jugoslavs.

72

It was natural that after these consultations and discussions with diplomats who at that time were playing a leading part in Rome, and who, by notifying their respective Governments to the same effect, were assisting us and our cause, I decided to act in accordance with their advice. I therefore made up my mind to hasten my departure to Paris, where I would deal with the most urgent matters. As I felt confident that before very long it would be possible to induce the Italian Government to take the final step, I planned to return to Rome within three or four weeks for the purpose of definitely settling our military problem in Italy.(31)

After discussing matters with representatives from among our prisoners, who had been released and were already working in the National Council at Rome, I decided in favour of accepting the compromise as indicated. It was clear to me that the Italians would be obliged to concede to-morrow what they did not concede to-day, and that they themselves would abandon their present attitude as soon as the progress made by our movement in France and elsewhere gave them an opportunity of doing so.

I therefore accepted everything I could. With regard to the formation of semi-military labour corps and the discipline to which the prisoners were to be amenable on their release, I made very emphatic reservations in the name of the National Council, so as not to prejudice its future principles or course of action. I formulated all these points in a written communication which was sent to General Giardino on October 8, 1917.

It was in accordance with the terms of this reply that, when leaving for Paris on October 10th, I instructed Hlaváček, who was in charge of the Rome branch of the National Council, to continue organizing our prisoners in the camps, and to assure them that the organization of the actual army was only a matter of time. On no account, however, was he to proceed with the formation of labour corps. My intention was, immediately on my return to France, to hasten the formation of the army in accordance with the scheme agreed upon, as in the meanwhile the first contingents from Russia were announcing their arrival. This would confront Italy with a *fait accompli* as regards the Czechoslovak Army in France, and judging from the situation in Rome, as I had seen it, I was sure that this was a new argument which would have a decisive effect in Italy.

I did not, however, return to Rome for the completion of the work I had begun there. On my return to Paris my time was fully occupied with urgent business until March 1918. Then, too, Štefánik, on his return from America, expressed the wish to go to Italy himself for the purpose of settling the military problem there. Under these changed conditions I accordingly devoted myself to military work in Paris, to the preliminary arrangements for the Congress of Oppressed Nations, which was held at Rome in April 1918, and also to our affairs in England.

ATTEMPTS AT CONCLUDING AN UNDECISIVE PEACE. ALLIED NEGOTIATIONS FOR A SEPARATE PEACE WITH AUSTRIA-HUNGARY

(a) THE YEAR 1917 A CRISIS IN ALLIED POLICY

73

The Allied Note to President Wilson was a great encouragement to all who wanted to fight to the end ; but for that very reason it stimulated the opportunists to press their peace negotiations. I cannot precisely say to what extent Vienna interpreted the wording of the note as a warning sign of her ultimate fate, and was thus frightened into repeated peace overtures, either with or without Germany. Nor do I know to what extent some of the Allied politicians considered that the note was to be regarded only as a threat to the Habsburg Empire which need not be carried out, but which could be used in the attempt to separate Austria-Hungary from Germany, and to obtain a separate peace with Vienna.

Having spent the month of January at Rome, I left on February 5th to visit Masaryk in London. During my stay in London, Svatkovsky came to Paris where, on February 10th, he had an interview with Dr. Sychrava, with whom he left a message for Masaryk and myself. Dr. Sychrava was startled by this interview. Svatkovsky spoke about Austria-Hungary in the same terms as in December, but he was more emphatic. The dismemberment of Austria-Hungary was, he said, to be postponed for some twenty or thirty years. "You Czechs," declared Svatkovsky, who had visited Izvolsky on the same day, had brought him news from Switzerland, and had received instructions from him, "cannot withdraw. You must aim directly and thoroughly for the destruction of the Empire. But the Entente and Russia are entitled to attempt a separate peace with Austria-Hungary and Bulgaria." He thereupon gave an account of the news which he had from Vienna. At the Court there was said to be a strong feeling against the Germans. The

Government circles considered that the Southern army, which was purely an Austrian one, could be relied upon for all eventualities. Andrássy was in Switzerland and Radev, the Bulgarian Minister, was there too. Svatkovsky had had an opportunity of a conversation with him at Geneva. It was possible to negotiate with them, and it seemed clear that such negotiations would take place. He added that Russia herself was so weak that any final victory on her part was now out of the question. Coming from Svatkovsky, this was a serious admission.

Dr. Sychrava showed Svatkovsky No. 79 of our Russian paper, *Čechoslovák*, which he had just received, and in which it was stated that "the public opinion of Slavonic Russia, which ought to have the initiative in Slavonic and consequently also in Czechoslovak affairs, unfortunately continues to be in a backward state." Svatkovsky's reply to this was a surprising one: "I, too, have reports on that from Vienna. Czernin recently expressed an almost identical opinion. In Vienna they appear to be aware that our success with the Allied Note to Wilson did not proceed from Russia. They conjecture that it was managed by England." He added that with regard to the peace negotiations a favourable moment was being awaited, and as far as possible it would be when the Germans had suffered some kind of military blow. The general plan would be that Russia would receive Eastern Galicia, Rumania the southern part of the Bukovina, while the share of Serbia would be Bosnia and Herzogovina. Arrangements would be made with Italy for minor concessions, as the latter country was unwilling to fight until the end. Some authorities wanted to let Austria have Upper Silesia in order the more easily to induce her to change sides, and they even reckoned with the possibility that Austria would fight on their side against Germany. We and the Jugoslavs were to receive a certain measure of autonomy within Austria. It was explained that the word "liberation" in the Allied Note to President Wilson was not to be interpreted in the sense of "independence."

At that time I saw no immediate and direct danger in Svatkovsky's statement. I, too, had not taken the wording of the note to President Wilson in the sense mentioned, as I had faith in the Allies. I was strongly under the influence of this success which we had achieved, and I myself had seen under what circumstances it had come our way. Nevertheless, I was taken aback when I noticed that just as Svatkovsky had made his statement, the *Matin*, which was in touch with influential persons at the Quai d'Orsay, and had rendered me so much assistance in connection with the note to Wilson, suddenly changed front and began to publish suspiciously Austrophile articles.

We soon ascertained through Osuský that the articles came from Switzerland, that they were directly connected with Svatkovsky, and that they coincided with the beginning of the peace overtures of Sixtus of Bourbon. Simultaneously with this, I observed a certain hesitation and uneasiness with regard to us in various French circles, including those who were well disposed to our cause. To-day, knowing all that was going on behind the scenes, we can form a correct estimate of these matters in their political aspect. I myself did not lose confidence. I regarded these symptoms as resulting from the numerous manœuvres on the part of Austrophiles in France, who were connected with certain prominent Russian circles. In my opinion the best course was not to worry about these matters, but to proceed unswervingly on our way.

(b) COUNT MENSDORFF-POUILLY'S MISSION

74

While Sixtus was negotiating, other more or less important attempts were being made. Some of them were actual attempts to bring about negotiations, while others were mere intrigues. Some of them emanated from authorized persons who were equipped with direct official instructions, but in addition to them there were, especially at Berne, Lausanne, Geneva, the Hague, and Stockholm, various agents and other unofficial intermediaries, all of whom, in one way or another, were endeavouring to bring the belligerent Powers into touch, directly and indirectly.(32)

On the Austrian side the most active part in this respect was taken by Count Mensdorff-Pouilly, the former Austrian Ambassador in London, and also by Count L. Skrzynski, at that time Austrian attaché at Berne. Mensdorff's first action was taken in March and April 1917. On March 10th the Austro-Hungarian Minister in Berne communicated a statement from Rostworowski and Haguenin to the effect that the French authorities would like to discuss peace problems with some representative of Austria-Hungary. At that time there was a feeling of great anxiety in France and in Austria-Hungary. Both these States were exhausted by the war, and after the tension which had been produced by the peace movement in the previous December, and the conflicts over the note to President Wilson, a strong reaction and weariness had set in on both sides, to which the uncertainty arising from the Russian revolution had added.

Czernin eagerly availed himself of the Rostworowski-Haguenin interview (this was at a time when Sixtus was busy with his peace scheme). On March 18th Czernin announced that he would send Count Mensdorff to Switzerland for the purpose of negotiating. The ostensible purpose of Mensdorff's visit was to inspect the Swiss hospitals for the troops of the Allies and Central Powers. Czernin also informed Berlin of what was being done, but Zimmermann, the German Minister of Foreign Affairs, displayed very little readiness to negotiate, although in the end he gave his consent with reservations. In no case must there be any discussion on the Alsace-Lorraine problem. Mensdorff left for Switzerland at the beginning of April and spent a few days there. The French delegate, however, who, according to the news from French quarters, was to undertake his mission with the knowledge of England, did not arrive. With regard to willingness for peace negotiations, Mensdorff could learn nothing more than Vienna had already been informed by the Austro-Hungarian Legation at Berne. I have been unable to ascertain how far Rostworowski and Haguenin were acting merely upon their own conjectures, or whether they really had any instructions from official quarters.

Nevertheless, a certain importance may be attached to Mensdorff's interview with Mrs. Barton at Geneva(33) on April 4, 1917. As a result of this interview, Mensdorff learnt the following facts, which he reported to Vienna: (1) France and England were willing to reach an agreement with Austria-Hungary, but they did not wish to negotiate with Germany. (2) The problem of Alsace-Lorraine must be settled to the advantage of France. (3) Austria-Hungary would have to separate from Germany if she desired to attain peace, for in Allied circles it was felt that Germany was making use of the Habsburg Empire as an emissary, through whose peace overtures she wished to arrive at negotiations for a general peace. Mrs. Barton also indicated to Mensdorff that it was of no use reckoning upon negotiations with the French delegate, as America's entry into the war had produced an encouraging effect in France and England. The result would be for some time to come that the most bellicose element in France would predominate.

The report of Mensdorff's interview, which was transmitted to Berlin, caused Zimmermann much uneasiness. At that time the authorities at Berlin were strongly opposed to any kind of concessions, as they believed in the success of the submarine warfare. They also underestimated America as a source of danger to them, and felt confident that the Allies would be weakened through the effects of the Russian revolution. Zimmermann expressed this point of view very emphatically to Prince Hohenlohe, the Austro-Hungarian Ambassador, who at once informed Czernin of the feeling in Berlin.

Czernin did not share Zimmermann's views in the least. On April 7, 1917, in the sense of the conversation which had taken place during Karl's visit to Hamburg, he sent Zimmermann a detailed statement which undoubtedly had considerable significance. This statement disclosed the situation at Vienna, and indicated the views which were held by Government circles in Vienna as to the destiny of the Empire. Germany must bear in mind—so declared Czernin—that Austria-Hungary was unable to continue fighting on account of her internal political and economic situation. Germany, too, he said, was in a similar situation, and the war must therefore be concluded by the summer of 1917 at the latest. Hence Germany would have to make considerable concessions on the Western front, or else the Central Powers would be compelled to conclude peace on more unfavourable terms. Austria-Hungary was willing to help in this, and had given proof of her willingness by the offers which she had made at Homburg (Czernin here referred to the concessions which Vienna had made for the benefit of Germany in Polish affairs).

Although the Mensdorff-Czernin scheme came to nothing, Vienna continued to pursue the same policy. New opportunities were sought in Switzerland, Holland, at Copenhagen, and Stockholm. The most important efforts were those made in Holland, where Count Szechenyi, with the help of M. Loudon, the Dutch Minister of Foreign Affairs, tried to get into touch with the British in August and September 1917. Czernin again decided that Mensdorff should be sent to Holland for the same ostensible purpose as that connected with his visit to Switzerland. Matters had already been definitely settled, but at the last moment the scheme proved abortive. These details indicate the general feeling among the authorities at Vienna in the summer of 1917.

75

Without awaiting the results of his peace efforts in the West, or comprehending the actual difficulties and obstacles which stood in the way of their realization, Czernin carried on the same manœuvres in the East. He thought that the Russian revolution and its consequences could be well utilized for the benefit of the Central Powers, even by diplomatic means, and that the precarious situation of Russia might cause the Russian revolutionaries to conclude a separate peace with the Central Powers, if skilful advantage were taken of the new circumstances. Czernin therefore, supported by Karl and Zita, with perseverance and skill continued his peace efforts.

From an international and also internal point of view, the spring of 1917 was certainly the final date for Austria to conclude a peace which would more or less maintain her existence, although, of course, with the loss of some of her territory. Czernin's whole policy shows that he realized this fact. Herein we find an explanation of the steps taken by Czernin from the outbreak of the Russian revolution to the victory at Caporetta. After the latter battle, and more particularly after the conclusion of peace with the victorious Bolsheviks, he slightly changed his attitude and procedure.

(c) OUR LIBERATION MOVEMENT ABROAD AND OUR POLICY AT HOME

76

I must now discuss our policy at home and its relations to our movement abroad. In the first place, this was just the period when our policy at home definitely emerged from its previous passivity. Then, too, the overtures for a separate peace with Vienna were made at a period when the Viennese Government was passing through the most critical phases of its existence during the war, and when its chief concern was to prevent anything from happening at home which might be detrimental to its peace efforts. Accordingly, there are a number of moves, especially those taken by Czernin, which must be explained in connection with the policy of the Czech delegates at Vienna in the spring and summer of 1917.

I have already explained in detail how we began our activities with the full knowledge and consent of the chief political personalities at home. All of them were familiar with the feelings and desires of the Czech nation at the outbreak of the war. Throughout the war, too, we were in communication with them. Our plan necessarily involved close co-operation with our politicians at home, and it was a condition for our success that we should not be disavowed by them in the sight of the Allies.

The Austro-Hungarian Government and the military command knew as well as we did that the feeling of the great bulk of the population was against Austria-Hungary. They therefore adopted terrorizing tactics, partly against the leading politicians, who were regarded as dangerous persons, partly against the more venturesome individuals or newspapers. Later on, these tactics were extended so as to include Czech books, Czech schools, and all aspects of the national culture and tradition in general. However, these facts are sufficiently well known, and I shall not dwell upon them here.

In our propaganda abroad we took full advantage of this situation. The official terrorism in Austria-Hungary served the interests of our cause. The first phase of our policy at home—political passivity accompanied by persecution of the bolder elements—provided our movement abroad with a proof of the revolutionary feeling of our nation, and we were able to confirm this by pointing to the wholesale surrendering of our troops to the Allies. So altogether, during the first two years of the war, our nation impressed itself favourably upon Allied opinion. The persecution of such politicians, journalists, and authors as Klofáč, Dušek, Machar, and Dyk, especially the trial and condemnation of Kramář and Rašín, supplied our propaganda with weapons which proved to be most troublesome to our opponents. We were also assisted very effectively in our work by the discussions and efforts in the political and economic circles of Austria during 1916, which aimed at bringing about a closer co-operation between Germany and the Habsburg Empire in political, and especially in economic, matters. In view of the fact that the Balkans and Poland were then dominated by the Central Powers, these efforts on the part of the German nationalists in Austria were a strong argument in our favour. The political schemes in Vienna to introduce German as the State language, to centralize Austria as a complete entity with the exclusion of an autonomous Galicia, to Germanize the administration in Bohemia, at the very moment when Wilson and others were beginning to discuss the self-determination of nations, strengthened our position abroad and showed that our propaganda against the Habsburg Empire was justified.

The second phase of our domestic policy from the end of 1916, however, caused us much alarm and anxiety at first, and serious political embarrassments later on. What we feared was that we should be disavowed, and in all the messages which we sent home we insisted that any step of this kind should be most carefully avoided.

When Koerber came into office and announced that he would govern with the Parliament, we realized that our internal policy would have serious troubles to contend with. Either each party would go its own way—in which case we feared that there would be manifestos of loyalty to the dynasty on the part of the Catholics and the Social Democrats, nor were we sure of the Agrarians and the Young Czechs—or else the parties would arrive at a joint compromise which would necessarily involve a basis of opportunist policy.

Nevertheless, we publicly welcomed the formation of the "League of Czech Deputies" and the "National Committee" on November 19, 1916. We interpreted this step as indicating that important internal events were in preparation. We drew attention to Koerber's measures as regards Poland and Galicia, which were to be excluded from Cis-leithania, and thus by bringing about the isolation of the Czechs in Vienna would facilitate the coercive nationalistic policy. We emphasized the fact that the formation of the bodies referred to constituted our defensive measures against the Germans, and that by causing Vienna fresh internal difficulties they would help to weaken the Central Powers in a military respect also.

From December 1916 until the manifesto issued by the Czech authors in May 1918, the problems of Czech domestic policy caused us much concern. What caused us particular embarrassment in the Allied countries were the acts of opportunism among certain of our Parliamentary representatives, and more than once we had to explain that the Czech nation itself was opposed to these time-serving leaders, and that it would subsequently call them to account. Official circles in France, Great Britain, and Italy did not allow these details to shake their faith in us. They were acquainted with the activities of our "Maffia," concerning which they received information from independent sources. In the same way their own news service enabled them to form an idea of the actual situation in Austria-Hungary. Nevertheless, the attitude of our political parties in 1917 caused them at various times to wonder whether we were only extremists who could not be regarded as advocating the wishes of the whole Czech nation.

Our misgivings increased when Clam-Martinitz became Prime Minister on December 20, 1916, and Czernin Minister of Foreign Affairs two days later. The establishment of this Government coincided, in point of time, with one of the peace moves of the Central Powers. From Prague we were receiving news about the coercion of our politicians, and the movement for the defence of Kramář and Rašín. We heard that Austrian Government circles were adopting a menacing attitude towards our people, saying that peace would soon be declared, and that they would then embark upon an anti-Czech policy which would involve the dismemberment of Bohemia, new language laws, and new administrative measures, unless the Czechs displayed proper loyalty towards the Empire. I included all these points in the memorandum which I submitted to the Quai d'Orsay on December 29, 1916, when the Allied reply to Wilson was being discussed. I had, of course, hoped that our success in connection with the note to President Wilson would produce a stimulating effect upon our politicians at home. Yet as early as January 14, 1917, the National Catholic Party repudiated the note as being hypocritical and tendencious. The League of Czech Deputies then held a long discussion on the attitude which it was to adopt towards the note, and on January 23rd a resolution against the note was passed and transmitted to Clam-Martinitz and Czernin. On January 30th Czernin gave an audience to repre- sentatives of the League, before whom he placed a new reso- lution, similar to the former one as far as the contents went, but couched in terms far more acceptable to the Government. Czernin asked the League to send him this revised resolution, and at a meeting on January 31st the League decided to do so. Czernin thereupon issued the resolution in its revised form. It ran as follows:

"With regard to the reply of the Entente States to President Wilson, in which it is declared that one of the war aims of the countries fighting against our Monarchy is 'the liberation of the Czechs from foreign rule,' the presidency of the Czech League repudiates this insinuation, which is based upon entirely false suppositions, and it emphatically proclaims that, as always in the past, so too at the present time and also in the future, the Czech nation envisages the conditions of its development only beneath the sceptre of the Habsburgs."

The first news that we in Paris received of this was by way of Switzerland in a telegram emanating from German-Magyar propagandist sources, precisely at the moment when Sixtus of Bourbon was beginning his activities in Switzerland, and when the Austrophiles in France and England had started an agitation against the war aims formulated in the note to Wilson. As can be imagined, this produced a painful impression upon Masaryk and the rest of us. Hitherto we had acted in concert with the politicians at home, but now this course of action had been interrupted. From what we knew of the feeling among our people, we judged that they had succumbed to strong pressure on the part of the Government. That is how we explained this regrettable occurrence to official circles and the Press in Allied countries. Fresh news arriving from Prague partly reassured us. Before long we heard that Czech public opinion was extremely dissatisfied with the resolution of the League and the National Council, and that it had shown its disapproval in an unmistakable manner.

The change in the international situation which was brought about by the entry of America into the war and the Russian revolution, was evidently the cause of the very marked change of tactics in Vienna with regard to the Czechs during March and April 1917. Czernin was laboriously seeking methods for reaching negotiations with the Allies; the Russian revolution, just as in 1905, was producing a disruptive effect upon Austria-Hungary, and Milyukov's proclamation on our behalf had evidently not failed to exert an influence upon Vienna. The Czechs at home, just like ourselves abroad, welcomed the revolution as a new political era for Russia, which would bring about an equally profound change in our own conditions. Under these circumstances, Clam-Martinitz could no longer reckon with the fulfilment of his anti-Czech schemes in Austria.

We, too, believed that these two great historical events would bring about important results. We knew that at that time the situation of Austria-Hungary was precarious in every respect, and we hoped that our politicians at home would attach the same importance as we did to the events in question. These hopes of ours were justified when, at the end of April, we came into possession of the first manifesto of the Czech League which displayed any considerable degree of determination. This manifesto, which was issued on April 14, 1917, while not actually opposing the Empire, nevertheless demanded that Austria should deal with the most urgent questions involving ideas of democracy, the Parliamentary system, and the revision of the Constitution on the lines implied by the self-determination of nations. It was clear that the wording of this manifesto had been prompted by the events in Russia.

77

I had heard on good authority that the Austrian Parliament was to be definitely convened for May 30, 1917, and as I wished to prevent any repetition of the previous political mistakes at home, I sent the following message to Prague in the second half of April 1917, after consultation with Masaryk :

In connection with the successes which we have achieved here, especially the note to Wilson, our work in Russia with Milyukov, as well as our work in Italy, America, and elsewhere, we urgently draw your attention to the fact that Austria is exerting every effort to save herself. Intrigues are of daily occurrence, and they are a source of much danger. We are almost powerless against them. Great sacrifices have been made by France, who regards Germany alone as the chief enemy, and to separate Austria from Germany would be a possibility to which France might be driven by circumstances for the purpose of terminating the war at an early date. It is only your opposition which can save us, as the formula concerning the self-determination of nations cannot be abandoned. If the Austrians were able to say that they are entitled to speak in your name, if you were to make a declaration of loyalty, if you failed to show clearly that you are opposed to Austria, you would deprive us of our last weapon, and justify the Entente in concluding with the dynasty a separate peace, in the framing of which we should not be able to express any opinion. The present situation makes it imperative for us to show whether it is the dynasty and the diplomats, or whether it is the nations themselves who are entitled to negotiate on behalf of the Austrian nation. Unless you make it clear at the present moment that the dynasty and its diplomats are not entitled to do so, we are lost.

We urgently draw attention to the fact that the victory is not yet completely gained. It would be a mistake to consider it a matter of course that Austria will be destroyed and you liberated. We still have powerful opponents who are producing proof here that the Austrian nations do not wish to be liberated. *Právo Lidu* is being read and quoted here as a proof against us that we are not entitled to speak on behalf of our people, who desire merely an Austrian Federation.

To-day, then, is the decisive moment. It is now no longer sufficient to repeat that your manifesto and your guarded attitude were the result of compulsion. We are aware that it is so, but the people here cannot understand it. When Serbia and Belgium have suffered so severely, they see no reason why our people should be so much afraid of prison or even greater sacrifices. You must speak your minds plainly and openly. Now, at the convening of Parliament, is the opportunity. Seeing that we need a decisive and unmistakable proof that the dynasty is not entitled to speak on behalf of the Czech nation, we call upon you to carry out the following unconditionally:

1. To grant no sanction either to the war or to the budget estimate, to the levy of troops, or to any single enactment of paragraph 14.[1] Further, to give no permission for the continuance of the war.

2. To demand the release of all deputies, freedom of speech for them, stoppage of treason trials, and freedom of the Press. By these tactics you will best prevent the convening of Parliament.

3. To demand permission for a number of people to come and consult with us and Professor Masaryk (more particularly if he too should receive an amnesty and thus be entitled to enter Parliament) on neutral soil, and reach an agreement on our policy as a whole. In no case will Masaryk return to Bohemia and enter Parliament.

4. At all costs to repudiate any disavowal of what has been done by us or the National Council.

5. To demand historical State rights without prejudice to the gaining of Slovakia, and without prejudice to the existence of Austria.

6. In no case must all our deputies attend Parliament. At least the Bohemian and Moravian radicals must abstain. Here it would not be understood how our people can attend Parliament without causing obstruction and disorder, etc.

7. To sum up: You must set forth the problem of Czech State rights. That means that as far as we are concerned the December Constitution does not exist. In consequence, you must not attend the Emperor's ceremony of taking the oath to the Constitution and the manifestation of loyalty. We therefore ask you not to attend Parliament for these

---

[1] The essential contents of paragraph 14 are as follows:
" If urgent circumstances in the interval between parliamentary sessions render necessary any measure requiring, in accordance with the Constitution, the consent of the Reichsrat, this may be done under the collective responsibility of the Cabinet at the orders of the Emperor, on condition that it entails no modification of the constitutional laws. . . . Enactments reached under these circumstances have the force of laws when they are signed collectively by the ministers." . . .

ceremonies, and we will see that this produces an appropriate effect here.

I therefore repeat that these are essential for our preservation, which to-day rests in your hands.

1. Not to vote with the Government on any point.
2. Not to be present at the manifestations of loyalty in Parliament.
3. The Radicals at least, if not all, must set up a passive opposition.
4. Not to disavow us.
5. To demand State rights.

Whatever you do, there must be no repetition of the mistake made in 1848. None of you must vindicate the existence of Austria. Remember that there is a revolution in Russia, and that Russia will be a republic.

Finally, it is our wish that influence should again be brought to bear upon our troops. If the Slavonic regiments on the Italian front were to offer resistance, this would be interpreted as showing Austria's vitality. It would therefore do us much harm. In this matter do all that you can.

78

On May 19th, on the initiative of Jaroslav Kvapil, the poet and dramatist, was published the proclamation of the 150 Czech authors who felt the same misgivings as we did abroad, and in trenchant terms called upon the responsible Czech politicians to speak and act in Parliament on behalf of the Czech nation as the nation really desired. And even though it was not stated in so many words, this declaration meant that the Czech parties in Parliament should declare themselves in favour of the programme of the Czech revolutionary movement abroad, and in favour of a restoration of the Czech State, including Slovakia, without the dynasty and irrespective of the Habsburg Empire.

In Paris we received a summary of the declaration only a few days after it was published, and shortly after that the full text. It made us feel that we need have no further misgivings as to the session of Parliament. We realized the difficult situation of our leading politicians at home, and we did not expect them to achieve impossibilities. All that we wanted was that they should not lose ground. In Allied circles we emphasized that our programme was identical with theirs, even though there was a divergency in our tactics. We also insisted that we had no desire to expose our people to persecution unnecessarily. We had reasons for believing that the position of Vienna would grow worse and worse, and we therefore felt confident that now we should not be disavowed, but that under the pressure of public opinion the manifestos from Prague would develop more and more on radical lines.

On the day before the opening of the Parliament at Vienna (May 29, 1917) the National Council issued a proclamation, drawn up by Professor Masaryk, in the form of a protest against the summoning of Parliament. It emphasized the illegal character of this proceeding. The mandates of the deputies had not been issued in time, and more than fifty of them were unable to exercise their Parliamentary functions. Moreover, the Constitution of 1867, which did not acknowledge the Czechs, was no longer in existence, having been infringed on several occasions by Franz Josef. There were also other grounds for protest. The Austrian Government had declared war without Parliamentary sanction and against the will of the Czech nation. In every possible manner it had persecuted the Czechs, had expended the sum of 60 milliards on the war, had refused to admit eight Czech deputies into Parliament, and was instituting new repressive measures against Czechs who showed any racial consciousness. By summoning Parliament, the Austrian Government wished to transfer responsibility for the war to the nations which it governed. It also wished to exact declarations of loyalty from them, and thus produce an influence upon the Entente to their detriment.

The Czech authors had repudiated the responsibility of the Czech nation for the war, and declared themselves in favour of independent Czech territories, together with Slovakia. As, however, any considerable anti-Austrian manifestos in the Czech areas would certainly have been suppressed, it was only the National Council in Paris which was free to display the will of the nation. It therefore protested against all Austrian intrigues, and declared that the resolutions of the Parliament at Vienna could not be binding upon the Czech nation, and it expressed an unflinching determination to achieve complete independence. This declaration of the National Council met with wide comment in the Allied Press.

The reservation of State rights which the Czech League, by arrangement with the National Council, brought forward in the Austrian Parliament on May 30, 1917, demanded State rights, and emphasized the principle of the self-determination of nations. It claimed a democratic Czech State, united with Slovakia. It did not contain any declaration against the Empire, but only against dualism, and it admitted the possibility of transforming the Habsburg Empire into a federated State comprising free national States.

The most important passage in this proclamation was as follows:

"Therefore in this historical moment, taking our stand upon the natural right of a nation to self-determination and free development, which in our case is strengthened by inalienable historical rights and by State documents which are fully recognized, we, at the head of our people, will strive after a union of all branches of the Czechoslovak nation in a democratic State, in respect of which it is not possible to leave out of account the Slovak branch, living as a complete unit coherently associated with Czech historical territory."

This was the passage in the proclamation upon which we based our propaganda. We explained to the Allied countries that the suggestion for a federated State was a purely tactical necessity, the purpose of which was to prevent any persecution on the part of the Austrian Government. This interpretation was corroborated by the attitude of the public at home, which, while evincing satisfaction at the outset, ignored the reference to the Empire and a federated State, but more and more laid stress upon that part of the proclamation which claimed a Czech State in combination with Slovakia.

Having thus interpreted the proclamation in a revolutionary light, and, moreover, having drawn attention to the fact that at the same meeting of Parliament the Jugoslavs, Poles, and Ukrainians had all emphasized their own national programme, we were justified in declaring to the Allied countries that the first plain symptom of dissolution had now made its appearance in the Habsburg Empire.

As I have mentioned, it was already clear to us then that with the progress of events, notably in Russia, our policy at home would assume an increasingly radical character. This assumption was soon confirmed. The refusal of the Czech League on July 12, 1917, to attend the discussions for revising the Constitution was a proof that by this time the majority of our politicians realized that the destiny of the Empire could be decided only by the results of the war. From then onwards we felt more at our ease, as we were able to explain all manifestations of our policy at home as indicating a revolutionary spirit.

(d) THE PEACE MOVE OF THE SOCIALISTS. THE CONFERENCE
OF THE SECOND INTERNATIONAL AT STOCKHOLM AND
CZERNIN'S PEACE POLICY. OUR SOCIALISTS AT STOCK-
HOLM

79

Almost at the same time as the Government at Vienna was
making the peace moves which I have described above, there
started an important international movement which was
prolonged until the autumn of 1917. It caused much agitation
in European public opinion, and it undoubtedly produced a
number of results which were beneficial to our cause. I am
referring to the attempt to summon a congress of the Second
International at Stockholm in the summer or autumn of 1917.

At the beginning of 1917, the remaining members of the
Central Executive Committee of the Second International,
joined by the Swedes, Danes, and Dutch (also the Belgian deputy
Huysmans), formed a Dutch-Scandinavian Socialist Committee.
This committee, with a view to bringing about the speedy end
of the war, addressed a special questionnaire to all the Socialist
parties which before the war had been members of the Second
International. The questionnaire contained three fundamental
queries:

1. Do the parties desire the re-establishment of the International?

2. Are they willing to attend an international Socialist
conference?

3. Under what conditions would it be possible, in their opinion,
to arrive at peace overtures and the end of the war?

In the Allied States all the Governments were unanimously
opposed to the undertaking of the Dutch-Scandinavian
Committee. The possible consequences which it involved were
against the Allied interests, needs, and plans at that time. It
was a source of menace to the Allies because it aimed at bringing
about peace during a period when their military position was
unfavourable. On the other hand, the whole of the circumstances
under which it was being held fitted in more or less with the
situation of the Central Powers. Czernin, who neglected no
opportunity for promoting his efforts towards a speedy peace,
realized that in this particular instance he would do well to
make use of the Social Democratic parties of the Central
Powers. In this he succeeded to a very large extent with the
Austro-Hungarian Socialists, and partially also with the Germans.

As it happened, this scheme was a considerable advantage

to our cause, as it rendered possible the dispatch of a Czecho-slovak delegation to Stockholm. The National Council at Paris conceived and carried out a scheme for utilizing the action of the Dutch-Scandinavian Committee. The representatives of our liberation movement, not being connected with any organized Social Democratic parties, could not expect to be admitted to the negotiations at Stockholm. We therefore suggested to the Socialists who had taken part in our move-ment in America, Russia, London, and Paris, to apply to the Stockholm Conference with at least a memorandum. This was done, and the committee in Stockholm placed this memorandum at the disposal of all the Socialist parties who attended the negotiations there. The branch of the National Council at Petro-grad made even more effective use of the Stockholm Conference for spreading information about our national plans and aims. Bohdan Pavlů proceeded to Stockholm, and shortly afterwards he was joined by Prokop Maxa, who spent some considerable time there. In accordance with Masaryk's instructions they discussed matters with various members of the conference, informing them of the state of affairs in Russia, and acquainting Socialist circles with our aims. The provisional Russian Govern-ment attached considerable importance to our action in Stockholm. Milyukov expressed full approval of it and granted a diplomatic passport to Pavlů and Maxa.

The delegates of the Czechoslovak Socialist Party were Antonín Němec and Gustav Habrman. They discussed matters at great length with Maxa. He placed before them a report on the various branches of our movement, accompanied by docu-mentary evidence. Maxa afterwards stated that the report impressed them all very much. Habrman and Němec expressed their complete approval, and Dr. Šmeral declared that he agreed with 75 per cent. of what we had done. The delegates rendered good service to our cause by giving an unbiassed account of the precarious conditions in Austria. The other Socialist delegates and also the journalists were greatly impressed by what they heard about the distress and national persecutions in Austria. Altogether, the activity of our delegates in Stockholm and the participation of our representatives from Russia promoted our revolutionary movement considerably. We were able to convey to our politicians in Prague a far more precise and detailed account of our work abroad than had been possible hitherto. There was a direct exchange of views and a removal of various doubts and uncertainties.

XII

ATTEMPTS AT CONCLUDING AN UNDECISIVE PEACE.
ALLIED NEGOTIATIONS FOR A SEPARATE
PEACE WITH AUSTRIA-HUNGARY—(*Continued*)

(*a*) THE PEACE NOTE OF POPE BENEDICT XV AND THE WAR
POLICY OF THE VATICAN. CZERNIN'S POLICY AND THE
CZECHOSLOVAK CAUSE

80

ONE of the characteristic symptoms of the situation in the
summer of 1917, and a classical example of the war policy of the
Holy See, was the peace note of Pope Benedict XV, issued on
August 1, 1917. It aimed at bringing about peace negotiations
and thus accelerating the end of the war. This brings it within
the scope of the present remarks, apart from the fact that there
was a close connection between the war policy of the Vatican
and the attempts to preserve the Habsburg Empire.

Here I should like to insert a few words about the general
policy and diplomacy of the Vatican during the war.

Pope Pius X died in August 1914, and his successor was
elected on September 3rd following. The new Pope, Giacoppo
della Chiesa, had been the deputy of Cardinal Rampolla, the
State Secretary of Leo XIII and later of Merry del Val, the
State Secretary of Pius X. From 1907 onwards he had been the
Cardinal of Bologna, and on being elected Pope he received the
name of Benedict XV. The war had brought the Catholic Church
into a very awkward predicament, not only in a political respect,
but also as regards its ecclesiastical, spiritual, and moral
mission. In a political respect it was between two fires, and if it
had unequivocally taken sides, the consequences would have
been very detrimental to its interests. From a spiritual and
ecclesiastical point of view, its position was no less difficult.
The war had disorganized the contact of the Vatican with the
priesthood and its other adherents in both camps, and in consequence of this its followers became more subject to the authority
of their respective States. Then, too, the moral disorder which
arose everywhere as a result of the war inevitably tended to

impair the influence of the Catholic Church. In every country the representatives of Catholicism were compelled to identify themselves with the war aims of that country, and this circumstance helped to undermine the international Catholic solidarity which had hitherto been so strong.

Benedict XV was elected Pope evidently because he had collaborated so long with Popes Leo XIII and Pius X, and with their two prominent State Secretaries, Rampolla and Merry del Val. The political and diplomatic tasks of the Church during the war exhibited such difficulties, as early as September 1914, that great reliance was placed upon the diplomatic and political experience of Giacoppa della Chiesa. Let me at once point out that Benedict XV did not fulfil these expectations. He had been a good official, capable of studying in detail the problems with which he was dealing ; he worked hard and was not impervious to new ideas, but he had no skill in politics. He succumbed completely to the influences surrounding him, and he never was able to cope with the situation during the war on the lines of the great political and diplomatic traditions of the Vatican. His war policy was therefore doomed to failure from the outset. When he was elected, it was considered in the Allied countries that his policy would follow the traditions of Leo XIII and Cardinal Rampolla, i.e. he would favour the Entente. This soon proved to be an error, and it became clear that there had been many changes in the Vatican since the time of Leo XIII. Parenthetically I may point out that the Vatican was simply unable to pursue a pro-Allied policy during the war, and it was equally unable to maintain an attitude of neutrality towards the Allies. This was due to the fundamental character of the war between the Central Powers and the Allies, the result of which was that the longer the war went on, the more did the interests of the Catholic Church lean towards the side of the Central Powers.

The war began with an ultimatum of the Habsburgs, the most Catholic of the great Powers in Europe, the traditional pillar of the Catholic Church, deriving support from the Vatican both within and without, and possessing a record of many years of service to the Vatican in international politics in the Balkans, in Germany, against Russia, against Italy, and within its own frontiers, against Liberalism and all progressive tendencies, against Orthodoxy and all schismatic movements. The war began against Orthodox Serbia, which was supported by

Orthodox Russia for strengthening its Balkan policy. The camp of the Habsburgs was shared by Germany, which, having long given up the "Kulturkampf," made use of the Catholic centre for the support of its autocratic policy, and adroitly promoted the Catholic element at home and abroad, especially in Turkey and the Far East. The other side comprised Protestant England, anti-clerical France, and Orthodox Russia, and this alone inevitably proved a determining factor with Conservative Vatican circles at the very outset. Orthodox Russia, before the war, was regarded by Catholic Rome as a bogey penetrating into Central Europe, struggling for influence in the Balkans, and harbouring designs against Constantinople and St. Sofia, while the whole of the Byzantine heritage—which incidentally France and England had assigned to Russia by the agreements on the dismemberment of Turkey in the spring of 1915—was no longer merely a bogey, but an immediate danger hovering above Rome. Anti-clerical pre-war France, which had carried out a breach with Rome, had ruthlessly imparted a lay character to schools, administration, and army, and had no representatives at the Vatican, would, in the opinion of several important Catholics, have expiated this policy by sustaining a defeat. Liberal England, the centre of unrestricted religious research and development, from which Protestant thought was disseminated throughout the world, formed a new danger to the policy of the Vatican. In fact, the Entente contained only two elements—and they were comparatively weak—which provided a counter-argument to these considerations on the part of the Vatican: Catholic Belgium, with its eminent Cardinal Mercier, and the French Catholics, with whom, however, their nationalistic tradition and their Conservatism soon proved too strong for their Catholicism, and resulted in openly expressed dissatisfaction with the attitude of the Vatican. Then the Entente was joined by anti-Vatican Italy which, during the war, never ceased to carry on its old struggle with the Vatican, and in the London Pact inserted an article making it impossible for the Vatican to take any share in the peace negotiations, and thus frustrating one of the chief aims of Vatican policy during the war.

When the United States entered the war and the Russian revolution broke out, the objections of the Vatican to the Quadruple Entente were strengthened by the final arguments which, as a matter of fact, had exerted an influence from the very beginning: Wilson's democratic ideology and his struggle against the dynastic autocracy of Central Europe, the subversive tendencies of the Russian revolution, and the definite acceptance of the principles involving the self-determination of nations. The latter item, in particular, was intended to bring about the dismemberment of the most Catholic of the great Powers, and the removal of the most Catholic of the dynasties, and the whole affair was entirely alien to the feelings, wishes, aims, and interests of the Vatican. Thus was accentuated the great divergency between the two belligerent parties; one side consisted of democratic France, England, Belgium, Italy, Serbia, joined later by revolutionary Russia, and the democratic United States, all of whom were waging war against the militaristic and dynastic autocracies of Central Europe. Accordingly the Vatican, as an inveterate champion and representative of tradition, of hierarchy, and of all autocratic, dynastic, and aristocratic principles, could not do otherwise than pursue the policy with which it had always been identified, and had always openly acknowledged. For reasons of its spiritual affinity it was antagonistic to those who represented the ideals and principles of modern democracy, involving respect for the individual, the spirit of tolerance in its fullest acceptation, and the interests of progress in political, economic, social, religious, and moral aspects of life.

For these reasons the Vatican could not look with favour upon the prospect of an Allied victory. On the other hand, its purpose would not have been served by an integral victory on the part of Germany and the Pan-German schemes in Central Europe, in Turkey, and the Near East generally. Nor could the Vatican be expected to approve of the presence of Turkey among the Central Powers. But compared with the misgivings which it felt at the thought of an Allied victory, this was a far lesser evil. What would have suited the Vatican best would have been peace on the basis of the *status quo* with a few minor changes, such as the restoration of a Catholic Poland, the removal of Russian influence from the Balkans, and a few territorial concessions from Vienna to Italy. Such were the ideas in the entourage of Benedict XV, and they may be taken as forming the broad outline of his war-time policy.

It should be added that the diplomatic relations of Vienna and Berlin with the Vatican were better than those of the Entente States. From 1907 onwards the influence of the Central Powers in the organization and diplomatic policy of the

Vatican had greatly increased. France, England, the United States, Serbia, and Italy, on the other hand, were entirely without any official representatives at the Vatican. Altogether, the Central Powers paid great attention to the political interests of the Vatican, while the Western States were inclined to regard it far more as a moral or spiritual factor. This was a great mistake on their part. It never was, and never will be, the Vatican's wish to renounce its political organization and its political influence. In this respect Benedict XV was a typical Pope. He systematically aimed at promoting the Papal authority in international politics. He was anxious to secure a share in the peace negotiations, and protested against Article XV of the London Pact, to which I have referred above. He would also have liked to obtain recognition of the Vatican as a political power through the membership of the League of Nations.

It was therefore a mistake for the States of Western Europe to expect that the attitude of the Vatican would be dictated by the spiritual interests of the Catholic Church. Benedict XV took the point of view that the Papal See could perform its spiritual mission effectively and independently, only if it had sufficient authority and political influence, and for that reason during the war he subordinated its spiritual mission to its political interests.

Such was the struggle which the Vatican itself waged during the war. I think I may say that as far as spiritual matters went the Vatican was on the losing side. By giving precedence to its political interests, it associated itself, although in a hesitant and guarded manner, with those who were the representatives of power and of the materialistic proclivities existing in the pre-war period, as embodied in their method of warfare, in their system of politics and diplomacy, and in their war aims. If the Vatican had been guided by its higher spiritual interests it would have sided with those who proclaimed respect for international agreements and the removal of autocratic tendencies.

Post-war events have shown that the Vatican did not lose by the victory of the Allies. This is a further proof that its policy during the war was an erroneous one, both morally and politically. This explains why the Vatican was so astonished at the defeat of the Central Powers, since until the very last moment it did not believe that such an eventuality was possible. It had assisted the Habsburg Empire right up to its downfall, and after the Peace Treaties were signed the Vatican expressed itself about them with such reservations that some of the Powers thought that the Papal See intended to discredit them.

81

All the above statements are confirmed by the actual policy of the Vatican during the war. Scarcely had the war broken out than Pope Pius X defined the first principle of Papal policy thus: As it had not been possible to prevent the war, everything must now be done to accelerate the restoration of peace. Although this seemed to be a purely impartial point of view, the circumstances caused it to be a harmful principle to the Allies only. The principle thus defined by Pius X was somewhat elaborated by Benedict XV, so that in its final form it comprised the following:

1. Impartiality to both sides.

2. The employment of all resources for alleviating the miseries of war, assisting prisoners, emigrants, inhabitants of occupied areas, women, children, etc.

3. Exertion of all efforts to conclude the war and prepare peace negotiations.

As I have pointed out, the first item on this programme was incompatible with the third one, but the most serious objection to the whole scheme was that the Pope had interchanged the word "impartiality" for "neutrality." A neutral is precluded from adopting an attitude to any action of the belligerents, however outrageous it might be. Impartiality, on the other hand, implies the passing of a moral judgment. In actual fact, Benedict XV assumed an attitude of moral neutrality towards the Catholic world, an attitude which was interpreted as being more or less "benevolent" neutrality towards the Central Powers.

At the same time, the philanthropic activity of the Papal See was carried on in a consistent and effective manner throughout the war, and it met with sincere recognition on all sides.

It was on September 8, 1915, that Benedict XV issued his first manifesto in favour of accelerating the peace negotiations, and he repeated this during the Christmas of the same year. In February 1916 he ordered public prayer for peace at an early date. The Vatican took the view that the less the number of belligerents, the sooner peace would be concluded, and acting on this principle it did everything in its power to prevent Italy from entering the war. The Vatican also endeavoured to induce the United States not to supply the belligerent countries with foodstuffs and munitions. As in actual practice these supplies were being sent only to the Allied countries, this impartiality was again being exercised for the benefit of one side.

In the early months of the war all the friends of the Vatican and the Catholic Church in the Allied countries expected that Benedict XV would express himself on the subject of violated Belgian neutrality, ill-treatment of non-belligerents, and the bombardment of French cathedrals. In this they were disappointed, as the neutrality or impartiality of the Vatican did not permit of any such course.(34)

When, in the summer of 1916, the Central Powers found it advisable to make peace overtures, they took advantage of the Vatican in carrying out their purpose. To-day it can be ascertained how the diplomats of the Central Powers, notably those of Vienna, caused the Vatican to associate itself closely with all their peace efforts. The peace offer which was made by the Central Powers on December 12, 1916, was dispatched by them to the Pope also. The Vatican unreservedly approved of Wilson's first note, dated December 18th, in which he called upon the two belligerent parties to announce publicly their peace terms.

In December 1916 Benedict summoned up enough courage to express publicly a number of views on the war, which though couched in general terms, were nevertheless sufficiently in the interests of justice. Thus he expressed his regret at the bombardment of open towns, at the removal of the civilian population from their homes, and at the evil effect of submarine warfare.

It was, however, in 1917 that the political and diplomatic activity of the Pope during the war reached its culminating point. The Russian Revolution had brought relief to the Vatican in one way, but in another it had proved a source of considerable alarm. While weakening the political influence of Russia, it threatened the social order by reason of its excesses, and the Vatican was extremely sensitive to both these results. The entry of America into the war caused serious disappointment to Catholic Rome, and the Vatican had exerted its whole influence to try and prevent this critical step. Then in the spring of 1917 came the Socialist peace movement, the progress of which the Vatican followed with great dissatisfaction, as it feared that should the scheme achieve even an apparent success, it would deprive the Pope of credit for a mission which he ought to be carrying out, and would thus tend to strengthen the prestige of international Socialism in general. Thus, from the spring of 1917 onwards, the Vatican was continually considering its active intervention with a view to peace negotiations. In June and July the diplomatic authorities of the Vatican closely investigated the situation on both sides, and on August 1, 1917, Benedict brought out his peace note addressed "To the heads of the belligerent nations."(35) This may be regarded as his most significant political action during the war. The note was transmitted to the respective States in the middle of August, and published on the 16th of the same month.

In his note Benedict began by referring to the three principles which he had formulated on becoming Pope, and which I have mentioned above. He emphasized that he had no special political purpose, but was prompted entirely by his feeling of duty. He proposed the following principles as being conducive to a lasting peace: (1) material force should be replaced by the moral strength of right; (2) armaments should be reduced to the minimum necessary for preserving public order; (3) armies should be replaced by arbitration bodies; (4) the freedom of the seas should be guaranteed(36) ; (5) mutual exemption from the payment of indemnities for damage incurred, except in cases where such compensation was agreed upon; (6) mutual evacuation of territories then occupied, i.e. Belgium, with guarantees for its complete political independence of both belligerent parties, evacuation of the occupied areas of France, together with the restoration of the German colonies. (7) The outstanding territorial questions between Austria and Italy, Germany and France, were to be considered in a spirit of reconciliation and with due regard to the desires of the nations involved; (8) the same spirit should be brought to bear upon the territorial aspects of the Armenian and Balkan problems, as well as the question of the former Kingdom of Poland.

Such, then, was to be the basis for establishing the future peace of the nations. Benedict's note produced a favourable effect chiefly in Vienna, since it was entirely in accordance with the aims and efforts of the authorities there. It was directed towards an early peace, and it said nothing definite as to Austro-Hungarian territory, nor did it refer in any way to the self-determination of nations, nor even to their equitable treatment. Official Berlin was more guarded, especially on account of the Vatican's unambiguous attitude towards Belgium. The German Press, especially that of the Right, objected to the note, although *Vorwärts* published an article on August 17, 1917, expressing approval of it.

In the Allied camp the note was immediately repudiated in a very emphatic manner. France was offended by it on account of Alsace-Lorraine, and also because it placed the attackers and the attacked on the same footing. Belgium was dissatisfied that the evacuation of her territories was conditioned by the restoration of the German colonies. Italy regarded the note merely as a manifestation of the peace terms of the Central Powers. As for England and the United States, they were equally opposed to the note, which they considered to be lacking in clearness. They also disliked the manner in which it evaded the most difficult problems, and failed to condemn several acts of violence committed by the Central Powers. Moreover, the compromises which it suggested would in their opinion soon lead to a new war. In all these States the Press was practically unanimous, and not even the leading Catholics ventured to defend the note, but on the contrary, as for example in France, they protested against it.

It was typical of the Vatican policy that Russia, although at that time still an Allied and belligerent State, had been omitted from the note, and it was not sent to the Russian Government. Evidently the peace envisaged by the Vatican would have been very markedly anti-Russian in character.

We in Paris looked upon the rejection of the note as a good sign. Just at the moment when the note appeared, I was making arrangements for my visit to Rome. I was therefore doubly interested in the whole matter. I saw that it promoted the policy of the Habsburg Empire, and I conjectured that, such being the case, I was hardly likely to meet with much success if I got into touch with the Vatican.

The main question which arose in the Allied countries was whether the note had been arranged beforehand with the Governments of the Central Powers. The general impression was that this had been the case. The English and Italian Press at once published reports to this effect, and the French Press copied them. The public in the Allied countries, on the other hand, immediately received an official intimation that the Allied Governments had had no hand in this undertaking. The

Vatican defended itself against this serious charge of favouring the Central Powers by pointing out that Benedict would not be capable of such an action, and that no agreement had been made with the Governments of the Central Powers. A letter containing these arguments was sent by Cardinal Gasparri to the Archbishop of Sens and published at Paris in *La Croix* on October 25th. The Vatican also availed itself of certain ecclesiastical dignitaries for the purpose of counteracting these suggestions. Thus, in England, it was Cardinal Bourne who was entrusted with this task.

To-day it is possible to state that the Vatican had exchanged views with Vienna and Berlin on the subject of its peace overture. Thus, it is an historical fact that at the beginning of August 1917 Mgr. Pacelli, the Papal Nuncio at Munich, transmitted to Dr. Michaelis, the Imperial Chancellor, a document containing almost word for word the concrete peace conditions as formulated in the note which was officially dispatched to the belligerent Governments two weeks later. It is likewise true that the German Government accepted Pacelli's memorandum as a Papal peace overture, prepared an answer, and passed the whole matter on to Vienna, where, on August 6th, Czernin expressed his approval of the answer given by Michaelis. He urged Berlin, however, to be more explicit in its reply on the subject of Belgium, in order that the Allies might not be able to deduce from it that Germany was contemplating annexation in any form. I do not know when and how Berlin conveyed to Pacelli the answer which it had prepared by agreement with Vienna. It perhaps regarded this step merely as an attempt to test the atmosphere in Berlin. The German reply to the memorandum was, on the whole, favourable, as was also the later official reply to the Papal note of August 1st. It seems evident that the Vatican took this step only in order to be certain how the Pope's official statement would be received in Berlin. It had no doubt that the note would be favourably received in Vienna, and it did not attach much importance to the opinion of Bulgaria or Turkey. But as far as I know, it did not show similar consideration for Allied opinion, which it sounded only indirectly through various unofficial sources of information.

The discussions between the Central Powers on the subject of the reply to the Papal note were difficult. Vienna had accepted the note with great satisfaction, and desired to reply unreservedly that it should be regarded as a basis for peace negotiations. It was anxious to induce Berlin to share this point of view, and in the end the German authorities gave Vienna the assurance that their reply would be identical as regards its contents, but that it would be more guarded in form. In particular, Berlin was not satisfied with the wording of the note on the subject of Belgium and the references to the Franco-German frontiers. Turkey very emphatically declined to consider any discussion about Armenia, and Bulgaria wanted the wording to be without prejudice to the possibility of a later annexation of Macedonia.

At length the Central Powers managed to agree upon the wording of their notes. The replies were separate in order that each country could be free to draw up its note in a manner most acceptable to its respective public. The Austrian and German replies were issued on September 19, 1917, and their reception in the Allied countries was extremely unfavourable. It was considered that they were insincere and that they concealed ideas of annexation. This applied particularly to the German note, which evaded any reference to the Belgian question.

The Vatican itself was highly satisfied with the reply from Vienna, but less so with that from Berlin, partly because the Kaiser himself had not answered. Nevertheless, the Vatican felt most hopeful that the replies would form the basis for further conversations.

The action of the Allies was most characteristic. France and England first of all agreed that they would not reply at all. Accordingly, France took no further steps in the matter, while England merely acknowledged the receipt of the note, and after Wilson's reply Lord Robert Cecil announced in the House of Commons that England associated herself with America in this respect. In Italy, Sonnino made a speech in the Parliament there on October 24th, 1917, rejecting the note and designating it as expressing the wishes of the Central Powers. In this speech Sonnino also, for the first time, publicly stated what many Catholics had hitherto only thought, namely, that the Pope, although considered as the supreme moral authority of the Catholic world, had never made any public statement as to who was guilty in the war and who not.

The Vatican replied to this rather half-heartedly, first of all in a letter from Cardinal Gasparri to the Bishop of Valencia, and then in an article published by the *Osservatore Romano*, which was a direct answer to Sonnino. Leaving on one side the justified objection to the general form of the note, the Vatican vindicated its avoidance of certain topics in its note of August 1st. The Pope, it was urged, was unwilling and unable to act as a judge or to discuss the question of innocence or guilt in a document, in which his sole purpose was to be an intermediary with a view to bringing about peace negotiations in the interests of all mankind. If he had acted as a judge, he would have defeated the aims of his peace movement at the very outset.

This statement should be carefully noticed. Although the Vatican does not expressly say so, it again draws a distinction between its spiritual mission and its political activity. In its former capacity it evidently associates itself with the duty of being the supreme protector of morality, justice, and right. In its capacity as a political factor, however, it feels itself entitled to act as any other political power would do. This twofold function naturally results in a twofold code of ethics, which forms the most distinguishing feature of the Vatican policy during the war. The conclusion to which this inevitably brings me is, that religious and ecclesiastical matters in general should be excluded from politics. The only possible solution of the problem of the Church in modern democratic States is the return of the Papacy to the spiritual mission which it followed in the early period of Christianity, and a free Church in a free State.

At the same time it would be political blindness not to see that the Papacy, the Catholic Church, and Catholicism as a whole constitute an important international factor, and that they will continue to be a powerful spiritual factor. It was these considerations which prompted me during the war to induce the Vatican to adopt at least a neutral attitude towards our movement, and for the same reason I have always been anxious since the war to keep up a positive policy with the Vatican. This means that I desire to defend the interests of the State resolutely and consistently wherever the policy of the Vatican may be at variance with them, while as regards the spiritual mission of the Vatican, it is my aim to preserve an attitude of tolerance and respect, demanding, of course, the same in return. This is the only possible positive ecclesiastical policy for our State, as for others. It seems to me that the development of the Papacy in the future will involve a gradual loss of political influence and a corresponding increase of moral and spiritual influence.

The King of the Belgians did not send his official reply until January 23, 1918, or six months after the Pope's note had been issued. This was because the Belgian Government was anxious to ascertain exactly what views the Allies would take, how the Central Powers would reply, and in general what effect would be produced by the action of the Vatican. Moreover, Belgium was in rather a difficult situation in this respect, owing to the Belgian Catholics who at that time constituted the decisive element in Parliament. The Belgian reply was courteous in tone, stating that due note had been taken of the Vatican point of view, which was identical with that of the Belgian Government, as far as Belgium was concerned. It referred also to the Pope's communication to the Belgian Government, in which he had stated that when speaking on January 22, 1915, about acts of injustice, he had had Belgium in mind as the victim of those acts. On all other questions the Belgian Government announced that it must first arrive at an agreement with its Allies before expressing its point of view. In conclusion, it emphasized the fact that it was not responsible for the infringement of neutrality, and pointed out in a very unambiguous manner that it would not accept any peace which did not offer it full restitution for the injustice which it had sustained, and an assurance that such acts would not be repeated in the future.

The most interesting diplomatic document, however, connected with the Papal note was President Wilson's reply, which was signed by State Secretary Lansing, and without any undue delay was dispatched on August 27, 1917. It emphasizes the fact that every honourable person must share the desire of the Vatican for an early peace, but that the peace programme formulated in Benedict's note represents a mere return to the pre-war state of affairs. President Wilson took the view that no just and lasting peace could be attained by this process, the aim of the war then being to remove the regime in Germany which was responsible for the whole disaster. Any negotiations with the autocratic German regime on the basis of the Papal note would mean giving it an opportunity of continuing its former policy. The new peace must be based upon the rights of nations and not upon the rights of Governments. The United States, the reply continued, had no special war aim, but merely desired the peace to be founded upon principles of justice and mutual trust. In conclusion, President Wilson again declared that he was unable to place any confidence in the word of the present rulers of Germany, and that any idea of peace negotiations was out of the question until the necessary commitments could be obtained from the nations of the Central Powers.

This reply was a severe blow to the Papal note. Immediately after it was issued we were able to observe the advantages which we were likely to derive from the Pope's action. The hopes of the Habsburg Empire had again collapsed, and the principles of democracy and the self-determination of nations had been emphatically enunciated by the most powerful authority in the Allied camp. At a time when the repeated attempts at a premature peace and the uncertainty as to what would happen in Russia were causing us serious concern, we were greatly encouraged by this circumstance.

82

In spite of this obvious failure, the Vatican did not give up hope of being able to bring about peace negotiations. The attitude of the Berlin Government on the subject of Belgium induced the Vatican to approach it again through Pacelli, with a view to obtaining a clearer expression of opinion. At the same time Benedict sent a personal letter to Emperor Karl, asking him to use his influence with Berlin to bring about a change of attitude as regards Belgium on the lines of the Papal note of August 1st. In the same letter the Pope urged Karl not to refuse discussions with Italy on the subject of the Trentino. Karl replied by letter on October 4th and promised that he would intervene at Berlin on the subject of Belgium, and declared himself ready to discuss the question of ceding a part of the Trentino in return for compensation in colonies. He concluded by saying that Austria-Hungary was willing to evacuate the Balkan countries under definite guarantees of safety. On October 24th the Pope wrote a letter of thanks for this favourable communication, and expressed himself as being gratified at Karl's attitude. This letter, however, reached Vienna at the time of the Caporetta victory, and in the meanwhile Kühlmann had replied to Pacelli on the subject of Belgium in less accommodating terms than those of Michaelis's reply to the Papal note of September 19th. Vienna, having occupied further Italian territory, was no longer disposed to negotiate with defeated Italy on the subject of the Trentino. In a speech delivered at Budapest on October 4, 1917, Czernin threatened that if the Allies did not accept the offers of the Central Powers, as contained in the Papal note and their replies, they would not regard themselves as bound by the proposals in question. The Pope, on the other hand, was well aware that without concessions on the part of Italy, at least in the Trentino question, there was no prospect of any early peace negotiations. The Papal Nuncio at Vienna and Mgr. Pacelli therefore intervened afresh. They applied to the Emperor Karl and the Government at Berlin asking them to assure the Pope that in no case did Vienna intend to retain any of the Italian territory recently occupied. Although Czernin and Karl assented to this, they made it clear that since Vienna had scored a military victory over Italy, no concessions as regards the Trentino could be considered.

This was the final step taken by Benedict in the autumn as a sequel to his peace effort, in which the Vatican counted mainly upon the assistance of Vienna and the German Centre (Erzberger). The Vatican was discouraged by its lack of success in this undertaking, and that is why nothing more was heard from Benedict during the rest of the war.

I will here add a few remarks about the Papal policy during the war, as far as it affected our movement. There can be no doubt that this policy was entirely opposed to our aims and aspirations. As general secretary of the Czechoslovak National Council I was familiar with the political tendencies of the Vatican during the war, and I at once realized the underlying principle of Benedict's peace note. The action of the National Council had to be arranged in accordance with this. We were not strong enough to undertake a struggle against the Vatican, and such a course would have done us harm among our own people, especially the Slovaks, as well as among the Catholics in the Allied countries. I therefore combatted the policy of the Vatican by showing what the Catholic Church meant to the Habsburg Empire, and how the Vatican was serving the political purposes of the Central Powers. In dealing with Benedict's peace note our course of action was the same as that adopted against all attempts at a premature peace, which were in the interests of Vienna and Budapest.

As I have explained elsewhere, it was my purpose to win over Catholic circles, just as all others, to the Czechoslovak cause. At the time when the Papal note was issued I was arranging my second visit to Rome, and in connection with this I made the acquaintance of Mgr. Ceretti, one of the most capable of the Vatican diplomats and subsequently the Papal Nuncio in Paris, to whom I was introduced by P. Quirielle. I had several conversations with him about the war, with special reference to Austria-Hungary and ourselves, and he struck me as being very moderate in his views. For the most part he listened to me with detachment, although in a number of matters he expressed his agreement with my opinions.

At that particular time I was finding a manifest sympathy for our movement among several leading French Catholics. Thus M. Trogand, the director of the Catholic periodical *Corresponant*, was then beginning to show a little favour to us in his paper, and we also received signs of approval from Mgr. Baudrillart, a prominent member of Catholic circles in France, and a man of learning and influence. The opposition to the Papal policy brought the Allied Catholics, especially those in France, closer to us. They regarded the unfavourable attitude of the Vatican to our movement as being equally biassed as it was in their own affairs.

While at Rome during September and October 1917 it was through Loiseau, as on my first visit, that my contact with the Vatican was maintained. On that occasion I was more guarded in my attitude, partly on account of the circumstances connected with the Papal note, partly also because, at a time when there was so much tension in the atmosphere, I did not wish, by my relations with the Vatican, to cause unnecessary offence among Quirinal circles.

(*b*) DIFFICULT SITUATION OF THE ALLIES IN THE AUTUMN OF 1917. FRESH NEGOTIATIONS TO SEPARATE AUSTRIA-HUNGARY FROM GERMANY. GENERAL SMUTS AND COUNT MENSDORFF-POUILLY

83

Czernin's policy, which aimed at taking advantage of every possible opportunity of peace negotiations, seemed, at the end of the summer of 1917, to be making favourable progress on account of the Socialist action at Stockholm, the Papal note, and the course of events in Germany and the Allied States This, however, was only of short duration. In a few months, after the victory at Caporetta and the conclusion of peace with the Bolsheviks, there was a turn of the tide which produced results entirely opposed to the policy of Vienna.

Ever since the outbreak of the Russian revolution Germany

had been in a state of internal dissension. Conflicts between political power and military power became more and more acute, and they led to differences between Berlin and Vienna. Bethmann-Hollweg realized that tactically Vienna was in the right, and that a more moderate policy would have been in the interests of the German Empire, but Hindenburg, Ludendorff, and the heads of the German Admiralty refused to give way. These disputes were complicated by an analogous struggle in Parliament. The whole of German policy was oscillating between two diametrically opposite tendencies. There was a moderate section which desired early peace negotiations, in which Germany would be satisfied to compromise, while the military authorities and the nationalistic politicians of the Right aimed at nothing less than a military victory which would enforce heavy peace terms upon their opponents.

The adherents of the former tendency, the most prominent representative of which was Erzberger with his group, started open Parliamentary warfare at the beginning of July 1917 against the military authorities and also against Bethmann-Hollweg, their objection to him being that he went too far in his concessions to the Chauvinists. In the middle of July 1917 Bethmann-Hollweg fell, and nobody in Germany was sorry for him, as he was equally disliked by the Chauvinists. Vienna alone attempted to save him, fearing that his successor might be even more dependent upon the supreme military command.

This proved to be the case, as the tactics of Michaelis soon showed. On July 19th, for the first time, the Reichstag passed a resolution that Germany desired peace, concluded by an agreement between the two belligerent parties. Michaelis, however, had not the courage, in the face of the military authorities and the reactionary parties, to give the Pope any definite assurance on the subject of Belgium when he was preparing his peace note in June and July. Kühlmann was in the same predicament with regard to the German reply to Benedict's note on September 19, 1917. In this internal struggle Vienna and the Vatican gave all possible assistance to the moderate tendencies, and in fact the whole of Erzberger's action had been carried out in agreement with them. It did not produce any substantial results, even when Michaelis also had to retire and was replaced on November 1, 1917, by Count Hertling, the Bavarian Prime Minister. Hertling also soon succumbed to the influence of the Supreme Command, and this final victory of the German

Chauvinists was rendered decisive by the developments on the battle-fronts and the political events among the Allies.

In October and November 1917 the situation of the Allies was, in every respect, an alarming one. In France the Government of Briand had been replaced on March 14, 1917, by Ribot's Cabinet, in which the Minister of Foreign Affairs was Ribot himself, and the Minister of War was Painlevé. Ribot's Government came into power at a juncture when the military and political situations were daily growing worse. The Russian revolution and its military consequences, the failure of Nivelle's offensive and the resulting war-weariness and defeatist propaganda in France, difficulties in Parliament, the peace overtures of Sixtus of Bourbon, quarrels with the Socialists on the subject of the Stockholm Conference, difficulties in Greek affairs, and disputes with regard to Italian policy—all this tended to weaken France both within and without.

Painlevé's Cabinet, which replaced that of Ribot on September 12, 1917, and in which Ribot continued to act as Foreign Minister with Painlevé as Minister of War, was in an even more difficult position. On the Eastern front there was now a continuous record of German successes. The proceedings at the Stockholm Conference, Benedict's note, and the increasing chaos in Russia were producing an atmosphere of pessimism in France during the autumn of 1917. The Bolshevik revolution and the events which followed it intensified this depression to the utmost.

From the moment when the separate peace between the Central Powers and Russia began to be talked about, there were incessant protests in France against the treachery of the Bolsheviks and Russia in general. What made matters worse was that there were still no visible results from American cooperation at the front, and everything tended to strengthen the movement for concluding the war by negotiation. Caillaux was carrying on propaganda in favour of abandoning the English alliance and arriving at an agreement with Germany for an advantageous peace. The French Parliament was also in a nervous condition on account of disputes with the Socialists. The first crisis of Painlevé's Government occurred on October 28th, and Ribot, as Minister of Foreign Affairs, was replaced by Barthou. Two weeks later the whole Cabinet fell, and was succeeded in the middle of November by Clemenceau's Government.

In Italy the situation was even more precarious. The vacillation of the Government, and particularly of Sonnino, on war aims; the twofold policy towards Germany and Austria respectively; the action of the Pope, which undoubtedly tended to exert a demoralizing effect on Italian public opinion; and, finally, the propaganda carried on by the Socialist neutralists—all this led to a profound crisis in home policy and lack of resolution at the front. The crisis developed towards the end of October 1917 into the fall of Boselli's Government, and to a far more serious complication, namely, the reverse at Caporetta in the last week of October. Nor was Orlando's new Government able to extricate the country from the effects of this disaster for some time to come.

In Russia and on the Eastern front, of course, the conditions were far more critical. The proclamation of the Russian Republic and the arrival of Kerensky's new Government could not counteract the increasing disruption in the army and in affairs as a whole. The chaos which thus ensued culminated in the Kornilov affair and then in the Bolshevik upheaval. At the beginning of December the new Bolshevik Government itself suggested the question of a military armistice to the Central Powers, and the necessary negotiations actually took place.

In England also these events naturally produced a profound impression. The greatest alarm was caused by the events in Russia and the possible consequences which might arise from them as regards the Far East and India.

The knowledge of these developments was naturally a source of encouragement to the German Supreme Command. As early as the summer of 1917 the German military leaders had decided upon a big offensive on the Italian front in order to reassure Czernin, who was urging the necessity to negotiate for peace without annexation or indemnities. Ever since May 1917 the authorities at Berlin had indicated to him that his fears were exaggerated, and the German victory at Caporetta went far to confirm their opinion. Then, too, the elimination of the Eastern front brought the separate peace with Russia, for which Czernin had made such efforts, and for which he had been willing to make such commitments beforehand. Now it was placed at his disposal unconditionally and without any commitments whatever. Hence the military victory of Germany against Italy and Russia, combined with the events in the Allied countries, denoted the political defeat of Vienna and of Czernin, who were compelled to subordinate their own views to those of the

German military leaders. As a matter of fact, Czernin's ideas as to the outcome of the war were not so far wrong, but it would appear that from this time onwards, although he did not avoid occasional peace moves, he gradually changed his former attitude and began to believe that an Allied victory was impossible. In March and April 1918 he was evidently of the opinion that the existence of the Habsburg Empire was no longer at stake. In accordance with this he modified his policy after the signature of the peace of Brest-Litovsk, and perpetrated a series of irreparable blunders which ultimately landed Austria-Hungary in ruin.

Such was the situation in which new secret overtures for a separate peace with Vienna were launched in the middle of December 1917. This time they emanated from the Allies, the initiative being that of Mr. Lloyd George. There is every indication that he undertook this step with the knowledge and approval of Mr. Balfour. I do not know whether the French Government received previous or timely information on this point, but as far as I have been able to ascertain it would appear that the French were not informed of Mr. Lloyd George's undertaking until the negotiations had been concluded. As regards Italy, London evidently hoped, after the Caporetta defeat, that the Italians would not be able to maintain so uncompromising an attitude as with the negotiations of Sixtus of Bourbon. The new negotiations began in the early part of November, but the definite proceedings did not take place until the middle of December. There was a meeting between General Smuts and Count Mensdorff at Geneva on December 17, 1917, but they led to nothing, just as those in December 1916 had done. As a result of this repeated failure it was now felt that all such attempts were useless. Thus, although in themselves they were a source of danger to our cause, their consequences hastened the solution for which we had been struggling, and again confirmed the argument with which we had identified ourselves towards the Allies throughout the war.

84

On December 5th Count Skrzynski, the Legation Counsellor attached to the Austro-Hungarian Legation at Berne, informed Czernin confidentially that Prince Djenal Tussum and Parodi, who was in the confidence of Sir Horace Rumbold, the English Minister, had indicated to him the desire of the British Government for its representative to meet the Austro-Hungarian delegate for exchanging views on peace questions affecting only those two countries. On November 11th Czernin expressed his agreement with this on principle, but with certain reservations, which showed that his opinion of the general situation had changed since the previous April. He was willing to accept any communication which the British Government might make to him, and Count Mensdorff-Pouilly could at any time proceed to Switzerland for this purpose. On December 1, 1917, Sir Horace Rumbold sent Parodi a letter, in which he repeated the former communication, and asked for the date when the delegate from Vienna would arrive. After long negotiations, during which the Austrians expressed their desire that the British Government should send somebody of the same standing as Count Mensdorff, who was the oldest and most important Austro-Hungarian diplomat, it was agreed that the British delegate was to be General Smuts, and that the meeting was to take place on December 18th at Geneva in the villa of the Austro-Hungarian Consul Montlong. General Smuts arrived at the stipulated time and he was accompanied by Philip Kerr, Lloyd George's secretary.

In his conversations, General Smuts showed a very strong anti-German attitude, but it would appear that he was far more indulgent towards the Habsburg Empire. His projected scheme with regard to Austria-Hungary involved something similar to the British Empire with the self-governing dominions, and at the conclusion of his interview with Mensdorff he repudiated the idea of dismemberment of Austria-Hungary.

Mensdorff's final suggestion was that General Smuts should meet Czernin himself, as the latter would best be able to decide whether Austria-Hungary could influence the Germans against the programme of German militarism. In accordance with the instructions which Czernin had given him, he endeavoured to prepare a way for direct contact between German and British diplomacy. When, however, General Smuts emphatically declined to have any dealings with the Germans, he did not insist, but again, acting on Czernin's instructions, intimated that it was useless to try and bring about a separate peace without Berlin.

85

This was Czernin's last peace overture. He undertook it in the conviction that every opportunity should be taken to end the war speedily and to save the monarchy. From the very beginning of his term of office as Foreign Minister at the end of 1916, Czernin was convinced that the war should be ended as speedily as possible, evidently regarding this as the only way of saving Austria-Hungary. It seems to me that of the Austro-Hungarian politicians during the war Czernin proved to be, relatively speaking, the best. It cannot be denied that he showed capacity as a politician and negotiator, with quite a good knowledge of the problems with which he was dealing. He knew that defeat would mean the end of Austria-Hungary, whose excessive dependence upon Germany he deplored. He rightly judged that this would prove one of the main difficulties to Austria-Hungary, both as regards Germany and also the Allies. In his capacity as Minister at Bucharest he realized in good time that Rumania would enter the war, and his reports on these matters were accurate, although the authorities at Vienna and Budapest attached no importance to them. He was quick to realize that the only possibility of successful negotiation with the Allies was to be moderate in his demands, and his policy was carried out in accordance with this idea. In all disputes with Germany he opposed the German Supreme Command, and in this, too, he was right. I do not think that he could have saved the Habsburg Empire, even if Vienna had paid more heed to him, but he would have been a more dangerous opponent to us. In my opinion, once the war had started, it was not humanly possible to save Austria-Hungary at all.

86

Though all attempts at a premature peace ended in failure, there was always the possibility that they might succeed, and this, of course, had to be reckoned with. Neverthelessi, I was a firm believer in our final victory. Considerations derved from the philosophy of history led me to feel sure that the peace moves in 1917 and the spring of 1918 would fail of their purpose. I regarded victory in our national struggle as being extremely probable because the military, political, and moral forces which had been let loose by a war between five European Great Powers, by the entry of America into the war, and by the outbreak of the Russian revolution had acquired such an impetus that the intervention of no personal will, however strong, could avert the destructive effects which they would ultimately have upon the Habsburg Empire. The opposition of the greater part of the nations within her borders to her rule was an elemental one, and her existence was increasingly threatened as the ideas associated with democracy and racial self-determination became more and more the driving forces of the contest. Then, too, I considered that this war, the greatest in history, must inevitably produce some vast and decisive results, or, if untenable compromises were made, their outcome would be internal upheavals after the war was over. For these reasons I felt convinced that Austria-Hungary could not survive, and that our cause would consequently be victorious.

In all the anxiety which I felt during these efforts to bring about a separate peace, when we were struggling against the intrigues of the Austrophiles, against the endeavours of reactionaries, against alarmists and opportunists, or against the scruples of persons who were conscientious enough, but who had an imperfect conception of the points at issue, the ideas which I have outlined above formed a great encouragement and hope to me, and they were confirmed by my daily experience during the war, as well as by the general course of the war and its results. It was my belief that the truth would prevail, but I did not expect it to prevail unaided. Accordingly, the struggle against all arguments in favour of a separate peace formed the basis of our work in 1917. I was aware that we could not reckon upon any sentimentality towards the oppressed nations on the part of Allied politicians if there was any serious question of peace with Vienna. In so terrible a war there was far too great a tendency to protect immediate interests, whether real or only apparent, and regardless of public declarations or promises. As I have said, I do not reproach the Allied politicians for this. The question was not merely a moral one. It involved a proper understanding of what any particular policy would lead to, as far as the Allied States were concerned, and specially an understanding of our argument that, in the end, it would be better for the Allies and Europe in general if the Habsburg Empire were to disappear.

Any compromise with Vienna in the summer of 1917 would have been an unmitigated disaster to us. By that time we had a political and military movement organized on a large scale, and as its leaders we had committed hundreds of thousands of our people and their families to a life-and-death struggle.

XIII

NEW GUARANTEES OF OUR VICTORY. ESTABLISH-MENT OF OUR MILITARY UNITS IN FRANCE AND ITALY

(a) CLEMENCEAU'S GOVERNMENT AND THE POLICY OF FRANCE AT THE BEGINNING OF 1918

87

ON November 15, 1917, Clemenceau's Cabinet came into power in France. It marked the end of hesitation, nervousness, and a lack of concerted plan in France and among the Allies generally. Clemenceau came into power with a programme, the main trend of which could be expressed as follows: "No further pacifist campaigns, and no intrigues to bring about an undecisive peace. Away with treachery, away with semi-treachery. We are waging war and nothing but war. What we want is a decisive victory."

This opens the last phase of the war, which coincides with the final establishment of our army in France, the Bolshevik revolution in Russia, and thus also a new turn to the whole of our military movement there. This, too, was the period which brought the final decision on our military movement in Italy.

As Prime Minister and Minister of War, Clemenceau immediately initiated a vigorous policy both in home and external affairs, and he remained faithful to this policy until the end.

Clemenceau deserves a large share of credit for the result of the war. He has been reproached with acting in an impulsive and ruthless manner towards men and events, but he is, and will remain, one of the great figures in the war. Behind an apparently rough exterior was hidden a refined and educated personality with a broad outlook and an ample store of experience. He knew that one of the great factors which often decides the course of action adopted by politicians is their lack of courage. Clemenceau never lacked courage or resolution, and that is why, although he made mistakes just as others did, he contributed so largely to victory.

He first of all brought about order in home affairs. He eliminated the direct and indirect causes of defeatism, and he concentrated around him a great majority of the Parliament whom he inspired with fresh confidence. As Minister of War he devoted himself chiefly to the preparation of victory, leaving the diplomatic side of affairs to S. Pichon, his Foreign Minister, although he himself decided, either partly or completely, about matters of high policy.

Under his regime the view which superseded all others was that the interests of all the Allies coincided; that there must be a united military and diplomatic front; that in order to solve the political war problems satisfactorily the main requirement was to end the war by a military victory in common. Towards the end of March, at the very moment when the Germans were taking the first steps for their last great offensive on the Western front, General Foch was appointed supreme Allied Commander. Clemenceau realized the necessity of sending the Italians reinforcements after the reverse at Caporetta, and in the same way he understood how essential it was for the Allies to put forth their utmost resources for the attainment of victory. He therefore supported the formation of a Polish Army and concluded negotiations with us for the establishment of a Czechoslovak Army. At a later date he saw the significance of our movement in Siberia, and he did everything in his power to enable our troops to reach France.

The negotiations between General Smuts and Count Mensdorff-Pouilly began before Clemenceau took office, and they were completed a month after he made his first proclamation in Parliament on the subject of undecisive peace and the alternative which he favoured. It may therefore be safely assumed that he was aware of these events. When Lloyd George made his speech on January 5, 1918, Clemenceau sent him a telegram of congratulation to which I have already referred. I have also given my reason for supposing that this telegram had no bearing upon the Austro-Hungarian question in a sense unfavourable to us.

By this time the French Government was conscious of its commitments to us. When Clemenceau came into power, the text of the decree authorizing the formation of our army, as well as the statutes of the army, had practically been completed by agreement with the preceding Government of Painlevé. In Russia the organization of the army was making satisfactory progress, while in Italy we were preparing the final decisive measures concerning our army there. In the United States we had started a recruiting movement for France, and about 2,000 of our troops were already waiting in barracks at Cognac for the final decision on our army in France. The development of affairs in Russia during December and January aroused the hope that about 50,000 of our troops would be able to proceed to France.

Such was the general view which was taken of our movement by official circles and the Ministry of War. It subsequently turned out that on a number of points the estimates made by them and us were too optimistic, but it meant a great deal to Clemenceau as Minister of War, who realized the full significance of Caporetta, who could see the military consequences of the collapse of the Eastern front, who in the meanwhile had only a few American regiments at his disposal in France, and who understood that France was at that very moment passing through the most critical juncture of the war in which every contribution to victory, however small, deserved to be appreciated.

The events during the first months of 1918 crystallized Clemenceau's policy. Czernin's speech on December 4, 1917, at Budapest, in which he made it plain that Vienna would act with Berlin until the end of the war; the Italian reverse, the consequences of which demanded a final military victory upon that front also; the armistice in the East, which merged into peace negotiations, and concluded on March 3, 1918, with the peace of Brest-Litovsk; and the peace concluded on March 7th at Buftei with Rumania, now completely humiliated and obliged to cede considerable areas to Austria-Hungary and Bulgaria ; finally, the preparation of a great offensive in the West and the danger of an approaching attack on Paris—all this, far from inducing despondency in a man of Clemenceau's temperament, on the contrary made him exert every effort to cope with all these problems in the only possible way, by achieving a final and decisive military victory.

In my opinion, the great political and military victories of the Central Powers at the end of 1917 and the beginning of 1918; their ruthless and, from a political and psychological point of view, faulty tactics, which culminated in the humiliation of Rumania and the Balkans; the assumption of control over Poland, the new Balkan States, and Finland; the separa-

tion of the Ukraine from Russia and its evident subordination
to Germany and Austria-Hungary; and, finally—as it appeared
in Western Europe—in the systematic exertion of political
influence upon the Bolshevik Government in Russia, formed
the greatest and indeed the decisive factor in convincing the
Allies that there must now be no wavering whatever, that all
reservations and illusions must be abandoned, and there must
be a concerted effort for victory on the military fronts. We
saw how the Eastern events and the peace negotiations with
Russia were reflected in the speeches of Lloyd George, Wilson,
and Pichon, in which they emphasized their own war aims, and
made it quite clear that the Allies would not recognize the
results which threatened to emerge from the negotiations at
Brest-Litovsk.

In April and May 1918 the two Anglo-Saxon powers definitely
associated themselves with Clemenceau's policy. The decisive
factor in bringing about this change consisted of all these
events; but our own political and military movement, as we
shall soon see, helped to a large extent in bringing about this
decision.

(b) The Decree for the Establishment of our Army in France

88

Towards the end of the first half of October I returned
from Rome to Paris, and then proceeded to London on
October 20th, as I had received an urgent summons from
those in charge of our interests there. After Masaryk's departure
to Russia our movement in England centred in a Press Bureau,
directed as a branch of the National Council by Vladimir
Nosek, in accordance with my instructions from Paris. Olga
Masaryk acted as a direct link between Professor Masaryk
and our London representatives, and the London colony,
under the leadership of Sýkora, Kopecký, and Pochobradský,
helped us in our work.

The progress made by our movement in France, Italy, and
Russia, taken into conjunction with the state of affairs in
England, demanded a more active procedure on the part of
the National Council in London. Messages from Wickham
Steed and Dr. Seton Watson had repeatedly urged me to take
steps in this direction. My negotiations for an army in France

and Italy, the direct invitations on the part of Sir Rennell Rodd and Sir Samuel Hoare, indicated to me the possibility of entering into immediate touch with Government circles, and of informing them what had been done on our behalf in France and Italy. At this time I was in touch with the British Embassy in Paris, and in particular I was on good terms with Lord Derby, the British Ambassador there.

Although the negotiations in London were brief, they denoted further progress in the development of our work in England; they inaugurated official relations between the British Government and the National Council. Hitherto the authorities in London had dealt with Masaryk mainly as a political personality. Their relations with our fellow-countrymen in England had been of an official character, but they were confined to administrative affairs, and involved the granting of preferential treatment in certain respects, without any kind of commitments on their part.

The present negotiations accordingly formed the preliminaries to the development of a concrete agreement at a later date. I spent several days in London, and met a number of officials at the Foreign Office. Sir Samuel Hoare, who had also come to London, introduced me to Lord Robert Cecil. This was my first meeting with this prominent English statesman, who at that time was Blockade Minister and who, a few months later, rendered us such great services by making a fundamental decision on the subject of our movement. I had two further interviews with him, and gave him the memoranda which I had prepared concerning the progress of our cause. I also explained to him in detail our opinion on Austro-Hungarian and other Central European matters. Even before this he had been favourably disposed towards us. He was personally acquainted with Masaryk, whom he esteemed highly. In the meanwhile I made no concrete demand, wishing merely to gain confidence for my subsequent action. From my talks with Sir Samuel Hoare and Lord Robert Cecil I gained the impression that they had confidence in me and also in our movement.

I returned to Paris on October 28, 1917, and immediately began to discuss our military affairs with Lieut.-Colonel Cros and Major Dresch. In addition to current military questions, largely concerning the organization of the detachment formed from the prisoners of war, who had arrived from Rumania in the summer of 1917, I at once raised the question of the decree which had been prepared. The Poles had in the interim made considerable progress with the organization of their army. They had volunteers from America and elsewhere, as well as a certain number of prisoners of war from among the German troops. They had thus been able to publish their decree on the establishment of their army as early as May 28, 1917.

Not wishing to postpone the matter further, I urged that there should be an agreement as to the wording of the decree. Lieut.-Colonel Cros placed before me a wording analogous to that of the Polish decree. I asked for a short time to think matters over, as I was anxious to secure certain changes, which I began to discuss after having conferred with the National Council. The Ministry of War admitted that the conditions in our case were different from those of the Poles, and so after a few days the wording of the decree was agreed upon. Meanwhile Štefánik informed me that he was returning to Paris, and I therefore decided to postpone the publication of the decree which the Ministry of War itself now began to urge. I preferred, however, to wait until Štefánik had returned (he actually arrived on November 18, 1917), because I wanted him, as a soldier, to give his opinion of everything which the National Council had done as regards military affairs during his absence.

Štefánik approved of the text which had been agreed upon, but he took exception to one important detail. The first article of the decree declared that the French Government was constituting the Czechoslovak Army. I had accepted this formulation because the Poles had also accepted it, and then, too, after my return from Italy, I shrank from the prospect of attempting to struggle for fresh concessions after all the negotiations on the army statute, in which the French Government had really shown considerable indulgence towards me personally. Štefánik was of the opinion that it would nevertheless be possible to secure an alteration in the decree by which the constituting of the army would be attributed to the National Council and the Czechoslovak nation itself. The political significance of this formulation is obvious at the first glance, and Štefánik rightly attached great importance to it.

Štefánik's negotiations on behalf of this new formulation

lasted until nearly the middle of December. At the beginning of December the military authorities in the Ministry informed me that, in view of the precedent with the Poles, the Government would not accept the formulation we asked for, but in the end Štefánik succeeded in obtaining at least a compromise. The French Government withdrew the formulation attributing the constitution of the army to them, but would not comply with the proposal to attribute the constitution to the National Council. All reference to the constitution of the army was therefore omitted from the first article of the decree, which now assumed the following neutral aspect : "The Czechoslovaks, organized in an independent army, and acknowledging the authority of the Supreme French Command in military affairs. . . ."

And so, on December 16, 1917, it was possible to publish two important documents relating to the establishment of the Czechoslovak Army, and negotiated by the National Council. The first one was a report of the Government to the President of the Republic, stating the political and military reasons why France had decided to organize a Czechoslovak Army. At my request, emphasis was laid in this report upon the participation of our volunteers in the Foreign Legion, and it was pointed out that other States had already permitted the dispatch of Czechoslovak troops to France for military purposes.

The text of the actual decree comprised the main principles already contained in the previous army statutes which had been arranged. It first of all announces the full political recognition of the National Council and the autonomy of the army. There were a number of details contained in the statutes, but for fairly obvious reasons they were not yet formulated in the decree. The decree was to be published immediately, the statutes at a later date. The decree relating to the Polish Army had been drawn up in its first form as early as the summer of 1917, when events were not so far developed as in December of the same year. To declare in the solemn form, which distinguished the decree drafted in the summer of 1917, everything that was contained in the prepared army statutes, would have been a political manifesto which the situation at that time hardly justified. Moreover, by its very character, the decree was meant to be only concise and general in tone. And then, too, the Poles, who were somewhat more advanced in their organization of an army, had accepted a similar wording some considerable time previously. It was out of the question then to demand more for us than the Poles had been granted, both out of consideration for them and for the French themselves.

The wording of the decree was as follows:

Art. 1. The Czechoslovaks, organized in an independent army, and acknowledging the authority of the supreme French command in military affairs, will fight under their own flag against the Central Powers.

Art. 2. In a political respect the management of this national army devolves upon the National Council of the Czech and Slovak territories, with headquarters in Paris.

Art. 3. The equipment of the Czechoslovak Army, as well as its further activity, is ensured by the French Government.

Art. 4. As regards its organization, control, administration, and legal jurisdiction, the same regulations will apply to the Czechoslovak Army as are current in the French Army.

Art. 5. The independent Czechoslovak Army will be recruited from:
  (i) Czechoslovaks now serving in the French Army.
  (ii) Czechoslovaks serving elsewhere, in as far as they are granted permission to be transferred to the Czechoslovak Army, and also volunteers who enter this army for the period of the war.

Art. 6. This decree will be carried out in accordance with ministerial instructions, which are to be issued later.

Art. 7. The Prime Minister, the Minister of War, and the Minister of Foreign Affairs, are each requested to carry this decree into effect, as far as it applies to himself, and it will be published in the official gazette of the French Republic and printed in the bulletin of laws.

Given at Paris, December 16th, 1917.

R. POINCARÉ,
President of the Republic.
G. CLEMENCEAU,
Prime Minister and Minister of War.
S. PICHON,
Minister of Foreign Affairs.

For this reason my efforts were more and more directed towards bringing about at an early date the signature of the statutes by the French Government and the National Council, as well as their publication. New circumstances made it desirable that a few minor additions should be introduced in them (for example, on the subject of the uniform, as demanded by Štefánik), so that, as I have already stated, they were not actually published until February 7, 1918.

These two documents, the decree and the statutes, are

unquestionably of great political significance. After Briand's promise to Masaryk, after the French action in connection with the note to President Wilson, after the signature of the agreement on June 13, 1917, by Albert Thomas and Masaryk, relating to the transfer of our troops to France, these two further commitments formed the successful culmination of our political and military work in France at a critical and decisive juncture.(37) And what lent it a peculiar significance was that it was signed by such eminent men as Poincaré and Clemenceau.

In a juridical and political respect, our French army was the first of our independent national armies. Our troops in Russia, who at that time were more important from a military point of view, still formed a constituent part of the Russian Army, a state of affairs which continued until February 3, 1918, when Masaryk declared them to be a section of our independent national army in France. The army in Italy was not established in its definite form until the agreement between Štefánik and the Italian Government on June 21, 1918. In constructing our French army, Štefánik and myself continually bore in mind the need for impressing upon the Allies that the whole of this military movement was a single one, and that our three armies were to be regarded as the constituent parts of one and the same military unit. That is why the gradual unification of the army in France and Russia was such an important process, and why it was equally important that Štefánik, when organizing the army in Italy, should secure from the Italian Government, as an expression of this uniformity, if only in a theoretical declaration, the recognition of General Janin as Commander-in-Chief of all our troops, including the Italian section, on condition, however, that General Janin would not in any way interfere with our military movement in Italy.(38)

This systematic military work in France coincided with a great international crisis, in which the fate of the Habsburg Empire was at stake. I was well aware of this, and that is why, during this period, the National Council exerted every effort to present our movement as a serious, well-developed, and powerful factor. The signature of the statutes by Clemenceau on behalf of the French Government, and by myself on behalf of the National Council was, to my mind, not merely a signature to military instructions, but also a binding diplomatic document of great political importance. I also hoped that before long more such documents would come into existence in France. Moreover, according to the reports from Rome, our success with the army in France had produced a marked impression in Italy, which was tending to bring about the recognition of our military efforts by the authorities in Rome.

(c) Difficulties of our Military Organization

89

Having secured the army decree and statutes, we immediately set to work on our military organization. This, however, leads me to say a few words about the progressive development of our army in France from the various categories of troops which successively joined it.

The first ingredient of our French army consisted of a group of prisoners of war, whom Štefánik had obtained from Rumania. They reached France in the middle of June 1917, and met with a hearty welcome there. They had an encouraging effect upon us in the National Council, and strengthened our hopes that more troops would soon arrive from Russia. The French military authorities, however, were not prepared for them and sent them to the department of Lande, situated south of Bordeaux, a sandy and unpleasant region. There they were allotted to a camp containing black troops and also Bolshevized Russian soldiers.

This produced a very distasteful impression upon our first troops in France. Apart from this, their juridical situation was not clear. They had ceased to be prisoners, but they were not yet free soldiers, for neither we nor the French could deal with the various legal and other problems involved before the question of the army decree and statutes had been officially settled. This uncertainty and the disappointment which it involved with regard to the position of the Czech soldier in the Czech Army—above all, in France—proved still more demoralizing to them.

There was a slight improvement in the situation when, as a result of the French recruiting mission in Russia, Captain Husák's contingent, numbering about 1,100 men, reached France by way of Archangelsk. These troops arrived at Havre on November 12th, where they were well received by the

French authorities, and were joyfully welcomed by myself and Dr. Sychrava on behalf of the National Council. In accordance with an agreement which we had made, the Ministry of War had prepared accommodation for our future forces at Cognac, in the environs of Bordeaux. Later on, arrangements were made for additional troops at Jarnac and Joinville, close by. The two detachments comprised sufficient troops to enable us to organize the first regiment, to proceed with the issue of the decree and the statutes, and to adjust their legal and material status. Immediately after my return from Havre I proceeded to Cognac to inspect the accommodation provided for Husák's detachment, and to ascertain by my own observation and by discussing matters with Husák what steps would have to be taken in the Ministry of War to secure effective organization.

From Cognac, where several days were spent with Husák, full of hope that the army would be rapidly established, I returned to Paris, where I met Štefánik, who had just returned from America (November 16th). Together we worked at the solution of the more urgent military questions. The first thing we did was to arrange for the Rumanian contingent to be transferred from their demoralizing surroundings to Cognac. Shortly afterwards a number of Czech officers from the Serbian Army arrived at Cognac, but they at once confronted us with a serious problem, since the arrival of Husák's detachment had at once brought us a surplus of officers, of which there had hitherto been a shortage. Here I may add that the problem of officers was one of our outstanding difficulties throughout the war. It was the cause of disagreements and ill-feeling, especially at the outset, even in France.

It was not long before there were fresh disappointments at Cognac. The army statute had been agreed upon as early as August, but we had aranged with the Ministry of War not to publish the decree until there was a considerable body of our troops in France. At the very moment when Husák's detachment arrived and the question was to be settled, the negotiations on the subject of the decree were delayed because Štefánik, as I have already mentioned, wanted to have the wording changed. Apart from this, the bureaucratic mechanism of the Ministry did not move with any rapidity even in dealing with matters relating to the military administration at Cognac, which were quite independent of any decree.

As a result of this, 2,000 of our volunteers at Cognac continued to remain in an ambiguous juridical situation, being neither soldiers nor prisoners of war. There was no proper administration or organization, there were difficulties with the living arrangements, the food, the command, and the French authorities. The majority of the troops who had arrived from Russia were already in regular military formation (many of them had taken part in the engagement at Zborov), and signs of disappointment soon began to make themselves evident among them. Six weeks spent in this uncertainty filled many with indignation, and demoralized others. Not having been fully acquainted with the status of our soldiers in France, they had come there full of enthusiasm, expecting to join an independent army completely established. It was natural that they soon began to lay the blame on the National Council and upon myself in particular. I at once realized this, and attempted to pacify them as far as I could, holding out hope to them that the army decree would soon be issued, that the conditions would be changed before long, that we had already achieved successes, and so on. But it took a long time before I could allay the agitation at Cognac.

The day upon which the decree was issued was a red-letter day both in Paris and Cognac. The soldiers became soldiers both legally and officially, they became Czechoslovak soldiers, and with enthusiasm they read the decree and the newspaper articles on the new army which had arrived to help France and the Allies. An eager start was made with the detailed organization and the internal administration of the army, as well as with preliminary arrangements for military training. Our troops threw themselves heart and soul into the work. It became necessary for them to make themselves acquainted with the organization and training in accordance with the terms of the army statutes. I therefore arranged with the Ministry for the appointment of a regimental commander, Colonel Philippe, and also for a number of French officers to be allotted to the regiment. On January 10, 1918, I accompanied them to Cognac in order to introduce the troops to their commanders and instructors, and to hear any applications or complaints they might wish to make. The National Council in Paris would then have to take any necessary steps with the Government, to whom it would transmit whatever details were in the interests of our troops.

On reaching Cognac I found that our troops, especially the officers, were in a despondent mood and showed signs of resentment against the National Council. Several weeks of uncertainty had produced a demoralizing effect; the unsettled financial conditions, the surplus of officers, and certain unfair arrangements with regard to the promotion or appointment of those who had already been officers; the disappointment prevailing in a corps of about 120 officers and cadets who had come from Russia on the understanding that they would serve in France as privates, and would wait until they obtained their nominations—all this was now intensified by a fresh disappointment. First of all, the French Ministry of War had decided that the command was to be restricted to French officers, the Czechs being allowed only to act as their assistants, and to learn their duties gradually. Our newly arrived officers from Serbia added to the number of those who were dissatisfied, or of those against whom a grievance was harboured by the officers not yet appointed, and then, to make matters worse, our officers had discovered that the process of appointment and the general procedure in France were far more difficult and far stricter than in Russia, and that they would not therefore be in charge of their companies, battalions, or regiments for very long.

The French Ministry of War had thus refused to grant our officers the same standing in the army as they had had in Russia, on the grounds that the fighting on the Eastern front was different from that in France, and that our officers were not qualified to prepare troops for the front. They were therefore to start from the beginning again under the leadership of French officers and then, in the course of time, they could be made independent. The feeling which this aroused among our officers was such that it was ready to break out at any moment. Such was the situation which I found on my arrival at Cognac, and it showed me what difficulties we were likely to encounter in organizing our army.

Owing to its political status the National Council was compelled to accept the ruling of the Ministry of War. In the first place, I had admitted that it was a reasonable one as far as the chief points were concerned, and besides this we had no particular interest in having our troops sent to the front at an early date. From our point of view it was more important to wait until our forces were sufficiently numerous to enable us to derive political capital from their military functions. But for our officers this decision of the Ministry was a severe blow. Their conclusion was that in actual fact we had no independent army in France, and this provided the malcontents with a plausible reason for starting agitation against the National Council, and arousing mistrust of its political leadership. A number of officers regarded the proposed arrangement as a personal humiliation to them in the eyes of the troops whom they had hitherto been commanding.

It can be well imagined that I had a difficult time at Cognac during my negotiations with Husák and all the rest. It is only fair to add that Husák himself, although he did not approve of what was being done by the Ministry, realized how matters were, and helped me to pacify the others. In order to achieve this it became necessary to use much personal influence, and also to give a long account of our actual situation in France. I spent three days at Cognac for this purpose, and our officers then resigned themselves to the situation. Nevertheless, they continued to be dissatisfied with Paris for a long time to come. The troops objected that we were arbitrarily carrying out the plans of the French Government with regard to them, irrespective of their own wishes. I knew that this was the case, but I would not give way. The French military authorities at first regarded with suspicion everything which emanated from Bolshevik Russia. They felt misgivings because of the brotherly spirit among our troops, and there were a number of usages which they regarded as the germs of military Soviets. On a number of occasions they told me their opinions of these matters. The Russian Army, especially since the revolution, had been regarded by them with considerable reserve, and this attitude was intensified in the case of our volunteers who had originally been organized in that army. They expressed an altogether non-committal opinion of their technical knowledge. The fact was that they had practically no acquaintance with us, and were cautiously observing how the conditions in our army would develop.

Our troops had arrived from Russia at the time of the Bolshevik revolution, and during the first weeks of their stay in Cognac even the population displayed an exasperating mistrust of them. This, however, did not last long.

This juncture was a decisive one for me. The time was now approaching when decisions of far-reaching political scope

would have to be made, and the conduct and development of
our army formed one of the factors which would influence the
measures taken by the Government, either for us or against us.
I realized that this was going to be an important test, not
only of the ability of our officers but of that of our whole
nation. I had already witnessed at close quarters how the
French military circles had ruthlessly disparaged the Polish
Army on account of various disorders and disputes whilst in
the course of formation, and I therefore determined at all
costs to prevent similar occurrences amongst us, and to show
that we were more disciplined, better prepared, and more
advanced generally. Realizing thus how fateful the consequences would be to us if at this early stage we were to make
the slightest blunder, I was uncompromising towards the
troops. I insisted that they should unconditionally submit to
all instructions from Paris, and in particular I prohibited them
from engaging in politics, for that was a subject about which
the Ministry of War was most touchy. And so for several
months there was continual tension between Cognac and
the National Council in Paris. I deliberately overlooked the
unpopularity among the troops which I had incurred at the
outset. My hope was that after a certain time they would
realize that I was in the right, and all the reasonable elements
soon did so. I must admit that I often subjected their patience
to a severe test, and this only makes their merits all the more
praiseworthy. I now affirm that our officers and men from
France reached the highest standard of all our troops, and
it was not long before the Ministry of War itself began to
confirm me in this view. Within three months our troops had
won the approval of the French Government, but the difficulties and the nerve-racking disputes which arose in connection with this military enterprise, taken in conjunction
with the increasing pressure of our work during the spring of
1918, caused me much weariness and distress.

90

These troubles of the National Council were increased by
the difficult conditions prevailing in our colony at Paris. The
colony had split up into various groups, one of which aroused
serious and indeed well-founded suspicions that it contained
Austrian spies. Being possessed of ample means, this group

was able to assist our volunteers in the French Foreign Legion, and incited a number of them against the National Council and against me personally by alleging that we did not desire the formation of an army, and that we were not disposed to admit volunteers from the Foreign Legion into it.

The question of these volunteers was one of the most painful problems which I had to deal with at that time. The reputation of the Foreign Legion is well known. The discipline in it was severe, and it contained representatives of every European nation. Owing to the conditions under which it was recruited, it included numbers of men whose moral characters were dubious. Life in these surroundings was a terrible ordeal to those of our troops who entered the Legion out of sheer enthusiasm, and were now spending their fourth year in it. They found scarcely any congenial spirits among the men serving with them, with the exception of a few of the French commanding officers. Moreover, owing to the enormous losses sustained by the French, the Ministry of War naturally tended to assign the most exposed positions to the Foreign Legion, which under these circumstances was destined to be wiped out.

The number of Czech troops in the Legion at this time was about 300, and it was only by means of the utmost self-restraint that they had managed to hold out so long there. They accordingly welcomed the establishment of a Czechoslovak Army as a release from what was nothing short of a hell upon earth, but their applications for discharge from the Foreign Legion encountered serious obstacles. The supreme French command had hitherto systematically opposed a transfer of any considerable number of troops from the Foreign Legion, fearing that if this were granted to one nation, the same request would be made by all the others, and this would have meant the complete disappearance of the Legion. My efforts to secure the transfer of our troops to our army naturally met with opposition for months at a time, and this difficulty was overcome only when we were in a position to point to the existence of our complete regiments, in which it was possible to make better military use of our experienced legionaries from the French front.

I here recall one of the saddest and most touching episodes of my life during the war. One morning, in the spring of 1918, at the time when this seditious agitation in the colony against me among the volunteers from the Foreign Legion had reached its height, I was visited by about eight of our volunteers, who were then serving their fourth year in the Foreign Legion. Their attitude was desperate and threatening. On the previous day they had been informed that within three days they would be sent to the trenches somewhere near Verdun, and they were afraid that this meant taking part in an attack which involved almost certain death. With mingled entreaties and menaces they called upon me to do everything in my power which would lead to their being transferred to our army. When they arrived, they were under the impression that I was opposed to this course. One of them, in his excitement, produced a hand-grenade, which he threatened to throw at my feet. Another bitterly reproached me for the treachery of which I had been guilty, and declared that they would refuse to obey orders. This agitated interview, which lasted for three hours, more than once assumed a dramatic character, but in the end they were entirely assuaged. I gave them an account of everything that I had done on behalf of the cause, and explained why success had not yet attended my efforts. I disposed of their mistaken conjectures, and made them understand that it was their duty to hold out, since by so doing they would render a great service to our cause. Within three days they went to the trenches in accordance with orders, but only one of them ever returned. He came to me a few days later in the Rue Bonaparte with a revolver and a bayonet, with which he wanted to kill me. He was at once taken away to a military mental hospital. He had escaped death at the front only a short while before the attack, by behaving in such a deranged manner that he was regarded as being of unsound mind.

Finally, however, we succeeded in getting our volunteers transferred from the Foreign Legion to our independent army, by which process the number of our troops was increased and the greater part of our men were saved from the Legion. It cost me much work, and aroused a great deal of resentment against me.

The number of volunteer troops in our army was increased also by a further step on the part of our French colony. When the army statutes had been signed, Dr. Sychrava undertook the somewhat difficult task of arriving at an agreement with all our colonies in France by which they would submit completely to the authority of the National Council, acknowledge its sovereignty as a national Government, and agree to the introduction of compulsory military service. With the help of certain members of the colony, notably the well-known artist, F. Kupka, this scheme had successfully matured by March 1918. The French authorities were greatly impressed by the manner in which the colonies submitted to the orders of the National Council, and also by the smooth working of the recruiting arrangements. Much credit is due to our fellow-countrymen in France who, with enthusiasm and a full consciousness of their national duties, did excellent work.

A further component part of our army in France consisted of volunteers from America, amongst whom there was a considerable percentage of Slovaks. The total number of these men was about 2,000. In view of the difficulties with which we had to contend in forming the various regiments, and also of our urgent need to place at least one division in the field in France, we greatly appreciated the services of these arrivals from America.

Finally, Italy too helped by sending 500 of our Italian troops to complete our French division, and received in return a few dozen of our trained officers from France.

From the above account it will be seen what great difficulties we had to contend with when collecting and organizing our army in France. In spite of the fact that our Russian Army never reached France in its entirety, we managed in the end to obtain four regiments, comprising about 10,000 men. By their presence on the Western front they enabled us to secure those diplomatic successes which the National Council in the summer of 1918 achieved for the nation.

(d) The National Council and the General Staff of our Army. General Janin

91

To the above account of the development of our army in France will now be appended a few remarks on its internal organization as it progressed under the management of the National Council after the signature of the army decree and statutes.

In January 1918 special premises in the Rue Bonaparte were allotted to our military authorities, the General Staff of our army being the first of these. Through Štefánik's action our first general was Maurice Janin, who had been the head of the French military mission in Russia, had rendered Štefánik much assistance during his first visit there, and altogether had done much for our cause in Russia at the beginning of 1918. Štefánik persuaded him to devote himself to the organization of our army in France, particularly drawing his attention to the heavy task which would await him before our troops reached France from Russia. Janin complied with this request and the Ministry gave its consent. From that time onwards all the internal organization of the army passed under his control, and his management of it, to which he devoted his full attention, was altogether successful. He himself was not satisfied with this activity, as he would have preferred a broader sphere of work. In the summer of 1918 he left with Štefánik for Siberia as the supreme commander of our whole army.

The personality of General Janin was of great importance to our movement. The General Staff was composed first of French officers exclusively, but later it comprised Czechs as well. Our special military delegate acted on it as a representative of the National Council. This officer, in his capacity as a military expert, was at the same time assigned to me as secretary of the National Council, and thus formed a link between us and the General Staff. These functions were first carried out by Colonel Chalupa and subsequently by Colonel Fierlinger. It was the duty of this officer to vindicate the Czech character of our army with the General Staff, to see that the terms of the statutes were strictly fulfilled, to satisfy himself that the army was sufficiently autonomous, and to report to the National Council on the general conditions prevailing in it. These duties were mainly of a technical description, as I myself was in daily touch with General Janin and the members of the staff, and I personally discussed with them all questions involving matters of principle.

Our two representatives, whose names I have mentioned, acquitted themselves most satisfactorily. Their relation to the National Council was that of a high official of the Ministry to a Minister. Altogether, at this time, the National Council, by its method of work and its contact with the French authorities and with our army, had acquired a governmental character, being to all intents and purposes a combination of a Ministry of Foreign Affairs and a Ministry of War. From the spring of 1918 the French authorities treated it accordingly on all occasions.

The General Staff, acting with me as the representative of the National Council, saw that the regiments stationed at Cognac and Jarnac were properly equipped by the Ministry of War, and arranged all the details concerning the utilization of the army at the front. In December 1917 and January 1918, after his arrival from America, and before his departure to Italy, it was mainly Štefánik, besides Dr. Sychrava and Colonel Chalupa, who took part in the daily conferences and discussions on all these questions in the National Council and with the General Staff. I, as general secretary, attended to that side of the work which by the army statutes was reserved for the National Council. In January 1918 General Janin, Štefánik, Dr. Sychrava, and Colonel Chalupa were much occupied with the negotiations and discussions involved by the preliminary arrangements concerning uniforms, flag, badges, etc. Much labour was also demanded by the daily process of inducing the French authorities to grant all the facilities which were necessary for carrying out the statutes. This involved continual visits every day to the various official military departments, and as long as Štefánik was in Paris I arranged with him that he was to attend to this part of the business.

At the beginning of the summer of 1918 the internal organization of our division was completed in its essentials, and so, from May onwards we were able to consider the question of sending our 21st regiment to the front. This was done in June 1918, and was made an occasion for a solemn presentation of the colours. Messages were sent by President Poincaré and S. Pichon, Minister of Foreign Affairs; these messages proved to be the starting-point which led to the recognition of our independence and of our provisional Government by all the Allies.

(e) THE TURN IN ITALIAN POLICY. IN FAVOUR OF AGREE-
    MENT WITH THE JUGOSLAVS AND SELF-DETERMINATION
    OF THE NATIONS IN AUSTRIA-HUNGARY

92

After the reverse at Caporetta, Italy found herself in a serious predicament as regards war aims. The internal difficulties of Italy, to which I have already referred, had reached their culmination just at this time, and it was under these circumstances that there were new secret negotiations with Austria-Hungary for the purpose of an agreement, in which the Italian war aims would necessarily have been abandoned. Indeed, the whole of Italian public opinion inferred from two important speeches by Lloyd George and Wilson on January 5 and 8, 1918, that this agreement had actually been reached. At that time the Government were naturally acquainted also with the details of Smuts' secret negotiations at Geneva. When on February 13th Balfour made his Parliamentary statement on the Geneva negotiations with Austria-Hungary, the full gravity of the events as far as Italy was concerned were plainly acknowledged in the Press there.

There was another reason, however, why the situation was serious for Italy. Wilson's speech containing the famous fourteen points made it clear that the London Pact between Italy and the Allies could not be carried out.(39) This was the most severe blow which had been sustained by Sonnino's policy, and Government circles, as well as public opinion, which had hitherto taken its stand completely on the London Pact, were perhaps even more affected by it than by the words addressed to Vienna. Nor was it essentially mitigated even by Wilson's declaration of war on Austria-Hungary after the reverse at Caporetta. This was the psychological moment for a fundamental change in the line of policy which had hitherto been followed by the Italian Government both in political and military matters. It would seem that to a certain extent the Government had become aware of the mistakes in its previous course of action, i.e. the waging of what was known as "our war" (*guerra nostra*), "the Italian War," the rejection of a common front, certain considerations shown to Germany, violent and unnecessary disputes with the Jugoslavs on the subject of the London Pact, signs of compromise with regard to the oppressed nations of Austria-Hungary, and altogether a marked hesitation to adopt a definite attitude towards the problem of the existence of the Habsburg Empire.(40) With this was correlated an uncertain and undecided internal policy. After the serious military reverse the greater part of public opinion realized this, and assigned the blame to the faulty and uncertain Government policy. Thus, all these last events were interpreted as being so many blows directed against Sonnino's tactics.

Accordingly, in the spring of 1918 matured that profound moral crisis among the Italians which lasted throughout the war and, in fact, continued to operate after it. The state of Italy after the war is largely due to that crisis, and the policy which has been carried out since then may be regarded to a large extent as merely a continuation of that vagueness and lack of determination which dominated Italian policy during the war. In this sense Fascism and the policy of Mussolini were a reaction against the earlier events to which I have referred.

As time went on, the reaction against all this became increasingly stronger. Even during 1917 it was manifested by a number of groups concentrated around the *Secolo* and especially the *Corriere della Sera*, and including such men as Senator Albertini, A. Torre, G. Amendola, and Professor Borgese. Similar tendencies showed themselves among the independent Socialists associated with Bissolati and his followers. Mussolini consistently adopted a similar attitude in his paper, *Popolo d'Italia*. In ultra-nationalistic terms he expressed his disapproval of the lack of resolution shown by the Government circles connected with the "Idea Nazionale." This policy was directed against Sonnino, and expressly criticized Orlando, the new Prime Minister, for his inability to break down Sonnino's opposition, and thus lead the whole of Italian policy in a direction which would enable it to emerge from the crisis.

In Parliament also there was a strong reaction in this respect, and endeavours were made to bring about, if not a strong mass movement, at least a Parliamentary grouping of considerable strength, which would give a genuine impetus to the policy of Orlando's new Government, constituted just at the period of the Caporetta offensive, and brought into power at the height of the crisis. Accordingly, in December 1917, a Parliamentary League of National Defence (Fascio della Difesa Nazionale) was formed, consisting of senators and deputies who desired to wage war resolutely until a complete victory had been gained.

For this purpose abundant influence was brought to bear upon the Press of certain parties. Meetings and demonstrations were arranged which soon made their influence felt upon public opinion. The league comprised the nationalists, the anti-Austro-Hungarian elements (Federzoni, Colonna di Cesaro), the Liberals connected with the *Secola* and the

Corriere della Sera (Albertini, Agnelli), and also the Socialist reformists (Canepa, de Ambris, da Viti de Marco, Salvemini, and others). This policy was resolutely and effectively supported in the *Popolo d'Italia* by Mussolini, who afterwards supplied direct assistance to our movement.

This group soon came forward as a factor with a new and definite programme, the chief items of which were as follows:

1. It desired to carry on the war energetically till the end.

2. It accepted the policy of dismembering the Habsburg Empire.

3. It realized the necessity of co-operating with the oppressed nations in Austria-Hungary, and even considered it right that Italy, in the sense of Mazzini's ideals, should place herself at the head of this movement against Vienna. Thus arose what was known as the Italian policy of nationality.

4. It declared a condition of success to be a settlement between Italy and the Jugoslavs on the basis of a reasonable compromise and amicable co-operation in the future.

5. From the preceding items it followed logically that support should be given to the Czechoslovak movement as well as to the Polish and Rumanian policy.

These ideas were nothing new at the time of the Caporetta reverse, either to those who advocated them, or to other political circles. They had been discussed long since. Bissolati had associated himself with them at the very beginning of the war, and from time to time thay had been proclaimed clearly enough by Albertini's group and those connected with the *Secola*. There were many members of Government circles who were not opposed to them on principle, but who had not sufficient confidence in their success, or sufficient courage to champion them. The political and military situation was not of the kind which would render these ideas suitable for popular consumption. They had been recommended to the Italians ever since 1915 by French friends of Italy and the Jugoslavs, and also by Wickham Steed, Dr. Seton Watson, and Sir Arthur Evans, in London. Štefánik and myself had also emphasized them during our repeated journeys to Italy. As I have mentioned above, Štefánik's visit to Italy in the spring of 1916 was specially devoted to these matters and they had been publicly advocated by Salvemini, da Viti de Marco, Zanotti-Bianco, and others from 1916 onwards.

The present political situation suddenly created a favourable atmosphere for this policy. The conditions in France were analogous, and it was therefore possible to rely upon co-operation with Paris. There also the slogan of a fight to a finish for the benefit of oppressed nations was gaining ground more and more, and the Italian public were not slow to notice the attitude of reserve which Paris adopted towards the two declarations of Lloyd George and President Wilson. The Franklin-Bouillon-Fournol committee for inter-Allied Parliamentary contact was working in close touch with a number of Italian politicians (Galenga, Ruffini, and others), and it formed the Paris headquarters of the movement for liberating the oppressed nationalities in Central Europe. This body directed all its activities in France in favour of war to the end, and more particularly in favour of anything which would render victory possible, including the fulfilment of the demands made by the Jugoslavs, the Poles, the Rumanians, and ourselves. I have already mentioned that after the outbreak of the Russian revolution this body started regular meetings with a programme involving mainly the Slavs and the other oppressed nations. Here, too, attempts were made to bring about an agreement between Italy and the Jugoslavs. The good personal connections which Franklin-Bouillon and Fournol had with a number of Italian politicians exerted an excellent influence in this respect. It was from this body that the idea of a congress of oppressed nations emanated in the autumn of 1917.

The situation in London was analogous. There this movement was concentrated round the *New Europe* group, which was often attacked for its uncompromising opposition to the London Pact, but in it Wickham Steed and Dr. Seton Watson frequently succeeded in moderating the attitude of the extreme radical Jugoslavs, urging matters as far as possible towards a reasonable compromise. Under Steed's influence discussions took place at London in the middle of December 1917 between certain Italians (General Mola) and Jugoslavs (Trumbić), which tended considerably to bring the two camps closer together. These discussions were followed with interest by the Italian, Serbian, and British Governments, the latter of which made no secret of its sympathy for undertakings of this kind.

In December and January this change of situation had created an atmosphere which induced influential political circles in Italy to try to translate it into concrete action. My negotiations in September and October 1917 at Rome on the subject of our army, and the journalistic campaign started by me and systematically kept up by our Bureau in Rome, formed a suitable basis for developing this new line of policy. In the course of December, with the help of the Italian circles which I have indicated, our prisoners of war, and the possibilities of our army, were written about and discussed as an almost general topic. When, on December 19th, our army decree was published in France, this campaign reached a decisive point. The manifestations in the Italian Parliament on behalf of our French army on December 20, 1917 (intended partly also as a demonstration against Sonnino), formed the most typical indication of how affairs were shaping.

Our movement was closely associated with the development of the new conditions in Italy after Caporetta. We must not, however, blind ourselves to the real meaning of these events. As far as the Italians were concerned, our cause occupied only a secondary position. Those who realized the importance of an agreement between Italy and the Jugoslavs in its bearings upon the results of the war and the policy of Italy after the war, began to pay attention to our movement so that they could take advantage of it for furthering their political aims as regards the Jugoslavs. To support the Czechoslovaks meant favouring the destruction of the Habsburg Empire and advocating this integral solution of what was for Italy the most important problem of the war. It meant also accepting, in consequence of this, the principles of the Corfu Pact for the unification of the Jugoslavs, and this, in its turn, demanded an agreement with the Jugoslavs themselves. It would have been too difficult a matter to demand outright a solution of the Jugoslav problem as early as December 1917. But to ask the Government for something on our behalf could not result in any opposition, for at least it did not involve any embarrassment to Italy. Such was the argument of those who were associated with this new policy, and such was the basis of their course of action.

Thus, at the beginning of January 1918, more decisive stress was being laid at Rome on our problem, and there was even a suggestion that it might be possible to arrive at Italo-Jugoslav negotiations by way of our National Council. We were to act as intermediaries in the manner which Štefánik had desired in the spring of 1916. On January 19, 1918, Hlaváček wrote to me from Rome to this effect, and added that the Parliamentary circles concerned would approach me in the matter. I did not reject the idea, but I maintained a guarded attitude as I always do towards anything which involves my acting as intermediary. This is always a delicate and thankless task.

Meanwhile, under the influence of this inner political development in Italy, a committee for Italo-Jugoslav agreement and for co-operation with the other Austro-Hungarian revolutionaries had been formed at Rome ("Comitato italiano per l'accordo tra i popoli soggeti aU'Austria-Ungheria"). Besides this, the Socialist irredentists from Istria and the Trentino, acting in collaboration with Bissolati's group, had formed their own committee with the same object in view.

Orlando, being a good Parliamentarian, realized the importance of this change of attitude among the prominent politicians and in the Press. He was naturally influenced by the declarations of the two Anglo-Saxon statesmen, and leaving Sonnino to continue in his attitude of reserve, he began cautiously to co-operate with these various political factors. His visit to Paris and London, upon which he was accompanied by Sonnino (in the second half of January), was undertaken partly through the effects of the two declarations referred to, and it confirmed him in his conviction that the change of attitude was necessary in Italy. On January 26, 1918, he had his first long interview with Trumbić, at which Wickham Steed was present. In a moderate but unambiguous manner Trumbić placed the wishes and principles of Jugoslav policy before him. The interview ended amicably in favour of an agreement between the two nations, and as a result of it Trumbić was invited to Rome. The Press comments laid stress upon this aspect of the negotiations.

At the same time more concrete measures were being taken by the Parliamentary circles in Rome, who were working on behalf of this new line of policy. On January 15th there had been a conference of Allied Socialist parties at Paris, and on January 20th the Allied Socialist congress was held at London. The Italian Socialists, Arca, Canepa, Lazzarini, Ciccoti, de Ambris, Sestan, and Agnelli came to Paris and asked me to arrange a meeting between them and the Jugoslavs there. On several occasions we met a number of Jugoslavs for political discussions, and at the same time we negotiated with the Inter-Parliamentary Committee with regard to the Congress of Oppressed Nationalities. The Italian politicians raised the question whether it would not be more advantageous to hold this congress in Rome, so as to influence the Government and public opinion, and thus accelerate the change in Italian policy. The problem was settled shortly afterwards when J. S. Gallenga, the Under-Secretary of State in Orlando's Ministry, came to Paris at the beginning of February. The effect of his participation in this movement was to indicate Orlando's official approval of the whole of the undertaking on the part of Italian Parliamentary circles and the representatives of oppressed nations. We met several times at the Hôtel Crillon and the composition of these meetings (Franklin-Bouillon, Fournol; Dmowski, on behalf of the Poles; Braghicesco, on behalf of the Rumanians; De Giuli, acting as deputy for Trumbić, on behalf of the Jugoslavs; and myself, on behalf of our National Council) was the same as that of the subsequent Congress of Oppressed Nationalities, the organization and agenda of which we arranged. It was decided that the congress would be held in Rome, that Gallenga, on his return home, would reach an agreement with his friends in Rome as to the method of procedure, and that in accordance with this we should then complete the definite preliminary arrangements, settle the agenda and course of action, besides arranging for the possible participation of official representatives from among the Allies.

There were difficulties both on the part of the Italians and the Jugoslavs. Trumbić was unwilling to proceed to the congress until there had been a definite settlement of the Italo-Jugoslav dispute, and we could not induce him to come to Paris for any conversation of a binding character. De Giuli, who, during the absence of Trumbić, was managing the movement of the Jugoslav Committee in Paris, merely accepted messages and passed them on. In the end it was agreed that, before a final decision about the congress was reached, the delegates of the Italian Committee should meet Trumbić and endeavour to bring about a preliminary Italo-Jugoslav agreement comprising the formulation of general principles, which would enable the Jugoslavs to attend the congress at Rome.

On the whole, it was easy to agree on the principles which

were to govern the participation of other representatives. They were discussed in detail, and settled without any great difficulties at our meetings in Paris. The decisions on this point were as follows:

1. Each of the oppressed nations should draw up its programme of political and economic independence.

2. War to the death should be declared upon the Habsburg Empire, which formed the obstacle to the free development of the small nations in Central Europe.

3. All the oppressed nations of Austria-Hungary should solemnly unite for a common struggle against their common enemy.

4. The action of the congress was, first and foremost, to assume the form of a public demonstration for the purpose of influencing the Governments and also public opinion throughout the world. Its aim was to emphasize the need for the Allies to put an end to negotiations on the subject of a separate peace, and also to overcome the lack of determination concerning Austro-Hungarian affairs in general.

Such were the matters which were discussed at our meetings in Paris. The initiative and organization of the whole scheme were due to the secretariat of the National Council on the one hand, and Franklin-Bouillon and Fournol (later also Albert Thomas) with the Italian Committee on the other. As I have stated, the Jugoslavs were waiting for a preliminary agreement with the Italians. The Rumanians kept solidly with us. The Poles promised their participation, but did not exhibit any considerable activity.

The only thing that remained was to arrange a preliminary Italo-Jugoslav agreement, and this was done at London in the second half of February. The Italian Committee sent A. Torre and Professor Borgese to take part in these negotiations, which were attended also by Gugliemo Emanuele, the London correspondent of the *Corriere della Sera*.

(f) The Italian Government Sanctions the Establishment of the Czechoslovak Army. Štefánik's Negotiations

93

Before the congress in Rome actually took place, the moment arrived when the Italian Government gave permission for our army to be organized in Italy. As I have explained, during my last visit to Italy in September and October 1916, the recognition of the National Council had been secured, and permission obtained to form semi-military detachments for work behind the front. As I was certain that this step would necessarily be followed by a further one, I instructed the branch of the National Council in Rome not to organize these labour detachments, but to continue working at propaganda on behalf of an army, and to await the course of events in France. I felt sure that this would settle the whole matter at Rome also, and it was my intention to return there and arrange everything on the French pattern. Through the work of our Press Bureau at Rome and—what was more important—independently of it, a number of Italian publicists made their appearance who realized the importance of our cause and, without any prompting, wrote articles on our movement. Those associated with the parliamentary action, which I have referred to above as a product of the Caporetta reverse, also began to pay close attention to our movement, which they used in support of their newly adopted policy, and also as a means of arriving at the Jugoslav problem. As a result of all these circumstances, our position in Italy suddenly became more favourable than it had ever been before. At this juncture, too, the publication of our army decree in France, and the reports on the attitude of the French Government towards our military organization there, proved of the utmost service to us in Italy. The whole of the Press dealt with this subject as being an important political event. There were demonstrations in the Italian Parliament (41) which promoted the popularity of our cause in Italy, in spite of the fact that to a certain extent they represented a protest against Sonnino's attitude towards the question of our army there. In some cases, those who identified themselves with our cause were prompted by a sense of rivalry with France. The latter country, although not possessing any considerable number of our prisoners, had nevertheless anticipated Italian action with regard to the Czechoslovak Army.

After an internal struggle among the Italian authorities, the question of our army was settled in January and February 1918. Štefánik left me to continue negotiations with the French Government on the wording of the statutes and the internal organization of the army, and then made arrangements for a visit to Rome. He shared my view that the Italian Government would ultimately give its consent and, after the publication of our army decree in France, Brancaccio held the same opinion. For several months I had been giving him detailed information about our negotiations in Paris, and he had passed this on to the Supreme Italian Command. We had good reason to believe that the Italian military authorities had practically decided at the end of January that our army was to be sanctioned.

This is indicated by the proposals of General Giardino in January and February 1918, to the Supreme Military Council at Versailles, and by the report which Colonel T. Marchetti, head of the Military Intelligence Section, submitted on February 5, 1918, to the Ministry of War and the Supreme Italian Command. It was here that our long contact with the Italian Intelligence Service stood us in good stead. Marchetti's report showed a great appreciation of our work, and also a considerable knowledge of the conditions in the Austro-Hungarian Army. He rejected Sonnino's international arguments against the formation of a Czechoslovak Army, and supported his proposals by referring to the examples of Russia and France.

At all events, by the beginning of February, the Italian command had formed a plan analogous to that previously adopted in Russia for utilizing the Czechoslovak military forces. The Italian commanders at the front had many opportunities of seeing how the Czechoslovak troops behaved there, and how they risked their lives in the interests of their cause. It was thus obvious that they would be reliable supporters of Italy against the Habsburg Empire, that they could supply useful information to the Italians, and that by surrendering they helped to demoralize the Austrian front. The natural conclusion from this was that Czechoslovak detachments should be established all along the front, as they would prove a greater advantage to Italy than a single military unit. The need for some such step as this became even more urgent after the retreat on the Piave. The only opposition to the scheme came from Sonnino.

94

All these events led me to consider the scheme for organized labour detachments as the last manœuvre for hindering the establishment of our army in Italy. This scheme was being carried out between the end of January and the middle of February under the auspices of General Spingardi, who was evidently acting in agreement with certain authorities at the Consulta and other opponents of our movement. Hlaváček, who was in charge of our Press Bureau at Rome, reported on January 27th that Spingardi had told him to arrange for the National Council to begin organizing military labour detachments for the second line, as the Government had issued an order that all prisoners were to be used for work of urgent necessity, and as within two months he would clearly be obliged to employ all the Czechoslovak prisoners for this purpose, it would therefore be better if these prisoners were properly organized, and could thus assist the Italian Army as free helpers. Hlaváček pointed out that this proposal concealed a threat. If immediate action were not taken to form Czechoslovak labour detachments, our prisoners would be sent with the rest to engage in the usual work.

Hlaváček considered that there was a real danger, and therefore asked us to lose no time in sending our national badges for the uniforms of our prisoners, which would designate them as Czechoslovak troops. After a conversation with Štefánik and Brancaccio in Paris I came to the conclusion that the whole thing was a mere manœuvre designed to frustrate the establishment of our army. It would have been a compromise which in any case would have delayed the fulfilment of our plans. Accordingly I decided, after consultation with Štefánik, not to send the badges, but to postpone the formation of the labour detachments, and to accelerate Štefánik's visit to Rome. We had hoped that he would be able to leave towards the end of January, but his departure was delayed until the middle of February. On February 12th a new letter arrived from Hlaváček informing me that two days previously he had been summoned to Spingardi, who had told him that the Supreme Command required about 5,000 of our troops for work in the war zone, not later than February 20th. If they were not organized by that time, they would proceed there as prisoners. Hlaváček added that he had intervened with the Ministry of War for the purpose of postponing matters, and that he had received a promise to this effect on February 11th. On the next day, however, Spingardi had again sent for him, and told him that he had new instructions to dispatch several thousand of our troops to the war zone by April 18th. These detachments, he said, were to be formed in accordance with the pre-arranged regulations, the officers were to be designated by the National Council, the Italian uniforms which had been prepared would be as good as new, and there would be distinguishing marks in the form of cockades, red and white in colour.

In the letter to which I have referred, Hlaváček mentioned the pressure which had been exerted, and he stated that, acting on the instructions of the National Council, he had opposed the whole of this method of dealing with the situation. These matters caused us much dissatisfaction in Paris. We felt sure that before long our military schemes would meet with success, and we were therefore afraid that the manœuvre with the labour detachments would either frustrate the establishment of our army or at least delay it. Štefánik, on receiving Hlaváček's report from me, hurried to Italy to do the best he could under the circumstances. He started on his task somewhere about February 20th, and without paying any heed to the question of the labour detachments he immediately concentrated his efforts towards securing permission to establish the army. He achieved this object towards the end of June, and this was his greatest success during his war-time activity. I do not know all the details of his work or the procedure which he adopted, and indeed they are not known to others either. As a rule he never used to record anything in writing, and he explained the details of his plans to his fellow-workers only in a fragmentary manner. I can therefore mention only what he himself told me, or what I was able to discover officially from occasional documents.

95

The actual character of Štefánik's scheme varied from time to time. At first, like myself in October 1917, he aimed at securing a substantial number of prisoners for our army in France. His later plan, however, was more ambitious in its scope. He considered whether it would not be possible to secure more easily the consent of the Italian Government to the organization of our army in Italy, if our troops from France were attached to the auxiliary French corps which were sent to help Italy after Caporetta, and were then supplemented from the ranks of our prisoners in Italy. I do not know exactly whether this idea originated with Štefánik or with the Italian authorities. I only know that Štefánik would have agreed to it, and that at first it met with the approval of military circles in Italy. Incidentally, I have ascertained that this solution was suggested by General Cadorna as early as January or February 1918 to the Supreme Military Council at Versailles. His successor, General Giardino, repeated the proposal on February 24, 1918, with a slight modification, his chief demand being that our troops in France should be sent to Italy, and Orlando in March 1918 again urged the French Government to express an opinion on this proposal. Štefánik's plan was a similar one, and as far as I can infer (I had an opportunity of discussing the point with him) it was conceived independently of the Italian suggestions. When, finally, it was submitted to me as Secretary of the National Council, after having been previously discussed by the French and Italian Governments, and by the military authorities at Versailles, I opposed it. The view I took was that if the situation were such as to permit it, Italy would in the end grant us our army. I was not opposed to this solution on principle, but I insisted that if we were to give our consent to such a change, Italy should clearly undertake to place at our disposal all our prisoners who were on Italian territory. In other respects I was opposed to the integral realization of this plan, as I regarded it as essential that at least a part of our troops should remain on the French front. Besides this, at the beginning of March, owing to the exacting demand of the French military authorities, the organization and training of our army had not made sufficient progress to justify the use of our regiments at the front. After consultation with General Janin we replied in this sense to General Foch. The plan accordingly came to nothing.

The negotiations which Štefánik began towards the end of February enabled him at least to acquaint himself thoroughly with the attitude of the Italian Government. Before the middle of March he had had interviews with Orlando, Sonnino, Bissolati, and Diaz, and he had also been received by the King. The reasons which Sonnino gave him to justify his opposition to the establishment of our army were as follows:

1. Humanitarian considerations: Italy could not guarantee ultimate success in the war, and was therefore unable to accept

a sacrifice on the part of people who, if they were taken prisoners, could be executed for their share in the military operations.

2. Fear of reprisals against Italian prisoners. Sonnino had mentioned this point to me as early as the previous September, when he had also indicated his scepticism as to the result of the war.

Orlando himself was, on the whole, disposed to grant Štefánik's demand. Diaz was non-committal as regards the political aspect of the matter, while from a military point of view he raised various technical objections (language difficulties, fear of desertion, espionage, etc.). Finally, on March 9th, the Italian High Command, without giving any details, informed Štefánik that the question would be submitted to the Supreme Military Council at Versailles for solution. Štefánik at once notified me to this effect. It was about this time that he fell seriously ill, and on March 21st he asked me to come to Rome at once and complete the work with him there. I was, however, so much taken up with military arrangements, with the preparation of the Congress at Rome, and the problem of transporting our troops from Russia, that I was unable to leave Paris.

The matters which had been referred to the Supreme Military Council included the above-mentioned proposals of Cadorna and Giardini. On March 16, 1918, I was approached for the first time by General Weygand, who inquired what attitude the National Council would adopt towards the dispatch of our troops from France to Italy. On March 22nd, as the result of a fresh demand from Rome, he addressed the inquiry to me officially.(42) As I have already mentioned, neither General Janin nor myself regarded the project as politically expedient or even, at that time, practicable. Surmising that Italy would in any case sanction our army, and that whatever happened, this would not be the most advantageous solution either for us or anybody else, I declined it.

And, as a matter of fact, almost immediately afterwards, on March 26th, I received the first news from Rome implying the hope that the Italian Government would accept our point of view. In reply to the objections which had been raised by Sonnino and Diaz in their interview with Štefánik, he furnished them on March 20th with a detailed account of our aims, in which he explained what we had hitherto achieved during the war, and what the other Allies had already done on behalf of our army. He also analysed Sonnino's objections and, in a detailed rejoinder, brilliantly disposed of them. He ended by demanding that a part of the prisoners should be sent to France, while the remainder should be organized as a military body in Italy, some of them being detailed for work on the second line of defence, and the others being used as fighting units.

Štefánik's negotiations doubtless involved great difficulties, but from the very start he had the military authorities on his side, and they had long been convinced that his proposals were sound. As a result of this circumstance, as well as his personal qualities and his skill as a negotiator, Sonnino's consent was practically secured in the early part of April. When I reached Rome about that time to attend the Congress of Oppressed Nationalities, Štefánik informed me that the Italian Government consented to the scheme, and that the only thing that remained was to formulate the wording of the necessary documents. I arranged with Štefánik that I was to devote myself to matters connected with the Congress, while he would continue his negotiations on the wording of the military agreement. This was drawn up on the basis of our army decree and army statutes with France. Štefánik contrived that it should be expressly designated as a convention between the National Council and the Italian Government, which, in a political respect, denoted a step farther than our statutes with France, although the latter was perhaps a more substantial document.

96

Before leaving the Congress at Rome, I again discussed with Štefánik all further details of organization, various suggestions as to the wording of the agreement with the Italian Government, and further plans concerning our army in Italy. It was just at this time that Captain Šeba, who had been sent by Masaryk to organize our work in Italy, arrived from Russia. Under Štefánik's guidance he immediately started work. Dr. Osuský, who had come to Rome for the Congress, also spent about two weeks in Italy to assist with recruiting arrangements in the prisoner-of-war camps. I myself returned to Paris as soon as the Congress was over.

Štefánik's negotiations with the Italian Government lasted

until April 18th. On the following day he notified the French Government and myself that the negotiations were concluded, and that the agreement would be signed at an early date. At the same time he forwarded me the text of the agreement. In his report on these negotiations, M. Barrère, the French Ambassador in Italy, stated that the agreement differed in a number of points from the scheme prepared by the Supreme War Council at Versailles, but that Štefánik had succeeded in maintaining the principle of Czechoslovak Army unity, and that this was about the maximum which could be secured from the Italian Government under the conditions then prevailing. M. Barrère also paid a warm tribute to the ability which Štefánik had displayed in his handling of these negotiations. In this connection I should like to remark that one of Štefánik's difficulties was the question of unity between our army in Italy and that in France and Russia. What Štefánik aimed at was a process of unification in accordance with our common scheme, if not in actual practice, at least in a formal manner, in order that the principle might be recognized by Italy. In the end he succeeded in bringing this about. The Italian Government recognized the principle of the uniformity of all our armies, but in the actual organization it stipulated for complete independence from Paris. In the same way the later recognition of General Janin as the Commander-in-Chief of our armies was only theoretical in character. It had political significance but no military application. Nevertheless, as Barrère rightly pointed out, this was as much as could possibly be secured at that time.

The text of the army agreement was signed on April 21, 1918, by Orlando, as Prime Minister, Zupelli, the Minister of War, and Štefánik. It contains a recognition of the autonomy of our army, which is subordinated to the authority of the National Council as a supreme administrative body, paying the military expenses from the sums advanced to it by Italy. It is stipulated that the army will fight side by side with the Entente against the Central Powers. The internal organization and the statutes are reserved for a later agreement. In addition to our own officers, appointed by the National Council, Italian officers were also to be allotted to it and an Italian general would be in command. The status of our troops was the same as that of the Italians. The agreement contained also an undertaking that the Italian Government would facilitate the departure of our citizens, i.e. liberated prisoners of war, to France, and that after the war it would give our troops the opportunity of acquiring Italian citizenship. By means of this formulation Sonnino aimed at maintaining his original point of view. He wanted our people to proceed to France, not as prisoners but as free citizens, and in this he was actuated by fear of reprisals on the part of Austria. He inserted the clause relative to the acquisition of Italian citizenship for the eventuality of defeat which would make it necessary for our people to remain in Italy.

Štefánik was anxious to supplement the agreement with the authorities in Rome by a personal interview on the subject. On April 25th he therefore proceeded to visit General Diaz, the Italian Commander-in-Chief, to whom he submitted a detailed analysis of the agreement, emphasizing two points : (1) the unity of our army in Italy with the rest of our troops, and (2) the employment of our army as a fighting unit at the front, in connection with which the National Council would not interfere with the tactical arrangements of the Italian military authorities. According to Štefánik's report, General Diaz expressed his agreement and altogether showed himself entirely favourable to our military undertakings.

In accordance with the terms of paragraph 3 of the military convention of April 21st, the agreement was supplemented by additional and more detailed instructions as to the internal organization of the army, methods of recruiting, the appointment of officers, etc., which were analogous to those contained in our French statutes. This was signed on April 30, 1918, by General Zupelli and Štefánik.

None of these agreements contained any express political commitments as regards our future independence. Sonnino, although he had taken part in the discussions at which their wording had been agreed upon, declined to put his signature to them, and avoided everything which might denote an undertaking with regard to us or the rest of the Allies on the subject of our future State or the destruction of Austria-Hungary. Nevertheless, these military documents undoubtedly represented a considerable advance towards the realization of Czechoslovak independence.

(g) The Organization of our Army in Italy. Its Share in Operations at the Front

97

The actual organization of our army in Italy proceeded very quickly. About March 10th more than 4,000 of our troops at Padula were constituted into labour detachments. As I have already mentioned, Štefánik did not oppose this scheme, as it was his intention later to transform the labour detachments straight away into a regular army. This intention was actually carried out.

When, in the early days of April, the Government gave its consent to the formation of an army, the systematic work of recruiting and organizing the troops began in earnest. It was directed largely by Captain Šeba, who formed a link between Štefánik and the camp where the army was being formed. Here the military experience which he had gained in Russia stood him in good stead, and later on he became the representative of the National Council with General Graziani's staff. After Štefánik's departure for Siberia I appointed him our military plenipotentiary at Rome.

The centre of the recruiting and organizing arrangements was in Umbria. The chief garrison was located at Foligno and individual regiments were stationed in the neighbourhood at Perugia, Spoleto, and elsewhere. The recruiting of our troops immediately after the army had been sanctioned was carried out rather hastily. From the report supplied to Štefánik by Captain Šeba on May 5, 1918, it appears that up to that date the number of Czechoslovak prisoners entered on the records of the National Council was 17,000, and 14,000 of these volunteered for military service at the first summons. It was from these men that our first division, 11,500 strong, was formed by the middle of May, the remainder being organized as reserves. This division comprised four regiments of artillery, each containing three battalions and each battalion four companies, one of which was a machine-gun company.

In Italy, as elsewhere, the question of officers long continued to be a sore point to us. Our officers there were enthusiastic but unprepared, and for a long time we had no training schools for them. All posts were occupied by Italians, and this caused much dissatisfaction to our troops. In France we had a surplus of officers, and it had been arranged that they should be transferred to Italy. For a long time, however, it was not possible to carry out this plan, although I still did not know what there was to prevent it.

General Graziani, whose appointment took place as a result of an agreement between General Diaz and Štefánik, was soon a great favourite with our troops. What they particularly liked about him was his straightforwardness and his unaffected regard for the rank and file, with whom he made a point of coming into contact. On the other hand they demurred to his attitude towards the influence of the Czechoslovak element in the army. He did not favour the exercise of authority by our people or any attempt to impart a Czech character to the internal affairs of the army. He also alarmed our officers by his evident tendency to engage in active service without sufficient preparation, and to embark on undertakings which were regarded as rash adventures.

In Italy, as in all the other centres of our activity, the Sokol movement rendered us valuable services. In the first place, the discipline in our volunteer corps was derived from that of the Sokol organization. Then, too, the aptitude shown in military organization and the rapid progress in training were due mainly to the experience acquired by the Sokols. It is therefore no exaggeration to say that the Sokol movement formed the basis upon which the success of our army organization was built up.

98

The military qualities of our army in Italy were attested by its record at the front. It is not my intention to discuss this in detail, but I will remind my readers that in its very first engagement, which took place on June 16, 1918, it acquitted itself with distinction. Our second share of active service, which was taken on September 22nd, proved to be the most important military achievement of our regiments on the Italian front. The Austrian forces made an attack on the Dosso Alto sector, which was being held by our division. After severe fighting, our troops drove the Austrians back, and inflicted considerable losses upon them. In the second half of October our troops were transferred to the Piave front, where they likewise won the approval of the Italians.

I must add a few words on the subject of our intelligence section, the organization of which had started as early as

January 1918. At first these sections were unconnected with each other or with the main body of our army, but when our military organization was completed, the National Council insisted that these formations should be incorporated with the national army as an integral part of it. This was done, and the 2,000 men who formed this unit distinguished themselves by their exceptional courage and the excellent results which they achieved. A greater proportion of them than of any other branch of our army fell into the hands of the Austrians, and met their end by execution.

99

After he had settled all the details necessary for the organization of our regiments, Štefánik turned his attention to a number of political matters. He first of all arranged with the Italian Government that the ceremony of presenting the colours to our 34th regiment should take place on May 24, 1918. This was attended by the whole of the Allied diplomatic corps in Rome and also by such ministers as Orlando, Sonnino, Bissolati, Nitti, and others. Speeches were made by Orlando, Mr. Nelson Page, the United States Ambassador, and also by M. Simon, the French Minister of the Colonies, who happened to be in Rome at the time. The ceremony concluded with a speech by Graziani and an address by Dr. Sychrava to our troops.

Štefánik now regarded his task of military organization in Italy as completed. It was his intention, after a short stay in France, to return to Italy to see how the organization was working. Before leaving Rome he therefore asked M. Barrère to obtain for him, as a French soldier, the sanction of the Ministry of War in Paris, and on June 6th M. Barrère made a most laudatory report on Štefánik's activity in Rome. As a result of this, Štefánik was able to carry out his intention, and by July 1st he was back in Italy again. On this occasion he dealt with a number of outstanding details concerned mainly with the administration of courts-martial.

In the meanwhile I had been continuing the organization of our army in France. In particular, I arranged for the presentation of the colours to our troops on the French front, analogous to that in Rome. On this occasion, too, there were enthusiastic demonstrations in favour of our movement. Representatives of the French Government confirmed the status of the National Council as the supreme executive body of the Czechoslovak nation. I then proceeded to London to negotiate with the British Government. At that time the National Council was beginning to concentrate its attention upon our movement in Siberia, the problem of our intervention in Russia, and the transport of our troops to France. Dr. Ivan Marković had just arrived from Russia with news on the situation which helped us to understand what had happened in Russia and Siberia with regard to our troops. I had discussed these matters in July 1918 with the Ministry of War and the Ministry of Foreign Affairs, who had urged that one of our representatives ought perhaps to visit our army in Siberia. It was also suggested that our Commander-in-Chief, General Janin, should also go there, partly for the purpose of provisionally directing the essential military operations, and partly to arrange on the spot the process of transferring our troops to the Western front. I reported these matters on July 24th to Štefánik, who at that time was in Rome. He immediately informed me that he was returning to Paris at the earliest possible moment, and that he was preparing to proceed to Siberia. He arrived in Paris at the beginning of August, at the time when I was in London discussing the question of our recognition with the British Government.

XIV

TRIUMPH OF THE POLICY OF SELF-DETERMINATION

(a) OUR CO-OPERATION WITH THE JUGOSLAVS

100

WHILE the idea of national liberation formed the theoretical basis from which the Congress originated, the preliminary arrangements in connection with it showed that the practical incentive which led to its being convened was the endeavour to settle the Jugoslav-Italian controversy. The other nations from Austria-Hungary were successively approached when it was realized, bit by bit, how the Jugoslav-Italian dispute was connected with the whole problem of the Habsburg Empire, and thus also with the future of the other Central European nations who were struggling for freedom. When, finally, our Italian friends understood Italy's direct interest in attempting, during the war, to settle her attitude towards the whole group of problems which would involve the dismemberment of the Habsburg Empire, i.e. the relation of Italy towards the Czechoslovaks, the Poles, and the Rumanians in their future independent status, they themselves acknowledged the necessity for common action on the part of us all.

In the early years of the war the need for such co-operation was not properly realized even by those nationalities whose interests were closely affected by it. The dismemberment of the Habsburg Empire was not looked upon as a problem of urgent political interest, especially as the *émigrés* during the initial period of their exile were absorbed almost entirely with organizing their own national movements. The mutual relationship and interdependence of all these problems in their earlier phases were not understood sufficiently as to bring about common and systematic co-operation on the part of all the interested nationalities.

The *rapprochement* of the Central European nations in their struggle for liberty was thus a gradual process, and it was not until the end of 1917 that there was any considerable amount of organized co-operation between them and Italy.

Between the Jugoslavs and ourselves, of course, there had been a close and amicable contact and work in common from the very beginning of the war. With the Poles, too, we had been in touch from the outset, and occasionally we had exchanged views with them while, notably after the outbreak of the Russian revolution, there had been a certain amount of co-operation between us. Until the Congress of Rome, however, there had been comparatively little contact between the Poles and the Jugoslavs, while the Rumanians did not join the movement until after their reverses in the first half of 1917.

Before describing the events associated with the Congress of Rome, I will say a few words about our co-operation with the Jugoslavs, Poles, and Rumanians during the war, both in its general aspects, and also with regard to my own part in it. I have already stated that we had shared activities with the Jugoslavs from the beginning of the war. This was a matter of course, being a natural consequence of the pre-war traditions and policy of the two nations. Our interests were identical, we were comparatively well-acquainted with each other, we had always taken action in common within the Habsburg Empire, and during the war Vienna and Budapest adopted the same methods against us. Masaryk, who was at the head of our movement, was personally acquainted with many of the Jugoslav politicians, and his pre-war participation in all their struggles formed a significant link between us. He was highly esteemed by the Serbs, Croats, and Slovenes alike, who valued his judgment and sought his advice. Masaryk himself has given a detailed account of his work with the Jugoslavs, and I will therefore refer to these matters only as far as I myself was concerned in them.

The Jugoslav problem presented more difficulties to the Allies than did ours or that of the Rumanians. Serbia had differences with Bulgaria and the Habsburg Empire, as well as with Italy. In addition, there were the problems of Montenegro and Albania, to say nothing of the internal dissensions among the Serbs, Croats, and Slovenes themselves. Little was known about these matters, and much propaganda work had to be carried on in order that the official circles, and also the public opinion in the Allied countries, might obtain a proper idea of the points at issue. The future of the Croatian and Slovene territories was, of course. closely bound up with that of the Habsburg Empire, and this circumstance united the work of the Jugoslavs with our own. Accordingly, from the beginning, we worked in common, transforming our two national problems into a single cause. Our work was carried on in the same surroundings, and we gained the same friends and helpers. We were in practically daily contact with each other, and this lasted until the end of the war.

We Czechoslovak *émigrés* were in the same position as the Jugoslavs from Austria-Hungary, who, to a certain extent, acted independently of the officially recognized Serbs. As compared with ourselves, however, they had the advantage, especially in the early part of the war, of being backed by an independent State already existing, but it was not long before differences arose between them and official Serbia, as well as with Italy, and hence also with the rest of the Allies. This made work difficult for them, and it also caused considerable embarrassments to Serbia and often to ourselves as well.

The Jugoslav Committee, under the leadership of Trumbić, Supilo, and Hinković, often reproached official Serbia, which for all practical purposes meant Pašić, for its lukewarm policy in the problem of unification. For some time Pašić was suspected by a number of people, including Supilo, of deliberately working for the unification of only the orthodox Jugoslavs. During the period from 1916 to 1917, Trumbić had similar misgivings, and on more than one occasion he confided to me his troubles in this respect.

What formed a more dangerous obstacle to the aims of our Jugoslav friends was the Jugoslav-Italian disagreement. The Allies had rewarded Italy for entering the war against Austria-Hungary by the London Pact, which was concluded on April 24, 1915. All the Jugoslavs waged a most resolute struggle against the Pact from its very inception. It thus gave rise to the protracted Jugoslav-Italian dissension, the history and consequences of which are now familiar enough, and it must be regarded as one of the great mistakes made by the Allies during the war.

The attitude of the Jugoslav Committee in both these matters was uncompromising. The policy which they consistently pursued involved complete national unification, as well as a logical application of the principle of nationality to the dismemberment of Austria-Hungary. It also emphasized the strength and significance of the Croatian-Slovene element, for which it demanded complete equality with the Serbs. The dispute was complicated by the action of the Croats in Austria, and particularly by the very vigorous manner in which the Croatian troops had fought against Italy. This circumstance was adduced against the Jugoslav Committee as a proof that the Croatians and Slovenes were really pro-Austrian. The Committee, on the other hand, made use of this to show that the London Pact was untenable, but many Italians regarded this proceeding of the Committee as implying approval of the anti-Italian attitude of the Croatian troops, for which they therefore blamed the Committee. This led to suspicions, recriminations, and personal attacks upon members of the Committee, whose work for several months was nullified as a result.

Our movement naturally sided on principle with the Jugoslav Committee, but we endeavoured to transfer the dispute in all its aspects to a tactical domain. We advocated the necessity for showing consideration towards official Serbia, and knowing that the friends of Austria-Hungary would use this against the Jugoslavs and ourselves, we tried to moderate the high feeling occasioned by the disputes. With regard to the differences of opinion concerning the equality of all three parts of the Jugoslav national unit, we suggested that the Jugoslavs should settle this matter after the final victory had been achieved. This was the principle upon which we acted in the Slovak question.

We urged the Jugoslavs to moderation in their dispute with Italy, in order that they might not arouse against themselves too great a prejudice, the effect of which would perhaps be to make the Allies dissatisfied with all of us, and possibly make them unwilling to continue against Austria to the end. Several times we pointed out that the downfall of Austria-Hungary was our chief purpose, and that for the sake of it certain sacrifices might have to be made to Italy. We judged that these sacrifices would be smaller if both sides could agree upon them of their own accord at a suitable moment, and that preparations ought to be made for this eventuality. We resolutely opposed the practice of continually reproaching the Allies for their blunder over the London Pact, and we also opposed anything which might be construed as an indirect approval of the action of the Croatian troops on the Austrian front.

More than once the Jugoslav Committee evinced disapproval of, or even dissatisfaction with, our policy, or with certain of our tactical moves. I always expressed our point of view with considerable reserve in order to moderate the conflict or to bring the two parties together. On the whole I followed the tactics of avoiding direct interference, and of bringing a conciliatory influence to bear upon the two parties by means of private conversations. It often happened that certain of the radical Italians asked me to express my views on these matters publicly, their ulterior motive being to use any of my statements against the Jugoslavs. I therefore always declined to follow their suggestion. A number of the Jugoslavs, on the other hand, considered that I was too cautious in my attitude. I consistently avoided any public declaration, my point of view being that in the disputes between the two Allies it was our function to draw attention, in a private and amicable manner, to possible reasonable and just settlements, and not to make any untimely public statements which would only extend the dispute by introducing some third Ally into it. When the proper moment came we would let both sides know our point of view, but we should then do so frankly. When the appropriate moment did come we fulfilled our duty towards the Jugoslavs accordingly.

Throughout these proceedings I laid stress, both privately and publicly, that as Slavs we had maintained, were maintaining, and always would maintain, a sincere friendship towards the Jugoslavs, and on account of these sentiments we should never deny that it was in our own interest for the conflict to be justly settled, and for the two nations to be brought together, in order that we later on might not find ourselves in a difficult situation on account of any trouble which might arise between them. In this way I succeeded, as General Secretary of the National Council, in warding off any serious disputes and conflicts which might have been detrimental to our movement.

The Jugoslav Committee found abundant support in France and England. In Paris particularly the Jugoslav cause was taken up by all those who were in contact with us as well. This applies especially to such Slavists as Denis, Gauvain, Brunhes, Eisenmann, and Haumant, together with quite a number of politicians and journalists. In England the Jugoslavs were assisted by Wickham Steed, Dr. Seton

Watson, Sir Arthur Evans, and a large number of the contributors to the *New Europe*. The Jugoslav-Italian dispute formed a subject of daily debates in these and other Allied circles throughout the period between 1916 and 1918, and there were times when these differences in opinion threatened to estrange the Allies, and to assist the friends of Austria-Hungary in the Allied countries to gain many adherents to the idea of preserving the Habsburg monarchy. This was a source of embarrassment to the Allied Governments even during their official negotiations, and there was actually a danger that their effective military co-operation might be impaired by it.

These matters caused us serious concern. The attitude I adopted towards them as General Secretary of the National Council coincided with that of Masaryk. Štefánik took more active steps and outwardly, too, he was more uncompromising. He did not disguise the fact that he disapproved of the radical tactics of the Jugoslav Committee, and on several occasions he had recourse to direct intervention for the purpose of inducing the Committee to make concessions. What led him to take this course was his more frequent contact with the Italians, especially the official and political circles in Rome. That is why Trumbić, Vesnić, and other members of the Jugoslav Committee several times openly opposed Štefánik.

101

As a representative of the National Council I began direct co-operation with the Jugoslav Committee on February 11, 1916, at a meeting with Trumbić, Županić, and Vošnjak, in Paris. In the course of time I made the acquaintance of Supilo, Hinković, Meštrović, Vojnović, Cvjetiša, Grigorin, and others. From March 1916 onwards our work together was systematic, close, and amicable. We were drawn together very much by our common labours and our common danger. Our friendships were personal, and they continued to be so throughout and also after the war. Of the Jugoslavs from Austria-Hungary, Trumbić was the one with whom I was most in contact, and I recall with pleasure the work which we carried on in common, as well as the anxiety and dangers which we shared. I shall never forget the touching moment when, in August 1918, he came to congratulate me on having achieved British recognition of the National Council as a *de facto* Government, and of the Czechoslovak nation as an ally. He regarded that as a decisive blow to the Habsburg Empire and as a victory for the Jugoslavs also.

In the second half of March 1916, Trumbić, Hinković, Štefánik, and myself frequently met to discuss the differences with the Italians. Štefánik strongly advised the two Jugoslavs to arrive at a direct agreement with Italy, and at the same time he negotiated to this effect with M. Vesnić, the Serbian Minister in Paris. In the spring of 1916 he had observed that political circles in Paris were beginning to be seriously alarmed at the Italo-Serb-Jugoslav disagreement, and he indicated to some of his French friends that we Czechoslovaks might be able to help in bringing about a settlement. He suggested that in view of his activity on the Serbian front and his visits to Italy, where he had gained a number of friends, he himself might find an opportunity of doing something in this connection. I have already stated that as a result of this he was entrusted with a non-official mission to Italy in March 1916, for the purpose of ascertaining the views of Italian circles as to the chances of a Jugoslav-Italian agreement. He had proceeded on this mission on March 24, 1916, but the Jugoslavs had looked rather askance at this undertaking, and from that time onwards they regarded Štefánik with reserve, considering him to be too pro-Italian.

Nevertheless, the co-operation between the Czechoslovak National Council and the Jugoslav Committee, both in Paris and London, became increasingly intimate. What differences there were, concerned chiefly tactics and methods of procedure. At a special meeting with Trumbić on April 16, 1916, we arranged a common programme and a practical course of action, to which we fully adhered until the end of the war. Our community of action was made more conspicuous when Denis extended the scope of our review, *La Nation Tchèque*, so as to include not only Czechoslovak matters, but also Jugoslav questions.

It was not long before the results of this became manifest. During his visit to Rome, Štefánik encountered strong opposition, which the political circles there explained to him as being due partly to the fact that *La Nation Tchèque* was adopting an anti-Italian attitude, and that they could not be expected to strengthen and support us against their own interests. Thus, from the intensified co-operation between the

National Council and the Jugoslav Committee, there emerged our first conflicts with the Italians, with the Jugoslavs, and partly also with Professor Denis.

On his return to Paris, Štefánik at once drew attention to these difficulties, and emphasized the need for observing greater caution. He even took the view that it would be necessary to explain in *La Nation Tchèque* that we could not make common cause with the Jugoslav Committee in carrying out their policy. He reminded us that even the friends of the Jugoslavs in Rome, notably Barrère, Loiseau, and Giers, the Russian Ambassador, were unable always to approve of the radical tactics advocated by the Jugoslav Committee. This was the origin of a number of misunderstandings and even disagreements amongst us. To-day, especially after the Jugoslav endeavour to achieve an amicable agreement with Italy, there can be no harm in mentioning these matters.

On May 18, 1916, I was invited to call on M. Vesnić at the Serbian Legation. I had been discussing these topics with him for a long time, but this was the first occasion upon which he raised any objections to Štefánik's policy. I then discussed matters with Denis to the same effect, explaining to him why and to what extent I was in agreement with Štefánik. We also considered the tactics of the Jugoslav Committee an unpractical one in certain respects, and detrimental to their own interests. I had heard various complaints on this score in Allied official circles. We took the view that between them and the Italians a compromise would have to be reached sooner or later, and that it would be dangerous not to prepare for it in good time, otherwise they would end by incurring a serious set-back by which they would probably lose more than if they agreed to a reasonable compromise involving some voluntary sacrifice on their part. On the other hand, I was bound to admit that Štefánik's policy went too far, and that some of the Jugoslav complaints were well-founded.

In June a number of objections were raised to Štefánik's policy by Trumbić, and again I had to admit that some of his remarks were justified. Štefánik, it should be said, believed that much would be accomplished as a result of the London Pact, and he arranged his tactics accordingly. He said that our duty was to save as much as possible for the Jugoslavs by means of a moderate attitude towards Italy, even if the Jugoslavs viewed the situation in a wrong light and occasionally complained about us. This was a subject to which Vesnić always recurred whenever I visited him. His most emphatic remarks about us were made during my visit to him on September 19, 1916. It was then that I intervened for the first time with the Serbian Government on behalf of the National Council, asking for the liberation of our prisoners of war from Serbia who, after the retreat through Albania, had taken refuge in France. M. Vesnić promised to secure the sanction of his Government for the liberation of about 4,000 of our prisoners, and he then took advantage of the opportunity to remind me once more of Štefánik's policy in the Jugoslav-Italian question. He asked in very emphatic terms that there should be no repetition of this, and I promised that I would speak to Štefánik about it. I did so, and although Štefánik maintained his previous point of view we agreed upon a tactical course of action which prevented any untoward incidents in the future. I may add that no further trouble occurred in this respect, with the possible exception of two episodes during the Peace Conference. On one of these occasions the Jugoslavs were offended at Štefánik's action and complained to me about it, while on the other occasion the Italians were dissatisfied with what I had done and took their grievance to Štefánik. Both these misunderstandings, however, were settled amicably.

Perhaps I ought here to say that the Jugoslavs, smarting under their grievances against the Italians, and distressed by their country's disasters, were not quite fair to Štefánik, who was prompted by the best of intentions, and who really desired to bring about a timely agreement between the Italians and the Jugoslavs. After my interview with M. Vesnić we noticed a definite abatement of the Jugoslav-Italian tension. Then the preparation for the Congress of Rome and the active part which we took in it met with the approval of the Italians also, while the success of the Congress itself for the Jugoslavs provided a concrete proof of the effective work which we had accomplished in common with the Jugoslav Committee.

Our relation to official Serbia and to the Serbs in general was marked by the same sentiment, and was directed towards the same purposes. Throughout the war we received friendly support from the Serbian authorities. In this respect I can pay a tribute to the Serbian Legation in Paris, where M. Vesnić, by means of his extensive connections and diplomatic experience, supplied me with information, advice, and direct assistance for several years. In the same way, M. Jovanović, the Serbian Minister in London, did much to promote our co-operation, and in Rome we were helped by the Serbian Minister, M. Antonjević, who had previously been a Legation Counsellor in London. In Russia also the co-operation between our organizing bodies and the Serbian authorities was very active, nor must we forget the joint effort of our organizations in America with the Serbian Legation and the members of the Jugoslav Committee there. Finally, let me mention that our military co-operation with Serbia was of the same gratifying character. The Serbian Government highly appreciated the services of our volunteers in its army, and later on readily granted permission for them to be transferred to our own army in France. In Russia our military co-operation with the Serbs was pervaded by the same spirit, and I need refer only to the excellent results of our joint activities in the Dobruja division under the leadership of General Živković.

Continual interest was evinced in our national cause by Alexander, the Serbian heir-apparent, with whom Professor Masaryk was in touch. Pašić, too, who during the war had a fairly accurate idea of how the military problems of Central Europe ought to be settled, found suitable opportunities for reminding the Allies of our claims. It was a long time, of course, before we could keep pace with Serbia in matters of high international policy. Serbia was an Allied State on whose account the war had started, and as such she had a Government, commitments from the Allies, and so on, while for a long time we were mere émigrés. Nevertheless, in 1918 we were now and then able to contribute towards a settlement of Jugoslav problems. Masaryk did much in this respect, while I endeavoured to act as advocate for the Jugoslavs in cases where they were being unfairly treated. I pleaded their case not only with the Italians, but also with the other Allies, and when in June 1918 I secured the recognition of the National Council at the Quai d'Orsay, I asked for a reference to the unified Jugoslav State to be made in M. Pichon's note, a request which was complied with. And there were several other instances.

Our relation to the successes of the Serbian and Jugoslav policy was fairly analogous to that in Polish affairs, although we were on closer terms with the Jugoslavs. When in August

1917 Pašić and Trumbić signed a joint declaration of the Serbian Government and the Jugoslav Committee at Corfu, we regarded this as one of the most decisive phases in Jugoslav policy and as an advantage to our own cause. It meant not merely a formulation of the future relationships between the three branches of the Jugoslav race, the principles of their future constitution and their existence in common, but also a great international manifesto for Jugoslav unity, and thus for the abolition of the Habsburg Empire. This declaration fulfilled its international mission perfectly, and its effects brought it within the scope of our own movement.

Our successes in the organization of an army and in the organization of the National Council and its branches, as well as in securing our recognition from the Allies, were welcomed by the Jugoslavs with a corresponding interest and gratification. Our recognition and the proclamation of our independent Government on October 14, 1918, were greeted by them as a victory of the Jugoslav idea. The Serbian Government, by a communication from Pašić, was one of the first to acknowledge our independence. At the Peace Conference also we took joint action in all common and fundamental problems. The treaties of alliance which were concluded later on between the two independent States, through the co-operation of Trumbić, Vesnić, and Ninčić, formed merely a logical conclusion to our common policy during the war.

(b) OUR CO-OPERATION WITH THE POLES AND RUMANIANS DURING THE WAR

102

The character of our relations with the Poles during the war was partly determined by the circumstances under which our two nations had lived before the war. In this respect the chief factor was the relation of the Poles to the Habsburg Empire and also to Russia. At the beginning they were indulgent towards Austria, or at least were little concerned with the problem which the Monarchy presented, while we were uncompromisingly anti-Austrian. Towards Russia, on the other hand, they became more and more uncompromising and remained so until the end, while we were endeavouring to find methods of reconciling our conflicting interests. Of course, the division of the Poles into an Allied camp and a camp of the Central Powers, by which they differed from us and the Jugoslavs, correspondingly characterized the Polish policy during the war, and exerted much influence upon our relations, especially as in the Allied countries many Poles were among the ranks of the pro-Austrians and pro-Magyars. These divergencies, however, were gradually modified by the events of the war, so that as our mutual interests ceased to be so diametrically opposed, a close relationship was established between us.

As a result of these divergencies of interest the official policy of our National Council did not, until the time of the Russian revolution, altogether harmonize with the Polish aims. What we then demanded was the unification of all the Polish regions of Russia, Austria, and Germany into a single State, with the widest possible measure of State autonomy under Russian suzerainty. We did not approve of the ambiguous policy of the Austrian-Poles, and we objected to the anti-Russian agitation which the Poles carried on in the Allied countries. It was our wish to be loyal to all the Allies, even though our attitude towards Tsarist Russia was a critical one. We therefore worked in favour of that maximum of the Polish claims which, before the outbreak of the Russian revolution, we regarded as compatible with the interests of all the Allies, as well as of the Poles themselves. In so doing we endeavoured to win the Poles over to our anti-Austrian attitude, and we managed to secure their support for agitation aiming at the destruction of Austria-Hungary. I never underrated the influence of the Poles, especially in this question. Among their *émigrés* there were many who sympathized with the movement for a separate peace with the Habsburg Empire, because they considered that only in this way would Germany be defeated and compelled to give up Posen and Silesia. On the other hand, they had no misgivings as to the future of Galicia, especially when they knew that the Emperor Karl was willing to let Poland have it in return for the protection of his monarchy. These Poles even regarded with sympathy the idea of a reduced Austria-Hungary, with which they thought that an independent Poland might be able to elaborate a political system, and thus better cope with both Russia and Germany. This was only a slightly different application of the Austrophile theory by which Vienna might counterbalance Berlin. Its advocates counted upon the assistance of the

Magyars, and we were only a subordinate factor in their calculation. At the same time, any degree of Polish opposition to the Habsburg Empire was of great value to our cause, since the fact that the Poles were on good terms with Vienna, and wanted to see her treated with consideration during the war imparted a sense of detachment to any anti-Austrian attitude they might adopt, and tended to confirm the justice of the policy pursued by the Jugoslavs and ourselves. The Poles, in their turn, were inclined to demur at what they considered the excessive moderation of our attitude towards Russia. Even those, such as Erazm Piltz, who showed much consideration for Russia and the Allies, in their confidential conversations with me made no secret of their intention to secure complete State independence at any price. This led to various minor misunderstandings between us. When the Russian revolution broke out it was followed by the proclamation of a provisional Government in Poland, and when the Russian front collapsed, it was clear that the last obstacle to the realization of Polish aims had been removed. From then onwards we worked in close agreement with the Poles, although we sought to moderate their territorial claims, and advocated the principle of a Polish State within ethnographical frontiers, with access to the sea at Danzig. (Of course we always realized that a strict application of the principle of ethnographical frontiers was never practicable, and that there would always have to be concessions on both sides.)

It was in the spring of 1918 that the first symptoms of the Teschen dispute made their appearance. I had several discussions with Dmowski about this, urging how essential it was to reach a timely agreement on the basis of a reasonable compromise in order to avoid trouble after the war. (It was always my opinion that the frontier between us should be formed by the River Vistula, which would then connect us also with the Baltic.)

Dmowski was the strongest political personality among the Poles who were working in the Allied countries during the war, while Piltz, by reason of his moderation, did most to further the interests of the Polish cause in Paris. He it was also, who had the best understanding of our common interests, and from the very outset planned his activity so as to facilitate co-operation with us. The most popular of the Poles, and the one who proved a great asset to his country, especially in America, was Paderewski, whom I did not meet until the Peace Conference.

My first meeting with Dmowski took place at Paris on May 18, 1916. I was immediately captivated by his shrewdness and the trenchant character of his political plans. He was well aware of our Russophile tendencies and at first he spoke guardedly, endeavouring to influence me by his moderation towards official Russia. At subsequent meetings, however, he became more and more radical, until he began an offensive against our line of policy by complaining of me and also of Masaryk, whose activities in London were, he alleged, not sufficiently favourable to the Poles.

I vindicated the tendency of our policy on the ground that we had to show consideration to the Allies and to Russia as well. At this period Dmowski was strongly opposed to the Allied policy, which in his opinion made too many concessions to Russia. He foretold and also desired the fall of Russia, and he himself told me that the day when the Russian revolution broke out was one of the happiest days in his life. He then began to advocate the theory that Russia was eliminated from European policy for another fifty years, and that France and the Allies must compensate themselves in Eastern Europe against Germany by means of a strong Poland. This theory met with much approval, and its prospects were further strengthened by the advent of Bolshevism. This policy, of which Dmowski was the foremost advocate, contributed largely to the subsequent advantageous position of Poland at the Peace Conference. Promoted by the further developments of European events, it rendered possible the later territorial extension of Poland, against which the Americans and particularly the English demurred for a long time at the Peace Conference.

It should be added that Dmowski had many opponents, particularly in London, where the chief of them was Mr. Lloyd George. This was due to his anti-Semitism, which he often exhibited rather ostentatiously, and his equally ostentatious nationalism. On the other hand, however, he understood better than the other Poles that in order to achieve the Polish aims it would be necessary to destroy Austria-Hungary, and in this respect he was always consistently on our side. We carried out a great deal of work jointly with the Poles during the war. From the spring of 1916, when I established official contact with the Polish National Committee in Paris, our central organizations there were in continual touch with them. After the Russian revolution our organizations in Russia also co-operated considerably with the Poles. For the reasons which I have stated above, our co-operation with them made slow progress, but it reached its culminating point in the spring of 1918, when we succeeded in inducing them definitely to oppose Austria-Hungary, and to take part in the Congress at Rome. From that point onwards our work together became systematic and effective.

Up till that time most of the Poles had gone their own way, as they did not wish to complicate their cause, which had been an international one from the very outset, and increased in importance as time went on, with problems which affected the rest of us. In the Jugoslav question they maintained an attitude of reserve, as they were unwilling to offend Italy. As regards matters affecting the Habsburg Empire, in addition to what I have already said, the Poles always proceeded with due consideration for the Austrophiles in the Allied States and also for the Vatican, because these circles, who were opposed to the dismemberment of the Empire, were at the same time almost entirely in favour of the Poles.

The development of events in the spring of 1918, however, showed the Poles that they too would have to share the struggle for self-determination and the ideas advocated by Wilson. As regards Russia, ever since the peace of Brest-Litovsk, the freedom of Poland in one form or another had been assured. Nevertheless, they realized that by associating themselves with our line of action they would be certain of the immediate union of all three portions of former Poland. Hence, from 1918 onwards the Poles in the Allied countries were entirely on the side of those who proclaimed uncompromisingly the policy of liberating the oppressed nations and abolishing the Habsburg Empire. The Congress of Rome gave concrete expression to this tendency.

On the whole, therefore, the policies of the Poles and ourselves, which had been divergent at the beginning of the war, became closer in the course of 1917, and from 1918 onwards coincided. The Teschen dispute was regarded as a subordinate question which could be settled on amicable lines. When our independence was declared in October 1918, the Polish National

Committee in Paris sent a special deputation to congratulate us, and to emphasize the need for political work in common after the war.

103

Our contact with the Rumanians during the war was naturally not so close as that with the Jugoslavs and Poles, but we laid the foundations of a common policy, which we have continued to pursue. From the first moment when they entered the war we sought contact with them in Paris and London, and our relations became even closer from the time of the Rumanian military reverses. In the winter of 1916, while on his way to Russia, Štefánik visited the Rumanian front, where he secured permission for several hundreds of our prisoners to be transferred from Rumania to France. An important visit to the Rumanian front was paid also by Masaryk in the autumn of 1917, his object being to discuss the question of using our troops from Russia there. He entered into contact with official circles, with the Government, and with the military authorities, and he was duly received as the representative of an Allied nation. Here I may add that our volunteers served side by side with those of Rumania in the Serbian division on the Dobruja front.

My own co-operation with the Rumanians was mainly of a propagandist character. From 1917 onwards I worked for several months in Paris with Senator G. Draghicescu, who was received there on the same terms as the Jugoslavs, the Poles, and ourselves. In the same way we co-operated with the Transylvanian representatives in Paris, at the head of which was T. Vuia, and also with the Socialist, Dr. Lupu, who was later a minister.

It gives me pleasure to recall my first meeting with Take Jonescu at London in October 1917. It was at the period when, after the collapse of the Russian front, nothing more could be done on the Rumanian front, and the fate of Rumania seemed to be sealed. On that occasion I met Jonescu, in company with the Rumanian minister, Titulescu. In discussing the situation we agreed that we should win in the end, and that after the war we should pursue a common policy in Central Europe. Jonescu, who was one of the most capable of the war politicians, had already met Masaryk. He had a high opinion of Pašić and was on terms of close friendship with Venizelos. He was one of those politicians with whom it was possible during the war to discuss all the post-war problems of Central Europe, and when he referred to our future joint activity I was able to agree with practically everything he said.

After the Rumanian catastrophe a number of other Rumanian politicians, especially from the Liberal camp, came to Paris. In the winter of 1917 my work brought me into contact chiefly with Florescu, a former minister, with Goga, who was subsequently a minister, and with the authoress Helena Vacarescu, all of whom, together with Senator Draghicescu, shared in the now highly developed activities of the oppressed nations of Austria-Hungary. They at once associated themselves with the movement inaugurated by Franklin-Bouillon and Fournol, and also with the preparations for the Congress of Rome.

When Rumania concluded peace with the Central Powers, the activities of their representatives abroad by no means came to an end. On the contrary, they realized that their only hope of national liberation and unification lay in the victory of us all. They therefore became even more closely attached to our movement, and in the end they achieved victory. In spite of the passing difficulties which were encountered at the Peace Conference between the Jugoslavs and the Rumanians on the subject of the Banat, and between the Rumanians and ourselves regarding Carpathian Ruthenia, this co-operation during the war prepared the ground for that post-war Little Entente policy at which Masaryk and the rest of us had been systematically working since 1917.

Thus, under the influence of the military events, the policy enunciated by Wilson, the Russian revolution, and the activity of all of us who were struggling for the liberty of oppressed nations, there gradually came into being that policy of self-determination which found its expression in the Congress of Rome and which in the course of the summer of 1918 became so obvious and essential a factor in Allied tactics.

(c) THE CONGRESS OF OPPRESSED NATIONS IN ROME. ITS INTERNATIONAL SIGNIFICANCE

104

After long and difficult discussions in London between Trumbić and A. Torre, an agreement was reached on March 7, 1918, about the terms for settling the Jugoslav-Italian dispute, and also about their joint anti-Habsburg policy at the Congress of Rome. At the same time, in the course of these discussions, principles were formulated for defining the co-operation of all the oppressed nations of Austria-Hungary, and the path to the Congress of Rome was thus opened.

We arrived at Rome on April 8th, and at once began to discuss the formal procedure of the Congress, which was solemnly inaugurated at the Capitol on April 9th, under the presidency of Senator Ruffini. It was attended by numerous Italian politicians, while Bissolati and Commandini sent congratulatory telegrams.

On April 10th, the four following committees began their work: (1) For propaganda; (2) for matters affecting members of the Austro-Hungarian nationalities who were military or civil prisoners of war in the Allied countries; (3) for the organization of a future Congress; (4) for formulating the resolutions of the Congress.

At the final plenary meeting, which was held on April 11th, there were special declarations from the representatives of the individual nationalities. Thus, Zamorski, on behalf of the Poles, emphasized the fact that while the main adversary of Poland was Germany, whose defeat was an essential condition for achieving the unity and independence of Poland, the Poles would nevertheless continue side by side with the other nations against the Habsburg Empire. Then Dr. Lupu and Senator Mironescu protested against the peace which had been signed at Buftei, and pointed out that the Austro-Hungarian Government, while speaking of peace without annexations or indemnities, was annexing extensive territories and at the same time taking possession of the main sources of Rumanian wealth. Trumbić next demanded the unification of all the Jugoslavs, emphasizing the principles of the agreement which had been reached with Torre, and declaring that the detailed discussions for a territorial agreement would have to be postponed until a later period. I myself, speaking on behalf of our National Council, laid stress on two points, which met with the approval of the Congress. (1) The struggle was not merely against Vienna, but also and equally against Budapest. As regards ourselves, the most important question was that of unity with the Slovaks. (2) The events which were then taking place within the Habsburg Empire formed the best proof that the Empire was slowly but surely collapsing.

Thereupon declarations were made by Senator Draghicescu, Franklin-Bouillon, Wickham Steed, and Albert Thomas, while the concluding speeches were delivered by Ruffini and Barzilai. The declarations of Franklin-Bouillon and Wickham Steed were particularly important. The former, as President of the Parliamentary Committee for Foreign Affairs, announced his authorization for stating that the French Government gave its complete sanction to the action of the Congress, and that, in view of the discussion just held on Czernin's last speech, he could give an assurance that the French Government and the French Parliament would never conclude a separate peace without Italy and the other Allies, great and small. Wickham Steed stated that he could confirm how completely the British Government approved of the Congress, and that the interview which he had just had with Sonnino enabled him to make the same statement as regards the Italian Government also.

The Congress was an undoubted success. The Governments of all the Allied countries had followed its proceedings with interest and understanding, the effects of which soon made themselves felt.

After the Congress was concluded, a joint delegation of the nationalities represented was received by Orlando, who in the presence of Bissolati made a speech identifying himself with the work of the Congress, and emphasizing the readiness of Italy to co-operate with the Jugoslavs and, in fact, all the oppressed nations.

In Paris the Congress had a good press, and in official circles it was regarded favourably. Clemenceau himself made this clear to us when, in the middle of April, we returned there from Rome. A delegation of those who had attended the Congress, comprising representatives of all the nationalities, and headed by Franklin-Bouillon, was received at a special audience by Clemenceau, to whom the results of the negotiations and the details of our further plans were submitted. Clemenceau very emphatically expressed his approval. He was generous with words of encouragement, and in particular he unreservedly condemned the Habsburg Empire. In this he was greatly influenced also by his conflict with Czernin, with which I will now proceed to deal.

(d) THE ARMAND-REVERTERA SECRET PEACE NEGOTIATIONS, AND THE CLEMENCEAU-CZERNIN-EMPEROR KARL CONFLICT

105

In the middle of June 1917, at a time when the negotiations of Sixtus of Bourbon had not been entirely disposed of, application was made, according to the official version of the Ministry of Foreign Affairs at Vienna, to Count Revertera, an Austrian nobleman, whose private circumstances kept him at Freiburg, in Switzerland, by a certain Swiss "throat specialist," to the effect that an important French personality had made important peace overtures to him, and asked him if he could communicate them to the Emperor. (I should add that the official French account differs from this Austrian version in attributing the initiative for the whole affair to Vienna.) At the beginning of June, Revertera notified Czernin of this, and received instructions to ascertain who the personality in question was, and at the same time to bring the proposals so that they might be submitted to the authorities in Berlin.

According to the Viennese version, Revertera discovered at the beginning of August that the personality referred to was Major Count Abel Armand, who at that time was in charge of the Intelligence Department at the Ministry of War, and who was said to be coming to Switzerland to negotiate with Revertera, bringing with him proposals drawn up by Thomas and Painlevé, and approved by Ribot and Lloyd George. He was said to be anxious to negotiate for a separate peace with Vienna. In the course of a conversation with Armand it was discovered that the general lines of the scheme proposed were very anti-German in character, involving, as they did, the separation of Bavaria from Germany, the division of Silesia, and the incorporation of Poland with the Habsburg Empire. These were evidently plans emanating from the French General Staff. Vienna was asked to cede the Trentino to Italy, Trieste was to become a free harbour, and the whole of the Empire was to be federalized.

Revertera received instructions from Vienna that the proposals made must be quite precise so that they could be submitted to Berlin, and that if Berlin agreed to negotiate on the basis of them, such negotiations would have to be carried out by responsible persons, possibly the two Foreign Ministers. Czernin at once proposed a meeting of the two ministers or their representatives at Vaduze, in Liechtenstein. Revertera, however, received an answer from Armand stating that the point at issue was a separate peace, and that for the present, at least, there could be no discussions of the matter with Berlin. He therefore returned to Vienna, where he informed Karl and Czernin accordingly, the result being that no information on the subject was transmitted to Berlin. Revertera then returned to Switzerland with fresh instructions.

On August 22nd Armand and Revertera met again. Armand produced his written peace proposals, which were so far-reaching in character (they involved the restitution of Belgium and the French invaded departments, with complete compensation, the ceding of Alsace and Lorraine, the neutralization of the left bank of the Rhine, the ceding of the Trentino and Trieste, the restitution of Rumania and Serbia, the establishment of an independent Poland as formerly constituted, the federalization of the Habsburg Empire, etc.) that it seemed as if the negotiations were not intended seriously. On August 28th Czernin informed Revertera that these proposals were not acceptable for any sort of negotiations, that it was impossible to transmit them to Berlin, and that any separation from Germany was entirely out of the question. Accordingly, there were no further negotiations.

But in the middle of September 1917 and again in January 1918, Revertera—according to the Austrian version—through the same channels, received a message that Armand was anxious to renew the conversations with him. Czernin sent Revertera instructions from Brest-Litovsk to the effect that he was quite willing for further discussions to take place, but it must be made clear to Armand that if France desired a genuine exchange of views, it would be best for a meeting to take place between the Foreign Ministers or their plenipotentiaries. This would at once make things clear.

On February 2nd Revertera and Armand had an interview, from the general purport of which, as reported by Revertera, it is clear that Clemenceau, like the preceding Government, was willing to negotiate with Vienna for a separate peace. What he wanted were counter-proposals to the last French peace offer of August 1917. He insisted upon securing Alsace-Lorraine, and emphasized the requirement that Austria-

Hungary was not to identify herself so completely with the imperialistic programme of Berlin, as Czernin was doing in his declarations. Thereupon Czernin, on February 22nd, requested Revertera to point out that there were no prospects of any serious negotiations until France renounced her claims to the annexation of Alsace-Lorraine. Revertera carried out these instructions at a meeting on February 25th. On that occasion he also furnished Armand with a written memorandum from which, however, it would appear that the Viennese version attributing the initiative for these negotiations with Paris is incorrect, and that on the contrary the whole scheme emanated from Vienna. Other indications lead me to believe that Revertera's action, which in point of time coincided with the final stages of the negotiations carried on by Sixtus of Bourbon, had the same basis and originated from the same circles as these did. In any case, Karl was closely associated with the action, which in its early stages was certainly not divulged to Berlin.

Armand then at once informed Revertera that under these circumstances Clemenceau would not embark upon the negotiations. Shortly after that, on March 4th, Revertera again received a message that Clemenceau would not entertain any peace offer which did not settle the question of Alsace-Lorraine.

From the official French documents, and also from the controversy which developed on this subject between Clemenceau and Czernin, emerged the following facts which tend to rebut the Austrian version and, I think, to confirm the conclusions which I have suggested above :

1. In his declaration of April, Painlevé stated that according to the Intelligence Section of the Ministry of War, the initiative came from Austrian quarters in June 1917, and that through the agency of a certain Swiss citizen, Count Armand was several times invited to meet his relative, Count Revertera (Armand and Revertera are, I believe, cousins).

2. From Clemenceau's declaration on April 8, 1918, it follows that the meeting was the result of Austrian initiative, and that Painlevé and Ribot gave their permission for Major Armand, of the Intelligence Department of the Ministry of War, to proceed to Switzerland. Although the negotiations produced no result, when Clemenceau, on November 18th, the day after his entry into office, was informed of the new *démarche* from

Switzerland, dated November 10th, he did not consider it desirable to interrupt the negotiations, as they might provide the Ministry of War with useful information. Major Armand therefore received permission to proceed again to Switzerland, after having been instructed by Clemenceau, in the presence of his chief, Colonel Goubet, that he was to listen to Revertera but to say nothing himself.

3. On February 25, 1918, according to the French version, Revertera, wishing to lay stress upon the purpose for which negotiations had been started, handed Armand a written explanation as follows: In August 1917 conversations were instituted for the purpose of securing from the French Government peace proposals for Austria-Hungary, which should be of such a character that they could receive the backing of Austria-Hungary.

From the above evidence it can be inferred that the initiative in June 1917 did actually emanate from Revertera, that the basis of the negotiations was identical with that underlying the activity of Sixtus of Bourbon, and that Karl was implicated in the matter. When Vienna saw the conditions upon which Paris insisted, and realized that they could not possibly lead to any results, the matter was dropped. It would also seem that in January 1918 the negotiations were started by Armand, but that Czernin at once insisted on discussing, not a separate but a general peace.

Thus, for the third time it was seen that the aims of Vienna and those of the Allies were still opposed. Clemenceau, without obviously pursuing such a purpose, received a fresh and decisive proof that such was the case, at a moment which was of particular importance to us. I should not here refer to these matters again if the negotiations between Armand and Revertera had not given rise to the well-known conflict between Clemenceau and Czernin at the very moment when international events were compelling the Allies to adopt a definite attitude towards the Habsburg Empire. This conflict was the last and culminating factor leading to the first mortal blow which was inflicted upon Austria-Hungary.

106

On April 2nd Czernin delivered a speech to a delegation from the municipality of Vienna which had important reactions both within the Empire and abroad. From the point of view of Austria-Hungary, the Habsburg dynasty, and the Foreign Minister himself it was a fundamental blunder. Although it did not actually decide the fate of the Empire, there could be no doubt that it facilitated and hastened the collapse of the Monarchy. It is difficult to estimate what could have been the immediate causes of so serious a mistake. In any case, it shows that at this period of his apparently great successes Czernin had entirely lost his balance, and was now incapable of any clear judgment about the situation of the Empire at home and abroad.

In his speech Czernin at first made a violent attack on our foreign movement. He referred to Masaryk in uncomplimentary terms, and pointed out that although equally such treacherous leaders were to be found both within the Empire and outside it, the Czech nation was loyal to Austria. These remarks produced a violent conflict within the Empire, in which the Jugoslavs and Poles made common cause with us. The Czech delegation protested in most emphatic terms to Seidler, the Prime Minister, who, without actually disassociating himself from Czernin's speech, endeavoured to tone it down in certain respects. Nevertheless, the speech provided our politicians and those of the Jugoslavs in Austria with a pretext for greater opposition to the Government, and for the manifesto against the Empire which occurred in April. The effect of the speech abroad was principally to provide our movement with the best possible tribute. The Allied Governments realized better than ever the extent to which Vienna was harassed by our movement, and Masaryk became an even more significant symbol of the struggle against the Empire.

There was a second noteworthy point in Czernin's speech which produced results of equal importance. His defence of Vienna and Berlin for a policy of annexation after the conclusion of the three peace treaties, by which the Central Powers and Bulgaria had come into possession of extensive territories, and his taunting of the Allies with the responsibility for the prolongation of the war, aroused more violent protests against him than against the Germans, who made no secret of their intentions and did not attempt to make them appear innocent by means of pacifist phraseology.

But the most important part of Czernin's speech was his reference to the secret peace negotiations with France. In order to brace the political circles at home to further efforts, and to explain why the war was being continued, why the last offensive had been launched, and why Vienna would remain side by side with Berlin against France until the end, he declared that Clemenceau had recently endeavoured to start peace negotiations with Vienna, but that Czernin had insisted on the need for first renouncing all claims to Alsace-Lorraine. As Paris had refused to do so, there was no alternative but to continue victoriously to the end. Here Czernin was evidently alluding to the interview between Armand and Revertera at Freiburg on February 2nd and 25th, to his instructions to Revertera, and also to the report which Revertera had sent to Vienna on the subject of his action. The blow which Czernin wished to inflict was aimed in two directions. It was intended to strengthen confidence at home, and to demoralize Allied public opinion, especially that of France, at the moment when the severest German offensive was being launched. It was also intended as a proof to Italy that she had been betrayed by France, who had been making peace negotiations without her knowledge.

As soon as this speech had been delivered, Clemenceau repudiated Czernin's version, and Czernin, who in the meanwhile had left for Bucharest to settle the peace terms with Rumania, immediately returned and started a controversy with Clemenceau. The latter, in a number of official reports, emphasized the fact that it had not been France but Vienna who had sought peace negotiations, and these attempts at a separate peace had been made on several occasions. At the same time he alluded to the intervention of Sixtus of Bourbon and to Karl's agreement with the French claims to Alsace-Lorraine.

This filled Czernin with consternation, and then ensued his controversy with Karl on the subject of the Emperor's well-known letter to Sixtus. Karl first of all repudiated to Czernin the authenticity of the letter, and sent a telegram in this sense to the Kaiser. Czernin made an official declaration accordingly, but when Clemenceau published a facsimile of the letter, Vienna had recourse to the explanation that the letter was purely personal and non-official, and that it had been forged. To all these evasions on the part of Vienna, Clemenceau replied with a severe indictment of Karl and Czernin. The whole world then saw that the Emperor had been lying, and that Czernin had fallen a victim to the results of this intrigue.

It is not quite clear whether he had been imposed upon or not, but there can be no doubt that at the moment when he was publicly testifying against Clemenceau he was quite aware of what was going on. The memoirs of Windischgraetz prove this.

Czernin fully realized what this moral catastrophe involved. Victorious Berlin would regard the affair as treachery at the moment when its armies were again approaching Paris. The Germans and Magyars in Austria would use this against him, so that his policy, the policy of the Empire, and the situation within it were all threatened. Czernin, who evidently at that period regarded himself as the protector of the Empire, now opposed all attempts at secret anti-German negotiations or at a downright separation from Germany on the part of Karl and Zita as firmly as he had shared their views in April 1917. It is said that he was now considering the possibility of forcing Karl to abdicate as a sequel to the affair. The matter ended, however, with his resignation on April 14, 1918. The net result of the episode had been to reveal to the Allied countries the deplorable character of Viennese policy. Czernin was the last Austro-Hungarian Foreign Minister who had any kind of Austro-Hungarian policy. His fall denoted the end of the Empire, and his successors, Burian and Andrássy, were merely liquidators of a ruined concern.

Austro-Hungarian policy could scarcely have sustained a severer blow than the incidents to which I have just referred. And when Paris, Rome, and London received further reports, concerning the telegram of Karl to Wilhelm on the subject of an indefeasible alliance between the two Empires and Karl's journey to Spa, followed by a new agreement of alliance by which Vienna entered into fresh commitments to Berlin, all the Allied Governments could only infer that any separation of Austria-Hungary from Germany was now out of the question, and that the war would have to be won by force of arms. As a matter of fact, the agreement at Spa was the closest military, political, and economic union which the two Empires had hitherto concluded. Vienna had up till then avoided such binding commitments, notably in economic matters, but at Spa Karl succumbed in this respect also. The further discussions as to the development of an economic union were carried out in all detail by the appropriate experts at Salzburg between July 9 and October 11, 1918. The fall of the Empire, of course, made these things null and void.

It was now felt that the Allied Governments had passed sentence on the Habsburg Empire. I myself drew this conclusion from the political events which immediately followed the news from Spa. On April 11th the French Government issued an official *communiqué* announcing that all the documents relating to the Clemenceau-Czernin incident were to be submitted to the Parliamentary Committee of Foreign Affairs. This was done a month later and, as we shall see, it led to declarations on the part of Clemenceau which proved decisive in their bearing upon the policy of France towards Vienna and ourselves.

Under these circumstances our work in Paris progressed admirably. I have already referred to the visit of representatives of the oppressed nations of Austria-Hungary, and it was upon this occasion that Clemenceau expressed himself to me in terms of particular approval concerning our military and political movement, emphasizing the necessity for transferring our Siberian army to France. Shortly after that I again applied to Clemenceau for an audience and for a more concrete discussion of our affairs, particularly as regards the status of our army and our political position in general. I was received on April 20th, when I gave Clemenceau an account of our various achievements. I asked him to agree to the recognition of Czechoslovak independence and of the National Council as a *de facto* Government. He expressed himself as being entirely favourable to my application on principle, but pointed out that before his sanction could take effect the preliminary arrangements would have to be duly made, and an agreement reached with the various authorities concerned. He was still reacting to the effects of his controversy with Czernin, and declared that he himself regarded the Czechoslovak question as settled, that he would recognize the National Council as a Government body, and that he was prepared to grant it the Government prerogatives for which I had asked—recognition of diplomatic representatives, passports, the grant of a loan, etc. A month later, at a fresh audience, he repeated and amplified his promise, giving also his consent to a procedure by which it could be carried into effect.

The important effects of these events was shown when, on May 10, 1918, Clemenceau submitted to the Parliamentary Committee of Foreign Affairs a report on the Sixtus of Bourbon incident and the Armand-Revertera negotiations. In outlining the fundamental features of the attempts at a separate peace with the Habsburg Empire, especially the last episode with Czernin and Karl, Clemenceau indicated the aims of the French Government. No real interest of France or any other Ally had been neglected. The negotiations could not have led to any satisfactory result, because there had never been any real possibility of concluding an acceptable peace with Vienna and isolating Germany. This was clear from the documentary evidence submitted. Clemenceau accordingly inferred that the only remaining possibility was to proceed to the last extremity against the Habsburg Empire, to support all the efforts of the Austro-Hungarian nations to secure their independence, and thus to accelerate the fall of the Habsburg Empire and, with it, the fall of Germany. The published *communiqué* on the subject of this meeting shows quite plainly the direction followed by the committee in its deliberations.(43)

(e) Last Attempts at an Agreement with Vienna on the Part of Great Britain and the United States

107

Similar conclusions as to the possibilities of a separate peace with Vienna were reached at this period by Great Britain and the United States, not through the influence of Clemenceau's policy, but as the result of other events which were no less important, but which concerned these two countries exclusively.

The whole of Lloyd George's action on the subject of Austria-Hungary in 1917 showed plainly that England would not have hesitated to make an agreement with Vienna if the opportunity had presented itself. This was shown beyond any doubt by Lloyd George's attitude in the Sixtus of Bourbon incident, his initiative for negotiations in December 1917, and his speech on January 5, 1918. In spite of the fact that the action of General Smuts and the public declarations of Lloyd George had produced no positive result, the Government was convinced in February 1918 that its procedure with regard to the Habsburg Empire was the correct one. When Balfour, on February 13, 1918, replied to a question which Mr. Whyte had asked concerning the negotiations of General Smuts at Geneva, he declared quite frankly that the Government considered it their duty to avail themselves of all means which, while adequately protecting the interests of the British Empire, would tend to shorten the war for the general advantage. He thus indicated that if it were possible to come to some arrangement with Vienna, and then more easily and quickly defeat an isolated Germany, London would endeavour to do it.

In spite of this, the latest events on the Eastern front, and the German offensive which was being prepared in the West, compelled the British Government to follow Clemenceau's example and, while not entirely ruling out the scheme in hand, to avail themselves of all possible resources for securing a military victory against the German and Austrian Empires. In the middle of February this led the British Cabinet to establish an extensive and systematic network of propaganda in the enemy countries for the purpose of undermining the enemy battle-fronts, and also of weakening the opposition behind the front among the population and the political circles. London was only now beginning what Germany had been doing for some time past, and it was also then that the Bolsheviks began the same kind of work on a large scale. By arrangement with the Governments in Paris and Rome, it was decided that a joint Allied system of propaganda should be started, and that the English side of it should be managed by Lord Northcliffe, who had recently returned from a mission in America.

Lord Northcliffe accepted Lloyd George's offer and, after conferring with Mr. Wickham Steed, he prepared a whole organization, the London headquarters of which were located at Crewe House. An inter-Allied agreement on the subject of joint propaganda was reached at a meeting in London, which was attended by Wickham Steed on behalf of England, Franklin-Bouillon and Moysset on behalf of France, and Callenga Stuart on behalf of Italy. All these close friends of ours were advocates of the policy which aimed chiefly at the destruction of the Habsburg Empire.

The preliminary arrangements for this scheme in London throw an interesting light on the policy of the British Cabinet at that juncture. Lord Northcliffe, having accepted the post as director of this propaganda, was advised by Steed to ascertain the precise political basis upon which his work was to be carried on. In a letter to Balfour on February 24th he rightly pointed out that the tendency of the propaganda would necessarily depend upon whether the Allies wished to make peace with Karl and his monarchy, without paying any attention to its internal condition, or whether their policy aimed at the destruction of the Habsburg Empire and the liberation of the non-German and non-Magyar nationalities within it. Balfour's reply, dated February 26, 1918, is a very instructive one. He stated that the British Government was still unable to make any definite reply to so far-reaching a question. They must first of all know what view was taken of this by France, Italy, and the United States. He added that it would nevertheless be possible to carry on the propaganda for the time being in such a way that neither of the two eventualities would be excluded. If propaganda was going to be carried on with a view to liberating the oppressed nationalities, and in such a way that the destruction of the Habsburg Empire seemed to be its objective, it might have the effect of forcing the Empire to decide more quickly in favour of a separate peace. If, nevertheless, this result were not to be reached, the dissolution and collapse of the Empire would accelerate the liberation of the peoples in it. Therefore, announced Balfour, although the propaganda must be carried on as though we wished to destroy the Empire, we must not in the meanwhile shut the door to any possibility of peace with Karl by any definite promise as to the liberation of the oppressed peoples.

Lord Northcliffe and Mr. Steed accepted this condition, although reluctantly, and asked that the Allied Governments should at least make no definite declarations in favour of the Habsburg Empire, but should, on the contrary, manifest their sympathies with the oppressed peoples. They added that in any case the Foreign Office would soon see that it had taken an incorrect view as to the method of procedure.

The British Government very soon received proof of this. At the conclusion of their meeting at Geneva in December 1917, General Smuts and Count Mensdorff-Pouilly had agreed that they would continue their negotiations if the Governments concerned wished to proceed in the same manner as before, i.e. with Sir Horace Rumbold and Legation Counsellor V. Skrzynski as intermediaries.

In accordance with this agreement, Mr. Phillip Kerr arrived at Berne on March 10, 1918, with new proposals from Lloyd George for further negotiations with the Viennese Government. Skrzynski at once notified Czernin, who, however, on this occasion very decisively instructed Skrzynski not to negotiate with Mr. Kerr. His reasons for this were, firstly, that London had divulged the Smuts negotiations which had actually been referred to in the British Parliament, with the result that Czernin had been attacked by Press and Parliament both in Germany and at home ; and then it was Czernin's view that both the previous and the present English overtures were merely an attempt to arouse nervousness and mistrust, for the purpose of separating Vienna from Berlin.

Nevertheless, Mr. Kerr found a means for reaching Skrzynski, who discussed matters with him, and he afterwards made various excuses to Czernin for having thus acted contrary to his orders. There can be no doubt that the people in Berne did not agree with Czernin's view of the situation, and considered that it would be advisable to meet Kerr. The latter again inquired whether Vienna would or would not make peace without Germany and cease to support German imperialism. Skrzynski, on his own account, could only say that he had received instructions from Vienna to negotiate with nobody, and that Vienna, as he himself knew, would in no case separate from Berlin. Thus Lloyd George's scheme again fell through.

On March 7th the Jugoslav-Italian agreement, to which I have previously referred, was signed at London provisionally by Trumbić and A. Torre, and this step was followed with interest and sympathy by the Foreign Office. The preparations for the Congress of Rome had been completed, and Steed left for France, partly to carry on the propaganda which had been arranged, partly on account of the Congress of Rome, as he judged from Balfour's letter that London would support all schemes in favour of the oppressed peoples if the consent of Paris and Rome could be secured.

During the Congress of Rome the British representative showed himself very favourably disposed to our movement. After the Congress he attended the demonstration which was held in connection with our army, and when the Prince of Wales came to Rome in May 1918 he was present at the demonstration in Augusteo, which Štefánik also attended. These were symptoms of a more resolute policy on the part of London. Then came the Clemenceau-Czernin incident, which definitely influenced British public opinion and Government circles against Karl and the Habsburg Empire.

I may add that when I went to London to negotiate for the

recognition of the National Council, Lord Robert Cecil assured me that under certain conditions the British Government would recognize our independence.

Thus we see that the month of April 1918 was a critical period in England, as elsewhere, in which events had matured sufficiently to settle the fate of the Habsburg Empire.

108

The same influences operated in the United States. I have already sketched the main outlines of President Wilson's policy towards the Habsburg Empire. On various occasions and in various forms he had repeated his principles: a struggle against the imperialism and autocracy of the Central European Governments in favour of their internal democratization and the self-determination of peoples, the allotment of Italian territory to Italy, of Polish territory to Poland, the reconstitution of Serbia and Rumania, the settlement of injustices, and compensation for devastated areas, the evacuation of occupied territories, the freedom of the seas, disarmament after the war, arbitration courts, the League of Nations. All this, however, did not necessarily mean the destruction of the Habsburg Empire.

The United States at this moment had no political scheme which would affect the existence of the Empire. Wilson's attitude towards Austria had not changed since he had declared war on her. Vienna therefore thought it advisable to pass from public declarations to secret negotiations.(44)

On February 17, 1918, Czernin, at the Emperor's request, sent to Prince Fürstenberg, the Austro-Hungarian Ambassador in Madrid, a telegram entrusting him with a long message from Karl to President Wilson. The Ambassador was instructed to hand it personally to King Alfonso, and to ask him on behalf of the Emperor to act as intermediary between Karl and President Wilson. At the same time Karl indicated his belief that the last declarations of Wilson and Czernin had cleared up the situation to such an extent that it was now possible for representatives of Karl and President Wilson to proceed to a direct exchange of views on the subject of peace.

In the message itself the Emperor based his argument on four principles expressed by Wilson in his speech on February 12th, and in accordance with them he explained his views on the war and the possibilities of peace negotiations.

Karl's proposal was that both sides should declare their readiness to renounce any kind of annexations or indemnities. He added that this would mean the complete liberation of Belgium. He expressed the opinion that the agreement between the views of President Wilson and his own was such as to make it possible to set about concrete negotiations. He concluded by proposing a meeting between the representatives of President Wilson and his own delegates.

Prince Fürstenberg delivered the message to King Alfonso on February 22nd, and three days later Alfonso informed Karl that he would willingly dispatch the message to President Wilson, and that he hoped for its success. At the same time he demanded the strictest secrecy in the whole matter. On March 2nd he sent Karl a fresh report on the audience of the Spanish Ambassador at Washington, giving an account of how the message had been delivered, and how Wilson had reacted to it.

According to the report of the Spanish Ambassador, Wilson, after thanking King Alfonso for delivering Karl's document, expressed great interest in the message, which seemed to him to be rather "transcendental," and announced that he would have to examine it carefully before replying. This was all the more necessary because this intervention had placed him in a somewhat awkward predicament; he was opposed to any kind of secret negotiations, and these were matters which interested all his other Allies. Besides this, any peace negotiations or settlements of territorial problems must be based upon the principle of national justice and not upon any secret agreements on the part of one side or the other. Nevertheless, it appeared that the Spanish Ambassador and King Alfonso were favourably impressed by the effects of the step they had taken. In Alfonso's opinion, Wilson would agree to a direct exchange of views, but would not enter into any discussions through the agency of delegates. Such a process would constitute actual negotiations, and Wilson would be obliged to notify his Allies about such a matter beforehand.

On March 5, 1918, King Alfonso handed Prince Fürstenberg Wilson's reply. In it Wilson first of all expressed his gratification that Karl accepted the principles which he had laid down before Congress on January 8th and February 11th. He pointed out, however, that there was no need to discuss them with the help of delegates, because they were so clear and pregnant that no representative of Wilson could elucidate them further. He said that he would like to see the principles of the other side formulated with equal clarity. In particular he would like to know what was meant by a settlement of Balkan problems, how Karl proposed to deal with the disputes concerning the Adriatic coast and those with Italy, what he understood by the satisfaction of the national aspirations of the Slavonic people in Austria-Hungary, and how he would handle the question of the non-Turkish nationalities in Turkey. Wilson assumed that as regards Polish and Belgian affairs his views were identical with those of Karl. He further assured Karl that he desired knowledge on these points, not for any reasons of tactics, but because he really wished to go into these matters. He said that he was anxious to discover a rational settlement, and to promote the chances of a quick and genuinely lasting peace.

In the opinion of Alfonso and his ambassador, Wilson's reply did not offer much ground for actual optimism, but it was nevertheless a good sign. Wilson, it appeared, had told the ambassador that he himself had typed out the whole of the reply in order that nobody could divulge the secret. An exchange of views conducted on these lines was not at variance with his opinions about public peace negotiations. If, however, the steps hitherto taken were to be changed into any form of explicit offer, Wilson would be obliged to inform the Allies about it immediately.

Karl and Czernin decided to reply to Wilson's question through the same channels as before. As early as March 9th they notified King Alfonso of their intention, and made the preliminary arrangements for it. On March 23, 1918, the lengthy text of Karl's reply left Vienna for Madrid, but the delivery of Karl's message was delayed in Madrid through what appeared to have been partly technical difficulties and partly political obstacles. King Alfonso seems at this juncture to have had difficulties with Dato, his Prime Minister, who was afraid that Alfonso's action would involve Spain in awkward consequences if the Allies got to hear of it.

In actual fact, as early as March 13th, the London newspapers reported that Karl was in touch with President Wilson. On the day before, the *Matin* had published a definite report from Switzerland stating that negotiations were proceeding between Karl and President Wilson. Even earlier than this, on March 9th, i.e. immediately after Wilson's first reply, the *Temps* published an unmistakable reference to King Alfonso, mentioning in its special report that Karl had applied to Wilson through the agency of a neutral sovereign. These matters were clearly a source of great embarrassment to the Government at Madrid, and it would appear that they caused a considerable delay in the subsequent proceedings and in the delivery of Karl's reply. Towards the end of March the whole matter was a current topic in the diplomatic circles of Paris and Switzerland, although the precise and detailed facts were not known. It was from these circles that we heard about the negotiations. There was a rumour in Paris that the Allied intelligence service had intercepted and deciphered telegrams which Alfonso had sent to Washington. We ourselves in Paris were very imperfectly informed about the matter. The newspaper reports had drawn our attention to it, but at first I did not place any credence in it, and even afterwards I did not consider that it was of any great importance. At that particular moment I was so taken up by work connected with our army, as well as the preliminary arrangements for the Congress of Rome, and I had such confidence in our early success with the transport of an army to France, that I now no longer regarded such a surprise as possible.

As a result of the diplomatic difficulties, and owing to the circumstance that Karl's message in its final wording was very late in reaching Madrid, the message was not delivered to Alfonso by the Austro-Hungarian Ambassador until the middle of April 1918.

This important reply of Karl to President Wilson, which was prepared after March 10, 1918, contains the following main ideas:

First of all, Karl emphasizes the agreement of his views with Wilson's principles, but he points out the advantages of verbal negotiations over lengthy correspondence. As regards the national aspirations of the Slav peoples, who are located in the neighbourhood of Karl's territories, he desires to offer them a helping hand, but he denies their right to shift nations and provinces from one State sovereignty to another without their will and, in fact, against their interests, since owing to the mixture of races in those parts of Europe it is impossible to settle racial questions so as not to infringe at the same time the equal national rights of other nations. On the shores of the

Adriatic, Austria, he said, was not pursuing tendencies at variance with Wilson's principles. He added that a direct conversation would be the easiest way for devising a means of removing antagonisms in the Balkans in the interest of the Balkan nations and in accordance with Wilson's wishes. In this respect it would be necessary to unite the scattered Bulgarian minorities by incorporating them with Bulgaria, and to ensure the possibility of economic expansion for Serbia and other States. As regards protection of the non-Turkish races in the Ottoman Empire, a solution could be found compatible both with Wilson's principles and with Turkish sovereignty. In reply to a direct inquiry of Wilson's as to what concessions to Italy he regarded as reasonable, Karl pointed out that the Italian demands for territory from the Brenner and Ljubljana (Laibach) run completely counter to Wilson's principles, since the population of these areas is largely German or Slav. Trieste, which is more Slav and German than Italian, had, he said, agreed with Austria, and he would regard its incorporation in Italy as a complete disaster. Southern Tyrol had never belonged to Italy, and the Italian elements which had settled there had done so only for the sake of an economic existence. In conclusion, he repeated the opinion that a settlement of this question in the spirit of Wilson's principles was possible only by direct conversation. The only obstacle to peace lay in the acquisitive aims of France and Italy, and if Wilson could induce them to abandon these, the doors of peace would open.

I have ascertained that Kühlmann was informed by Czernin about this second message. The second phase of his action was thus proceeding with the knowledge of Berlin. This was Czernin's customary method of procedure. He began some scheme on his own account, so as not to be interfered with by Berlin, and then he waited for a favourable opportunity of notifying Berlin in such a way that his action could be regarded as correct.

In the meanwhile, however, since Wilson's first reply, the peace of Brest-Litovsk and also peace with Rumania had been concluded. Then followed Czernin's well-known speech at Vienna on April 2nd, as well as his conflict with Clemenceau. This brings us to Czernin's resignation on April 14th, to which I have previously referred, and to the reappointment of Burian as Minister of Foreign Affairs three days later. On

April 21st Burian sent Prince Fürstenberg a telegram instructing him not to send Karl's message to Washington for the time being, if it could not be done by a special courier, as the Spanish cipher was known to the Allies.

President Wilson probably never received Karl's second message. The Clemenceau-Czernin incident and everything which followed it, the new agreements on the occasion of Karl's visit to Spa, the new commitments and the greater dependence of Vienna upon Berlin no doubt deprived Karl and the Government at Vienna of any opportunity or desire to continued any such scheme.

On my return to Paris I was asked to call upon Mr. Sharp, the American Ambassador. At that time I was in continual contact with Mr. Frazer, his Counsellor of Embassy, and in fact with the whole of his staff, to whom I had been systematically furnishing reports on our work in the Allied countries and on the conditions in Central Europe ever since the autumn of 1917. I regularly used to receive invitations to visit the Embassy whenever anything of particular importance had happened, and in the second half of April Mr. Sharp had twice asked me to call upon him in connection with the Clemenceau-Czernin conflict, as he was anxious to obtain details about the state of affairs in the Habsburg Empire, the Congress of Rome, and the stage which our movement had reached in France. At first Mr. Sharp had been totally ignorant of Central Europe and our affairs, which he had accordingly regarded in a very naïve manner, but when he became acquainted with our movement, the organization of our army and our political and military activities in the Allied countries, he at once became an enthusiastic supporter of our national demands. I am unable to say whether he had any influence on his Government and on President Wilson. On the occasion of my second visit he read to me the telegrams which he had sent to Wilson on the subject of our affairs. They constituted an enthusiastic plea on our behalf, and a demonstration of the fact that nothing more could be done with the Habsburg Empire, that the nations in it were gradually liberating themselves, and that the Allies in Europe were clearly directing their policy in accordance with this circumstance.

These successes were, of course, supplemented first and foremost by our intensive action in the United States themselves. Masaryk had reached Chicago on May 5th, and his arrival had become known throughout America on account of the enthusiastic welcome which was extended to him by the American Czechs and Slovaks. From that moment he began a systematic activity on behalf of our political aims, and he collaborated with the representatives of the nations who, like ourselves, were counteracting the efforts of the pro-Austrians and the pro-Magyars. In his *Making of a State*, Masaryk has given a detailed account of this activity, and, in particular, he explains the whole basis of the Austrophile tendencies in America.

If I again consider what happened in the first four months of 1918 as regards Austro-Hungarian affairs—Lloyd George's final attempt at negotiations with Austria-Hungary on March 10th, Karl's attempt at peace negotiations with President Wilson in February and March 1918, which on April 21st, after the Clemenceau-Czernin conflict, was abandoned as the result of Burian's orders—I again arrive at my former conclusion: the Allies had realized that secret negotiations would lead to nothing in 1918. On the other hand the conclusion of peace in the East, and the final desperate offensive of Germany in the West, had impressed upon the Allies two facts which were essential to a proper understanding of the war: Russia, whose intrusion into Central Europe they feared, and whose possible expansion had hitherto formed the argument of many for preserving the Habsburg Empire, had now collapsed; on the other hand Germany had acquired a mastery over the whole of Central and South-Eastern Europe. At length it was fully understood what we had meant when we had said that Austria-Hungary no longer constituted that counterpoise against Germany in Central and Southern Europe which, according to French conceptions, she should still have been in the last century, but she was, on the contrary, a link and an auxiliary factor for German expansion towards the south and the east. It is impossible to exaggerate the significance and the scope of these facts in their bearing upon the change which Allied policy underwent in this question.

109

On May 10, 1918, I sent our political circles in Prague the following brief political report, which gives a clear idea of our situation in the Allied countries at that time, and shows the political progress which had been made in the preceding months:

1. Our political situation is excellent. The Clemenceau-Czernin conflict has definitely destroyed all links with Austria-Hungary, against whom they will now proceed here resolutely and with full strength. The war may drag on for about another year and a half, and this must be reckoned with. In France and Italy our position is very good, and in England they are now resolutely moving against Austria. In France, within about three months, we shall have some seventy or eighty thousand troops.(45)

In Italy our division is already at the front. The formation of the army is being carried on energetically by Colonel Štefánik, who completed the chief negotiations with the Italian Government on the subject of the army. Professor Masaryk has reached America from Russia, and he will stay there for some time. At the present moment he is in Chicago.

2. Our movement is at its best in France. Here the National Council is in a strong position, it is exercising supreme rights as regards the Czech Army, it is recognized by the Government as a supreme governing body, and after the arrival of our troops from Russia it will have even more power. The Congress of Rome has strengthened our position. Co-operation has been arranged between all the Austro-Hungarian peoples, and this was of great significance here.

After his return from Rome Dr. Beneš, with the other delegates, was received by Clemenceau, who definitely informed him that France would not desert the Czechs, and spoke about our troops in terms of high commendation. At the last military conference at Abbeville our army was likewise a subject of discussion, and it was referred to with approval. If you at home can also continue as hitherto in a relentless struggle, there is no doubt that we shall win the day.

3. Therefore be prepared for fresh political successes on our part. After our return from the Congress of Rome, Clemenceau and Pichon promised us emphatically that they would give us a declaration, and acknowledge us as completely independent. Clemenceau expressed himself similarly on the Commission which dealt with Emperor Karl's letter, and announced that they would recognize and proclaim the independence of the Austro-Hungarian nations. Our work on this matter is now making rapid headway in Paris. We are sure that the result will be satisfactory, and that in a short time we shall attain recognition. Be prepared for it.

4. It is therefore of enormous importance for preparations to be made at home also. You must do more, not only in political matters but also in other directions, to harm and destroy the whole position of Austria-Hungary. It is essential for the people there to see that we are working with all possible resources. Masaryk will arrive in Europe within eight weeks.

(f) The Struggle for the Principle of Self-determination within the Habsburg Empire

110

The report reached Prague shortly after the celebrations at the National Theatre in May, at a time when within Austria-Hungary the same development in the struggle against the Empire and for self-determination was being completed, as had just been successfully achieved in the Allied countries. It assumed forms which were more and more revolutionary in character, and which only in a few cases for tactical reasons were still thinly disguised. The parallel action and the direct co-operation of the revolutionary movement abroad, with the political action which was directed in the same spirit within the Empire, was now beginning to be carried into effect. The struggle for the principle of self-determination was thus started to its fullest extent within the Empire also.

The slogan of self-determination was first uttered by our politicians in the proclamation of the "Czech League" on April 14, 1917. Here, evidently under the influence of the Russian revolution, they appealed for "the application of democracy, of Parliamentarianism, and the revision of the constitution on the lines of self-determination and the requirements of nations in the Habsburg Empire also."

Under the influence of the Czech's authors' manifesto and of public opinion, which received it with enthusiasm, the proclamation of the Czech deputies in the Viennese Parliament on May 30th went even further. It appealed primarily for the principle of self-determination, from which it then deduced the need for a national Czechoslovak State. This was all the more important because analogous proclamations were made by the Poles, Jugoslavs, and Ruthenians, so that from this time onwards the action taken by these nations was uniform or parallel with our own. Allied public opinion interpreted this as a profound crisis, going to the very roots of the Habsburg Empire. The succeeding events tended only to strengthen this impression. Our propaganda was continually striving to hasten this crisis at home, while demonstrating in the Allied countries that the Habsburg Empire was moving towards its inevitable collapse. It was naturally our most earnest wish that nothing should happen at Prague and Vienna which might discredit our interpretation of events and the efforts we based upon it, and in our messages to Prague we gave the most emphatic expression to this desire.

Of course, we made the most abundant use of every proclamation and every action emanating from our deputies, our politicians, our Press, and our authors. The declaration made by Clam-Martinic on June 12th, in which he repudiated the declaration of the opposition on May 30th, and insisted that the only programme of the Government was Austria and her inviolable unity; Dr. A. Stránský's reply, which immediately followed, and which culminated in the declaration that none of the racial problems of Austria-Hungary would be solved in the Parliament at Vienna; the speeches of the Czech deputies, Stříbrný and Kalina, together with the proclamations of Korošec and Lazarski on behalf of the Jugoslavs and the Poles respectively—we exploited all this material for the purpose of showing the Allies that what had been advocated by President Wilson on the subject of the freedom of nations found warm response within the Habsburg Empire.

The fall of Clam-Martinic on June 22, 1917, confirmed this impression, while the further steps taken by the Czechs and Jugoslavs against Seidler's new Government made our work all the easier. The declaration of the Czech deputy, Staněk, on June 26th, declining to vote for Seidler's Government or for any other which would not recognize the principle of self-determination; the declaration of another Czech deputy, Prášek, who spoke against the alliance with Germany, and who expressed the solidarity of all the Czech deputies with those of their colleagues then in prison; the proclamation against dualism and in favour of the establishment of national States; the proclamation of the Czech deputies Bechyně and Zahradník, in the same sense—all these things were quoted by us as further serious symptoms of the approaching collapse.

The further progress of events assisted our efforts even more thoroughly. Czernin continued his attempts and manœuvres to conclude peace with revolutionary Russia, and issued declarations that he accepted the views of the Russian revolutionary Government on the subject of peace without annexation or indemnities, guaranteeing freedom for all nations. He himself compelled Parliament to debate the principles proclaimed by the Russian revolution, and this led to questions and proclamations by the deputies, Soukup and Daszynski, demanding that the nations themselves, and not merely the Emperor, should have a decisive voice in the peace negotiations, the terms of which must be based upon the principles of self-determination.

Czernin was perturbed by this move. He feared that it might weaken the Empire at the peace negotiations, which he now believed to be close at hand, and accordingly, on June 27th, he caused Seidler to deliver a declaration in Parliament, which aroused great attention both within the Empire and abroad, and proved of no little service to our propaganda. The declaration ran as follows: "The assumption expressed in the interpellation made by Deputy Daszynski, implying that the Imperial and Royal Government would acknowledge the right of self-determination as a basis for a permanent peace, is an error. The Imperial and Royal Government takes its stand upon the basis of Article V. of the Constitutional Law of December 21, 1867."(46)

At the moment when a severe struggle on this subject was being waged in Russia between the Government and the extremists, at the moment when President Wilson was solemnly proclaiming this principle of self-determination, when it was gaining influence and strength in the Allied countries, Czernin's proclamation served admirably to throw light upon the state of the Empire and the intentions of the Government at Vienna and the Central Powers in general. And in this respect Vienna was considered to be far more moderate than Berlin. The Allied Governments, when speaking about the freedom of nations, had in mind not merely the nations within Austria, but chiefly Belgium, Poland, Serbia, and Rumania, who at that time were in the hands of the Central Powers. The Seidler-Czernin proclamation was taken as indicating what the Governments of the Central Powers would do in this respect if they were to remain masters of the situation.

The Czech deputy, Dr. Baxa, made a speech on June 28th, in which he pointed out that as a logical result of this policy the Czech question and the other racial problems would not be settled in the Empire itself, but at a general peace conference which would decide the future of the small nations. Then came a new declaration by Staněk, published in the newspaper *Az Est*, emphasizing the programme of Czech

policy as regards the incorporation of Slovakia into the Czech
State. Both these items enabled us to show how far the struggle
for the principle of self-determination had proceeded, the
inference being that it would cease only when the Empire
had succumbed. This was confirmed even more strikingly by
the fact that on July 5th our deputies, associating themselves
with Dr. Stránský's very emphatic manifesto in the constitutional committee, declined to take part in the work of
revising the constitution, their reason being that they were
awaiting the Peace Conference. The decision of the Government
to prorogue the session of Parliament on July 15th, because its
meetings were giving more and more proof of internal disruption, satisfied us completely. On the other hand we felt
some alarm at the amnesty which, at the beginning of July
1917, was granted to the political offenders, and particularly
to the Czech deputies, Kramář, Klofáč, and Rašín. We were
not sufficiently familiar with the details of the situation, and
we did not know whether there might not be some systematic and decisive political scheme behind this step. We could
not help wondering whether any definite guarantees had been
given in return for the amnesty, or whether it might even
denote a turning-point in the line of policy at Prague. When
immediately afterwards references began to be made to
Seidler's resignation, and to the preparation of a coalition
Cabinet, we felt convinced that danger was really imminent.
We knew that the "Czech League" had previously stipulated
an amnesty as the chief condition for any kind of Parliamentary co-operation with the Government, and that our
deputies had frequently intervened in this sense. The persecution at home had hitherto been our strong political argument,
of which we should be deprived if an amnesty were granted.
And if on top of this there had been a change in our line of
policy, it would have been a severe blow to the whole of our
movement.

The fears with which these events inspired us were
accentuated by the international situation at that juncture.
We were aware that there had been attempts at secret peace
overtures, we knew of the war weariness in France, and of the
willingness in London to reach an agreement with Vienna. This
was at the time when the negotiations of Sixtus had not yet
come to an end, and we also knew that the Pope was preparing
some action. Any change in our line of policy at home, and

acceptance of responsibility for the whole policy of the Empire seemed to us a direct support to the movement for a separate Allied peace with Vienna.

III

On July 12th I sent the following report to Dr. Šámal, in Prague :

I must ask you most emphatically, and in the interests of all our successes gained hitherto, to be uncompromising and, in particular, not to enter any ministry. As the situation is now developing, Austria will become weaker and weaker. So will Germany. They will be defeated, and when this comes about you must not be involved in any responsibility for the war. Here this would be understood as work on behalf of Austria. Therefore, no coalition ministry on any account.

This is all the more important because we have arrived at matters of far-reaching significance. Our army has at length been sanctioned. Masaryk has arranged in Russia for the Government and the military authorities there, with the consent of the Soviets, to send thirty thousand of our volunteers to France. Štefánik has gone to America, and has already secured Wilson's consent for the recruiting and transport of Czech volunteers to France. Dr. Beneš is negotiating with the Italians for the release of Czech prisoners of war, and the Italian Ambassador in Paris has assured him that there will be no fundamental obstacles; Sonnino himself will ask only for conditions which can be easily fulfilled. We hope that by the autumn we shall have forty to sixty thousand troops in France, apart from our volunteers in the Russian brigade, which is already fighting, and has achieved great successes.

Our movement to-day is very extensive. We have two millions of our people adequately organized, and the Allies have a good opinion of us because of the correct and orderly manner in which our policy is carried on. If you do not make any political blunder, we shall gain our purpose. There are still many here who would be willing, in case of peace, to make some compromise with Austria which would not give us what we want. For them, any compromise of yours with Austria would constitute a reason for saving Austria. It is absolutely essential for our policy to be reciprocal, and for you not to disavow us in any way. The voting against the budget produced an excellent impression —those are the lines on which you must continue. Our aim must be absolute independence, and we shall ourselves decide as to alliances and federations. That is the point of view with which we have consistently identified ourselves. You must not do anything to disavow us, or else we should lose all our prestige. It can now no longer be said that you cannot speak out, since the deputies went so far in their proclamation.

In other respects also our work proceeds well. The prisoners of war are already well organized in France, and we are beginning the same work in Italy. In Russia order has at last been attained. Professor Masaryk has been there since May, and has achieved real successes. He has done much work there with Sir George Buchanan, Albert

Thomas, and Vandervelde. He was with the General Staff, and negotiated with the Ministers Lvov and Tereshchenko on the subject of our army. He put matters straight in the internal affairs of our organization. In America our people have accomplished a great deal of work. By means of collections they have made it possible for us to work successfully, and full recognition must be given to the enormous amount of work which they have done. With the Slovaks we are working in complete harmony.

The military situation is good on the whole. France is the weakest in this respect, and the English and Americans are our chief hopes. The sacrifices of the French are already considerable. They would therefore gladly accept a possible peace with Austria in order to terminate the war more quickly. Hence the danger of any compromise with Austria is greater than would appear. Only if you hold out and help us to show that Austria cannot be saved from collapse will they keep on until the end.

There are two more points which must be added:

The Slovak question will be solved favourably for us on the condition that you do not withdraw. Here the feeling is decidedly in favour of uniting us with the Slovaks in order to give us more power against the Germans. If you do not desert them, they here will not desert us.

A second question: If the Government should want to exploit the case of Dürich, remain completely calm. The dispute about Dürich will do no harm to our work and success. On the contrary, Dürich had to go because he had compromised himself completely with the old regime in Russia, and his departure strengthened our inner situation with regard to both French and Russian opinion, particularly the latter, because they objected to our connections with reactionary circles. So if the Government and the police should exploit this against us, you will know what view is to be taken of the matter.

I emphasize, then, these points: (1) No co-responsibility. (2) No coalition ministry. (3) Not to desert the Slovaks. (4) Not to negotiate with Austria for a compromise or to disavow us.

This report gives a good idea of our wishes, fears, and opinions at that time. It reached Prague somewhere about July 25th.

Here I should like to add something further with regard to our mutual news service between Prague and Paris. After the war I ascertained from my friends in Prague which of the reports actually reached them. Nearly all of them arrived safely. They were eagerly awaited, and their arrival caused much satisfaction. The receipt of most of them was notified to me during the war, just as we in Paris were able to confirm the receipt of news from Prague. From the summer of 1917 we again had a safe and uninterrupted connection by way of Switzerland and also Holland; from the spring of 1918 communications were carried on very quickly, so that as a rule it was easy to arrive at an agreement. In Paris I always had the impression that the National Committee in Prague was proceeding at this period in concert with us, upon the basis of our continual contact. I had at least reports from Dr. Šámal to the effect that he and Dr. Štěpánek regularly delivered our reports to the narrow circle in Prague which was preparing for the possibility of revolutionary action, and from which he kept us supplied with news, thus co-ordinating the whole of his work at home in the authoritative political circles with our activity in the Allied countries.

This is borne out by a number of important messages which, by that time, I had received from Prague. Thus, before my report of July 12th reached Prague, I received on July 17th a message from Prague which had crossed with mine and which, to a certain extent, formed a reply to my reports.

This message contained the following main political reports:

The necessity of the closest possible co-operation between the committee at Prague and the persons who in the Allied countries are directing the movement for the liberation of the Czechoslovak people, has caused the Czech political leaders to consider sending from time to time reports on the political situation in Bohemia, on the resolutions arrived at, etc. They, on their part, desire to receive absolutely reliable news about the steps taken and the results achieved by the organization abroad, in order that they may arrange their further proceedings accordingly. All instructions coming from the Allied countries will therefore be welcomed.

From the newspapers you will have learnt about the declaration which was made in the Reichsrat and by which the representatives of the Czech people claim the re-establishment of an independent Czechoslovak State. All the Czech political parties decided in unison to make this proclamation, the chief purpose of which is that the voice of the Czech nation should be heard in the Allied countries. Under the present circumstances, particularly in view of the state of war which prevails, it was not possible to proclaim openly in the Reichsrat that by independence the Czech nation understands separation from the Monarchy. The Czech political leaders are of the opinion that at the moment of peace negotiations the Czech question will be discussed as a European question, and the Allies will not permit it to be regarded as an internal affair of the Austrian State. In any case, the Committee at Prague asks to be kept informed about this matter, and also about the effect which the declaration produced in the Allied countries.

This report and the further events at home came as a great relief to us, showing, as they did, that our misgivings had been ill-founded. We attributed this in a large measure to the services rendered by the delegates of the Social Democratic Party who went to Stockholm, and the reports on the international situation and the whole of our movement which they brought home with them. We accordingly explained in Allied circles that the amnesty was a proof of the weakness and chaos prevailing in the Habsburg Empire, the precarious conditions of which it would render even more critical. This opinion of ours was confirmed by the fact that the Emperor's attempt to form a new coalition Cabinet proved unsuccessful after the express refusal of the "Czech League," which continued its previous attitude against Seidler's new Cabinet of officials. The latter Cabinet was appointed on August 30, 1917, for the purpose of carrying out the revision of the constitution upon the basis of national self-administration, while preserving State unity.

Under these circumstances our work in the Allied countries was not disturbed by any fresh fears. The return of Klofáč to the leadership of the party; the formation of a Czech State Rights Parliamentary group on September 26, 1917, consisting of the Young Czech, National Socialists, State Rights and People's Progressive parties; the election of Habrman as President of the Social Democratic Party on October 18 ,1917; and, finally, the attempt to found a large bourgeois party known as the Czech State Rights Democratic Party, with a pronounced anti-Austrian programme—all these events adequately indicated to us the direction in which matters would now proceed at home, and gave us every reason to believe that from that time onward the two constituent portions of our national policy, at home and abroad, would, little by little, merge outwardly also into one.

112

After the Bolshevik revolution in Russia and the first attempt to arrange an armistice between Russia and the Central Powers, an opportunity presented itself for imparting to the progress of events at home a clear public expression which produced excellent results. In the peace offer made by the Bolsheviks to the Central Powers there was an express reference to peace without annexations or indemnities, and in accordance with the principle of self-determination. Seidler, speaking in Parliament about the negotiations with the Bolsheviks, stated that the Austro-Hungarian Government would accept the offer on the condition that both sides agreed to abstain from any interference with the internal organization of each other's States. The "Czech League" realized clearly what this implied, and on December 4th Klofáč and Staněk headed delegations calling upon the Government to admit representatives of the non-German nationalities to the proposed negotiations, and to base these negotiations on the principle of self-determination. The same demand was then made by the "Czech League" and also by the Jugoslav Parliamentary group. When, however, in the second half of December the Armistice had been arranged and definite peace negotiations began, Czernin, at Brest-Litovsk, made a declaration against the Russian attitude towards self-determination, and this was greatly resented by the non-German nationalities.(47)

Political circles in Prague seized this opportunity to incite a strong protest against the policy of the Empire, and this led to the convening of the general Diet of the Czech territories which was held at Prague on January 6, 1918. The Declaration which was passed on this occasion constituted an emphatic demand for Czech State independence within the historical frontiers and including Slovakia. It emphasized the principle of self-determination in the revolutionary sense with which Russia had imbued that term, and it demanded the representation of the Austrian nationalities at the Peace Conference. This declaration was repudiated by Seidler in Parliament on January 22nd, and this assisted us greatly in our movement.

The struggle between Vienna and Prague was now carried on quite openly, and in spite of the fact that the "Czech League" and the official policy of the Czech deputies kept within certain limits, so as not to be exposed to unnecessary persecution, Czernin notably was well aware that declarations of this character might be an indirect obstacle to his negotiations with the Allies. Believing that after the conclusion of peace in the East, and after the German offensive in the West the Central Powers would achieve a final victory, and evidently judging that it was necessary once and for all to suppress with a firm hand any such attempts, he delivered the speech already referred to on April 2, 1918, in which he made a violent attack on the Czechoslovak movement at home and abroad.

This speech had disastrous consequences to him, not only in foreign countries, but also in Prague, where it produced the effect of strengthening the resolution of Czech political circles. Czernin had attempted to draw a distinction between the leaders of the Czech nation, who were carrying on a policy against the Empire, and the Czech nation itself, which he described as being still loyal and Austrian. In order, therefore, to show the unity of the whole nation against Vienna and against Czernin's policy, the Czech politicians in Prague convened a special demonstration of all classes of the Czech people. This demonstration, to which the Jugoslavs were also invited, took place at Prague on April 13, 1918, and the chief feature of it was a solemn vow made by all the representatives of the nation, by which they confirmed their adherence to all previous manifestos, and entered into a national commitment not to give up their struggle until the aims formulated in the previous manifestos had been achieved.

This April demonstration formed a landmark to us in our efforts abroad. Czernin's speech had inflicted a severe blow upon the Empire from the Allies' point of view, while at home the whole nation had responded to it by an open adherence to the revolutionary programme. Nothing more was now needed for the success of our work in the Allied countries. We saw that the psychological and moral development of affairs at home had been completed, and that it was now only a question of the actual material collapse of the Empire.

Under these circumstances we were deeply gratified by the first Slovak demonstration, which was held on May 1, 1918, at Liptovský Svatý Mikuláš at the instigation of Dr. Šrobár, and which demanded the recognition of the principle of self-determination "not only beyond the frontiers of our Monarchy, but also for the nations of Austria-Hungary, and hence also for the Hungarian branch of the Czechoslovak stock." We adduced this as a proof that the Slovaks were at one with us, and that they desired Czechoslovak unification against the Magyars.

This is the conclusion which I should draw from the whole of this development:

The month of April 1918 was the decisive point in the struggle for the self-determination of the Austro-Hungarian peoples, within the Empire also. For the Czechs it meant— especially when taken into conjunction with the May-time manifestos—the culminating period of their resistance to Vienna. The Jugoslavs were advancing solidly with us, while the Poles now regarded their separation from the Empire as practically certain. And everything which followed merely tended to confirm and emphasize the April events.

113

It will be more convenient here to complete this chapter on our home policy, although by doing so I slightly anticipate the course of international events.

On May 1st the following report was sent to me from Prague by Dr. Štěpánek, who, with Dr. Šámal, Rašín, Kvapil, and Scheiner, was then in charge of the activities of the "Maffia":

After having placed our own political action on a firm basis, a process which cost much endeavour but which showed unexpectedly extensive results, and after having achieved an absolutely fraternal association, not only with the group of Jugoslav deputies, but also with the political headquarters of the Jugoslavs at Zagreb, we have now for some time been engaged upon the establishment of a league of oppressed nations within the Empire. The relevant dates indicating the progress of this movement were May 30, 1917, January 6th, and April 13, 1918. First and foremost we endeavoured to win over Polish political circles to a joint action, and thus to follow the Socialist groups and the Pan-Poles who have already come over. The prospects of success are good, for the common danger constitutes a real common basis. . . . I will only add that on May 16th there will be celebrations at the National Theatre, which will be attended by large Polish and Jugoslav deputations. Important confidential political conferences have been projected, and according to present arrangements their continuation will be organized partly at Zagreb and partly at Cracow. The Ukrainians, Italians, and Rumanians have also been invited to Prague, and we hope that they will come.

It is evident that this forms an analogy with the Congress of Rome, and our policy here is thus parallel to that abroad. Our programme will naturally remain always the same—an independent Czechoslovak State in connection with which, however, out of regard for present and future Allies, a lesser emphasis will be placed upon historical rights, but there will be a generally acceptable formula of self-determination as regards the economic and other essential requirements of the State, with assurances for the linguistic minorities. Further, in every direction, a joint defensive and offensive movement against Austria, i.e. a federative State, Bohemia, Poland, and Jugoslavia as a fulcrum with great powers of international leverage. All this, of course, is only a rough sketch. The exact programme accepted by all representatives can be communicated only by word of mouth. It is necessary, therefore, to reply as promptly and favourably as possible to the inquiry about transport by submarine.(48)

From all this it will be seen that the political situation with us is a favourable one. On all sides there is a resolute spirit of sacrifice and self-confidence, enormous activity and unity. In our next we shall reply to the inquiries contained in the letter of February 18th.

I made abundant use of this report in official circles, and when it was confirmed by the news which arrived in the following week, it naturally provided a fresh proof of the agreement, co-operation, and mutual confidence between the National Council and our home policy in Prague and in the Empire generally. More than this we did not need to establish our credentials in the Allied countries.

The fall of the Empire was to be brought about by a military blow which would reduce Austria-Hungary to such straits that, at the moment of the approaching catastrophe, our people at home could give the Empire its last blow by an internal upheaval. We in the meanwhile aimed at making all political preparations, constituting a national army and Government, gaining recognition, becoming Allies, attending Allied conferences.

The further events at home, such as the first enactments of the May Government for setting up local governing bodies in Bohemia, the struggle against which was started by the Czechs and Jugoslavs, joined later by the Poles; the resolution of the "Czech League" to indict the Government; the resignation of Seidler and the appointment of Hussarek's Cabinet on July 24, 1918, which two days later continued the movement for the administrative division of Bohemia, merely showed that the process of collapse was spreading.

On July 13th came the establishment of the National Committee, which issued an emphatically revolutionary manifesto denoting full and unreserved unity with our movement in the Allied countries. This was of great political significance to us in its bearing upon our contact with Prague. In this manifesto the Committee stated that it would "gather and direct all spiritual, moral, and material forces in the nation for attaining the right of self-determination in an independent democratic Czechoslovak State, with its own administration beneath its own sovereignty." From the "Maffia" I then received reports on the work of the National Committee to bring about the expected catastrophe of the Empire. This work included political preparations, economic and financial measures, as well as the action of the Sokols in military affairs.

From the time of the May celebrations I had no further alarm about the situation at home, although in none of my reports to Prague did I omit to insist that there should be no negotiations with Vienna. My purpose in doing this was chiefly to support our radicals at home against the opportunists there. Nor did I have any further difficulties compelling me to explain or excuse to the Allies what was happening in Prague or Vienna. Only once, in August 1918, I found myself in difficulties during the negotiations with Balfour to secure our recognition by Great Britain. I shall refer to this later.

Of the other events at home I made use only of the manifesto of our deputies in the Vienna Parliament at the beginning of October, when we had proclaimed Czechoslovak independence, and it was again necessary to make it clear that we were taking this step with the knowledge and approval of our politicians at home. I pointed out that the President of the "Czech League" had openly referred in Parliament to our army and to the National Council as being the factor which, in spite of the opposition of Vienna and Budapest, would represent the Czechoslovak nation at the Peace Conference.

NEGOTIATIONS WITH THE ALLIES FOR THE TRANSPORT OF OUR ARMY FROM RUSSIA TO FRANCE AND FOR OUR POLITICAL RECOGNITION

(a) Negotiations in Paris and London for the Preservation of our Russian army. Allied Resolutions for its Transport to the Western Front

114

THE Bolshevik revolution showed the Allies, as early as November and December 1917, that they could no further count upon the military assistance of Russia. The preparations of the Bolshevik Government for concluding peace, which began with the application for an armistice with Germany on December 3, 1917, naturally confronted the National Council with the question as to what was to happen to our legions in Russia. If peace were concluded, our purpose in Russia would be at an end, and our only salvation would be to transfer the whole army rapidly to France.

From June 1917 onwards much work was being done in connection with the transport of our prisoners of war from Russia to France, as arranged by Masaryk with Albert Thomas and the Russian Government. Captain Husák reached France with his contingent in October 1917, and a second contingent, commanded by Captain Gibiš, arrived at Cognac in February 1918. From the summer of 1917, in the prisoners' camps and among our soldiers throughout Russia, the desire to reach France became more and more pronounced, and in proportion as the disorder and chaos in Russia increased, this demand became more and more emphatic. The Bolshevik revolution had made it imperative for us to leave Russia. When, therefore, in January and February 1918 the Bolsheviks had gained control of Moscow and Kiev, together with the whole of the Ukraine by a gradual process, Masaryk's chief concern was to ensure the safety of the army, and to arrange for its departure

in accordance with the agreement with France. With this end
in view he had given telegraphic instructions on November 7,
1917, the day of the *coup d'état*, to Jiří Klecanda, the authorized
representative of the National Council on the General Staff,
and through him to Prokop Maxa, the commissary of the
Czechoslovak Army, that under all circumstances they were to
maintain neutrality towards internal Russian disagreements.
Then, after his arrival at Kiev, he made an arrangement with
the Ukrainian Government then in power, by which the Czechoslovak Army should continue to receive supplies of all necessities. Finally, he discussed with the representatives of the Allied
Powers, especially with the French representative, the methods
by which the continued safety of the army corps was to be
secured, and he urged that the troops should with the least
possible delay be transferred from Russia to the Western
front, although some of the Allied representatives wanted our
army, jointly with the Rumanian, Ukrainian, and Polish troops,
to renew the military action against Germany.

The measures taken by the Soviet Army against the Ukrainian
Government, however, soon created an entirely new situation,
making it even more urgent for our departure to be accelerated.
As a result of pressure from the Soviet authorities, the Ukrainian Government on January 24th declared the independence of
the Ukraine, and began to negotiate with the Germans. But
before these negotiations were completed, the Soviet troops,
under the leadership of Muravyev, drew near to Kiev and
started a resolute offensive. This caused the leaders of the second
Czechoslovak division, in accordance with the principles which
Masaryk had insisted upon, to begin negotiations with the
Soviet leader for neutrality. An agreement was reached in this
respect at Yagotin on January 31, 1918, and on the following
day there was a supplementary agreement making the terms
of the settlement applicable to all the Czechoslovak contingents.

It was under these circumstances that on February 7th
Masaryk, as President of the Czechoslovak National Council,
proclaimed all those Czech troops in the various regions of the
former Russian State as being a component part of the Czechoslovak Army in France. When, on the next day, Kiev was
occupied by the Soviet Army, negotiations were at once started
between the National Council and the Soviet commander,
Muravyev, who received representatives of the Allied armies
and with them Prokop Maxa, the Czech representative. On

Sunday, February 10th, the negotiations were completed. Kotsiubinsky, the military secretary of the Ukrainian Soviet, and Muravyev, the Soviet Commander-in-Chief, assured Masaryk, who was present on that occasion, that they would fully recognize the armed neutrality of the Czechoslovak troops, and that they would give instructions for all necessities in the way of equipment, money, and food supplies to be issued to our army. The only stipulation made by the Soviet was that the Czechoslovak Army should continue to maintain order wherever it was garrisoned.

On this occasion Masaryk also discussed with Muravyev the question of transferring our army to France, and of its recognition as a component part of the Czechoslovak Army in France. Muravyev admitted the Czechoslovak point of view in this respect also, and gave permission for the troops to be transferred, but he stated that it was not within his jurisdiction to make any authoritative decision on this point. He evidently made inquiries in Moscow, for on February 16th Masaryk received a communication from him stating that the Commander-in-Chief had no objections to the departure of the Czechoslovak contingents to France.

The rapid advance of the German troops on Kiev made an immediate solution imperative in this sense. Our troops, who were handicapped in the Ukraine by their lack of proper equipment and artillery, as well as of reliable supplies and good lines of communication, could scarcely venture on further fighting with the well-prepared Germans. The first encounters with them began on February 24th. Four days later the Germans were already in Kiev, and from March 8th to March 13th violent fighting took place at Bakhmatch, where the Bolsheviks, who were opposed to the policy of the Germans in the Ukraine, fought successfully against them in common with our legionaries.

I shall not discuss the question why our troops did not immediately act against the Bolshevik revolution in Russia. I have no personal experience of the local conditions prevailing there, and what information I received on the subject was only of an indirect character. Masaryk himself has given a documentary account of this in his *Making of a State*.

On March 7, 1918, Masaryk left Moscow on his way to Vladivostok, Tokio, and America. Immediately after the fighting at Bakhmatch our troops left the Ukraine for Russia proper, and in accordance with Masaryk's instructions prepared for the journey to France by way of Siberia and Vladivostok. On March 15, 1918, Prokop Maxa, the commissary of the Czechoslovak Army, was informed that the Soviet Government had given permission for this journey, in which connection the Soviet Commander-in-Chief, Ovseyenko, had expressed the wish that Czechoslovak troops should hand over part of their arms to the Soviet Army. On March 16th, therefore, Major-General Shokorov, the commander of the Czechoslovak Army Corps, gave orders for preparations to be made for departure. At the same time instructions were given that any part of the equipment which would prove a hindrance on the journey was to be voluntarily given up to the Soviet Army Command. In a special order, which was issued publicly, Ovseyenko expressed thanks for this equipment, and on the same day issued an order to all commanders and station-masters instructing them not to hinder the movements of the Czechoslovak Army Corps, but to expedite them in every possible way. By March 18th, however, the situation in Moscow had changed, and the military authorities began to make difficulties about the departure of our troops to Omsk, their explanation being that the Czechoslovak Army might join Semyonov or the Japanese. Fresh negotiations were therefore started with the Soviet Government, who on March 26th again granted permission for the Czechoslovak Army to proceed to France, not as a fighting unit, but as a group of free citizens carrying a definite quantity of arms to protect themselves against the attacks of the counter-revolutionaries. On this occasion also an agreement was reached for the removal of the greater part of the Russian officers in our army, and the Council of People's Commissars undertook to grant our troops "all possible assistance on the territory of Russia, provided that they maintain an honourable and sincere loyalty."

Thus began that remarkable march of our revolutionary army across Russia and Siberia to the Western front. On its way eastward the army was joined by further detachments of our people, who had hitherto been prisoners of war, or who were scattered in small groups over Siberia. At the end of May the total number of troops who were ready for transport to Europe was about 45,000, according to the statistics of the French authorities.

115

The events connected with negotiations about our army after the outbreak of the revolution in Russia, the disputes about their transport, their action against the Bolsheviks and their preparations for the journey to Europe were strongly reflected in the negotiations with the Allies in Paris and London. I conducted these negotiations from the end of 1917 until our legionaries finally returned home, and the proceedings which they involved were of great importance in their bearing upon the recognition of our independence.

We of the National Council in Paris regarded the return of our troops as an essential condition for the whole of our success in France and, indeed, in Western Europe generally. For this reason, from the time when our army decree had been published, all our efforts were concentrated upon the transport of our army from Russia to France. From the spring of 1918 onwards I experienced for months at a time an alternation of hopes and disappointments, and I used all the resources at my disposal to promote the success of the scheme. As an example of the anxieties which this entailed to the National Council, I will mention only the case of the inaccurate report from Russia, notified to us officially from the Ministry of War on March 4, 1918, and signed by General Foch. This report alleged that Masaryk had made an agreement with the Bolshevik Government by which our troops were to remain in Russia, and the French Military Mission there had accordingly suspended all preparations for transferring them to France. On March 11th de Margerie sent me from the Quai d'Orsay an official communication on this alleged compromise.

It soon proved, however, that the report was based upon an error, and that General Niessel, from whom it had emanated, must have misunderstood Masaryk's negotiations with Muravyev. But from the resulting conversations at the Ministry of War and the Ministry of Foreign Affairs, as well as from the official documents and the reports which General Janin gave me on the subject of his discussions with the General Staff, I realized what attention the French were giving to the problem of our troops, what policy they were pursuing in this matter, and what political successes it would be possible for us to achieve in Paris and with the rest of the Allies as a result. Incidentally this shows also how mistaken were the views of those who blamed us for what they regarded as the ill-conceived scheme of transferring our troops to France. It was precisely this scheme which saved the integral character and the cohesion of our army, which without it would have been dispersed in the Soviet ocean. And from de Margerie's letter it is plain what the Western Allies would, in such a case, have thought of our action.

I therefore set to work again with fresh enthusiasm to arrange the organization of our French army, and to prepare for the arrival of our legionaries from Russia. Štefánik, in the meanwhile, had proceeded to Italy, and my work was carried on in conjunction with General Janin, who had established his General Staff in the Rue Bonaparte, not far from the premises of the National Council. After his return from Russia, Janin was able to occupy quite an important post in the French Army.

It was in March 1918 that I began to carry on regular negotiations with the French and English authorities about the use, transport, and organization of our army in Russia and Siberia.

On April 1st an inquiry from London, relative to the use of our army in Siberia, was handed to me by the French Government. In it the British War Office stated that our army, then on its way to Vladivostok, numbered about 40,000 men. Trotsky, it was said, had demanded that it should remain in Russia to form the nucleus of the reorganized Russian Army. Our troops had declined to do this, but the British War Office was doubtful whether this army, which possessed real military significance, could actually get to Europe. It ought, therefore, to be used in Russia or Siberia. The English military authorities held the opinion that it would be possible to occupy Siberia in the region of Omsk, or else to proceed to Archangelsk where a military base could be established, from which communication with Siberia could be maintained by way of Perm. Finally, it might be possible to pass beyond Baikal and join Semyonov, and this latter solution was the one which the English favoured.

I at once discussed the matter with General Alby, Chief of the General Staff in the Ministry of War. Together with him, and then with General Janin, I drew up a reply which was sent to Clemenceau on April 2, 1918. In this communication I opposed the use of our troops in Western Siberia, and I would have permitted them to be sent to Archangelsk only for the sake of more rapid transport to France. It was my wish that if the case arose, they were to remain in Eastern Siberia only until the vessels for their transport were ready. This was the policy consistently followed by the National Council in Paris from Febuary 1918 until the end of the war and beyond it.

By the terms of our agreement with the French Government, signed in our army statute on February 7, 1918, the Allies were not allowed to make use of our army without our consent. The point of view of the National Council was thus decisive, and, as a matter of fact, it coincided with the wishes of the French Government at that time. Accordingly, the French authorities continued to make preparations for the transport of our troops. On April 11th the French military attaché in Moscow reported that conflicts had arisen between our army and the Bolshevik authorities.(49) He further stated that it was difficult to decide whether our troops would, under such circumstances, actually reach Vladivostok. Trotsky had given orders for their advance to be stopped, and there were continual differences of opinion about their disarmament. On this point he mentioned that the Czechs had realized the danger of such a course, and had therefore declined to give up their arms. In spite of Trotsky's orders they were proceeding eastward, and he laid stress upon the fact that their one desire was to get to France.

At this juncture the Paris Government and the General Staff asked the American Government on April 20th to make arrangements for a supply of vessels at Vladivostok. They also applied to the French and English authorities for vessels which could be sent to Archangelsk for a similar purpose. This, I believe, was the first official suggestion on the part of the French Government that a section of our army might perhaps be transported by way of Archangelsk.

116

Thus the question of our army became an important factor in the policy of the Allies and their conduct of the war. Everything which came from Russia was loyally brought to my notice by the Government, so that on the whole I was kept informed on all points in quite a detailed manner, and my official point of view on behalf of the National Council was consulted. I was often in a serious dilemma; I had little direct contact with our army in Russia on account of the physical difficulties involved. From time to time I received a message from Masaryk, which enabled me either to understand or occasionally only to surmise the chief things which were going on. It was in accordance with these circumstances that I made my arrangements and decisions in Paris. Beyond this I had only the official Allied reports. This inadequacy of communication was a great handicap.

On two occasions there were differences between us in Paris and our leaders in Russia and Siberia. At the beginning I agreed to the plan of transporting a part of our army by way of Archangelsk, because I saw that the Governments in Paris and London approved of it, and also because I had confidence in the French official reports. Our military leaders, however, expressed themselves against it. It is difficult to say which of the two views was the right one. When I ascertained how our troops were situated I defended their point of view before the Supreme Military Council at Versailles.

The second case was rather more serious. The decision of the executive committee of the army on July 7, 1918, to set up an anti-Bolshevik front in the Volga area, to begin an advance against the Soviets and to proceed further into Central Russia, seemed to me a political and military blunder, and I still think so. I was always in favour of resolute defensive action against the Bolsheviks, of establishing a firm front to cover the gradual evacuation, thus making it possible for our troops to leave Siberia by gradations and in good time without any detriment to their morale. The scheme which had been started, however, was not adequately prepared. It counted upon Allied help which could not be given, and was stimulated partly by the insistence of the anti-Bolshevik elements in Russia, partly by unfounded reports about Allied intervention which was alleged to be already in progress. Moreover, the hopes of any adequate help from Russian quarters proved to be vain. The scheme was therefore doomed to be abortive.

In view of the controversy about the use of our army and our policy in Siberia and France at this time, I draw attention to an official telegram concerning an interview which Masaryk had with M. Regnault, the French Ambassador in Tokio, just about this period in the middle of April. It is an extremely valuable document, and gives a good idea of our plans with regard to the army in Siberia, and of Masaryk's views on the situation in Russia at that time. The telegram runs as follows:

Tokio, April 15, 1918. M. Masaryk, President of the Czechoslovak National Council, who after a long journey in Russia has just arrived here, made the following statement to me:

If the Allies recognize the Bolshevik Government, Lenin, who is an honourable man, will be glad to seek in the Quadruple Entente a factor of resistance and help against German aggressiveness. With the help of France and the United States he would re-establish the army and construct the railways.

An international company should aim at purchasing wheat and petroleum, and transporting them northwards for sale to the Russian peasants in exchange for footwear, clothing, and agricultural implements. The German invasion is certainly limited only to the Ukraine, Finland, and the border provinces of the Baltic, which are already regarded as lost provinces. If these disputes and struggles are settled, the Germans will have a free field for exploiting Russia.

Nothing can be expected from the social revolutionaries, who are the opponents of the Bolsheviks. As regards the monarchist movement, it is obvious from the failures of the Cossack generals that they would not gain any adherents.

M. Masaryk added that if he were granted a free hand in carrying on recruiting activities among the Czechoslovaks, of whom he has 50,000, this would be worth while because he would thus gain the confidence of the Maximalists. He would be unwilling to interfere in the internal policy of Russia, and emphatically declined to subordinate the troops to the orders of generals.

I informed him that according to the newspapers his troops had been disarmed, and the officers had received orders not to leave Russia. In his opinion the first point is of no consequence, because France needs men and not arms. It is necessary to save these men from being given to Austria, and from having to keep on fighting against the Allies. The prohibition to leave Russia applies only to the Russian officers and not to the foreign *cadres*.

My informant stated that he is able to despatch these troops to France, although he is aware of the difficulties involved by the preparation. It would be necessary to establish seventy trains passing through Russia and Siberia; this problem can be solved only with the assistance of Russia. Further, it would be necessary to have from twenty-five to thirty vessels; this would be the affair of the Allies. He himself is willing to organize the enlistment of a further detachment numbering 50,000 men.

(*Signed*) REGNAULT.

This telegram, and still more the memorandum on events in Russia which Masaryk prepared in Tokio for President Wilson and handed to Mr. Morris, the American representative there, aroused some resentment in Paris, and in certain military circles made matters difficult for us. The Allies in Western Europe were not familiar with the situation in Russia. Western Europe had been anxiously following the attempts of Kornilov,

Alexeyev, Semyonov, and other generals to restore the army and to wage war on the Bolsheviks. Archangelsk had been occupied by the Allies, and there had been a suggestion of possible help to those elements who were well disposed to the Allies, although nobody desired intervention on a large scale, for which there were no adequate resources at that time, in view of the decisive German offensive on the Western front. On the whole, however, there was a firm belief that a change would soon ensue.

In France, under the pressure of the German offensive, there was ill-feeling against the Bolsheviks, who were regarded there as traitors, agents of Germany, destroyers of the common front, destroyers of Russia, propagandists of peace without annexations and indemnities, and of revolution in the armies. In France there were many who had confidence in the generals, the monarchists, the cadets, and the social revolutionaries. The views expressed by Masaryk as to the possibility of negotiations with Lenin and as to the duration of his regime, and the scanty hopes which Masaryk placed in the success of the other anti-Bolshevik factors, caused astonishment in some quarters and anger in others. Some of the Paris papers, such as the *Echo de Paris*, published a telegram from Washington containing a summary of Masaryk's propaganda, together with an attack on him and us.

From Regnault's telegram I realized what the point at issue was, and I began to make Masaryk's point of view understood in political, journalistic, and official circles of Paris. To some extent I succeeded in this, but I was unable to set Štefánik's mind at rest for long. He was greatly influenced by the impression which he had formed in certain military circles, where Masaryk's attitude was condemned. He himself, as regards Russian affairs, had accepted the view current in those circles, and at that time he was decidedly in favour of intervention. I ought to add, however, that Štefánik subsequently changed his views on Russia.

Even at that time I was convinced that Masaryk was right, and I therefore identified myself with his opinions, in spite of the contrary attitude of Štefánik and a number of the English and French authorities. (Here I may mention that in French military and political circles there were many who shared Masaryk's views in this respect.) Subsequent events proved that Masaryk was entirely right.

In spite of these differences of opinion as to the development of affairs in Russia we were all united on the subject of our army, and the French Government itself took no steps which were at variance with the terms of our agreement.

When, on April 20th, I was received by Clemenceau, he emphasized to me this direction of his policy, and referred in very eulogistic terms to our Siberian troops, adding: "They are admirable soldiers. I should like to have them here at the front at all costs. Fifty thousand of your people in France will be the best guarantee of our victory and yours."

This was at a time when, after the Congress of Rome had come to an end and the Clemenceau-Czernin controversy was over, our situation in France and with the Allies generally was a very favourable one. The negotiations for transferring our troops from Russia to France strengthened our position still more. We were constantly in touch with the French and English authorities on this subject, which came up for discussion at various inter-Allied conferences. I participated in these indirectly. General Janin and myself, on behalf of our General Staff and the National Council respectively, first of all conferred with the French Government, and then in a number of cases I negotiated direct in London with the British Government. The matter under discussion was then transferred by the Governments concerned to the agenda of the Allied conferences. The first occasion when the problem of our army thus became a subject for Allied consideration was at the military conference held at Versailles on April 27, 1918, as the result of French initiative. The military representatives of France, Great Britain, Italy, and the United States (Generals Belin, Sackville-West, Bianchi d'Espinosa, and Bliss) here prepared a collective note for the future conference of the Supreme Allied Military Council on the situation of our troops in Siberia. They demanded their transfer to Europe at the earliest possible date, those west of Omsk by way of Archangelsk and Murmansk (the latter base to be held by them provisionally for the Allies) and those east of Omsk by way of Vladivostok.

A few days afterwards, on May 2nd, the Supreme Military Council held its fifth session at Abbeville, and was attended by the military and political representatives of the Allied Powers (Clemenceau, Pichon, Foch, Pétain, Belin, Lloyd George, Lord Milner, Sir Douglas Haig, General Sackville-West, General Bliss, Orlando, Sonnino, etc.). Among other important questions, it dealt also with the transport of our troops from Russia, and it passed the following resolution (No. 3):

The Supreme Council, in approval of Circular Note No. 25 of the military representatives, has decided:

1. That the British Government should take all steps to ensure the transport of the Czech contingents now at Vladivostok.

2. That the French Government should assume responsibility for these contingents until the moment of their embarkation.

3. That the British Government should notify M. Trotsky of the concentration of the Czech divisions at Murmansk and Archangelsk, not belonging to the army corps which left Omsk for Vladivostok.

This resolution of the Supreme Council established officially a unified course of action for the Allied Governments with regard to the events in Siberia, and this strengthened our status in the Allied countries. The resolution was communicated to the National Council and the General Staff of our army in France, and also to the Allied representatives in Moscow. Further steps were immediately taken for carrying out the terms of the resolution. Representations were made to the Bolshevik Government by the Allied representatives in Russia (General Lavergne and Mr. Bruce Lockhart). On May 7th the authorities in Paris received a message from General Lavergne to the effect that the Bolshevik Government had agreed that the section of our troops who had not yet crossed the Omsk line should be transported by way of Archangelsk, entirely in accordance with the Abbeville resolution, and General Ogorodnikov was said to have non-officially sanctioned the guarding of the White Sea harbours by our troops. These arrangements were looked upon as a great concession on the part of the Bolsheviks, indicating their willingness for an agreement with the Allies. With the help of Sadoule, Lavergne had secured from Trotsky the sanction for allotting to our troops a part of the war material located in Archangelsk.

In view of these favourable circumstances I considered that the moment had now come for discussing all these questions direct with the British Government. Since my last visit to London the situation in England had changed considerably to our advantage. In Russia the British were taking an active part in the scheme for safeguarding our troops, in which they were deeply interested. This is shown by an inquiry addressed by the War Office to Paris on April 1st, and also by the devoted services which were rendered to us in Moscow by Mr. Bruce Lockhart.

In Paris I was in continual contact with Lord Derby, the British Ambassador, whom I kept informed of the progress of our movement. I had occasion to ask for his intervention in London on our behalf, and he always readily complied with these requests. It was after consultation with him that on May 7, 1918, I proceeded to London for the purposes of negotiation.

(b) OUR MILITARY ACTION IN RUSSIA AND THE SIBERIAN ANABASIS

117

The agreement reached by Masaryk with Muravyev on February 16th and by the branch of the National Council with the Moscow Government on March 26th regarding the disarmament, neutrality, and transport of our troops to France, had met with unexpected obstacles almost immediately. The precise character of some of them has not yet been made clear by documentary evidence, although the conditions then prevailing provide a satisfactory clue to their psychological and political origins. Our first transports, on their progress eastward, had encountered difficulties at the end of March in Penza from the local Soviets, whom the Central Government at Moscow had allowed a sufficient degree of autonomy to make decisions in accordance with their wishes and requirements. The local Soviets feared our troops as an armed force which might upset their authority, the result being that at every station of any importance difficulties arose, and it became necessary to hold continual negotiations to secure consent for further progress eastward, which was to be granted in return for the surrender of arms. This aroused the suspicion and opposition of our troops who, having from the beginning been mistrustful of the Government and the local Soviets, regarded all these proceedings as a source of danger to the army, increased, moreover, by the continually developing agitation of the Communists in our army, who were trying to incorporate it with the Red Guards.

In the early days of April the tension on both sides increased. The Central Soviet Government was undoubtedly in a dilemma because the Germans and Austrians, seeing in our army the only military unit in Russia with any degree of cohesion, and fearing that our troops might actually reach France—which would mean a real danger, especially to the Habsburg Empire—

had secured a clause in the peace of Brest-Litovsk by which Russia undertook not to allow on her territory any foreign or Allied armies, and they then exerted a strong pressure in this direction upon the Soviet Government. They hoped that in this way they would succeed in dispersing our army, and it seems that the Central Powers also instructed the Austro-Hungarian and German prisoners of war, especially in Siberia, to promote this policy.

Thus the lack of confidence on both sides, which was, I think, quite natural and comprehensible, increased until the inevitable conflict ensued. As early as April 13, 1918, at a military conference between a part of the leaders of our first division the majority were in favour of not handing over arms in future to the local Soviet authorities in accordance with the agreement between us and the Bolsheviks, but to proceed forcibly eastward, using, if necessary, other means than negotiation. The congress was, however, a confidential one, and officially the army knew nothing about its resolutions. The military leaders themselves had not trusted the Soviet authorities from the very beginning when the agreement of March 26th had come into force, and on their own initiative they had retained a quantity of arms exceeding the stipulated amount. The branch of the National Council was aware of this and tacitly sanctioned it. In other respects, however, both the branch of the National Council and the leaders of the army corps endeavoured loyally to fulfil the terms of the agreement with the Bolshevik Government.

Nevertheless, our army managed to proceed eastward during the month of April, although its progress was very slow and precarious. At the beginning of April some of the Allied military authorities devised a scheme by which a part of our army was to be transported to the Western front by way of Archangelsk. But this plan aroused fresh suspicions, uncertainty, and disputes in the ranks of our troops.(50) They had formed the idea that this was a trick on the part of the Bolshevik Government to divide them into two camps. They were also afraid that if the journey were made by sea from Archangelsk the Germans would get to know about the departure of the vessels and would sink the transports. It was certainly a tactical and political blunder that the Allied plan was not notified in time and in sufficient detail either to the Czech military leaders or the branch of the National Council in Moscow, but the negotiations on this subject were carried on between the Allied representatives in Russia and the Soviet authorities direct, and as a result of the agreement between them the Central Soviet Government issued an order that further transport by way of Irkutsk was to be stopped. This order gave rise to the most varied conjectures among our troops, especially as at the same time the Soviet Government issued another order relating to the transport of German prisoners from Eastern to Western Siberia.

This decision caused much unrest among our troops, and it was not allayed even when inquiries in Moscow from the French representative there showed that the transport of the army located westward from Irkutsk was to be carried out by way of Archangelsk and Murmansk at the wish of the Soviet Government and the Allies. When this had been ascertained, the Moscow branch of the National Council decided to comply with this wish, and started negotiations with the Soviet Government on the necessary procedure. The essential details had already been arranged with the army commissary when unexpected events upset the results of the negotiations. For while these had been in progress, the now well-known incident at Chelyabinsk had occurred on May 14th. A Magyar prisoner of war had provocatively, and without reason, wounded a Czech soldier, whereupon our troops had retaliated by executing the offender. The Soviet authorities had then intervened and arrested several of our troops, and after unsuccessful attempts to secure their liberation by negotiating with the local Soviet authorities, the troops decided to free them by forcible means. Urged by the rank and file, the leaders sanctioned this step, and placed themselves at the head of the movement, as they feared that if it were carried out in a disorganized manner serious complications might ensue. They occupied the town, liberated the prisoners, and at once departed. The incident gave rise to serious military and political dealings between us and the Soviet Government, and had a considerable influence upon the development of our action in Siberia. In itself it was of no great significance, but it was one of those factors which bring accumulated tension to the breaking-point.

118

Although this tension did not lead to open hostility it caused both sides to make preparations for possible conflicts. The military congress summoned at Chelyabinsk, and started on May 18th, in accordance with the instructions given to the delegates, resolved in its negotiations on May 20th to decline to proceed to Archangelsk, since it regarded this scheme as a Bolshevik trick against the army. On the same day Trotsky ordered the arrest of Maxa and Čermák, the delegates of the Moscow branch of the National Council, who on the following day were to have made a definite arrangement with him for adjusting the progress of our troops eastward. Maxa and Čermák then sent a message to our troops urging them to keep to the agreement and to surrender their arms, as that would be the only course by which they could reach Vladivostok. Our troops, however, thought that this message had been sent as the result of pressure from the Soviet Government, and they refused to obey it. At the same time our military leaders intercepted Aralov's telegram instructing the Soviet authorities to call upon the Czechoslovaks to organize themselves into labour brigades and to enter the ranks of the Soviet Red Army. This naturally aroused indignation among our troops, and on the next day, May 23rd, the military congress decided to inform the Bolshevik Government that they would cease handing over their arms to the Soviet authorities, and that they would force their way eastward. Evidently, as a reply to this resolution, Trotsky issued, on May 25th, the order to disarm the Czecho-slovaks forcibly and to shoot all those who did not submit, the remainder to be interned in prisoners' camps. On the same day, May 25th, evidently as a result of telegrams from Aralov and Trotsky, the first Soviet attempt was made at Maryanovets, near Omsk, to disarm a military transport, and on the two following days similar attempts were made at Irkutsk and Zlatoust, near Chelyabinsk. On the same days, in accordance with the resolu-tion of the Chelyabinsk congress of May 23rd, Captain Kadlec and Captain Gajda decided to proceed eastward at their own discretion and to occupy Mariinsk and Novo-Nikolayevsk.

Thus began the Czechoslovak action in Siberia. On May 27th Chelyabinsk was occupied, on the 29th Penza was captured, on the 31st Tomsk, on June 6th and 7th Omsk, on June 8th Samara, and on June 19th Krasnoyarsk. The Czechoslovak action was at once resolutely opposed by the French military repre-sentatives, Vergé and Quinet, following the instructions from Paris by which they had been urged to secure the transport of our troops to France, and fearing that a conflict with the Bolsheviks would frustrate the realization of this scheme.

This throws a clear light upon our policy in Russia and in

France, and it provides an answer to both schools of thought, i.e. those who blame us for not having intervened, and those who attack what they call our interventionist policy. It also answers those who explain that our action at that time in Siberia was the decisive factor which caused the Allies to adopt a definitely favourable attitude towards our movement. With regard to the view that our diplomatic recognition by the Allies and the decision as to the fate of the Habsburg Empire were brought about by our Siberian action against the Bolsheviks, I would say this: It by no means implies a disparagement of the great importance of our Siberian action if I state that this is not the case. It is an inaccurate conjecture. I was discussing the question of our Siberian army in Paris, and I saw every day the great importance that France attached to the transfer of our troops to the Western front, but not to their employment in Siberia. I negotiated in Paris, London, and Rome on the subject of our recognition, and in none of those centres was the question of our action against the Bolsheviks in Russia raised either by me or by the Allied Governments in this connection. This particular problem was always settled solely and exclusively within the limits of the general Allied policy towards the Habsburg Empire.

The army in Siberia played, of course, an important part, and in the course of my negotiations I always used it as an argument in our favour, just as I did our military movement in Italy and France, or the resistance of our nation to the Austro-Hungarian regime at home. In Paris no particular importance was attached to the incident at Chelyabinsk, and the action at the end of May was regarded as local in character. Our army in Siberia contributed towards our recognition and the decision as to the Habsburg Empire mainly by its mere existence. Its eastward march fitted in admirably, of course, with our strong propaganda in Western Europe and the United States. By this I do not mean that it did not render important services to Allied policy as a whole, especially by holding the Siberian line and preventing the return of the German and Austro-Hungarian prisoners, some of whom, at least, could have been used for military purposes again by the Central Powers. In my opinion, it is often forgotten that our Siberian army was our strongest political factor at the end of the war and during the Peace Conference. I made use of its retention in Siberia to win our peace terms.

Against the attempts of the Central Soviet Government to disarm our troops and prevent them from proceeding to the East, the Allied representatives in Moscow, prompted by our action in Siberia, undertook a joint *démarche* on June 4, 1918, by declaring that as the Czechoslovaks were to be regarded as a constituent part of the Allied Army, any attempt to disarm them would be treated as a hostile act against the Allies. This was opposed on June 8, 1918, by Count Mirbach, the German Ambassador, who lodged a protest with the Soviet Government, demanding that the transport of our troops to the Western front should not be allowed, on the ground that it would infringe the commitments of the peace of Brest-Litovsk. On June 13th Chicherin, on behalf of the Soviet Government, replied in a note to the Allied representatives that the Czechoslovaks were supporting the Russian counter-revolutionaries and that, as this involved intervention into the internal affairs of Russia, the Soviet Government must insist upon their being disarmed.

The warfare which had arisen between our troops and the Bolsheviks accordingly continued. Towards the end of April 1918 the newspapers announced that the first consignments of our troops had reached Vladivostok. Thus, from the beginning of May, they were distributed from Rtishchev, Penza, and Samara up to Vladivostok, and afterwards, when fighting began, they formed three groups: The Penza group in Central Russia as far as the Urals; the Chelyabinsk group from the Urals to Omsk; and, finally, the eastern group reaching from Omsk by way of Irkutsk as far as Vladivostok. They had not yet gained possession of the Siberian Railway, having occupied only some of the main junctions. The sections between these junctions were in the hands of the Bolsheviks and their local authorities, who thus prevented the Czechoslovaks from occupying the line. Being continually harassed by the local Soviets, and fearing that they might be split up into separate groups without any mutual contact, the Czechoslovaks, especially after May 3rd, were anxious to establish an uninterrupted connection between the separate military groups, and also to secure continuous occupation of the railway line so as to be able to reach the sea without delay.

The struggle for the Siberian Railway was therefore continued. On June 29th Vladivostok, at the eastern extremity of the line, was occupied, and on July 4th Ufa, on the western extremity, was captured. Within two days both our military groups, those of Penza and Chelyabinsk respectively, achieved the desired connection, and on July 7th the most important decision of our military leaders was reached. The executive committee of the Penza military group instructed Lieutenant Čeček to change the objective of his operation. The Penza Corps was not to continue its progress eastwards, but to remain where it was, and act as an Allied advance-guard for establishing a new Eastern front against the Germans. A report now reached Vladivostok that our second military group had been hindered in its free passage eastwards by the interference of Bolsheviks and prisoners of war. The Vladivostok group therefore decided, towards the end of June, to proceed to the help of their comrades. They refused to embark on the vessels which were now ready, and returned westwards, gaining possession of railway stations as they went, and occupying the eastern part of the Siberian railway line.

This is the beginning of the actual anti-Bolshevik action of the Czechoslovaks. It constituted a change of military and political plans and aims. The results showed themselves immediately. Our troops proceeded to attack Syzran, Saratov, and Kazan, advancing from the Ural base westwards. On August 6th ensued the long-prepared intervention of the Japanese, the original aim of which was to assist the Czechoslovaks in occupying the railway and reaching Vladivostok. In the course of events, however, the Japanese intervention changed its character, and assumed the form of an occupation of the eastern part of Siberia, partly to prevent the Bolsheviks from penetrating to the Far East and partly to secure a basis in the Far East for undertaking any extensive anti-Bolshevik operations which the Allies might decide upon.

Thus, as events developed, the Czechoslovaks, at the beginning of August, were distributed all along the Siberian line, continuing to engage in small-scale hostilities, and gradually occupying the important railway centres. At the most westerly extremity of the territory occupied in European Russia, at Kazan, Penza, and Samara, their regiments faced Bolshevik Russia and the Red Guards. On August 28, 1918, Jan Syrový was appointed supreme commander of our army, all the Russian officers, with very few exceptions, having left. In the middle of September the whole of the Siberian railway line was in the hands of our troops, and partly in those of the Japanese.

At the same time, however, it was reported that the Bolshevik Government, having completed its military preparations, was inaugurating an advance against our legionaries.

At the beginning of October 1918 our troops on the Volga front realized that in their exposed position they would not be able to hold out for long against the pressure of the Bolsheviks. They were disappointed because no help had arrived from the Japanese or the rest of the Allies, and they saw that the anti-Bolshevik Russians were incapable of rallying for any firm resistance which might lead to a restoration of the Russian State authority. It was under these circumstances that on October 4th our troops began to retreat, first from Syzran then from Kazan and Samara. Our army was now wearied and discouraged, but the turn of the tide on the Western front in Europe, the recognition of the National Council in Paris as a Government, and the collapse of the Central Powers at the beginning of November 1918 saved the situation.

Koltchak's *coup d'état* on November 18, 1918, removed our troops from military co-operation with the Russians. Not wishing to bear any responsibility for the internal events in Siberia, they gradually left the Volga front, handing it over to the Russians, and retaining only the railway for their own purposes. At the end of December the Czechoslovaks had definitely withdrawn from the Volga area. On December 30th Ufa was lost, and at the beginning of 1919 Generals Štefánik and Janin withdrew all our troops from the Russian anti-Bolshevik front. By this time, too, the Czechoslovaks, knowing that the war was at an end, and that their country had been liberated, were anxious to reach home with as little delay as possible.

The above is a concise account of our Siberian anabasis. It was a remarkable exploit from a military and a human point of view, while in a political respect it was of great significance. In Bohemia, Moravia, and Silesia our common soldiers had joined the Austro-Hungarian regiments, they had then passed over to the ranks of the Russians, and after severe hardships and sufferings the greater part of them, amid the chaos of revolution, had entered the improvised volunteer organizations, in which for some time they fought against the very people whom they had just left. Then, under the auspices of their great leader, they set out on their march across the vast spaces of Russia and Siberia; they occupied close upon 8,000 kilometres of railway, little by little, fighting against all kinds of hostile forces, until at last, after traversing the entire globe, they might reach the Western front in Europe to take part in the battles for their nation's freedom. In many respects their story is a unique one, and while this long series of adventures and vicissitudes was in progress they improvised, not only the military organization, but also the economic and educational aspects of their legions. Their leaders were men who, though fundamentally non-military in their inclination, adapted themselves with the determination and energy of their race to the rigours of the situation.

On the whole our troops may be taken as representing the chief features of the Czech national character. They exhibited its vitality, its perseverance, its common-sense methods of handling a situation, but at the same time its tendencies towards contentiousness and undue sensitiveness. This, incidentally, applies also to the majority of our troops in France and Italy.

General Syrový was a favourable type of the Czechoslovak leader. He inspired the confidence of the rank and file by his straightforwardness and sound judgment. The troops knew that a man of this kind would never lead them into rash and aimless adventures. By his military achievements, which can be appraised only in a more specialized account of our anabasis in Siberia, he rendered invaluable services to our liberation movement.

(c) First Negotiations with the British Government for the Recognition of the Czechoslovak National Council

119

After Masaryk's departure for Russia in May 1917 I visited England from time to time for the purpose of keeping in touch with our friends in London, and ensuring that the London office of the National Council continued to work in uniformity with the secretariat in Paris. Masaryk had entrusted me with the management of our political affairs during his absence, and had given me authority to carry on any negotiations which might be necessary with the Government in London. Here, too, Olga Masaryk participated in our political work. As I have already mentioned, I left for London on May 7th, as I considered that after recent events this was a suitable time for attempting to improve our position still further by direct negotiations with the British Government.

I remained in London until May 19th, and the negotiations which I conducted during that period with Lord Balfour and Lord Robert Cecil represent the first decisive step on the part of England which promoted our national and political aims. I was asked to call on Lord Balfour on Friday, May 10, 1918. Having been introduced by Mr. Wickham Steed, I outlined the situation in Austria-Hungary, and particularly in Bohemia, giving also an account of our movement abroad, with special reference to the attitude of the French Government towards our efforts. At the same time I asked for the recognition of the National Council as an outward sign that the British Government was in agreement with our war aims. I also asked for our army to be recognized to the same extent as in France. Finally, I pointed out that Great Britain had already made a number of concessions to the Poles, and that we were equally entitled to some such consideration. At Lord Balfour's request I then submitted two memoranda in which I had explained the juridical situation of the National Council in France and Italy, and the significance of the military instructions signed by Clemenceau on February 7th.

Knowing that the British were guarded in their attitude towards Austro-Hungarian affairs, and not wishing therefore to precipitate matters, I asked only for an undertaking that the British Government would not oppose the policy of the other Allies in our affairs, and that it would at least follow their lead in anything which was done on our behalf.

After our first interview Lord Balfour declared that he personally was an adherent of the anti-Austrian and anti-Hungarian policy. He fully recognized our endeavour to establish an army in France and Italy, and admitted that we had formed the only element in Russia which had shown itself able to cope with the Bolshevik chaos, and had held out longest on the Eastern front against the Germans. Having then asked for a written statement of the questions which I had submitted to him, he promised that within the next few days he would be able to tell whether he could sanction our policy by recognizing the National Council and granting an open documentary undertaking with regard to our military aspirations. I reminded him that the French Government had already promised me a public political manifesto on our behalf at an early date, and also its agreement with any joint Allied manifesto in our favour which might be made. I therefore asked him that, should there be any negotiations with the Allies on this subject, Great Britain might not oppose an Allied collective manifesto of this kind.

I negotiated also with Lord Robert Cecil, to whom I submitted the same demands. The negotiations at once took a very favourable turn. Lord Robert considered the possibility of a political manifesto which would apply to our nation and our army, and he linked this up with the general question of the use of our troops within the scope of Allied military operations as a whole. He took the view that a manifesto of this kind could not be regarded as a promise that fighting would be continued until we were liberated (as in the case of Belgium), but merely the eventual recognition of the sovereignty of the National Council and of our army as an Allied army. I expressed my agreement with this conception of the situation.

The decisive negotiations with Lord Robert Cecil on the subject of political recognition and the utilization of our army took place on May 15th and 17th, when I explained our point of view to him: The Czechoslovak National Council had made an arrangement with France by which our troops, numbering about 30,000 at a minimum, were to be transferred to that country. We insisted upon carrying this out, although we were to fight also on the Eastern front if it should be renewed. The transport of these troops, however, would have to be taken into account, and in this respect Britain, in particular, was to afford assistance. In view of the precarious conditions of our troops in Siberia, it was desirable that they should receive moral encouragement by a solemn declaration recognizing the unity of our army on all fronts. This would acknowledge us as Allies on an equal footing with the rest of the minor Allies.

In my decisive interview with Lord Robert Cecil on May 15th, when for the first time he admitted the possibility that Great Britain would recognize us as Allies actually during the war, it seemed to me that there was a marked divergency of views between France and Britain as regards our Siberian army. France, needing at home every possible soldier, took her stand upon the resolutions passed at Abbeville, and demanded the transfer of our Siberian army to the Western Front. The British, as I then conjectured, fearing the pressure of the Bolsheviks eastward, had, for the time being, exhibited merely a tendency to maintain our troops in Eastern Siberia chiefly to limit the advance of the Bolshevik military action and propaganda towards the Far East, and also with a view to the possibility of renewing the Eastern front against the Germans.

Lord Robert Cecil asked me direct whether we would not prefer to leave our troops in Siberia for these purposes. I answered him by explaining our point of view: We wanted to arrange the transport of at least 30,000 of our troops to France in accordance with our original agreement. We had, of course, no objection to an arrangement by which our troops in the East would, jointly with the Allies, renew the Eastern front against Germany, if any such Allied action were really to be reckoned with.

Although the whole matter was left at this stage, I regarded these negotiations as a considerable success for our cause in England.(51) At a second interview on May 17th Lord Robert Cecil spoke in even clearer terms than before, indicating his resolution not only as regards us, but also in the affairs of the Jugoslavs and of Austria-Hungary in general.

During my visit to England on this occasion I met also Lord Milner, to whom I was introduced by Lady Muriel Paget. I asked him to enter into official touch with our army by assigning a military attaché or possibly a military mission to it and also to the National Council in Paris. I also asked him to allow all the Czechoslovak soldiers in the English and Canadian Armies to be transferred to our army in France.

The result of these negotiations was favourable on the whole. Demand after demand was complied with by the British authorities, just as I had been promised by Lord Balfour, Lord Robert Cecil, and Lord Milner. A few days after my visit, on May 22, 1918, Lord Robert Cecil made a speech at a demonstration to commemorate the entry of Italy into the war; and on behalf of the British Foreign Secretary he expressed his gratification at the agreement reached between Italy and the Jugoslavs as a result of the Congress of Rome, and he stated that one of the aims of Allied policy must be the liberation of all oppressed peoples from the Austro-Hungarian yoke. He also expressed his satisfaction at what Italy and France had conceded to the Czechoslovaks, a remark which tended to emphasize still further the significance of our negotiations in London.

In accordance with the undertakings entered into by Lord Balfour and Lord Robert Cecil, the Foreign Office in London transmitted to the National Council in Paris a communication confirming its policy towards us, recognizing the National Council and our army, and stating that in this respect it would adopt the same measures as the other Allied countries. The British War Office also complied with all my requests. It appointed a special military mission to be assigned to our army, at the head of which was General Spears.

The Foreign Office communication is as follows:

FOREIGN OFFICE,
June 3, 1918.

SIR,

In reply to the memoranda with which you were so good as to furnish me on the 10th and 11th instant, I have the honour to assure you that His Majesty's Government, who have every possible sympathy with the Czechoslovak movement, will be glad to give the same recognition to this movement as has been granted by the Governments of France and Italy.

His Majesty's Government will thus be prepared to recognize the Czechoslovak National Council as the supreme organ of the Czechoslovak movement in Allied countries, and they will also be prepared to recognize the Czechoslovak Army as an organized unit operating in the Allied cause, and to attach thereto a British liaison officer so soon as the need for this may arise.

His Majesty's Government will at the same time be prepared to accord to the National Council political rights concerning the civil affairs of Czechoslovaks similar to those already accorded to the Polish National Committee.

I have to add that the above decisions have been communicated to the Allied Governments concerned.

I am, sir,
Your obedient servant,
ARTHUR JAMES BALFOUR.

DR. BENEŠ,
    THANET HOUSE,
        231, STRAND, LONDON.

(*d*) NEGOTIATIONS CONCERNING THE PROCLAMATION OF THE FRENCH GOVERNMENT. THE CONFERENCE OF VERSAILLES, JUNE 1918. INTERVIEW WITH ORLANDO AND SONNINO

120

I returned to Paris on May 20th. One of my fellow-travellers on this occasion was the English general, Delmé-Radcliffe, who was conveying to the French Government the reports from Lord Robert Cecil on the results of my negotiations in London. As far as I could judge from my conversation with General

Radcliffe on the journey, Lord Robert Cecil, on behalf of the British Government, had indicated the possibility of an agreement with France on the subject of our Siberian army and its utilization in accordance with the British point of view, as suggested to me in London. On the following day I was summoned to the Quai d'Orsay, where, in discussing the matter with Pichon and Berthelot, I clearly realized the divergencies on this point which had arisen between the two Governments.

My point of view coincided on the whole with that of France, where public opinion and the majority of the politicians regarded the position in Russia and on the Eastern front as hopeless. They had little confidence in the possibility of renewing the front there, and considered these attempts as a scheme whose chief purpose was to protect the interests of the British Empire.

On the following day I was sent for by Clemenceau who, as Minister of War, discussed with me the question of our Siberian army and my negotiations on the subject in London. His attitude in this respect was identical with that of Pichon and Berthelot. In the course of this conversation I emphasized our political aims to Clemenceau, who repeated the promise which he had made to me a month previously after my return from Rome. He also referred me to Pichon who, he said, shared his views on this matter, and he spoke in such emphatic and decisive terms that I considered it essential to quote a portion of this interview in the report which I sent immediately afterwards to Prague, in order to encourage our people there to continue their struggle against the Empire.(52)

It had been arranged between the British and French Governments that, in the week between May 20th and 30th, a special conference was to be held in London as a preliminary to the Allied conference which was to be held at Versailles on June 1st, and at which, it was assumed, the question of a joint policy in Austro-Hungarian and Polish affairs was to be discussed. In view of this fact, the subject of our army would have to be discussed between France and Britain almost immediately.

In view of the fact that our 21st regiment, which was stationed at Cognac, was very shortly to proceed to the front, the French Ministry of War suggested to me that this would be a suitable opportunity for organizing the demonstration which had been proposed, and that on this occasion the French view of the Czechoslovak question could be solemnly pronounced.

This was all the easier because, in the meanwhile, the organization of the Polish Army in France had made considerable progress, and an analogous demonstration was just being prepared in favour of the Poles. Accordingly, a fundamental agreement was reached on this point, and the details were to be arranged subsequently between the Ministry and myself. The date of the demonstration was fixed for June 15th.

Ever since the Congress of Rome I, in common with our friends in Paris and London, had not lost sight of the possibility of a collective Allied declaration in favour of the oppressed peoples. The recent negotiations in Paris and London, and still more the events in Siberia, had increased my hopes of the success of such a scheme. The Chelyabinsk incident, its immediate consequences, the arrest of Maxa and Čermák, and Trotsky's order to disarm our troops had resulted in a situation which tended to imperil the scheme for transporting our army to France, and for this reason the attention which Paris was devoting to the matter had been redoubled. It was just about this time that I had applied to Berthelot for help in this connection, and the joint Allied intervention had taken place at Moscow on June 4th.

121

The preliminary Franco-British conference was held at London on May 26 and 27, 1918. Those present included Lloyd George, Balfour, Robert Cecil, and Field-Marshal Wilson, representing Great Britain; and Pichon, Paul Cambon, and a number of military authorities, representing France.

At the conference it was agreed that on the subject of our army the resolutions of the Abbeville conference should, on principle, be adhered to, i.e. our troops were to be transferred as soon as possible from Russia to the Western front, while in the Far East the Allies would make common cause with them, and co-operate with them as necessity arose. The transport was to be effected partly by way of Vladivostok and America, partly by way of Archangelsk. If necessary a portion of the army would remain in Russia to hold the Archangelsk base. These questions were to be discussed at the forthcoming meeting of the Supreme Military Council at Versailles.

The possibility of an Allied declaration in favour of the Austro-Hungarian nations and on the Polish question was also discussed in some detail. Such a declaration would form the first public evidence that the Allies had now definitely ceased to contemplate the possibility of preserving the Habsburg Empire. According to my information, the British Government accepted the French proposal that such a declaration should be made, the nations in question being the Poles, Czechoslovaks, and Jugoslavs. With regard to the latter, however, it was emphasized that any definite decision on their question could be taken only after Italy had been consulted, and this was to be done also at the Versailles conference.

As previously arranged, the conference was held on June 1, 1918. After a discussion on Austro-Hungarian and Polish affairs, the following joint declaration was issued:

> The formation of a unified and independent Polish State, with a free access to the sea, constitutes one of the conditions for a permanent and just peace and the rule of justice in Europe.
>
> The Allied Governments have with satisfaction taken note of the declaration of the State Secretary of the United States, and desire to associate themselves with it, expressing their keenest sympathies for the national aspirations of the Czechoslovak and Jugoslav peoples.

The incomplete character of this declaration caused general disappointment. The original plan of all those who had attended the Congress of Rome was to secure from the Allies a common programme which should apply to all the oppressed nations in equally emphatic terms. Its purport was to be a definite condemnation of Austria-Hungary, the overthrow of which it should tend to bring about. We were hoping that this idea would emerge triumphant from the Versailles conference, and that the Allies would finally give open expression to a policy which they were individually carrying out with us against the Empire. France had given us a promise in this respect, and was working on behalf of this scheme. Our negotiations with England as to the utilization of the Czechoslovak Army, together with Lord Balfour's letter which was the sequel to them, and also the proceedings between the French and British Governments at the London meeting, had likewise given us hope that the British point of view in matters of Central European policy was now firmly established.

But as will be seen from the wording of the declaration, it was very moderate in tone, and it was formulated divergently for each of the nations concerned. It had been accepted as a compromise after a long debate on account of the opposition of the Italian delegates who at that juncture were unwilling to go to greater lengths. But it did not amount to very much, and as far as we were concerned it was of less consequence than Lord Balfour's letter. The Allies were merely repeating the proclamation made by the United States Department of State to their Governments on May 29, 1918, which happened to reach Paris while the conference was being held, and thus provided a temporary solution of the political difficulty encountered at the conference. The most that can be said of this declaration is that it forms an outward and visible sign that the Allies had changed their policy towards the Habsburg Empire, and it expresses the developments which had taken place in this respect during the months of April and May 1918.

122

The declaration of the Versailles conference caused dissatisfaction in all those political circles in Paris, London, and Rome which were working for a decisive policy against Austria-Hungary. The unsatisfactory character of the declaration was attributed mainly to the negative policy of Italy towards the Jugoslavs, but a number of our mistrustful friends were also inclined to wonder how far this result was due to the concealed activity of those who within the Allied ranks were seeking to save the Habsburg monarchy.

I myself expressed our sense of disappointment immediately after the conference to the Italian Ambassador in Paris, pointing out that the Italian policy had hindered the advance of our cause with the Allied Governments, and that Italy should have been the very country to support our anti-Habsburg policy in France. As a reply to my intervention with the ambassador I received on June 4, 1918, an invitation from Orlando to an audience at the Italian Embassy in Paris. This took the form of a long conversation at which both Sonnino and Bonin Longare were also present, and it was one of my most interesting political experiences during the war. The two Italian ministers formulated to me the principles of their attitude towards Czechoslovak affairs, and the extremely cordial and friendly conversation with them left me with a clear impression that Italy was particularly anxious not to be in any way a hindrance to the progress of the Czechoslovak movement for liberation. The ministers gave me the following account of the attitude they had adopted and the measures they had taken hitherto in matters concerning Austria-Hungary:

(a) They were opposed so far to any collective declaration on the part of the Allies because the Jugoslav-Italian dispute had not yet been definitely settled.

(b) They had no objection if one or other of the Allied States were to adopt a decisive attitude on the Czechoslovak question, but they desired to reserve independence of action for Italy. The Versailles conference had been unable to arrive at any decisive manifesto on behalf of the Czechoslovaks because this would have meant a similar manifesto for the Jugoslavs. It had been impossible to draw any distinction between the two cases. But the Jugoslav questions had not yet reached a sufficiently advanced stage to make possible any decisive manifesto in their favour. Sonnino, in particular, emphasized the fact that this did not at all imply that Italy was opposed to the Czechoslovak demands. On the contrary, as early as April 21st, Orlando and Štefánik had signed the agreement relating to our army in Italy, and on May 24th a demonstration had been arranged in Rome, when the colours were handed to the Czechoslovak regiment, on which occasion Orlando had made a speech expressing good will to the Czechoslovak cause.

(c) Italy did not wish to create a situation prejudicial to Jugoslav interests by a manifesto on behalf of the Czechoslovaks. Nor did she wish, in such questions as this which were so important to her, to be à la remorque d'une autre puissance, i.e. to be towed along by another Power. She would make her decision in these questions according to the circumstances dictated by her political needs and interests.

(d) When I insisted upon the community of our interests, both Orlando and Sonnino laid stress upon the identity of Italian and Czechoslovak interests with regard to Austria-Hungary, and stated that they were genuinely concerned for the liberation of the Czechoslovak people. Orlando, at the same time, asserted that in Czechoslovak matters Italy was resolved to go to the last extremities, that she would make her decision to this effect at the appropriate moment according to the political situation, and that in any case she would demonstrate her favourable attitude towards the Czechoslovak cause by her action.

(e) Recognition of the National Council by Pichon's Note. Balfour Associates Himself with the Manifesto of the French Government. Wilson's New Proclamation

123

Under these circumstances what I aimed at was rather that the French Government, apart from the other Allies, should carry out the terms of its own declaration. After the disappointing results of the attempt to obtain a joint Allied declaration for all the oppressed peoples, I decided to leave this scheme alone and to secure recognition at least for ourselves. With this end in view I therefore redoubled the preliminary activities in the secretariat of the National Council which were being made for the handing of the colours to our 21st regiment. It was the plan of the French Government that on this occasion the President of the Republic should deliver an important speech by which France would be definitely identified with the idea of a Czechoslovak State. I gratefully accepted the French plan which had been arranged and carried out in the same form with the Polish Army, but I could not help thinking that after the proceedings at the Versailles conference it was hardly enough for our purpose. Moreover, I had always given a slightly different interpretation to the promise which Clemenceau had made in April 1918. I therefore wanted something beyond a mere demonstration, however important it might be in a propagandist and political respect. My purpose was to secure a binding political and diplomatic charter as a responsible Government, which would give us a full and final recognition of national independence and sovereignty. Such a document as this would be a substitute for the joint Allied declaration which we had hitherto been unable to obtain.

The question as to what was to be included in the French manifesto formed the subject of long discussions at the Foreign Ministry with de Margerie, Berthelot, and Degrand, the result of which I summarized in a communication to the Ministry. In this document I asked for the following details to be included in the declaration:

(a) The recognition of our historical rights to a State within its historical frontiers, and a substantiation of our claim by reference to the action of our soldiers, our people, and our politicians against Austria-Hungary during the war.

(*b*) An express reference to the Slovaks to make it clear that one of the points at issue was the destruction of Hungarian unity and the union of the Slovaks as inhabitants of a component part of the historical areas in a single Czechoslovak State.

(*c*) The recognition of the National Council as representing the sovereignty of the whole nation, so as to make it clear that a Czechoslovak State was gradually being established with all appropriate attributes, and that the National Council was the first ingredient of its future Government which would later on be set up in its own country.

(*d*) The alignment of our question with that of the Jugoslavs and Poles in order to accentuate the international importance of this document, and to emphasize the solidarity of all three nations in the struggle against the Habsburg Empire.

Up to the last moment before the demonstration took place the Quai d'Orsay raised a number of objections to my demands.

There had never actually been any rooted objection to the declaration. The only point was to find a suitable opportunity for it, and to decide upon its form and substance. On June 26th I had a long discussion with Degrand on the subject of its exact wording, and on the following day he asked me to call at the Quai d'Orsay, where he submitted for my approval the definite text which the Ministry proposed to send me. The presentation of the colours had been arranged to take place on June 30th at Darney in Alsace, and on the day before leaving to take part in the ceremony, Pichon, in accordance with the agreement between us, sent me a declaration which manifested so generous an attitude towards our cause that it had an overwhelming effect on us in the Rue Bonaparte when we received it on June 29th at about one o'clock in the afternoon.(53) Again and again in my excitement I read the words: " The Government of the Republic will make its utmost efforts in order, at a given moment, to fulfil your aspirations for independence within the historical frontiers of your territories." Again and again I read the words acknowledging our rights, expressing the desires and obligations of the French Government, acknowledging our activities, efforts, and struggles. And I felt that now we had reached an important stage in the struggle, in the victorious struggle.

The attitude of the French Government towards our inde-

pendence was exhibited with equal clearness and emphasis in
President Poincaré's speech also. This speech, to which I should
like to add a few remarks, formed the culminating point of the
presentation of the colours to our 21st regiment. The ceremony
itself was attended by the President of the Republic, the Minister
of Foreign Affairs, Ministers Leygues and Lebrun, military
representatives of the Allies, representatives of the municipality
of Paris, General Castelnau, General Janin, and others. I first
delivered an address to the troops on behalf of the National
Council, and this was followed by the President's speech. I still
remember most vividly the preparation for this ceremony. It
was the first occasion during the struggle for our independence
upon which I found myself in an official situation as a representative of the independent State. It is therefore not surprising
if I still recall with emotion that memorable ceremony at Darney
on June 30th: the spectacle of our troops marching past the
President, the ministers, and generals, and proclaiming their
vow, the officers with drawn swords and the rank and file by
raising the fingers of their right hand, that they would return
home as free men or else die on the French battlefield. I experienced similar emotions on the Italian front in the Tyrolese Alps
at the beginning of October 1918, and also on the French front
in Champagne with the army of General Gourand, when on
November 8th I paid a visit to our troops at Terron. It was at
Darney that for the first time I felt confident of victory, while
in the Alps above Rovereto I surmised the approaching end of
the Habsburg monarchy, and at Terron it was my privilege to
inform the troops that we had been victorious in our struggle
for freedom, and that they were to prepare for the journey to
their liberated country.

124

As I have already pointed out, I was at that time concerned
about something more than a merely French proclamation.
Being always preoccupied by the necessity for a clearly formulated common policy of the Allies, and still feeling some
misgivings as to various peace manœuvres with Austria, we
continued to seek a method of securing, either directly or
indirectly, an Allied commitment of solidarity against Austria-
Hungary. The endeavour to obtain a collective declaration of all
the Allies in favour of all the oppressed peoples had not been
successful, as we have seen, and to begin with I therefore

restricted my plan to a collective proclamation on behalf of Czechoslovakia. Should this fail, it was my intention to adopt the tactics of obtaining recognition from the Allies individually and successively by using the successes achieved with one for obtaining similar concessions from another. Accordingly, in my personal negotiations, and also in my note of June 26th, I had asked the French Government on the occasion of the manifesto for Czechoslovakia not only to grant us its special diplomatic charter, but to induce the other Allies to associate themselves with the French manifesto in some form or other. I pointed out that, as far as Great Britain was concerned, the preliminaries had been prepared, as Lord Balfour's letter sent to the National Council on June 3rd stated that Great Britain would grant Czechoslovakia the same recognition as the other Allies did. As for Italy, I knew from my recent interview with Orlando and Sonnino that, owing to their dispute with the Jugoslavs, the Italians would not modify their attitude towards a collective Allied declaration on behalf of all the nations of the Habsburg Empire, but I hoped that the Italian Government would not regard it as prejudicial to Italian interests merely to associate itself with the French manifesto for the Czech cause.

The French Foreign Ministry granted me its sanction for the proposed measures, and on June 27, 1918, I arranged with de Margerie and Degrand the wording of the telegrams which were to be sent to London and Rome respectively. In these telegrams the French Government notified the two Allies what it proposed to do on behalf of the Czech cause within the next few days, and asked them to associate themselves by declarations of their own with the speech of the President of the Republic at the ceremony of presenting the colours to the Czechoslovak Army on the French front. At the same time I approached Lord Derby, the British Ambassador in Paris, and Bonin Longare, the Italian Ambassador there, asking them to use their influence to secure the support of their Governments for our demand. I also informed Mr. Sharp, the American Ambassador, and Mr. Frazer, his Counsellor of Legation, about what had been done in connection with the ceremony of presenting the colours.

The British Government, in fulfilment of Lord Balfour's promise to me, replied on July 1st by a special communication to Pichon. This was a reply to Pichon's telegram, the contents of which were analogous, and it was of great importance to us since it showed that England was maintaining the line of policy she had adopted. It also indicated the hope of Great Britain that the French policy towards the Czechoslovaks would be applied also to the Jugoslavs and Poles, the reference to whom in the French and English telegrams was intended as a reminder to Italy. This was the period at which a severe diplomatic struggle on the Jugoslav question was being waged in Paris and London with the Italians, and the successful progress of our cause was thus helpful to the Jugoslavs also.

125

Our confidence in the approaching victory thus became stronger and stronger, and was confirmed by the further course of events. The most striking of these was the new declaration of the United States Government, which now made its appearance at the most opportune moment. It will be remembered that under the influence of the Congress of Rome the United States Government had made a declaration of sympathy for the Czechoslovak and Jugoslav causes, and this was taken as the basis for the Allied declaration at the Versailles conference on June 1, 1918. On the same day upon which the telegrams of Pichon and Balfour were issued, we unexpectedly received from Washington this new declaration which formed a supplement to, and a commentary on, the previous American declaration of May 29th. In it the United States Government definitely identified itself with our claim to complete independence, and coming when it did, immediately after Pichon's declaration, it brought us fresh encouragement in our struggle against Austria. I regarded it as a further indication that the end was now approaching.

The official relations between the National Council and the Serbian Government, the Russian Embassy (which had been officiating in Paris since the time of Kerensky's regime), and with the Polish National Committee, made it necessary for me to inform them of the declaration of the French Government and all the developments which had arisen from it. I did this in a communication in which I undisguisedly expressed my assurance that these events denoted the approach of our national victory. I received replies from Vesnić, the Serbian Minister; Maklakov, the Russian Ambassador; and Dmowski, the President of the Polish Committee, all of which tended to strengthen our confidence.

Baron Sonnino, the Italian Minister of Foreign Affairs, did not associate himself with the French declaration. His point of view, as expressed to me in a conversation at the Italian Embassy on June 5th, was to be applied also to the present case, as I now realized.

(f) My Message to Prague

126

After having completed all the negotiations in Paris, which I have previously described, and while preparing for my journey to London, where I intended to start analogous proceedings for securing recognition by the British Government, I sent the following message to Dr. Šámal in Prague on July 8, 1918:

"On June 28, 1918, we attained our greatest political success hitherto. Pichon sent Beneš a letter in which he recognizes us as independent, emphasizing all our historical rights and also the Slovak question, and engaging France to take every step to enable us at the Peace Conference to achieve all our aims. The National Council is, moreover, regarded as the delegation of a provisional Government, and Pichon also draws attention to the necessity of a joint policy with the Jugoslavs and Poles. As a result of the letter it has been arranged with the Foreign Ministry to establish an actual State structure so that we may at once come into existence *via facti* as a State, and proceed to the peace negotiations as such.

"The idea with regard to the delegation of a provisional Government denotes, as far as we are concerned, that the other portion of this Government exists in a latent form at home, and will at once be established there as soon as it is necessary and possible. Hence the importance of unity and co-operation with us. It would be fatal for you to do anything not in accordance with our policy here, otherwise we should be compelled to leave the whole matter and resign. It would be a catastrophe if there were no unity now when we have achieved all our political aims.

"Regard the National Council, therefore, as the first ingredient of the Government which, at the first opportunity, will be formed at home. This ingredient here now represents the whole Government. Explain this idea to all our parties. We here are advocating it, and accordingly we can justifiably advocate all the interests of the nation as an actual Government, besides at once creating a whole State mechanism long before the Peace Conference. We shall set up a Legation and Consular service, together with a financial system, and we shall have a State loan.

"Pichon's letter is a commitment and a total recognition of our rights and demands, denoting the absolute victory of our policy here. Hence we shall act accordingly, but you at home must also proceed on the same lines. England has likewise given her recognition and sanction to this policy. There is thus no need to have any misgivings in a political respect. In Italy General Štefánik (he has just been appointed General) has achieved great successes, involving the absolute recognition of our rights to such an extent that we have even our own jurisdiction. Everything, then, is going very well here. Masaryk is in America. He has spoken several times with Wilson, and informs me that our cause there has been won so completely that Wilson and the American Government have promised not to make any fundamental decisions on Austro-Hungarian affairs without us or without our approval.

"In a military respect our cause is doing well; we have a total of about 120,000 men under arms,(54) and our chief concern is to have as many of them as possible at the moment of the negotiation. Austria has sustained a crushing defeat in Italy, and her loses are said to amount to 270,000. Here the military point at issue now is that of intervention in Russia, which will certainly be undertaken, and in which we will play a definite part. The decisive factor is American help, which is being counted upon here a great deal. That will decide the war. Be prepared as far as possible about the end of November for the possibility of a blow against Germany and Austria. In any case, we shall certainly let you know all details in good time.

"It is impossible to reckon with certainty upon a great blow against the Central Powers in the spring, but at that time we here must take into account the possibility of a revolution in Austria. Let everything be prepared in this sense. Have absolute confidence in our victory, in spite of the fact that the military situation is now grave. Politically we have gained such prestige that we cannot be deserted.

"We ask you to cause the action of the Catholics for the dynasty to be stopped, as that is doing us great harm here. Inform the Socialists that we are now backed by the chief set of Socialists in Italy, France, and England, and that they are co-operating very well with us, esepcially in France (Albert Thomas).

"Masaryk will arrive in Paris in the second half of August. There is no need to have any fears about our army in Russia. Hitherto they have gained the day everywhere, they are supported by the Allies, and the reports in the German papers are tendencious or fabricated.

"We need news from you about the economic position of Austria-Hungary and Germany, the results of the harvest, the present military strength of Austria-Hungary, and the possibility of a revolt or sabotage. We are sending almost immediately a scheme for direct action."

All my messages home were written in moments of feverish work or under the impending events relating to our cause. This is clear, I think, in the above report. In particular it shows how the political plans and views as to our further procedure were assuming a precise form, and how the decisive moment for the proclamation of our freedom was being consciously and systematically prepared. That was always most in my thoughts, and in Paris, London, and Rome my chief purpose was that when we did make a declaration of independence, it would not be merely a theoretical step, but a real political success and a death-blow to the Habsburg Empire.

XVI

OUR RECOGNITION BY GREAT BRITAIN. THE
BRITISH DECLARATION OF AUGUST 9, 1918.
RECOGNITION BY JAPAN

(a) THE ALLIES AND OUR ARMY IN SIBERIA. THE QUESTION
OF INTERVENTION IN RUSSIA

127

THE month of July 1918 became a period of decisive change in
the action of our Siberian troops. While I in Paris throughout
April, May, and even June had based my political negotiations
on the question of transporting our Siberian troops to France,
the development of events in Siberia was such that, at the
beginning of July, and especially in August, I had to adopt a
slightly different line for the continuance of my political
campaign.

The opposition of our troops to the local Soviets on May
25th, 26th, and 27th, and the struggle for the occupation of the
Siberian Railway in the first half of June, caused the French
authorities in Russia and also in France to consider for a short
time some new military scheme in Russia.

The question of intervention in Russia was as old as the
Bolshevik revolution itself. I have already mentioned that
the British military authorities had something similar in view,
i.e. some kind of "small" intervention at the outset, by which
they desired, on the one hand, to preserve access to Russia by
way of Archangelsk and Murman, on the other hand to check
the advance of Bolshevism to Baikal, where they feared its
effects upon their policy in the Far East. They carried out this
"small" intervention by their own means and methods from the
very beginning. Then when they saw the increasing strength
of the Czechoslovak Army they at once considered the possibility
of using it for these purposes. The objection of our troops, who
wished to proceed to France, and the French policy on the
subject of our army, which was in agreement with the consistent
policy of our National Council, caused the English also to assent
to the transport of our troops to Europe. Having sanctioned this

policy at the Supreme Military Council and at the conference in Abbeville, they kept to it loyally till July 1918, although some of them in the Far East never lost sight of their own aims in this question, and continued to work on behalf of them.

In the period immediately following the Bolshevik revolution, the French also, from time to time, considered the possibility of intervention. The Press discussed the matter frequently, for the general opinion was that the Germans were helping Bolshevism to power, and that they had had a direct hand in creating it for the purpose of destroying Russia and the Eastern front. Official circles were afraid that the Bolsheviks would negotiate directly with the Germans, or that the Germans, owing to the weakness of the Bolsheviks, would gain control of Russia with all its material resources. Others again regarded intervention as being desirable, because after the Bolshevik revolution and the collapse of the Eastern front the Germans would concentrate their whole strength on the West. Intervention in Russia thus denoted mainly an attempt at renewing the Eastern front against the Germans.

It would be wrong to suppose that the idea of intervention in Russia, originating or upheld in Western Europe, was caused, notably in 1918, only by opposition to the Bolshevik revolution or by the effort to bring the bourgeoisie to power in Russia. Originally, more thought was given to the Germans and to the struggle against them by way of Russia. It was not until after Koltchak's anti-revolutionary activities that the idea of anti-Bolshevik intervention began to gain ground in Western Europe, for it was then that the direct action of the Bolsheviks, their propaganda and their attempts to undermine the morale of the Allied armies, began to produce definite effects.

In our Czechoslovak circles, both political and military, the situation at the beginning was fairly clear. Although immediately after the Bolshevik revolution there were Czechoslovaks who held that it would be possible to defeat the Bolsheviks and who, if they had had their way, would have brought about the destruction of our army with all its inevitable consequences to our aims, Masaryk realized at once the impossibility of all such schemes, and therefore opposed them rigidly from the very start.

From the moment when, in February and in March 1918, the transfer of our troops to France had definitely become the order of the day, no serious-minded person amongst us reckoned with the possibility of intervention in Russia. The one endeavour was to reach France as rapidly as possible. It was a straightforward, simple, sincere, and consistent policy without any ulterior motives. This continued until the beginning of July. Even when at the end of May 1918 our troops in Siberia were compelled to fight their way from station to station, even when in June, during their struggle against the Soviets, they occupied various towns on the Trans-Siberian Railway from Samara to Vladivostok, they had no wish to carry out anything which could be described as intervention, their only purpose being to proceed eastwards and reach France that way.

It is true that the Czechoslovak Army contained a number of Russian officers who were predisposed in favour of intervention, and tried to influence our troops accordingly, but this was only at the beginning, and they did not remain for long. It is also true that during their advance eastward our troops showed their sympathies with the local non-Bolshevik elements, especially those with democratic tendencies. But the whole of the army, being fundamentally and emphatically opposed everywhere to the methods and policy of the Bolsheviks and to Bolshevism as a whole, profoundly shared the sentiments of the Russian revolution, disliked the old regime, and would have done nothing which was deterimental to this point of view. For this reason our troops instinctively resolved not to interfere in Russian affairs, thus acting in accordance with Masaryk's express instructions. Moreover, they had ample opportunities of seeing how incompetent and unprepared the anti-Bolshevik elements among the Russians were.

128

The French and English Governments at this period also consistently pursued their policy as regards the transfer of our troops to the Western front. Throughout the month of June and at the beginning of July also negotiations in this sense were carried on with me in the National Council. The meeting of the Supreme Military Council at Versailles passed a resolution on June 1st to continue the preparations for the transport of our troops, as already agreed upon at Abbeville and in London, and also decided what vessels were to be sent to Vladivostok.

The instructions sent in the first half of June from Paris to London, Washington, Tokio, and Moscow indicate the realization of this programme. The negotiations of the Allied representatives at Moscow in the first half of June were directed towards the same purpose, i.e. to secure for the Czechoslovak troops a peaceable departure from Russia and Siberia.

On the other hand, General Lavergne, the French military attaché, in his telegraphed report from Moscow on June 1, 1918, made the first reference to the possibility of intervention in Russia, in view of the fact that a conflict had arisen with the Czechoslovak Army. It was obvious that he personally desired such a course. This telegram also illustrates Trotsky's hostile attitude towards our army, as well as the feeling of mistrust entertained by our troops towards the Soviets. It also draws attention to the conciliatory attitude of Chicherin, who was anxious to avoid any conflict with our troops or with the Allies. Altogether the telegram makes it plain that the Soviet Government, the Allies and our army were equally uncertain which policy would have to be decided upon, and what would be the proper course to adopt.

When our troops took possession of Samara and Krasnoyarsk, it seemed as if the Allies were hesitating and considering whether the attitude they had hitherto adopted towards the transfer of the Czechoslovak Army ought not to be changed. They did not decide in favour of intervention, but realizing that for the moment no reliance could be placed upon the transport of our troops by way of Archangelsk, and that it was not possible to begin with the embarkation at Vladivostok, they decided in favour of half-measures. On June 20th Paris sent the first instructions to General Lavergne. In view of the fact that as a result of the recent developments in Russia the Czechoslovak regiments had come to a standstill, the *status quo* was more or less to be maintained, i.e. the positions occupied were to be held, and although there was to be no intervention, nothing for the meanwhile was to be done which might prove detrimental to the possibility of intervention in the future. General Alby, by whom the instructions were signed, also demanded that the Czechoslovaks should not allow themselves to be disarmed, and that those who had reached Vladivostok disarmed should be supplied again with rifles and ammunition. General Janin and myself gave our consent to these arrangements.

It was about the same time, towards the end of June, that our military command in Vladivostok decided on the need for returning to Irkutsk for the purpose of assisting our second military detachment, which had been blockaded between

Irkutsk and Vladivostok by gangs of Bolsheviks and prisoners. There was no ulterior motive in this decision, and it did not imply any attempt at intervention. But its direct consequence was to hold up the transport from Vladivostok, which had already been arranged by the Allies; and the Japanese, the English and the French were at once officially notified that, for the time being, the transport of the Czechoslovaks from Vladivostok would be abandoned.

It should be added that the French Government nevertheless regarded this decision as provisional, and continued to negotiate with the British Government for securing vessels to transport our troops. The question of the return of our regiments from Vladivostok to Irkutsk caused the Allies some concern as to what was about to happen in the Far East and in Vladivostok itself if a free field were left for the agitation of the revolutionary Soviet elements, and what would happen if our troops were actually cut off from the Vladivostok base. As a matter of fact, our military command in Siberia, fearing the possibility of such a development, had negotiated with the Allies on that subject. On July 12th the British Government notified Paris that, should this occur, a battalion of soldiers sent from Hong-Kong and about 1,000 troops from the "Suffolk" would be landed at Vladivostok. The French Government associated itself with this manœuvre, and sent a battalion of its troops from Northern China and Indo-China to Vladivostok for the purpose of securing peace, order, and a military base for our army.

In his communications to London M. Pichon also emphasized that the real purpose of these measures was to maintain the Vladivostok base for the security of the Czechoslovak Army, and not for intervention in Siberia. He said that it was all the more necessary to lay stress on this point because at that particular moment negotiations were proceeding between Japan and President Wilson with regard to a definite form of intervention by Japan, which must not be confused with the projected landing of French and English troops.

These matters were progressively notified to us, and in the course of July they formed the subject of negotiation in the National Council. Having no detailed news from Vladivostok and Siberia, and being without any direct connection with them, I was dependent upon the reports of the Allies. I found it difficult to reconcile myself with this state of affairs. Rightly or wrongly I did not think then that the Siberian undertaking would be of much use to the Allies from a military point of view. I could have seen some point in a united intervention on a large scale with definite political aims, directed towards the construction of an Eastern front. I knew, however, that for a scheme of this kind there was neither the determination nor the resources, and I feared the effects of any vague and half-hearted action for the Allies and for Russia, to say nothing of ourselves, since our troops would fall a victim to it. I therefore continued to lay stress upon our line of policy: We would not interfere in Russian affairs, and in any case we were anxious to transfer our army to France. For I considered that our best course was to have the greatest part of our army in Europe, where a decision would be reached as to the fate of the Habsburg Empire.

129

Here I should like to insert a few remarks about the policy of the Soviet Government at that time. All indications show that this Government, as long as it feared a German invasion, which might lead to its destruction, aimed at being on good terms and even co-operating with our troops and the Allies. The guiding idea of the Soviet Government was obviously to pursue a course which involved the least menace to its authority, and at that moment, not having any other interest or purpose than to maintain its position, the Soviet Government was prepared to keep in with all those who made such a course possible, and to proceed against any who endangered it.

That is why at Bakhmatch the Bolshevik troops kept on our side, and that is why, during the struggle for the Ukraine, they advanced against the Germans. In the same way Antonov-Ovseyenko, the military representative of the Soviets at Kursk, made friendly declarations concerning our troops. The Germans soon became aware of this. Their policy, prompted also by other considerations, before long was directed so as to avoid, as far as possible for the time being, any menace to the Soviet regime. The consequence was that the Soviet Government, seeing that for some time there was no immediate danger to be feared from Germany, became aware that the possible sources of danger comprised the Allies and our troops.

Thus, by its mere existence, our army became a serious problem to the Soviet Government. The Government at Moscow was familiar with the tendencies of our troops, who had no great liking for the Bolshevik regime. Moreover, the

German and Austrian Governments were urging the Soviets to disarm the Czechoslovaks in accordance with the terms of the Brest-Litovsk peace treaty. It would have best suited the wishes of these Governments if the Czechoslovak Army had been demoralized, disorganized by attacks from gangs of prisoners, or even scattered and possibly added to the ranks of the Communists. They would, in fact, have welcomed anything likely to prevent our troops from reaching France. All this led to ever-increasing conflicts on the railway route along which our army was advancing, and these conflicts were intensified by the anarchy within Russia, and the inability of the Central Government to compel the local Soviets to adopt a uniform course of action against the Czechoslovaks.

It cannot be doubted that at first the Soviet Government was actuated by a sincere endeavour to assist our army in proceeding as quickly as possible from Russia and Siberia to France. But it had no confidence in our troops, continually fearing as it did their intervention in internal affairs. Hence the demand for their disarmament, the main purpose of which was to minimize this manifest danger to the Soviets. Later on Trotsky, and especially our Communists, hoped that it would be easy to disorganize and bolshevize the disarmed troops. It was naturally an attractive undertaking for the Bolshevik doctrinaires to prevent the transport of our troops to France, and thus to make it impossible for them to have any further share in the imperialistic bourgeois war of Western Europe.

From the development of events it is clear that if the Soviet authorities had straightforwardly assisted us in our journey eastward, the instructions and aims of the Allied representatives in Siberia would not have been modified, nor would there have been any partial intervention by Japan. The mutual distrust between the Bolsheviks and ourselves, the misunderstandings to which it gave rise, the later insincere and ambiguous policy of the Soviet authorities, with the resulting misgivings of our troops as to the safety of the whole army—all this inevitably resulted in warfare. If the actions of all the parties concerned are closely scrutinized, it is impossible not to assign the original and main responsibility for the whole conflict to the Soviet Government and its representatives.

Thus it was that, in the second half of July, the idea of a Siberian intervention had come to a head among the Allies. President Wilson, after some hesitation and after making certain reservations, arrived at an agreement with the Government at Tokio on the conditions of Japanese intervention. The concluding stage of these proceedings was reached on August 2, 1918. The Japanese Army progressively occupied the eastern part of Siberia, and our army held the remaining part of the Trans-Siberian Railway. Both forces then mutually supported each other as military allies.

(b) RECOGNITION BY GREAT BRITAIN. OUR FIRST TREATY WITH THE BRITISH GOVERNMENT

130

Having completed the negotiations concerning Pichon's note of June 28, 1918, and being continuously occupied with the progress of our military affairs in France, Italy, and Siberia, I was anxious to take advantage of the favourable atmosphere in London, where as a result of the military and political events from May to June there had been an unmistakable stiffening of the anti-Austro-Hungarian line of policy. This, of course, was to our advantage, and I therefore hoped that it would be possible to induce the British Government to give more definite expression to its attitude towards us, in the form of a solemn public declaration analogous to Pichon's letter, and covering a wider scope than Mr. Balfour's letter of June 3rd.

There were two former diplomatic documents of the British Government which served me as a formal basis for undertaking this action: Mr. Balfour's letter of June 3, 1918, and Mr. Balfour's telegram of July 1, 1918, addressed to the French Government with reference to Pichon's note giving the sanction of Great Britain to the French decision. I considered that the situation as a whole was now sufficiently advanced for the settlement of something definite and permanent as regards our cause. It seemed to me that the time had now come to embody the results of everything we had hitherto achieved in the form of a decisive diplomatic document which, from the point of view of international law, would denote the establishment of a State and Government of an independent nation.

This aim was prompted also by our continual endeavour to manage our movement so as to achieve the establishment of a provisional Government before the war had ended, so that we should be actually in existence at the time of the Peace Conference, and thus automatically attend the peace negotiations, not as a section of a defeated State forming the subject of deliberations, but as an Allied nation which had helped to bear the brunt of the war. This was a point which I always emphasized, that we were fighting of our own accord, without guarantees or commitments from the Allies; that we were fighting with our own resources for our independence.

When I survey the details of our political and diplomatic activity abroad during the war, it seems to me that our greatest success lay precisely in the fact that long before the end of the war we managed to achieve full recognition as an Allied and belligerent nation. This proved of enormous advantage to our State as soon as the negotiations for an armistice began, and also later at the Peace Conference. How great this advantage was can be gauged if we try to imagine what would have happened at the Peace Conference if, the differences of interest and opinion among the Allies being what they were, and in view of the Allied unfamiliarity with conditions in Central Europe, they had negotiated about us and not with us. This danger was particularly great in our case because the whole of our territory was located within the Habsburg Empire. We were thus less favourably situated than the Jugoslavs of Austria-Hungary or the Rumanians of Transylvania with a State behind them, which, when the war ended, would represent and advocate their interests on an internationally legal basis.

131

The moment which I chose for my negotiations was very favourable. It was the first time that during four years of warfare the Allies were at a decided advantage in the field. The end of July, when I left for London, marked the beginning of the victorious struggle which formed the last momentous episode of the German offensive of March 1918, and which Marshal Foch regarded as the first step to the military victory of the Allies. In Paris the political circles and all those who had any inside knowledge of the situation breathed a sigh of relief after the second battle of the Marne. The Allied Governments now realized that the last stage of the war was at hand. Any lingering doubts as to victory were disposed of. Such was the impression with which I left Paris on my way to London, and this impression was strengthened in London—in that calm London which had stoically received all bad news from the front, and which had produced an overwhelming effect by its composure when everybody else was overwrought.

The Foreign Office was thus able to listen to my request at a moment when there was no more doubt that the tide of war had definitely turned in our favour. But the situation was favourable to us in other respects as well. Our troops in Italy had already been engaged at the front, and our French brigade had just been prepared for transfer from Alsace to Gouraud's army in Champagne for the purpose of taking part in the operations on the most difficult sectors of the front. The British Government itself was just negotiating with the Government of the United States and with Japan for the occupation of Siberian territory in the Far East in which Great Britain had special interest. Our army, whose operations were the subject of daily reports in the Press, had gained considerable popularity both for itself and for our cause, and now naturally occupied an important position with the Allied armies also.

Such, then, was the situation, such were my reflections and hopes when, in the last week of June 1918, I called on Mr. Balfour at Downing Street for the second time during the war.

132

While waiting in Mr. Balfour's drawing-room and preparing to approach him with my petition, it suddenly flashed across my mind—as often during the war at moments which were important or decisive in their bearing upon our national cause—how strange human destinies could be. As a young student I had devoted much time to English history, and I had become attached to the personalities of the great English statesmen. I had traced the growth of British world-power in the last few centuries, and I regarded the leading politicians of the British Empire as incorporations of this power. When in 1906 I paid my first visit to London, England produced an enormous impression upon me. I again studied its history, and again I became aware of the prosperity, influence, and power which the British nation had derived from the judicious, skilful, and purposeful policy of its statesmen.

I often used to think that in Trafalgar Square and on other prominent London sites there ought to be monuments, not of the English admirals and soldiers, but of the English politicians. I also felt, rightly or wrongly, that the strong and sometimes, perhaps, too self-centred statesmanship of Great Britain, rather than the strength of armies and military victories, was the source of the British world-empire.

These impressions of mine coincided with the ideas I had formed in my student days, when I used to read the biographies of British statesmen. William Pitt, Castlereagh, Canning, Palmerston, Lord Salisbury, Gladstone—all these great figures appeared to me, a young student and a member of a small nation in Central Europe, who, from his youth upwards, had devoted careful thought to the destiny of his own nation and its struggle for existence, in an impressive and alluring light, by reason of the determined and yet humane manner in which they pursued their aims.

By a strange freak of destiny and under circumstances altogether curious and unexpected, I suddenly found myself now face to face with the successors of those historical figures, successors concerning whom history—whatever judgment it may pass on them—will one day declare that in the greatest war that the world had hitherto experienced they helped to control the destinies of the British world-empire, and they had a share in deciding the fate of half the globe. I could not help recalling my early impressions, which had left such vivid traces on my mind and in the light of which I still regarded British policy.

It was with these sentiments that I carried on negotiations during the war, during the Peace Conference, and also later with Mr. Balfour, Lord Robert Cecil, Lord Curzon, and others. I regarded them as prominent figures in the Great War. Lord Balfour, whose mild stoical scepticism, rarely showing itself, but nevertheless acting strongly within him, I observed whenever I began to speak to him about political matters, was always thoroughly familiar with the topics forming the subject of his negotiations. Outwardly he produced the impression that, like other Englishmen, he was slow in taking in the points that had been explained, but he grasped the essentials of questions with exceptional rapidity, with equal rapidity he discovered his opponent's weaknesses, and in the course of debate he managed to direct the argument straight towards them. He had a brilliant capacity for finding his way about when dealing with a problem, and particularly for forming a rapid and final judgment about persons. He will certainly occupy a permanent place among the great English statesmen. I had opportunities, especially later on at the Peace Conference, of seeing with what psychological skill he was able to estimate and classify the individual representatives of the nations concerned, and how, in accordance with the opinion he thus formed, he found an appropriate attitude towards each one in his political dealings with him.

To the psychologist it was a sheer joy to observe how Mr. Balfour, in moments of excitement, dispute, or heated argument, by his composure and by uttering a few words contrived to restore matters to their right proportion. He applied, so to speak, cold poultices to the heads of excited politicians, even when he revealed much human understanding of their conflicts and their agitation. I always esteemed his high intelligence and his cultivated mind, and it was gratifying to me that during several years of sincere co-operation he counted me among his friends.

In Lord Robert Cecil I at once recognized an idealist, always engaged on an internal struggle between his fanatical desire to show good will even to his opponents, and the need for considering the immediate interests of British politics, which from time to time imposed upon him the duty of refraining from action and keeping silence precisely on occasions when he was anxious to do just the opposite. This first impression was confirmed later on, notably during the long period of my co-operation with him in the League of Nations. His idealism brought him near to me, and from the very first I became so closely attached to him that the memory of the support he gave to my work and that of my friendship with him during the war, during the Peace Conference, and later, will always be one of the most pleasant features of my political activity.

This man who, by many people in England, was regarded as an unpractical or naïve idealist could, on occasion, by his intelligence and where need was, also by his understanding of exclusively British interests, show himself so excellent a tactician and so practical an advocate of his country's welfare while maintaining his idealism, that often he seemed to me an excellent indication of how British politicians endeavour to make British statesmanship coincide with gentlemanly conduct.

From the first moment I approached these two statesmen with feelings of respect for the power and influence which they represented, but also with a complete frankness which placed me completely in their hands. I not alone had confidence in their honesty, but I was also a firm believer in their British political common-sense and also in the strength of the facts and arguments which I had submitted to their Anglo-Saxon mentality. And I had taken great care not to ask anything of them which would not have been compatible with the interests of Great Britain. I soon felt that they, on their part, had confidence in me, and that however far-reaching my demands often were, they appreciated the direct and detached manner in which I always endeavoured to act where our cause was concerned.

At a critical moment in the history of our national movement I now stood before these two men, anxious to convince them that for a moment they should use their great influence and their extensive power on behalf of our national cause. I proceeded to do this with a feeling of confidence that my request was not only in our own interests, but was of general advantage to the Allied cause. My hopes were not disappointed, either by Mr. Balfour or Lord Robert Cecil.

133

As during my negotiations in May, I now explained to Mr. Balfour quite frankly what the Czechoslovak National Council was aiming at—a final settlement of its international position in a juridical and political respect. On the strength of the events which had occurred concerning us within the past two months, I placed before him a whole scheme involving the integral recognition of the National Council as a Government, the recognition of Czechoslovak independence, the recognition of the Czechoslovak nation as an Allied nation, and also, from the point of view of international law, as a belligerent nation. Finally, I asked for an explicit statement declaring all our armies in France, Italy, and Russia a single whole, fighting on various fronts.

I supplemented my memorandum by a verbal explanation, in the course of which I could see that Mr. Balfour regarded my demands as excessive. He at once quite frankly mentioned a few serious objections, the most important of which were as follows:

(*a*) He was not certain whether it would be possible without any reservation to declare the National Council a Government, and thus establish a State, the territory of which was occupied by the enemy, to whom it still thus belonged both in international law and in actual fact. There was no analogy or precedent for such a case in history.

(b) If Czechoslovakia were to secure recognition, what were the Allies to do afterwards regarding the Poles and Jugoslavs? The Allies were unable, for obvious reasons, to establish a Polish State immediately; the Polish problem was still too complicated, and the form of its final solution uncertain. It was not clear what steps would be taken in this matter by the Central Powers, by Soviet Russia, or by Poland as then already established by the Central Powers. Then, in Mr. Balfour's opinion, there were difficulties equally great, if not even greater, on the subject of the Jugoslavs. This problem was complicated by the fact that an independent Serbian State was already in existence, that there were serious differences with Italy, and that the question of the Jugoslav Committee differed in character from that of the Czechoslovak National Council. Moreover, what of the Rumanians? And even that did not exhaust all the difficulties of the Austro-Hungarian problem. Hence, to detach the Czechoslovak question from the whole set of Central European problems, and to settle it as an isolated item, as I was asking him to do, was very difficult, if not impossible. That would not lead to a solution of the Austro-Hungarian problem. All these points would have to be carefully considered.

(c) Mr. Balfour acknowledged the work of the National Council, our political efficiency, and the achievements of our troops. But when I explained to him about our opposition to Austria at home and the establishment of the National Committee in Prague, he quite openly expressed to me his doubts as to what extent our National Council really represented the opinion of the Czechoslovak nation, and how far it was legally entitled to act on its behalf or to become its Government. The question was whether we were backed by the nation at home, or were only political *émigrés* with radical views, as *émigrés* generally are.

134

I endeavoured to dispose of all Mr. Balfour's objections partly by word of mouth, partly by a new memorandum which I submitted to him at a subsequent visit. He seemed to be fully satisfied by a detailed account of the latest phase of our policy at home. I pointed out that the best proof of our ability to speak and act on behalf of the nation lay in the fact that about a hundred thousand of our volunteer troops in the Allied countries already fully recognized us as their supreme authority.

Further, I mentioned that our movement abroad had met with the approval not only of political circles at home, but also of the masses of the population there. Mr. Balfour who, as an Englishman, appreciated plain facts, was particularly impressed by my reference to the hundred thousand volunteers fighting on the three Allied fronts.

In my accompanying memorandum I dealt chiefly with the objections of an international character. I also approached a number of influential persons in London, including Sir Eric Drummond, who was then Mr. Balfour's secretary, and who is now General Secretary of the League of Nations. I also had an important interview with Lord Milner, the Minister of War. It was at that time, too, that I first had dealings with Sir George Clerk, who later became British Minister in Prague. He was interested in the Central European situation, and particularly in Polish affairs.

Our friends, Mr. H. Wickham Steed and Dr. Seton Watson, were naturally anxious as to what the Foreign Office would say in reply to my demand. At that time they were both working at Crewe House, and in this capacity they were in a position to influence official circles. Mr. Steed generously and devotedly helped me by direct interventions. He approached people whom he knew in Downing Street and elsewhere, making it possible for me to meet various important officials. He also indicated what should, and what should not be included in the memoranda. He arranged fresh meetings, and when I received unsatisfactory answers he devised new methods of approach and new statements of our case.

Mr. Balfour recognized the validity of the arguments in my second memorandum, and at a new interview he told me that in principle he was in agreement with the idea of issuing a British declaration on our behalf; but, as at the previous discussion in May, he referred me to Lord Robert Cecil for a further and more detailed discussion of the matter.

I submitted to Lord Robert Cecil the above-mentioned memoranda, and also the draft of a declaration which I had sketched out on leaving Paris. In this draft I made the same demand as that contained in M. Pichon's letter of June 28, 1918, but I couched it in more emphatic terms and in a more juridically explicit form. I referred to the historical State rights, to the resistance of our people and troops to Austria-Hungary during the war, and to the manifestos of our politicians in

January, April, and May 1918. I demanded the recognition of the three Czechoslovak armies as a single independent army of an independent nation, whose destinies were now guided by the Czechoslovak National Council in Paris as the provisional Government of a new independent Allied nation.

Lord Robert Cecil considered that the draft was too emphatic, lengthy, and theoretical. At our very first interview he told me that the British Government would scarcely go to such lengths. He promised me that I should soon receive the Government's reply to my proposal, and two days later he placed before me his own draft based on the memorandum which I had given to Mr. Balfour. I was disappointed, however, by its moderation; the scope of its contents was smaller even than that of M. Pichon's letter. It was much shorter than my original draft and in this, incidentally, it was superior. It left on one side our historical arguments, and emphasized chiefly the facts connected with our movement abroad, the importance of which it acknowledged, but it did not even mention the words "sovereignty," "State," or "Czechoslovak Government." It took over from my memorandum and draft the passages emphasizing our political and military movement, as well as the juridical and political character of our three armies which, as Allied armies, were waging regular warfare against the Central Powers.

In view of this situation I at once took Lord Robert Cecil's draft as a basis for further discussions, and submitted to him a new and more emphatic counter-proposal which was a revised version of his own draft. I accompanied this by a further commentary in support of our claim. In order to secure Lord Robert Cecil's consent I not only drew attention to what we had already attained in France, but I also explained in detail the juridical aspect of the agreement which Štefánik had made with Italy in April and June 1918, and I laid particular stress on all the prerogatives which had been granted by Italy to our army and our National Council. I completed this commentary by a proposal which might serve as a compromise, to the effect that it might be possible to make a declaration couched in more moderate terms as regards the National Council as a Government, but that, on the other hand, the British Government might make an agreement with the National Council in which the supremacy of the National Council and the Czechoslovak nation, as well as its relationship to the Allies, could be mentioned more clearly and emphatically than would be possible in a public declaration under the circumstances then prevailing. It would be a special convention between the two parties constituting a commentary on the British declaration, the political and juridical implications of which it would express in detail. I prepared an outline of these juridical consequences, and at once handed it to Lord Robert Cecil, with a demand that if the British Government consented, they should be formulated as articles of a convention which would then be signed by both parties as a valid and binding document. The wording was as follows:

The recognition of the sovereignty of the National Council would have these consequences:

1. From an international and juridical standpoint the Czechoslovak territories would occupy much the same position among the Allies as Serbia and Greece.

2. Their armies would cease to be dependent upon the French and Italian Ministries of War, they would be solely under Czechoslovak administration, and would be recognized on an equal footing by all the Allies.

3. The Czechoslovak territories would have their own budget for the maintenance of administration and armies. They would ask the Allies for a political loan, in which England also would participate.

4. The Allies would negotiate direct with the provisional Government on all questions concerning Czechoslovak affairs.

5. The Czechoslovak territories would be represented at Allied conferences except those definitely reserved for the great Allied Powers.

6. A diplomatic, consular, passport, and courier service to be established for the Czechoslovak territories; all Czechoslovaks recognized as such by the Czechoslovak authorities would be treated as Allies in the Entente countries.

7. In order that the Allies might receive adequate guarantees, a mixed financial commission would be set up to control the Czechoslovak budget, covered by the Allied loan.

Lord Robert Cecil promised that he would again consider the matter, discuss it with Mr. Balfour, as well as the other members of the Government, and would give me a definite answer at the earliest possible moment.

The subsequent negotiations proceeded rapidly. Lord Robert Cecil recognized in principle all my objections. A few days later he summoned me again to the Foreign Office and placed before me a revised draft of the British declaration which had met with Mr. Balfour's approval. In its essentials our new counter-proposal had been accepted with insignificant changes.

I therefore expressed my agreement on behalf of the National Council.

As a characteristic change in our proposal, it is worth mentioning that the British Government declined to say unreservedly that it recognized the Czechoslovak National Council as an interim Government; for this it substituted a phrase recognizing it as a trustee of the future Czechoslovak Government. This was a compromise which we reached after a lengthy discussion with the assistance of Mr. Steed, who had proposed it. In no case did I wish to assent to any formula not expressly mentioning, on the one hand, the Czechoslovak State and Government, and, on the other, the National Council as the depository of national sovereignty. Mr. Steed's formula contained both these points.

The declaration which, with a special letter from Mr. Balfour, was officially handed to me from the Foreign Office on August 9, 1918, ran as follows:

DECLARATION

Since the beginning of the war the Czechoslovak nation has resisted the common enemy by every means in its power. The Czechoslovaks have constituted a considerable army, fighting on three different battlefields and attempting, in Russia and Siberia, to arrest the Germanic invasion.

In consideration of its efforts to achieve independence, Great Britain regards the Czechoslovaks as an Allied nation, and recognizes the unity of the three Czechoslovak armies as an Allied and belligerent army waging regular warfare against Austria-Hungary and Germany.

Great Britain also recognizes the right of the Czechoslovak National Council as the supreme organ of the Czechoslovak national interests, and, as the present trustee of the future Czechoslovak Government, to exercise supreme authority over this Allied and belligerent army.

A. J. BALFOUR.

August 9, 1918.

(c) IMPORTANCE OF THE BRITISH DECLARATION

135

I regard the negotiations which resulted in this declaration as the most important political activity of the National Council during the war. Of all the Allied declarations hitherto, that of Mr. Balfour had the widest scope in its bearings on international law. In this respect it constituted the actual recognition of the independence of our nation (including the Slovaks) while the war was still in progress, and its removal from Austro-Hungarian domination.

During my last visit to Lord Robert Cecil we were still concerned with the settlement of the British-Czechoslovak Agreement. In principle, Lord Robert Cecil assented to a formulation of the juridical and political consequences of the new British declaration. He also accepted the demand for a special agreement, acknowledging that it was expedient for ambiguities to be avoided by means of a precise formulation of the political and juridical consequences which proceeded from the British declaration, but which could not be embodied in it.

Just before my departure from London on August 10th, I gave my assent to the wording of the proposed agreement as formulated by Lord Robert Cecil in articles according to my suggestions quoted above. It was decided that the text of the agreement, the actual preparation of which would involve a short delay, was to be signed in about a fortnight, and that the British Embassy in Paris would notify me when I was to proceed to London for the signature. This stage was reached on September 3, 1918.

I do not think it is necessary to analyse in detail the juridical aspect of the British declaration, and especially of this agreement. In addition to what I have already said, I should only like to emphasize that by Article 6 of the British-Czechoslovak Agreement, giving us the right as an Allied nation to attend, during the actual war period, all Allied conferences where our interests were involved, it was my purpose to establish a basis for the entry of Czechoslovakia, first of all to the inter-Allied conferences and thus automatically with the Allies to the Peace Conference. In this my expectations were entirely fulfilled.

By the financial control which I offered it was our purpose to give England a full opportunity of examining our management of affairs, which would be equivalent to a guarantee of our credentials. By arranging for a permanent representative to be accredited to the British Government, and by establishing a consular and passport service, I aimed at taking the first practical step for our independent existence as a State in a palpable manner.

It will be seen that the British-Czechoslovak convention is an important document with regard to the creation of our State. From it can be demonstrated how our State was established deliberately and step by step, by laborious creative work, which had been planned with due regard to the political and psychological factors involved. This process of our gradual recognition by the Allies and our establishment by successive stages during the war provides much material which can be studied with advantage by all those who are concerned with the theories of sociology, law, and statesmanship.

It was clear that after these conversations the establishment of the Government and the State was only a purely formal matter. I indicated to Lord Robert Cecil that this step would soon be taken, and that we should do so at a moment when the circumstances seemed to make it desirable. Thereupon, even before proceeding to Paris, I instructed V. Nosek, who was in charge of the office of the National Council in London, to make all arrangements for securing legation premises, setting up a passport service, etc. This, of course, was to be done in consultation with the British Government.

Having negotiated the declaration and the British-Czecho-slovak convention, I left for Paris with very definite plans as to what my further steps were to be. I had decided to co-operate with Professor Masaryk in rapidly constructing our State, in producing the greatest possible number of *faits accomplis*, in setting up all the external emblems and institutions of a State which, under the circumstances then prevailing, could be realized. The whole of my activity from the London negotiations to the period immediately preceding the Armistice was directed towards this end. I had in view the situation of Belgium and Serbia, States without territory, with only a small army, with a Government in exile, and burdened with difficulties of all kinds. It was my aim to secure for Czechoslovakia the same juridical position as that of these two States, so that there could be no withdrawal, whatever might happen in the Allied countries or in Central Europe. In this I was prompted not merely by the fact that from July onwards the Allies had crushed the German military front, while the Austrian front in Italy had collapsed in a similar manner, but also by an observation of how matters were developing within the Habsburg Empire. I felt that we must now be prepared every moment for all possibilities.

On leaving London I asked Lord Robert Cecil to notify officially to the other Allies the agreement which we had reached. I was anxious that, by so doing, the British Government should emphasize the scope of all these arrangements. Lord Robert Cecil promised me this, and the Foreign Office made the necessary arrangements through diplomatic channels.

136

The far-reaching importance of the London agreements was realized in all Allied circles, both among the Government authorities and the politicians. It was not long before I myself saw clear indications of this. I will just mention two of the most typical cases.

As on all similar occasions I informed the French and Italian Ambassadors, as well as the Serbian Minister in London, about the proceedings. I was particularly anxious that Italy, having a direct interest in Austro-Hungarian affairs, should have a precise knowledge of the situation, and should realize that we were undertaking no steps which were not in accordance with her interests. For this reason, as soon as I arrived in London at the end of June, I quite frankly explained to Marquis Imperiali what my purpose was, and I asked him to use his influence for me with the English Government, while notifying to his own Government my proceedings in London. Marquis Imperiali was willing to help me, but at the same time he doubted whether the English Government, which hitherto had shown itself somewhat conservative as regards Austro-Hungarian affairs, would show any readiness to take so decisive a step openly. This view was in accordance with the policy of Rome and particularly with that of Sonnino. At that time there were considerable differences of opinion on this subject in the Roman Cabinet, but they terminated with the well-known Italian *communiqué* passed on September 9th and published on September 22nd, in which Bissolati's point of view in favour of Jugoslav unity was adopted with the more emphatic action in Austro-Hungarian affairs which it involved. I am inclined to think that our successes in London made this decision possible and, in fact, helped directly to bring it about. It should be remembered that the British Government at that time, as Mr. Balfour and Lord Robert Cecil pointed out to me, did not agree with Sonnino's policy in Jugoslav affairs, and on account of Italian opposition were unable to do anything decisive for the settlement of the problems which they presented. The assistance given to us, however, tended, in my opinion, indirectly to further the progress of the other questions. In this sense it is possible to interpret Mr. Balfour's speech at a public meeting held on July 25th at the Mansion House in favour of the war aims of Serbia and the Jugoslavs. His emphatic and non-compromising remarks directed against the Habsburg Empire, and delivered in the presence of several ambassadors, including Marquis Imperiali, were more than significant, and were taken as a clear indication of the policy being pursued by the London Cabinet in Austro-Hungarian matters.

Here I may point out that as soon as I received Mr. Balfour's declaration on August 10th, I sent a copy of it to Marquis Imperiali who, surprised at this step on the part of the British Government, went to Mr. Balfour to satisfy himself as to the British point of view. According to the report which reached me from a semi-official quarter, he asked Mr. Balfour whether the British Government realized the consequences of the arrangement with the Czechoslovak National Council. Mr. Balfour's reply is said to have been "Yes, we considered the matter for a very long time. We hesitated before deciding to adopt this course. But there is no other possibility. This means the destruction of Austria-Hungary."

The British declaration occasioned a certain amount of surprise in French Government circles also. In Paris they fully realized the political and military bearings of these decisions. As far as I could see, however, they did not at first understand the formula about the unity of our three armies. They were afraid that without their knowledge or consent I may have completed some new arrangement about our Siberian army or agreed that England was to make fresh use of it. As this army formed a part of our army in France, and was still mainly dependent upon the French military command, this interest on the part of the French Government can be readily understood. It was because Paris was not acquainted with the details of the London negotiations that the publication of the British declaration, which had been telegraphed to the Havas agency in Paris, was held up until my return there. When I arrived on August 12th I was at once sent for by Clemenceau at the Ministry of War, and then by Pichon and Berthelot at the Quai d'Orsay to give an exact account of what had happened in London. The matter was quickly explained, the declaration was published, and the representatives of the French Foreign Ministry did not conceal their satisfaction at the course which the British

Government had adopted. They also took the view that Austria-Hungary was settled as far as England was concerned.

While still in London I had informed Professor Masaryk in Washington of what had been done. On behalf of the National Council he sent a telegram of thanks to Mr. Balfour, and the representatives of the Siberian army sent the National Council in Paris an enthusiastic manifesto expressing their gratitude and devotion.

It would appear that the greatest surprise, if not alarm, was caused by the British proclamation in Vienna, where it became known on August 14th. It was at once forwarded to Burian, the Minister of Foreign Affairs, who at that particular moment happened to be conferring with the German Ministers and the Kaiser at Spa. There, too, they realized the significance of this document, especially as Burian asserted so unequivocally that the Habsburg Empire would not hold out for more than another two or three months. In any case, the Government at Vienna took an unprecedented step as regards our movement abroad. It attempted, in a special *communiqué*, to weaken the effect of the British declaration upon public opinion in the Czech territories. How far matters had gone is shown by the fact that this Austrian manifesto passed almost unnoticed in the Allied countries.

(*d*) NEGOTIATIONS WITH JAPAN

137

I had taken advantage of my stay in London in August and again at the beginning of September 1918 for the purpose of attempting to discuss the question of our recognition also with Japan. At that time there was very close contact between the National Council in Paris and the Japanese Government. As early as 1916 Professor Masaryk had been in touch with Japanese official circles in London, and Štefánik, in the course of his journeys, always made a point of establishing contact with them in one form or another.

I myself was in communication with the Japanese in Paris and in London. Most of my dealings were with Mr. Ito, an Embassy official, first in London and then in Paris, as well as with Count Matsui and Viscount Chinda, the Ambassadors in Paris and London respectively. In accordance with my custom, from the year 1917 onwards I kept them systematically informed of the progress being made by our movement, and of our negotiations with the Allies.

Until the end of 1917 the direct interest which the Japanese had in our movement was not very extensive. But from the time of the Bolshevik revolution in Russia this direct interest increased considerably; and when our army in Russia became a factor of importance, and the Allies decided to transfer our troops by way of Vladivostok to France, the Japanese became our immediate military collaborators and were, in fact, more directly interested in our proceedings than some of the great Allied Powers.

Professor Masaryk's visit to Tokio in April 1918 had a decisive influence in this respect. His personal intervention, his negotiations with the Minister of Foreign Affairs and other authorities, the appointment of our representative at Tokio and the activity of our first military contingent in the Far East, so consolidated the relations which had already been established in Japan that our political and military importance was soon recognized at Tokio.

From May 1918 the Allies began official discussions with the Japanese Government concerning the supply of vessels for the transport of our troops from Vladivostok to France, and also on the subject of equipment, supplies, medical services, etc. The Ministry of War at Paris kept me systematically informed about the progress of our affairs in Tokio, so that I was able to hold parallel negotiations on these subjects with Count Matsui.

When I was certain that England definitely intended to recognize the National Council, I visited Viscount Chinda, the Japanese Ambassador in London. I informed him how far the negotiations between Great Britain and ourselves had proceeded, and I mentioned that I proposed to ask the Japanese Government to follow the example of Great Britain in this respect. At Viscount Chinda's request I gave him a written statement on this subject, and promised that before my departure from London I would let him know the results of my negotiations with Mr. Balfour. This took place verbally at a fresh visit on August 10th, and on the following day I supplied him with a written account of the proceedings.

Viscount Chinda promised me that he would intervene in Tokio, and assured me that the Japanese Government would certainly grant us the same concessions as we received from London. I again visited Viscount Chinda on September 1st, when I returned to London for the signature of the British-Czechoslovak Agreement. He informed me that Tokio consented to the recognition of the National Council. Japan definitely regarded us as a military and political ally, and her dealings with our army in Siberia would be in accordance with this principle. The exact wording of the declaration had not yet arrived, as Tokio required beforehand not only the text of the British declaration of August 9th, but also a copy of the agreement which London had just prepared for signature.

The Japanese agreement was actually handed to me by the Japanese Embassy in Paris on September 11, 1918. It is not so definite as the British declaration. This can be accounted for by the guarded attitude which Japan adopted to European questions in general.

XVII

PROCLAMATION OF CZECHOSLOVAK INDEPEN-
DENCE. THE FIRST CZECHOSLOVAK GOVERN-
MENT

(a) RECOGNITION OF THE NATIONAL COUNCIL BY THE UNITED
STATES ON SEPTEMBER 2, 1918. OUR FIRST TREATY
OF ALLIANCE WITH FRANCE. AGREEMENT WITH MASARYK
AS TO THE PROCLAMATION OF INDEPENDENCE

138

AFTER the events which I have just described, our cause made
rapid progress in Paris, London, and Rome towards its final
success. Foch's counter-offensive in July produced the first
military results which pointed to a definite turn of the tide in a
military respect. Nevertheless, not having any detailed knowledge of the situation in Germany, and being aware of our own
difficulties, we felt sure that the war would continue until the
spring of 1919 at the least. We supposed that by that time all
the promised American troops would be in France at the front,
and that only then would it be possible to carry out successfully
the last decisive onslaught against Germany and Austria-
Hungary. We therefore distributed the rest of our work in
France, England, and Italy accordingly.

Our main concern was to be recognized as an independent
State among the Allied nations before the war was over, and
this had been achieved to an adequate degree as a result of the
last negotiations in England. France, Italy, and America had
raised no objections to this decision, and I therefore devoted
all my endeavours to induce the French and Italian Governments to confirm this state of affairs by new diplomatic documents and by a mutual agreement with us direct.

Having returned from London to Paris in the middle of
August, I at once started to try to bring about the signature
of a political agreement analogous to the one with England.
For this purpose I negotiated with Degrand, Laroche, and

Berthelot, to whom I submitted the unsigned text of the Anglo-Czechoslovak Agreement; and after exchanging views on this subject I suggested that the Quai d'Orsay itself should formulate the draft of an analogous Franco-Czechoslovak Agreement, having special regard to the position of France towards our movement. I emphasized the necessity of clearly formulating in such an agreement, not only our share in the inter-Allied conferences, but also our territorial demands, with a view to securing, if possible, the support of France for them at the coming Peace Conference. Finally, I aimed at arranging for the French Government to grant a formal and public proclamation of the National Council in Paris as the Government of the Czechoslovak State.

Berthelot entrusted the elaboration of the first draft of the agreement to M. Fromageot, the legal expert at the Quai d'Orsay, and to M. Degrand, his secretary, from whom I received it towards the end of August during my stay in London. But before these negotiations had entered on a decisive phase, matters took a new turn which was of great importance to us. This was the proclamation of the United States Government on September 2, 1918, concerning our liberation movement. This declaration defined our precise position among the Allied States, and solemnly confirmed the assurances which we had received from the European Allies :

WASHINGTON,
September 2, 1918.

The Czechoslovak peoples having taken up arms against the German and Austro-Hungarian Empires, and having placed in the field organized armies, which are waging war against those Empires under officers of their own nationality and in accordance with the rules and practices of civilized nations, and Czechoslovaks having in the prosecution of their independence in the present war confided the supreme political authority to the Czechoslovak National Council, the Government of the United States recognizes that a state of belligerency exists between the Czechoslovaks thus organized and the German and Austro-Hungarian Empires.

It also recognizes the Czechoslovak National Council as a *de facto* belligerent Government, clothed with proper authority to direct the military and political affairs of the Czechoslovaks.

The Government of the United States further declares that it is prepared to enter formally into relations with the *de facto* Government thus recognized for the purpose of prosecuting the war against the common enemy, the Empires of Germany and Austria-Hungary.

Since the end of June 1918 Masaryk had been systematically furthering the anti-Austrian trend in the official policy of America. In the course of July he had negotiated with the United States chiefly on the subject of our Siberian army and the method of supplying it with help, in which respect Wilson identified himself with the Allied action in Siberia. It was at this moment that the National Council was granted recognition by Great Britain, and Masaryk naturally used this as an argument when negotiating with Mr. Lansing for a similar recognition on the part of the United States. Mr. Lansing accepted Masaryk's point of view, and based his proclamation on the wording of the agreement which we had obtained from Mr. Balfour. He then submitted it for Masaryk's approval before making it public on the date mentioned. The declaration recognizes the National Council as a *de facto* Government, and regards it as being in a state of war with the Central Powers. It declares, moreover, that the Government of the United States is prepared to establish relations with this *de facto* Government for the purpose of carrying on hostilities against the common enemy. This was the first time that the expression "actual Government" was unreservedly applied to the National Council in a solemn commitment by a State so important as America.

There can be no doubt that the step taken by Wilson reacted favourably upon the further action of the Governments in London and Paris. When, on September 3rd, I signed the British-Czechoslovak Agreement in London I was able to show Lord Robert Cecil the American declaration as a proof that the Government at London had acted wisely, and when I was negotiating in Paris for a Franco-Czechoslovak Agreement, the American declaration made it possible for me to demand various commitments which, after Wilson's action, the French Government was willing to grant me.

139

When I returned to Paris on September 5th, I found the situation there slightly changed. General Štefánik had arrived from Italy towards the end of August, and was now preparing for his journey to Siberia. On seeing my plans and also the proposal drawn up at the Quai d'Orsay, he expressed certain reservations. He did not consider that matters were sufficiently mature to make it possible to form an actual Government so early. Altogether, he entertained doubts as to the whole political character of the agreement, and he wanted us to conclude an agreement in Paris on the subject of the National Council and our army, analogous to the one which he himself had signed with Italy on April 21 and June 30, 1918.

I found it impossible, however, to find acceptance for Štefánik's point of view. He himself, immediately before his departure for Siberia, vainly endeavoured to persuade Fromageot. Berthelot regarded Štefánik's views as impracticable. He agreed with the scheme originally drawn up, which was analogous to the agreement with Italy, and he agreed also that a provisional Government should be constituted at a favourable opportunity. He therefore asked me to arrange for the National Council to arrive at an agreement in this sense with Fromageot and Degrand. I acted in accordance with Berthelot's wishes, especially as Štefánik, seeing the views which predominated at the Quai d'Orsay left me with complete freedom of action in this respect. What I aimed at was that the original draft which Degrand had shown me should, on the political side, be brought as close as possible into line with the memorandum which had been submitted to the Quai d'Orsay.

In my interviews at the Ministry I had laid stress upon the following points:

1. There should be a settled formulation of our military assistance to France and the Allies, which would place us on an equal footing with them, and by which France would undertake, by way of reciprocity, to promote the reconstitution of our free State, and to allow us a free decision with regard to our army.

2. The National Council should be not merely the representative or the basis of a future Government, but an actual provisional Government, which in the agreement was to be recognized as the *de facto* Czechoslovak Government.

3. There was to be a binding declaration on the subject of our future frontiers and the whole of our territory.

4. There was to be a confirmation of our share in inter-Allied conferences, and official diplomatic relations were to be instituted between the new Government and the French Government.

There was another question which was no less important, and which emerged as a necessary and logical result of the new agreement and the new juridical relationship between France and ourselves. This was the question concerning a new and special military agreement instead of the hitherto existing decree issued in December 1917. This decree was no longer in accordance with the juridical state of affairs which had now been arranged, or with the stage which our political and juridical independence had now reached. It was therefore my aim that our army should be dealt with in a manner analogous to the juridical status achieved by our cause as a whole. This, however, was a very delicate matter, and I had to proceed with extreme caution, as otherwise the military circles would have opposed us. I also wanted to take advantage of this opportunity for emphasizing the fact that we ourselves would maintain our army and Government, and that after peace was concluded we would defray all expenses.

The extent of these demands can be grasped by anyone with a sense of politics. They show the logical and systematic manner in which our progress was made. Every fresh set of negotiations, every fresh diplomatic document necessarily denoted progress in the construction of our State. I hasten to point out that I never concealed any of these plans from the Allies, nor did I ever confront them unexpectedly with anything. I quite frankly explained our aims to them and always let them know the real purpose which I had in view.

The wording of the agreement, which complied with all the fundamental points in my demands, provided me yet again with an indication that we were proceeding on the right lines. We had achieved everything which could be achieved and which at that period we needed. Negotiations were completed about September 10, 1918.

140

Together with the accord on the text of the agreement, the Quai d'Orsay took due note of my information that at an early date we intended, in a formal and public manner, to announce the establishment of a provisional Government and to appoint diplomatic representatives. This was to be done at the moment which we should consider the most suitable according to the circumstances.

I therefore made the final preparations for this concluding phase of our diplomatic struggle for an independent State. In notifying Masaryk about all the important developments which ensued during my negotiations, I still had to arrange with him in detail for the course of action and the principles which we should follow in taking our final steps, for the persons who were to be taken into account in this connection, and for the exact juncture at which the matter was to be completed. From the reports which he was sending from Washington I observed that we were acting in complete agreement, and the Washington recognition of September 2nd showed me that there also matters had come to a head.

It was also my concern to prepare this final phase for our army too, as I was anxious for the proclamation of independence and a provisional Government to take effect not only before the Allied public, but also at the front and in the garrison centres amongst our troops, so as to impart a solemn and truly national character to the whole proceedings. I had also thought that it might be possible to choose November 8, 1918, as a symbolic day for this purpose. I was prompted to this far-reaching initiative, partly in realization of my complete agreement with Masaryk, partly in realization of the responsibility which was then resting upon me. Masaryk was at Washington, Štefánik on his way to Siberia, but the decision on the whole undertaking could be reached only in Europe, in accordance with the situation in Paris, Prague, and Vienna. I therefore acted with great care and consideration, but at the same time in a determined manner, such as is necessary at critical moments of this kind.

And so on September 13, 1918, I sent the following telegram to Masaryk in Washington:

In consequence of negotiations carried out in Paris and London their Governments fully accept principle of complete recognition of our Government. I have made an agreement with Ministry of Foreign Affairs enabling us at once to organize our central administrative body, the Czechoslovak Government, with regular diplomatic service. Seat of Government should be Paris, and we should have same status as Belgian Government with all advantages and entire public recognition internationally.

I submit this matter to you with my personal opinion of these questions: In view of situation here it would be good to set up a ministry under your presidency, with headquarters at Paris. It would be necessary to set up, beside the presidency of the ministerial council, also a Ministry of War and of Foreign Affairs. I do not know your opinion as to distribution of portfolios. I think that it will be essential to set up these three ministries, and as regards the others we should keep to the opinion that they are to be given to political leaders from Bohemia.

We could, in addition, set up State secretariats for finance and the interior.

The minister who might be in Paris in absence of the others could, for the interim, manage the remaining ministries. It would also be necessary to establish legations at Rome, Paris, London, Washington, and Tokio, and also to appoint our representatives to the Serbian Government, with the title of Chargé d'Affaires, at least for the time being. . . . In view of situation I am compelled to begin making these new arrangements now. Considering the last declaration and the situation as a whole, I regard it as somewhat dangerous not to start without having our juridical status precisely defined, or without immediately transforming the National Council into a regular Government. I see from the Austrian papers that our people at home are reckoning upon this. Kindly let me have a telegraphic reply to all these questions, and inform me of your fundamental views.—BENEŠ.

I received a reply on September 26th through M. Vesnić, the Serbian Minister. Masaryk expressed his complete satisfaction with everything we had done in Paris, and at the same time he declared himself entirely in agreement with the scheme for constituting a Government and with the other measures proposed in my telegram. The date upon which this reply was dispatched was then taken as the date when the provisional Czechoslovak Government was constituted.

141

Having thus completed all necessary preparations, and after obtaining the requisite consent of all the parties concerned, I considered it essential to send a final detailed report to Prague, and in this way prepare our political circles at home for all that was now to ensue. In a message which I sent on September 11, 1918, I summarized the facts and the contents of the document defining our international status, and I emphasized the unequivocal character of the Allied declarations in order to counteract any contrary statements on the part of the Austrian Press and Government which might be calculated to mislead our people at home.

In my message to Prague I also referred to our decision concerning the immediate development of a State organization, with a regular Government and the whole of the diplomatic apparatus. As a provisional step, the Government was to consist of a Prime Minister, which post had been accepted by Masaryk, Minister of War (Štefánik), and a Minister of Foreign Affairs (myself), while the remaining portfolios were to be assigned to politicians in Bohemia. I emphasized the fact that we regarded ourselves as a constituent part of the provisional revolutionary Government existing *de facto* in Bohemia, and I called upon them at home to maintain this conception, so that whatever might happen in Bohemia there would be no break in the unity between us in this respect.

Under no circumstances (I wrote) must there arise any dissension or schism between us. Nor must there be one Government coming into existence here, and another Government among you. Whenever a Government is to come into existence in Bohemia, the step must be taken in agreement with us, in unity with us, and in continuity with us. . . . It is out of the question for the Allies to instigate any negotiations whatever with Austria-Hungary. This is an eventuality which need not be feared. Nor need there be any misgivings as to whether the Allies intend to fight to a finish. It would therefore be a suicidal policy on our part to make any arrangements with Austria. For these reasons we consider it essential for you, at the right moment (we do not wish to decide this, as you will be in a better position to judge), to refuse point-blank to enter Parliament, and also to break off all relations with Austria-Hungary. You would thus demonstrate that you understood what was meant when the Allies proclaimed us an Allied nation.

At the same time we urge you not to provoke the Germans or anybody else to a premature revolt. Any revolution which is to come, and for which you should be prepared and organized, must take place in agreement with us. The chief military move on the part of the Allies will not be made until the spring. By that time we shall be adequately organized, and as a Government we shall be able to reach a definite political and military agreement with the Allies on the subject of the plan for overthrowing Austria-Hungary by an external offensive and an internal revolution.

I concluded my message by giving concise information as to the stage reached by our movement abroad and the position of our troops, especially in Siberia. I dispatched the message on September 5th, and accelerated as much as possible the realization of all the plans referred to, in view of the Allied military situation and our agreement with the Allied Governments, and particularly in view of what was then taking place in Austria-Hungary. The reports of critical happenings there were so precise that I was prepared for the utmost possibility, especially as a number of messages arriving from Prague via Geneva referred to the possibility of an impending military capitulation on the part of the monarchy. I was somewhat disturbed by rumours that the Austrian Government were preparing to revise the constitution. From time to time statements emanating from pacifist quarters were published, from which it appeared that Lammasch or Redlich would be appointed to the Preparatory Commission for drawing up the new constitution. At another time there was a rumour as to the promising progress made by the preparations for dividing Bohemia into administrative areas, and the measures adopted later by the Austrian Government showed me that Vienna was determined to take some decisive step without awaiting further developments. I therefore realized that we had no time to lose, and I made a special point of this in my telegram to Masaryk. Not wishing to be taken unawares by the course of events, I urged our business forward. The political situation in the Habsburg Empire, as well as the state of things on the various battle-fronts, tended only to confirm me in these proceedings.

On the Western front Foch's victorious advance, initiated by the offensive on July 18th, proved to be the beginning of the end of the Central Powers from a military point of view. Four consecutive German offensives in March, April, May–June, and July, on a larger scale than anything of the kind hitherto attempted in the war, indicated an extreme and final effort on the part of the Central Powers. These offensives used up enormous supplies of material, and entailed the sacrifice of hundreds of thousands of lives, without producing any success. The exhaustion of supplies and food-stuffs had reached its culminating point, and a renewal of the raw materials which had thus been used up was out of the question. The losses sustained in this final exertion of strength could never be made good, and the military and economic resources of the Central Powers could now only continue to diminish until they were exhausted.

The Allies, on the other hand, had at this juncture just reached a far more favourable situation, especially through the collaboration of America. Their resources were increasing, while those of the Central Powers were on the decline. The last effort of the Central Powers, at a moment when they were still in the ascendancy, proved unsuccessful. The inference was clear that a military catastrophe on the part of the Central Powers was now only a question of time, and it would evidently not be long in coming.

142

While the Central Powers were thus being overtaken by a complete military disaster, the internal situation of the Habsburg Empire was moving towards ruin with redoubled speed. At the time when I had secured our recognition by Great Britain, it was clear to the Government at Vienna that a catastrophe was inevitable unless peace could be made at the earliest possible moment. At a meeting between the two Emperors and their Ministers at Spa on August 14, 1918, Burian expressly declared that if the war were not ended within two months, the Habsburg Empire, being exhausted in every respect, would be unable to hold out. On his return to Vienna, Burian, just like Czernin at an earlier period, clutched at every opportunity for bringing peace negotiations within reach of the Empire. Burian's official peace proposal was made on September 15th in a note which he sent not only to the neutral States and to the Papal See, but also to Germany, Bulgaria, Turkey, and the Ukraine. In it he proposed that the competent States should, at the earliest possible date, meet together for an exchange of views as to the basic principles of the coming peace. It would not be in the nature of actual peace negotiations, nor would it denote a suspension of hostilities, but it would merely be a *rapprochement* for elucidating a number of points at issue and thus accelerating the arrival of the peace negotiations themselves.

The Allied Press immediately rejected this proposal, which it unanimously interpreted as a fresh proof of the chaos and exhaustion prevailing in the Habsburg Empire. At that time I was negotiating with the French Government on the subject of our agreement, and I at once saw that Burian's proposal was not viewed with any great favour. What a great contrast there was between this and the reception accorded to the first attempt of this character in December 1916 and also to Czernin's attempts in 1917.

At first a certain amount of surprise was occasioned by the fact that the note was dispatched by Vienna alone, without the other members of the Quadruple Alliance; and a number of Austrophiles in Allied circles endeavoured to show that this was a fresh symptom of conflict with Berlin, so that it would be a good opportunity to make another attempt to separate Vienna from Berlin. It soon appeared, however, that this was a preconcerted manœuvre, and the Allied answers, which were not long in making their appearance, came as a severe blow to the Habsburg Empire. As early as September 16th Balfour replied that any conversations, such as those suggested by Burian, could serve no useful purpose, and that the proposal made by Vienna would not mean peace, but an armistice leading soon to a new war. Immediately afterwards Lansing replied on behalf of President Wilson in terms which left no doubt that the latter, having publicly entered on a commitment to destroy the Hohenzollern autocracy, meant this to include all that the Habsburgs stood for. "The American Government," declared Lansing, "has already on several occasions most precisely defined the conditions which would allow it to discuss peace. It therefore does not intend to deal with any proposal whatever for a meeting in a matter on which it has already indicated its point of view and made so plain and sincere a decision."

Finally, Clemenceau delivered his answer, which was couched in the most emphatic terms, and was thus typical of his activity throughout the war. On the assumption that the Austrian offer had been made with the consent of Berlin—as was actually the case—he first of all turned his attention to Germany. He recalled various objections which the Allies had raised to her policy, diplomacy, and conduct of the war, and he concluded with the drastic declaration:

Germany desired to enforce the end of the war by military power. Let her wish be therefore fulfilled. The most fearful account is tendered from nation to nation. It will be paid.

We now realized how we were situated. We saw that our cause was in no danger when such replies as these were made to the Austrian offer. We understood, too, that such replies would inflict a further severe blow on the Habsburg Empire, the inner disruption of which would thus be accelerated. The Austrian Government would certainly be compelled to take further steps, involving possibly constitutional reform in agreement with the various nationalities inhabiting the Austro-Hungarian Empire.

The series of replies to Burian were completed two days later by Sonnino's reply, which was of a special character. In a simple *communiqué*, issued by the Stefanio Agency, Sonnino laconically stated that as the other Allies had already explained in detail the condition upon which the future peace must depend, any kind of negotiations would be superfluous.

Rarely has any diplomatic action ended in such material and moral failure. And the further course of events resembled more a tragi-comedy than a politico-diplomatic attempt to secure peace. Burian had received no favourable replies from the Allied camp, but Berlin, Sofia, and Constantinople had all expressed their approval of the Austrian offer. Accordingly, Burian thought that he might as well continue discussions with the Allies at least in the newspapers and official *communiqués*, now that they had refused to parley with the Austro-Hungarian Government. The Viennese Press announced that Parliament would deal with Burian's offer, and that the Austrian nations would show the Allies, who were unwilling for peace, that it was only the Central Powers who were striving to bring about a genuine peace among nations.

The discussion on the peace offer thus proceeded parallel with the continuing military defeat on the Western front and in the Balkans. The news on September 26th that the Bulgarians were asking for a separate armistice without their Allies, and that the Central European Quadruple Entente had ceased to exist, produced the alarming impression in Vienna that the moment of definite defeat was now at hand. The Government and all the authorities were aware that they would now have to adopt their final safety measures. In their opinion, although peace would be secured on severe terms involving territorial losses and the necessity to federalize the Empire in some form or other, they would, nevertheless, be able in the end to save the general framework of the Empire and the dynasty.

At the Ministerial Council on September 27th Burian, in the presence of Karl and General Arz, Chief of the General Staff, stated that the defeats on the Piave, the reverses in Albania, together with the events on the Western front, had so shaken the nerves of the population throughout the Empire that the Bulgarian catastrophe must be regarded as the last straw. Moreover, danger was threatening from Rumania, the Jugoslavs would again become a menace to the Empire from the South, and Turkey was now cut off. Under these conditions it was again necessary to make a peace offer to the Allies by October 15th at the latest, and Hohenlohe had already received instructions to start negotiating with Berlin on the subject of the new offer. The new adjustment of the Empire was also a more urgent matter now than it had been before. The war could not be continued beyond the end of the year. This information was also conveyed to Berlin. General Arz confirmed this in his statement, with which the ministers expressed their agreement.

It was under these circumstances that on September 28th I signed our agreement of alliance with France, arranged for a Government to be constituted and a proclamation of independence to be issued, besides settling with the Italian Embassy in Paris the details of my journey to Rome for completing similar negotiations with Italy. I left for Rome on the evening of October 1st in a very hopeful mood. Although I saw that events were taking a precipitant course, I still did not believe that the end of the war was at hand—in fact it is hardly likely that such a belief was entertained by anyone around us in the Allied countries or even in the camp of the Central Powers. From the circumstances as they were then I judged that we had a few weeks for realizing all our plans, and I wanted to make all preparations so that the solemn day for the proclamation of our national and State independence should fall on November 8, 1918.

(b) My Third Journey to Rome. Draft of an Agreement of Alliance with Italy. Visit to the Italian Front

143

Having obtained Masaryk's consent to my proposed course of action, I made all the necessary preparations in Paris, and then turned my attention to Italian affairs. I regarded it as essential to proceed in Italy on the same lines as we had followed in France and England, i.e. by preparing the ground for realizing our political plans, partly by a political agreement, partly by personal interview.

The dispute between Italy and the Jugoslavs was still exerting a considerable influence on our affairs. Since the British proclamation on August 9th with regard to us, and the progressive collapse of the enemy front in the Balkans, this dispute was tending rather to become more accentuated against Sonnino. At the beginning of September, through Bissolati's initiative, the Jugoslav question had become a subject for official negotiations within the Italian Government. Finally, the protracted dispute was settled by Sonnino's withdrawal, the credit for which is due to Bissolati and Orlando. On September 8, 1918, the Italian Government passed a resolution that Italy would identify herself with the principle of complete liberation and unification of the Jugoslavs. This resolution was, for a time, withheld from the public, but through official diplomatic channels it was transmitted to the Allies. This was a victory for the Jugoslavs and all their friends, a victory which had been won with difficulty, and which was received in all the Allied countries with much gratification.

Under these circumstances I felt sure that I should meet with no opposition. I had discussed things in detail first of all with the Italian Ambassador in Paris. I had given him a full account of my negotiations with the French Government, of the plans which the National Council had in view for the definite establishment of a provisional Government, and I had asked him to secure a favourable attitude on the part of Italy towards these plans. After reaching an agreement with him I handed him, on September 24th, a comprehensive memorandum on the position of our movement at that time and particularly on its future development, which I asked him to transmit to Orlando, relying on the amicable attitude which the latter had shown towards us on various occasions.

I left for Italy on October 1, 1918, immediately after the French Agreement was signed. My intention was, after arriving at a political agreement at Rome, to proceed to the front, and to arrange with those in charge of our troops there what should be done as soon as the provisional Government had been proclaimed. The process of constituting the Government was to be accomplished by a special solemn declaration which, as previously arranged between us, was to be prepared by Masaryk and published simultaneously in all Allied countries at the moment when the Government had been constituted. These proceedings were to culminate in solemn ceremonies at the front among the troops in France, Italy, Russia, and Siberia, and also by celebrations in the colonies, especially in America. As I have already mentioned, we had contemplated fixing the proclamation of our independence for November 8, 1918, the anniversary of the battle of the White Mountain.

144

While travelling to Rome I decided to visit our troops on the Italo-Austrian front, and this visit was one of my war experiences which I recall with the greatest pleasure. I started from Verona for the front by Lake Garda, and it is still with emotion that I remember the sight of the Alps occupied by our troops. Our cars passed through places where suddenly on the slopes there appeared hundreds of green uniforms and Italian hats with the red-white cockade. Farther on we unexpectedly passed from the mountain defile into a broad cavity, above which, in an amphitheatre, were assembled about 2,000 of our troops in a deluge of flags and waving hats. There was a long outburst of cheering, and I was then deeply moved as they intoned the strains of our national hymn, accompanied by the regimental band. The commander of the sector, having learnt about my visit, had rapidly organized this touching celebration which among these mountains at a height of several thousand feet, impressed me as few things have done in my life. I was greeted by several of those who had attended my university lectures. They were all filled with resolution and confidence, and they reminded me of the veiled suggestions which I had managed to embody in my lectures and which they had thoroughly understood.

During these moments there passed through my mind the memory of all that had happened from 1914 until October 1918, i.e. from the time when I had been creeping through the streets of Prague with treasonable documents in my pockets; when I had received messengers from Switzerland with suspicious luggage; when, as an outlaw, I had succeeded at the eleventh hour in escaping across the frontier; when I had begun my life of hardship in Paris, right up to that very moment when our national army were greeting me with songs and rifle salutes as a representative of our national Government, with a general of an Allied Great Power, and when, only a few miles away, the Austro-Hungarian military forces were awaiting an attack which was perhaps to have fatal consequences for them.

Amid the cheering of the soldiers we continued our journey until, in the vicinity of the front lines, I went with General Graziani and a number of officers into the trenches, which were a few hundred paces from those of the Austrians. We were standing immediately above Rovereto. General Graziani explained the position to me, and pointed out the scene of the recent conflicts, where several hundred Austrians had been captured. He also showed me another place where a number of our troops had been taken unawares and had defended themselves to the last with hand grenades rather than be taken prisoners. Now and then we heard the sound of firing, but on the whole the front at this point was quiet after the fighting which had taken place there in the preceding days.

We returned by another road along the front and around the

lake until we reached Spezzia. There we spent some time discussing the problems of military organization, the grievances of officers and men, and similar matters. There were difficulties with our troops and there were difficulties with Graziani, who in many respects was apt to be stubborn. I had some long talks about this with Colonel Vitalini, who understood the situation, and told me quite frankly how matters were. Our troops, he said, were full of enthusiasm and devotion to their great cause, but it had been, and still was, enormously difficult to agree on the ways and means for achieving their great ideals. Nevertheless, in the end we did agree. I promised to intervene at the Ministry in Rome, to improve the material situation of officers and men, to replace a number of Italian officers, and to emphasize in certain matters the Czech character of the army. Graziani also assented to our point of view and promised improvements. Early on the morning of the third day I started on my way back to Verona, where I spent some time in a hospital among our wounded.

While in Verona I heard about the further rapid development of military and political events, especially in the Balkans. After the Bulgarians, the Turks had capitulated. An inter-Allied conference had been hastily convened in Paris for the purpose of discussing the question of an armistice, with which the Allies were confronted as a result of these recent events. I also heard that before leaving for Paris with Sonnino the Italian Prime Minister, Orlando, had made an important statement in Parliament on the international situation and on the policy of Italy, in the course of which he had referred to our affairs in very definite terms. From the report of Orlando's statement which had been handed to me, I judged that it corresponded not merely to the memorandum which I had sent from Paris, but also to the agreements concluded with England and France, as the opposition had blamed his Government for allowing themselves to be forestalled in connection with our affairs by the two Allies who had less direct interest in the Habsburg Empire. For that reason also Orlando had made a special point of emphasizing the importance of the agreements signed in April and June 1918, and he announced that the concessions now being made by France and England had been granted to the National Council by Italy as early as the spring of the same year.

I at once telegraphed from Verona to Orlando thanking him warmly for his statement, and emphasizing the fact that I was just returning from the Italian frontiers, where our troops were defending Italian soil as if it were their native land. On the same day I left for Rome. Now that the fundamental sanction of the Government was confirmed by a public statement in Parliament, I inferred that I should be able to conclude all arrangements with the Consulta and the Ministry of War, which were necessary for realizing our political and military plans. When I reached Rome, however, the circumstances had changed. The recent international events had imparted a new direction to the development of our affairs also.

Orlando and Sonnino had already left Rome when I arrived, and I therefore first discussed questions relating to our army with the Ministry of War, and satisfactorily settled all the grievances of our regiments. I then proceeded to the Consulta and discussed with Demartino the question of a possible agreement and the proclamation of our independence. Demartino assured me that Orlando's declaration in Parliament was an affirmative reply to my proposals concerning the proclamation of independence and an Italo-Czechoslovak agreement, and that there was no dissent either as regards the matter itself or the methods of dealing with it. He added, however, that it would be necessary to agree about the details and the text of the agreement, in which connection the minister would have to be allowed the final decision. I agreed to this, and at the same time proposed that I would shortly submit my draft of the agreement to the Consulta, so that everything could be prepared before Sonnino and Orlando returned.

I also notified M. Barrère and Sir Rennell Rodd of my proceedings with the Italian Government, and through Sir Rennell Rodd I was able to inform Masaryk about the new situation. The victories in the Balkans, the fall of Hertling, the appointment of Max of Baden as his successor, and the armistice overtures made to Wilson by the Central Powers made it clear to us that fateful decisions were at hand. In this sense I telegraphed on the morning of October 10th, before leaving Rome, to Masaryk in Washington that the decisive moment was approaching, that Rome agreed to our plans, that we should evidently be prepared any day for a proclamation of independence, and that therefore it was necessary to draw up the required declaration immediately and send it to us in Paris.

My negotiations with Demartino on the subject of the Italo-Czechoslovak agreement had not yet been concluded, when I received from Dr. Sychrava a telegram of alarm urging me to return at once to Paris, because matters were in preparation which might have very far-reaching and even dangerous consequences for us.

(c) DECLARATION OF INDEPENDENCE AND ESTABLISHMENT OF THE PROVISIONAL CZECHOSLOVAK GOVERNMENT. RECOGNITION OF THE NEW GOVERNMENT BY FRANCE

On arriving in Paris on Sunday, October 13th, I found the atmosphere there charged with excitement. The political world and official circles were thinking of nothing else but the Allied discussions and negotiations concerning the events which had happened in the meanwhile, and which were of vital concern to us also.

In the face of these events and reports I asked myself what we should do under such circumstances, and how they might affect the preparations which we had just undertaken and the plans connected with the declaration of independence, which we had intended to realize within the next few weeks. I conferred with my friends in the secretariat of the National Council. The news from Austria concerning the plans of the Viennese Government made me feel uneasy, but, on the other hand, the news as to the action of the National Committee in Prague, which had also just arrived from Geneva, gratified us. At the same time the uncertainty as to how President Wilson intended to reply to Austria-Hungary was a source of anxiety to us and our friends. His reply to Germany had been couched in severe terms, and on the whole, in a number of circles in Paris, it was not expected that he would be severer to the Habsburgs than to the Hohenzollerns. This being the case, a number of our friends began to fear that the idea of a separate action with Austria-Hungary might again emerge. They found a reason for this conjecture in the circumstance that the repetition at Paris on October 15th of the congress of Austro-Hungarian nations which had been held in Rome, had been postponed in view of the fresh developments and also at the request of the French Government. Our French friends asserted that this had been done at the request of England. During this time it may well be imagined what tension there was amongst us in the Rue Bonaparte. Not knowing exactly how things were, we of the

National Council also shared—some more, some less—these various fears regarding the possibility of a compromise. We all realized, too, the momentous historical significance of the decisions which were being made. On my arrival the first thing I did was to report to my colleagues in the secretariat on affairs in Italy. We then discussed what we should do next, and we all agreed that I must first ascertain from all our friends what the situation was, and what steps were being prepared.

Accordingly, I made inquiries on these points from M. Vesnić, who had taken part in the Allied negotiations, and who at once gave me news which set my mind at rest. I also approached several French friends and then, on the morning of October 14th, I called on Berthelot at the Foreign Ministry, and reported to him about my Italian visit, at the same time letting him know that all preparations had been made for carrying out our plans. I asked him to inform me how matters were being viewed in Paris. In consideration of the agreements which we had hitherto made with the Allies, I questioned him directly about the negotiations with Austria and again insisted upon the necessity for the Allies, now more than ever, to hold out until the end. He replied emphatically and without hesitation: "There can be no question whatever of any serious separate negotiations with Austria. The forces which have been let loose cannot be held up. Nothing can avert the downfall of the Central Powers; Austria is condemned to destruction and cannot be saved. Even if an attempt were made in one quarter or another at some sort of negotiations, it would merely be an insignificant intrigue. The elemental forces and fateful influences which are now at work can no longer be mastered by human beings."

Such was Berthelot's diagnosis. His conviction as to the outcome of the war and the fate of the Central Empires had, as a matter of fact, been always very firm, even at the most critical periods of the war. This opinion I shared with him.

145

The discussion between President Wilson and the German Minister of Foreign Affairs was followed by the whole world with close and anxious attention. It was felt by everybody that each of President Wilson's replies was pressing the German Government more and more into a tight corner. As I have already stated, the fact that President Wilson was not replying to Austria-Hungary while carrying on this exciting diplomatic duel with Berlin, made me wonder the whole time whether this implied that discussions with Vienna were proceeding elsewhere and on different terms. There were various indications which led me to suppose that Vienna, while approaching Wilson officially, openly, and in concert with Germany, was intervening secretly either in France or England, possibly in both countries. The success of such proceedings was improbable after the reply which Clemenceau and Pichon had recently made to Karl. Nevertheless, the situation seemed to me somewhat dangerous, chiefly on account of the uncertainty as to whether these happenings denoted the end of the war or not.

This led me to continue my previous course of action with the greatest determination and more rapidly than hitherto. I accordingly decided on the immediate realization of the plan which I had prepared for November 8th. The reassuring results of my interview with Berthelot were calculated to strengthen me in this resolve rather than otherwise; and in the course of the interview itself I asked him what the French Government would do if I were to notify it officially that the Czechoslovak Government had been appointed and Czechoslovak independence proclaimed, or if a Czechoslovak diplomatic representative were to be immediately accredited to it. The answer which I received from Berthelot was the only one which I could possibly have expected from him and from a representative of the French Minister at that time: "French policy is based upon the previous agreements with the National Council. France has plainly indicated her attitude by means of the documents which she has signed, and she will keep her word. If the Government is notified of any decision on the part of the National Council, it will certainly at once adopt a favourable attitude towards anything of the kind." In reply to my further inquiry, Berthelot assured me that if I sent him the notification immediately I should certainly receive the French official reply on the following day.

I returned to the secretariat of the National Council in the Rue Bonaparte, and at once prepared an official note concerning the establishment of an interim Government. At six o'clock in the evening I handed a copy to the Quai d'Orsay and also to the diplomatic representatives of the Allied Powers in Paris. I announced that on September 26th (the date of Professor Masaryk's telegram sanctioning the realization of the plan) we had established an interim Czechoslovak Government, and that we were now publicly proclaiming the formation of an independent Czechoslovak State.

Together with this note I sent to the Allied Governments separate communications with regard to the accrediting of our diplomatic representatives in Paris, London, Rome, and Washington. These communications were also dated October 14, 1918.

146

I based the juridical justification for this step mainly upon the declaration of the United States and on the agreements with England and France. My reasons for this were as follows:

(a) At that time the United States had so great a prestige among the Allies that I regarded this as the best step on tactical grounds.

(b) It was in the declaration of the United States that for the first time, in reference to the National Council, use had been made of the phrase "*de facto* Government" without any provisos.

(c) I regarded Pichon's letter of June 28th as tantamount to recognition on the part of France, and the declaration of the British Government on September 9th as analogous to it.

Wishing to obviate any further controversies with the Allied Governments concerning the justification for this step, I was anxious to have the support of diplomatic documents unreservedly binding the Allies and devoid of any juridical ambiguities.

Masaryk's functions in the interim Government were important both to us and to the Allies. From the very beginning he had managed the finances of our movement, and we were all confident that his great authority would rule out the possibility of any recrimination in this respect. He was appointed head of the State mechanism and President of the Government for reasons which are too obvious to need explanation.

In accordance with Berthelot's promise, M. Pichon replied to me as Foreign Minister of the new Government on the next day, October 15th, granting full recognition to State and Government. In a second communication of October 16th, M. Pichon notified his acceptance of Dr. Lev Sychrava as our diplomatic representative.

(d) President Wilson's Last Blow to the Habsburg
   Empire. Recognition of the Provisional Government
   by Great Britain, Italy, and the Other Allies

147

While this was being enacted at Paris, on the other side of
the Atlantic was being prepared the concluding scene of the
great historical tragedy, culminating in the downfall of the
Habsburg Empire with its fifty millions of inhabitants. Professor Masaryk was just preparing his Washington declaration,
while directly and indirectly using all the influence at his disposal in order that the reply of the American Government to the
request of the two Central Empires should accord with our plans
and demands. It was at this decisive moment that we received
the first reports about the text of Karl's manifesto issued on
October 16, 1918, and dealing with what was termed the
federalization of the Habsburg Empire. This occurred when we
were about to have our Washington declaration printed, and
when President Wilson was preparing his reply to Austria-
Hungary. In spite of the firmness of our international position,
we could not underestimate this interplay of circumstances.
Professor Masaryk therefore intervened direct with the Washington Government, asking that the reply should not affect our
interests. He also sent President Wilson a copy of our Washington agreement on October 17th, and at the same time he
influenced the Press and official circles to interpret Karl's
manifesto correctly as a last attempt to save the Empire which,
on account of its inconsistency, insincerity, and inadequacy (it
did not deal with the problem of the nationalities in Hungary
or with the Jugoslav problem, etc.) could not be taken seriously.
We adopted similar measures against the manifesto in Paris
also, and before long nobody doubted in any quarter that Karl's
effort was a failure. Even in countries such as Sweden, Norway,
Holland, and Switzerland, which so much sympathized with
Vienna, the Press unanimously agreed that the manifesto would
serve no purpose. If, they said, it had made its appearance a
year sooner, then. . . .

President Wilson acknowledged the receipt of the Washington
declaration in a letter sent to Masaryk on October 18, 1918, in
which he informed him that he was greatly touched by our pro-

clamation of independence, and that Masaryk would certainly be satisfied with the reply which, at the same time, was being sent to Austria-Hungary. This reply was handed to the Swedish Legation in Washington for transmission to the Viennese Government.

Meanwhile, we in Paris, knowing that Wilson was about to make public his reply to Austria, were impatiently awaiting the telegram from Washington. At last, on October 20th, at three o'clock in the afternoon, I had a telephone call from Mr. Frazer, Counsellor of the American Embassy, who informed me that the reply had just arrived from Washington, and that at the Ambassador's instructions he was officially communicating it to me. At the same time he congratulated us on our new success. The afternoon papers on the same day published the text of the reply:

WASHINGTON,
October 18, 1918.

To MINISTER OF SWEDEN FROM DEPARTMENT OF STATE.

SIR,

I have the honour to acknowledge the receipt of your note of seventh instant, in which you transmitted a communication of the Imperial and Royal Government of Austria-Hungary to the President. I am instructed by the President to request you to be good enough, through your Government, to convey to the Austro-Hungarian Government the following reply:

"The President deems it his duty to say to the Austro-Hungarian Government that he cannot entertain the present suggestions of that Government because of certain events of utmost importance which, occurring since the delivery of his address of January 8th last, have necessarily altered the attitude and responsibility of the Government of the United States of America. Among the fourteen terms of peace which the President formulated at that time occurred the following: 'The peoples of Austria-Hungary, whose place among the nations we wish to see safeguarded and assured, should be accorded the freest opportunity of autonomous development.' Since that sentence was written and uttered to the Congress of the United States, the Government of the United States has recognized a state of belligerency exists between the Czechoslovaks and the German and Austro-Hungarian Empires, and that the Czechoslovak National Council is a *de facto* belligerent Government, clothed with proper authority to direct the military and political affairs of the Czechoslovaks. It has also recognized in the fullest measure the justice of the nationalistic aspirations of the Yugoslavs for freedom.

The President is therefore no longer at liberty to accept a mere 'autonomy' of these peoples as a basis of peace, but is obliged to insist that they, and not he, shall be the judge of what action on the part of the Austro-Hungarian Government will satisfy their aspirations and their conception of their right and destiny as members of the family of nations."

(*Signed*) LANSING.

This was the last Allied step which exerted any influence on the critical orientation among the Allies, and exercised a definite decision on the subject of our independence. Allied Government and official circles, Press and public opinion looked upon it as the last word. All that followed Wilson's note consisted merely of a political or juridical supplement to it.

148

After the recognition of the interim Czechoslovak Government by M. Pichon's note of September 15th, further recognitions soon followed which confirmed our juridical status, especially when the situation had been made clear by Wilson's reply to Austria-Hungary. On October 21st the Italian Ambassador, Bonin Longare, informed me by letter that the Italian Government was officially recognizing the Czechoslovak Government, and that this would in due course be communicated to me by a special note from Sonnino. This was done on October 24th, and a further communication on the same date sanctioned the appointment of Dr. Borský as our representative to the Italian Government.

The British Government, by a communication from Mr. Balfour on October 23rd, merely confirmed the receipt of my note of October 14th, and by a special communication from Lord Derby, the British Ambassador in Paris, sanctioned the appointment of Dr. Osuský as our representative in London.

On behalf of the Serbian Government the Prime Minister, M. Pašić, on October 24th sent me a note in which he acknowledged our Government, and at the same time expressed the great gratification of the Serbian people, its King and Government, at the recognition which we had been granted by the Allied Powers. He further expressed his satisfaction that our two nations would continue the same close relations which they had observed in the course of the war. On October 17th the Russian Embassies in Western Europe issued a *communiqué* by which the Russian provisional Government in Siberia recognized the National Council as the legal Government of the Czechoslovak State, and expressed the hope that both nations would in the future co-operate fraternally in close unity as hitherto. Replies were received to our note of October 14th also from the Belgian and Greek Governments on November 23rd and 24th respectively, both granting us recognition. Thus, by October 24, 1918, our independence was unreservedly recognized by all the chief Allied States. Our struggle for liberation had ended in victory.

XVIII

OUR MOVEMENT ABROAD MERGES WITH THE EFFORTS AT HOME. THE COLLAPSE OF AUSTRIA-HUNGARY AND THE *COUP D'ÉTAT* AT PRAGUE

(*a*) THE DELEGATES OF THE NATIONAL COMMITTEE MEET THE MEMBERS OF THE INTERIM CZECHOSLOVAK GOVERNMENT AT GENEVA. TWO MANIFESTOS BY THE PRAGUE DELEGATION

149

AMID the feverish activity entailed by the organization of the newly recognized State after October 15, 1918, some of the daily papers in Paris published the unexpected news on October 23rd that the Viennese Government had granted permission to the leading Czech politicians to proceed abroad, and even to get into touch with the members of the provisional Czechoslovak Government. At first we could not believe this. We knew, of course, that Austria was in a bad way, and we ourselves had asked for this very step to be taken in Prague, but we had not expected they would allow such a course so soon, and we were therefore not certain what might be behind this decision on the part of the Viennese Government. Later, we ascertained that Vienna, still believing that the Allies were anxious to preserve Austria, hoped that the Entente would bring its influence to bear on the politicians from Prague and on the interim Government at Paris so that the Czechs might be satisfied with autonomy or federalism as a solution of their question. At the end of October the Viennese Government was making efforts through Count Skrzynski in Berne to reach an agreement with Paris in this sense, but these efforts were unsuccessful. By that time the orientation of the Allies was on entirely different lines.

When the report was confirmed to me by Dr. Osuský from Geneva I informed the French Government, and added that the representatives of the interim Czechoslovak Government had decided to proceed to Geneva to negotiate with our politicians there. The first section of the Prague delegates, comprising Dr. Kramář, Dr. Preis, Dr. Šámal, and others, reached Geneva on the evening of Saturday, October 26th. They had been accompanied on their way through Switzerland by Dr. Osuský, who had given them the earliest news about the general political situation. I myself arrived at Geneva on the following Monday morning, October 28th.

This meeting at Geneva had, I think, considerable historical importance. The conference began on the same afternoon, and the questions which were discussed can be classified into three groups:

(*a*) My colleagues and myself supplied the delegates from Prague with a detailed account of the international situation in general. The Prague delegation on their part explained to us the situation at home, the military and political state of Austria, the economic conditions there, and the anxiety of our people as to what might happen in the immediate future should Austria-Hungary collapse.

(*b*) The second part of the discussion was concerned with the arrangements for establishing our independent State, the form of which was discussed in detail. We also considered how, at the moment of the capitulation of Austria-Hungary, the transition to a Czechoslovak regime was to be carried out.

(*c*) The concluding part of the conference was devoted to the conditions of an armistice for Austria-Hungary and the wishes of our people at home, which after my return to Paris I was to place before the Allies.

It seemed to me that on a number of questions the Prague delegates were a little uncertain, and that on the whole they had no very clear idea of our affairs abroad during the war. They were all convinced of the forthcoming collapse of Austria-Hungary. They referred to the desperate economic conditions, the exhaustion of the population, the demoralization of the army, the grim humour prevailing among the Czechs and especially in Prague, the perplexity of Vienna, and the attempts of the Government there to win over the Czech politicians. M. Klofáč told me about his last interview with Karl, from which he discovered that the Emperor's only wish was for everything "to be liquidated peaceably." They all, without exception, however, were alarmed about what might happen at the last moment. M. Habrman expressed this vigorously by saying that, "when the brute was at its last gasp it would lash out and avenge itself on us with terrible butchery." The rest feared that "when breaking-point had been reached," German troops would occupy the Czech territories, and that this would be a source of the greatest danger to us. A third serious danger to all consisted of the anarchy of Bolshevism, which was feared not so much among the Czechs, as in Vienna and Budapest. The only remedy lay in rapidly improving the food supplies.

On the whole I saw that the certainty of our final victory was tempered by fears of a German occupation and of hunger riots, especially in Vienna, as well as by the consciousness that Austria was still in existence, and that the delegates would have to return there. They had no definite plan as to further international action, which they left entirely to us abroad. For the eventuality of Austria's collapse, however, they had, as we shall see later, a fairly detailed scheme providing for the practical transition from the old monarchy to an independent State. In reply to the report of the Prague delegates I gave them a full account of what we had been doing abroad during the war. I should add that the discussions were not carried on with the usual formalities of meetings, but were rather in the nature of amicable conversations. Resolutions were passed with the proviso that they were to be submitted for the approval of the political parties and the National Committee at home. My own statement was couched in optimistic terms, and the gist of it was that our cause had been won, that we were already existing as an independent State and nation, that I had no further misgivings as to the result of the war, and that we should obtain far more than we had ventured to hope in 1914. The delegates, who hitherto had not been aware of our achievements in detail, and who were not acquainted with the wording of the documents granting us recognition, were both surprised and gratified to learn about these matters.

150

After we had exchanged information, I approached the delegates with a number of questions and requests. First of all, I explained that it was necessary for the Allies to see that there was complete agreement between ourselves and the politicians at home, and that our movement abroad was backed by the whole nation. Recalling the reports as to the Austrian efforts to obtain a declaration in favour of the Empire from our politicians, I urged the delegates that nothing was to be done at home which might be used against us. For this reason I asked whether the delegation was entitled and willing there and then to make definite binding decisions on behalf of the nation, in accordance with which we could continue negotiations with the Allies. What I asked for, in concrete terms, consisted of the following:

(a) A solemn testimony that the Czech nation was giving its full assent to the whole of our policy, that it was opposed to the Habsburgs now and for all time, and that it no longer recognized the existence of the Austro-Hungarian Empire.

(b) A declaration that our politicians at home, and therefore also those whom they represented, approved all the steps which we had taken in our activity abroad, and that they would accept all the commitments which we had made towards the Allies on behalf of the National Council and the interim Government. The Prague delegation pointed out that although they were not expressly authorized to take such a step, they were entitled to do so in view of the situation at home, and accordingly they at once replied in the affirmative to both the above-mentioned points. It was therefore decided that a statement to this effect should be drawn up in writing, and Šámal, Kalina, and Habrman undertook the task of wording it. On the following day the text of it was duly approved, and on the day before my departure for Paris it was signed. We also arranged that I was to hand one copy of the declaration officially to the Allies, but that, out of consideration for the delegates who were returning to Prague, it was not to be published until the conditions in Austria made such a course desirable.

The Prague delegation was so impressed by the documentary and other evidence of what had been achieved by our movement abroad, that on their own initiative they decided to place on record their special recognition of the work done by Masaryk, our troops, and the others who were concerned in our movement. Accordingly, without the knowledge of the Paris delegation, they drew up a statement expressing the sentiments of the nation in this respect. Before my departure to Paris they handed me a signed copy of this manifesto with the request that its contents should be conveyed in a similar form and at the appropriate moment to all those for whom it was intended.

Thus, after having been recognized by the Great Powers, the interim Government at Paris received its final and most important token of recognition from Prague. The unity of our struggle for liberation at home and abroad was in this way solemnly confirmed.

(b) Discussions as to the Republican Form of the State

151

Another important item for discussion involved the form of the Czechoslovak State and the establishment of a definitive Government at home. The majority of the delegates held the view that the CzechoslovakNational Council and interim Government had probably incurred obligations with some of the Allies which involved a monarchist form of State. I therefore explained that we had never undertaken any commitments in this sense. In particular, all statements as to Masaryk's negotiations on the subject of Prince Arthur of Connaught were without foundation. At one time General Štefánik had shown some inclination for an Italian dynasty, but not even here had there been any definite undertakings, and the question of a Russian dynasty had ceased to have any meaning as far as we were concerned since the outbreak of the Russian revolution. I myself was offered the opportunity of discussion on this subject on two occasions. As early as 1917, indirect overtures were made to me to discover whether it would not be possible to save the Czech crown for some Habsburg Archduke. I made it clear I did not take such discussions at all seriously.

Thus we were entirely free, and the nation and political circles possessed full liberty to please themselves as to the form of the State. I also pointed out that the Washington declaration definitely announced that our State would be a republic.

This being the case, the discussion on this point was not protracted. Habrman, speaking for the Social Democratic Party, expressed its desire for a democratic republic, a single chamber, and election of the President by the people. If the independence of the State rendered a monarchy imperative, his party would accept it, but very reluctantly. He was, therefore, particularly gratified to hear that we were in no way committed on this score. Dr. Kramář declared that he personally was in favour of a monarchy, but, he added (and I made a note of the exact words he used), "If it is to be a kingdom, it would have to be extremely democratic, as in England." From a private conversation about Russia, which I had with him on the same day, I gathered that he had in mind a monarchy governed by one of the Russian Grand Dukes, his assumption being that the conditions in

Russia would soon change and that after the rapid fall of the Bolsheviks the Romanoffs would return to the throne.

The establishment of a definitive Government in Prague, as soon as the regime in Austria came to an end, also formed the subject of detailed discussions. As regards this, the President of the Republic, the Prime Minister, and the two ministers of the interim Government were the chief items of the debate. All the members of the delegation considered it as a matter of course that Masaryk should be President of the new State. In the same way it was a foregone conclusion that the Prime Minister of the definitive Government was to be Dr. Kramář. The only point about which there was any uncertainty among some of the delegates was the choice of the future Minister of the Interior.

The Prague delegates also laid emphasis on the question of the Germans in Bohemia. It was recognized that in this respect we must proceed cautiously so as not to create any prejudice for ourselves when vindicating the historical frontiers of the Czech territories. We therefore unanimously passed a resolution that the definitive Government should include one German as a regional minister without portfclio.

It was further agreed that the two ministers of the interim Government should continue to exercise their functions as Minister of War and Minister of Foreign Affairs respectively in the definitive Government. I should here add that these negotiations were a friendly exchange of views, and were not regarded in any way as final decisions. The subjects dealt with were to be fully discussed in Prague, both by the National Committee and the political parties who were then to express their final opinion in accordance with the situation at home.

(c) Discussions on the Coup d'État in the Czechoslovak Territories. The Attitude of Prague Towards the Armistice Conditions

152

No less interesting was the debate on the manner in which the transition from the Austro-Hungarian regime to the new Czechoslovak State was to be carried out. From what the delegates said on this subject it was clear that our people at home had given the matter close consideration and were adequately prepared for the eventuality. The information thus gained was extremely valuable to me in my further activities in Paris.

In our discussions the change of regime was envisaged as involving, first and foremost, definite general revolutionary measures. All constitutional laws hitherto existing would cease to exist, and they would be replaced by emergency regulations which the National Committee would issue as decrees. A legislative commission would, however, be immediately set up to prepare and arrange detailed enactments, and to carry out the functions of a Parliamentary body until the constituent assembly had been convened.

Similar proceedings would be taken in economic matters. All the economic enactments would remain in force, and a number of the war-time arrangements would provisionally be retained (the distributing centres for sugar, clothing, cotton, potatoes, coal, etc.). On the day when independence was declared, all unrestricted export and import would be suspended and would then be sanctioned only by the Government. At the same time an import organization would be set up which, with the assistance of the banks, would deal with the import of raw materials, would restrict the import of luxury goods, and would attend to the supply of food, clothing, and employment. There would be a department to prevent profiteering, which would be punished by the confiscation of the offender's property. The prices of commodities would be adjusted by the State.

It would be necessary to make immediate preparations for establishing a National Bank and a new currency. We contemplated adopting the franc and forming an agreement with the States comprised in the Latin Currency Union. The Austro-Hungarian Bank would be liquidated and its branches in the Czech territories taken over by the State. The Austrian banknotes would, for the time being, remain in circulation, but they would have to be quickly superseded by Czechoslovak banknotes, which would then be the only legal tender. Joint-stock companies with their works on our territory would have to transfer their headquarters to us and become amenable to our control. Their board of directors would have to contain a definite percentage of our citizens. The rules and regulations concerning taxation would continue to hold good.

Mines and spas would at once pass over into State administration. The appropriate ministry, acting in co-operation with the Ministry of Social Welfare, was to make the necessary arrangements for safeguarding the interests of owners and workmen.

Land reform was discussed in some detail and in a very radical spirit. All privileges connected with large landed estates, entail, freehold, and ecclesiastical property were to be abolished; further, it was proposed to set up a National Land Bank which was to be entrusted with dividing up the landed estates into allotments, the subsequent sales to be carried out under close State supervision.

All munition factories would be handed over to State administration. Social policy was also discussed in detail, together with various questions affecting Allied property which had been confiscated by Austria-Hungary. For carrying out all these plans it would, of course, be necessary for us to secure the assistance of the Allies, both directly and indirectly, the essential point being that the Armistice conditions should be favourable to our plan. Our delegates were particularly concerned with the problem of a rapid military occupation of Austro-Hungarian territory if and when the final catastrophe ensued. One of the conditions which they were anxious to secure as being advantageous to a successful course of events was that Allied troops, and our own as well, should be promptly sent to the Czech territories; that a number of railway routes should be occupied; and that, in general, communications with the Allies should be secured in good time.

Much concern was caused to our delegates by the prison camps, especially those containing Russians and forming Bolshevik centres. They were also anxious to obtain Allied protection against a possible invasion by Mackensen's German army on the Rumanian frontiers.

These questions were all connected with the important problem of the food supplies. The delegates urged the necessity for relieving our own population from the hardships they were suffering, and also for preventing the possibility of hunger riots, especially in Vienna where, in the opinion of them all, the danger was most acute. They impressed upon me the need for drawing the attention of the Allies to these matters and for taking them into account when an armistice was under consideration.

Finally, we discussed the economic and financial affairs of Austria-Hungary and their bearing upon the interests of our State. This had particular reference to the pre-war and war debts of the monarchy, and the possibility of our obtaining financial assistance in the form of a loan from the Allies or by means of economic co-operation with them.

(d) COLLAPSE OF THE HABSBURG EMPIRE

153

While we were discussing the questions concerning the establishment of our State, events were developing with such rapidity that the climax, which we had not expected for weeks or even months, surprised us in the middle of our conference.

As I have already pointed out, Karl's manifesto proposing the federalization of the Empire had satisfied nobody, either in Austria-Hungary or elsewhere. Abroad it was regarded as a plain sign that the beginning of the end was at hand, at home it merely caused fresh indignation and protest, while among the troops it resulted, first of all in uncertainty, then in confusion, and finally in a complete collapse.

At Prague the National Committee met on October 19th, and from that date onwards continued in permanent session. It repudiated the Emperor's manifesto very decidedly, and proclaimed that "For the Czech nation there could be no discussion with Vienna on the subject of its future." The statement of the National Committee contained also the following: "The Czech question has become an international one . . . and cannot be settled without the sanction of that internationally recognized part of the nation which is beyond the Czech frontiers. It is the duty of the National Committee, on behalf of the whole of the Czech people, to declare that there can be no other settlement of the Czech question than absolute State independence. The National Committee therefore publicly protests against the efforts being made in Magyar quarters to persuade the world that our Slovak brethren do not desire to form a single national State unity with the nation of which they are an inseparable branch. The Slovaks, ill-treated and reduced to silence by unexampled Magyar coercion, cannot freely make known their desires. . . ."

During the same period, on October 17th, 18th, and 19th, the Jugoslav National Committee met at Zagreb and issued a manifesto signed by the representatives of the Slovenes, Croats, and Serbs in Austria-Hungary. Like the manifesto of the National Committee at Prague, it unanimously repudiated Karl's proposals, and demanded the unification of all Jugoslavs in a single free State. Although both these manifestos were confiscated, their contents became known in Switzerland just after October 24th, and they provided the world with a further indication that the end of the Habsburg Empire was at hand.

Wilson's note of October 18th was published at Vienna on the evening of Sunday, October 20th. It was received with consternation in some quarters and resignation in others, while among the representatives of the subject peoples it caused enormous satisfaction. It provided the Magyars with an incentive for hastening their separation from Vienna, which was carried out two days later.

On the afternoon of October 21st the Austrian National Assembly met and passed resolutions which make it clear that the Austrian Germans themselves were gradually preparing for any eventuality. The Assembly, comprising the German deputies from the Austrian Alpine regions, demanded the creation of a German-Austrian State which was to incorporate the Sudetic Germans. This, of course, presupposed some kind of agreement with the other national States established on the territory of the former Empire.

These details were reported in the Allied countries on the following day, and were interpreted there merely as a proof of the advancing process of collapse. The events in Hungary in the eyes of Allied public opinion also constituted a severe blow to the existence of the Empire. When after the publication of Karl's manifesto the Hungarians at once drew their own inferences from it, these developments were taken to mean that all bonds between the nations were gradually falling, and that the dynasty was being hurled to and fro by revolution without being able to brace itself together for any deliberate action. These signs of dissolution now became more and more frequent. Thus, on October 26th, we learned in Paris that four days earlier Dr. Stránský, referring to the results of Wilson's note during the debate on Burian's motion for establishing a permanent Parliamentary committee of twenty-six members to be in permanent touch with the Government, made the following statement: "We Czechs will not participate in the elections to the Committee . . . because the Entente has recognized our National Council in Paris as a Czechoslovak Government, and the Czechoslovak Army as the army of the Czechoslovak State. All this has been done with a view to the peace negotiations. We deputies cannot therefore anticipate the action of the Entente, and we are not entitled to act of our own accord." Then there came the news that on October 23rd a commission of delegates for foreign affairs had met at Vienna to examine Wilson's note, and that on this occasion the Czechs and Jugoslavs had announced that for reasons of principle they would not take part in the discussions. About the same time we learnt that Burian had resigned, a course which was followed also by Hussarek and Weckerle. Then came the news that Professor Lammasch had undertaken the task of negotiating with individual politicians for the purpose of forming a Cabinet "of order and liquidation." In the Allied Press this confused record of events left only one impression: the approach of the end, the downfall of the Empire, chaos, revolution, a struggle of all against all.

154

Concurrent with these decisive political events, the whole situation on the battle-fronts was moving rapidly towards the inevitable end. From the Balkans the Allied troops were advancing at such a rate towards the frontiers of the Habsburg Empire that the Magyars were beginning to clamour for the return of their regiments from the Italian front. In the concluding days of October the Turks were sustaining such severe defeats that they too appealed for an armistice, which was signed at Mudros on October 30th, and in the meanwhile the retreat of the German Army on the Western front was continuing. By the beginning of November the German line was approaching the Moselle, and was thus near its own frontiers. The collapse behind the front and the political upheavals were merely the direct result of the military defeat.

As regards the Austro-Hungarian Empire, the operations which had a decisive effect upon events were those on the Italian front, where the offensive which ensued on October 24th was bound to complete the overthrow of the Empire. It would be unjust to Italy to underestimate the significance of that last offensive, which was carried out by fifty-one Italian divisions, three English, two French, one Czechoslovak, and one American regiment. The opposing forces consisted of fifty-one Austro-Hungarian divisions.

Even before the offensive was begun there were signs of revolt in the regiments composed of Croats, who refused to go into the front line. On October 24th two Magyar regiments, the 22nd and the 25th, also refused to enter the fighting zone, and demanded that they should be sent to Hungary to defend their own country. This request was granted by the Emperor, and then other regiments, especially after the Piave defeat, imitated the example of the Magyars, so that the collapse of the army was precipitated like an avalanche. The Austro-Hungarian army began to disperse in confusion. One part was captured, while another part threw away its arms and seized upon whatever means of transport it could find. These troops, crowded together in cars, railway trains, and lorries, swarmed along, congesting all the railway lines, stations, and roads, and here and there destroying whatever stood in their way. And while this complete military collapse was in progress, news arrived from Pola that the Austro-Hungarian fleet had revolted. On October 30th it was handed over to the Jugoslavs.

(e) THE COUP D'ÉTAT AT PRAGUE ON OCTOBER 28, 1918, AND OUR GENEVA NEGOTIATIONS

155

The events at Prague between October 28th and 30th formed a connecting link in the great chain of circumstances constituting the downfall of the Habsburg Empire. Each of those who took part in this huge drama played his part as the instrument of a destiny which some interpret as the irresistible development of historical forces, others as the divine purpose of Providence. And as regards the events in Prague their relation to our national cause is that of a logical conclusion to the vast struggle which demanded so much exertion and sacrifice, self-denial, and firmness of will. This last phase had been so well prepared by the preceding events that, at the moment when the time came to act, there could be no doubt of immediate success, provided that sufficient skill and determination were brought to bear upon the task. The results show that this was indeed the case.

On October 25th a meeting was held at the Hôtel Continental in Vienna between our Geneva delegates and the Poles and Jugoslavs. On the same day the delegation proceeded to Geneva and Dr. Rašín returned to Prague. This was the time when news had reached our politicians and, in fact, all persons of authority in the Empire, that an Austro-Hungarian military collapse was imminent. On October 26th Rašín refused the appeal for help which General Boroević had made to the Prague National

Committee, his answer being that Austria-Hungary must first capitulate. On the same day the Austro-Hungarian Ministry of War was negotiating with the National Committee on the subject of joint action concerning the food supply, and the National Committee decided to co-operate with the Corn Exchange. On the evening of October 27th Tusar telephoned to Dr. Rašín about the disastrous situation on the Italian front, whereupon Rašín immediately settled with Scheiner that arrangements should now be made because on the next day "things were going to happen." The Germans in Bohemia, being also aware of the critical situation of the Empire, held a meeting at Dresden on the same day to discuss the question of help for German Bohemia in case there should be a catastrophe and a revolution in Bohemia.

Early on the morning of October 28, 1918, the chief members of the National Committee learnt the contents of Andrássy's note (Tusar had telephoned about it to Rašín during the night and the newspaper *Bohemia* had brought out a special early morning edition containing full details) as well as the capitulation of Vienna. This news at once became the starting-point for decisive action on the part of the National Committee. Švehla, together with Dr. F. Soukup, on behalf of the National Committee, took charge of the Corn Exchange, which formed the headquarters of the food supply for the whole country. Immediately afterwards the Václav Square, where the inhabitants of Prague learnt the joyful news in front of the offices of the *Národní Politika,* was filled with cheering crowds and the houses were decorated with flags. In this atmosphere of excitement the National Committee met at 11.30 a.m., and at noon Švehla, Rašín, Soukup, and Stříbrný proceeded to the Governor's residence and to the central administrative offices, where they demanded that the administrative authority should be surrendered to the National Committee.

The news of these events reached Vienna shortly after midday at the moment when Lammasch, the new Prime Minister, was taking his vow of loyalty to the Emperor at the Hofburg. The Emperor at once began to discuss the situation with Lammasch and Andrássy, and these discussions were continued at the first meeting of the Lammasch Cabinet which was held on the same day at five o'clock in the afternoon. Coudenhove, the Governor of Bohemia, was present, and from the Council Chamber telephoned to his deputy, Vice-President Kosina, instructing him to refuse to hand over the administration to the National Committee.

Meanwhile, in Prague, during the afternoon, the military authorities endeavoured to moderate the excitement of the crowds, who had already begun to pull down the Austrian emblems. The Magyar troops who were garrisoned in Prague were sent to patrol the streets. The military commander, however, who had been instructed by the Ministry of War to co-operate with the national committees for the maintenance of peace, acceded to the request of the National Committee in Prague and recalled the troops. The National Committee thereupon undertook the task of maintaining order in the city, largely with the help of the Sokols. The enthusiasm of the people was thus allowed free play, and October 28th was duly celebrated as the first day of national liberty. In accordance with the prevailing mood the National Committee, at seven o'clock in the evening, issued the first law of the Czechoslovak State. It runs as follows:

The independent Czechoslovak State has come into being. In order that continuity should be preserved between the juridical order hitherto existing and the new regime, in order that no confusion may arise and that there may be an undisturbed transition to the new life of the State, the National Committee, as executor of the State supremacy, enacts as follows on behalf of the Czechoslovak nation:

Article I

The State form of the Czechoslovak State will be decided by the National Assembly in agreement with the Czechoslovak National Council in Paris as bodies expressing the unanimous will of the nation. Before this is done, the State supremacy will be exercised by the National Committee.

Article II

All imperial and provincial laws will continue to remain in force until further notice.

Article III

All autonomous bodies, all State, district, municipal, and local institutions are answerable to the National Committee, and until further notice they will continue to carry out their duties in accordance with the existing laws and regulations.

Article IV

This law comes into force from to-day onwards.

ARTICLE V

The presidential board of the National Committee will be responsible for the carrying out of this law.

PRAGUE, *October* 28, 1918.

ANTONÍN ŠVEHLA.   DR. ALOIS RAŠÍN.   JIŘÍ STŘÍBRNÝ.
DR. F. SOUKUP.   DR. VAVRO ŠROBÁR.

At the same time the National Committee issued a proclamation to the people, calling upon them to maintain order and to show themselves worthy of the freedom which had crowned their efforts.

156

On the evening of October 28th the first attempts were made by the National Committee, with the help of the Sokol organizations, to form its own military units. Dr. Scheiner, Dr. Soukup, and Dr. V. Pospíšil negotiated with General Kestřánek, at the military headquarters, to obtain for the National Committee full authority over the Czech troops. The negotiations concluded after midnight in an agreement, the chief terms of which were announced by the military commander in his orders on the following day.

The Czech troops, wearing the distinctive mark of the national colours, were to be under the control of the National Committee which appointed Dr. Scheiner as their commander. The foreign garrison would continue to obey the orders of its military commanders, but it was to be used only after agreement with the National Committee. The circumstance that the military command in Prague at the critical moment showed its willingness to give way to the National Committee had an important bearing upon the ease with which the *coup d'état* was carried out.

On the morning of October 29th Coudenhove arrived in Prague. He was taken into custody and then was escorted by the Sokols to his former headquarters, which he was not allowed to leave, although enjoying freedom of movement in other respects. At midday a deputation comprising four members of the National Committee came to renew negotiations with him. It was then arranged that he would recognize the National Committee as "the executive organ of the nation's sovereignty," and that he would acknowledge its "joint management of the public administration." The staff and administration of the

State services were to continue unchanged, although Coudenhove himself decided to resign his post, as he was unwilling to
co-operate with the National Committee.

On the same day, in the afternoon, the Ministerial Council
met at Vienna, and sanctioned the arrangement which had been
arrived at in the morning between the National Committee and
Coudenhove, who was given provisional leave. Lammasch and
several members of the Cabinet, however, severely criticized the
action of the military authorities for having given the various
military commands authority to co-operate with the national
committees on the previous day, without having obtained
beforehand the sanction of the civil administration. In fact,
the Cabinet declared that the military authorities were entirely
to blame for what had happened at Prague.

At five o'clock on the afternoon of October 29th the Ministry
of War issued its long overdue reply to the proposals of the
military command at Prague. For the greater part it approved
the agreement between the military command and the National
Committee, but on the most important point it disavowed the
attitude of the military authorities in Prague. It declined to
permit the formation of a special Czechoslovak Army from
officers and men offering themselves voluntarily for service, and
gave instructions that all were to be retained at the duties undertaken under the terms of their military oath until they could be
properly demobilized and allotted to the new national States.
The Ministry further announced that they were sending General
Bardolff to Prague to superintend the military arrangements
there, and that until he arrived the command were not to enter
into any further arrangements with the National Committee
unless the Ministry had previously given its sanction.

157

The military command at Prague thereupon endeavoured to
withdraw that part of the agreement with the National Committee to which the Ministry objected, and it therefore prepared
a proclamation of martial law against civilians who incited
soldiers to infringe their military oath. It also freed officers from
their vow to the National Committee, and refused to permit
Dr. Scheiner to continue his official activity at the military
headquarters.

This denoted an opposition, at least for the time being, against
the formation of a special military force taking its orders from

the National Committee. The fundamental point at issue was whether the liquidation of the old order in the Monarchy would be carried out in accordance with the contents of the Emperor's manifesto, or at any rate with the possibility of preserving the dynasty within the new States, or whether it would be accomplished according to the desire of the nationalities for complete independence and separation from Vienna and Budapest.

In the evening General Kestřánek paid a visit to Coudenhove, and about the same time the National Committee received news that the military command at Litoměřice was preparing to take measures against the *coup d'état* at Prague, and that the Prague military headquarters also contemplated upsetting the agreement with the National Committee. Telephonic communication between Vienna and Prague was therefore cut off to prevent any further arrangements from being made. On the morning of October 30th Dr. Scheiner, Dr. Soukup, and Stříbrný went to the military headquarters, and by their decisive action, with the assistance of the first armed Czech troops, they succeeded in frustrating any further attempts to stem the course of affairs at Prague. At half-past nine Vienna was informed that the military authorities in Prague had failed to recover their mastery of the situation, and that the National Committee now had the military command also in its power. Vienna could do nothing but accept the news with resignation, since equally grave reports were arriving from the other parts of the Empire, while from Budapest the news was graver still.

On the preceding day what was known as "Deutschböhmen" and "Sudetenland" had been constituted, and when the Austrian National Assembly met on October 30th it sanctioned this step and designated Sudetenland as a constituent part of a new German Austria. Meanwhile, at a meeting in Ústí nad Labem (Aussig), it was announced that the German Government had promised help, and if need be, a military occupation for Deutschböhmen. On the following day the Government of Lammasch handed over the political administration of this new State to the State Council of German Austria, and thus began the struggle between the Government at Prague and the Germans in Bohemia on the subject of Deutschböhmen and Sudetenland.

The critical moments of the National Committee, October 29th and 30th, had now been overcome, and October 31st was the day upon which constructive work and the development of the new administration may be said to have started. From the very outset Dr. V. Šrobár had associated himself with this work on behalf of the Slovaks. By the declaration made at Turčiansky Svatý Martin on October 30th, the whole of Slovakia officially associated itself with the Czechoslovak national and State unity. The National Committee rapidly organized the food supply, the railways, the postal services, the national defence, and the Press. In this respect the early days of November passed off fairly quietly. The chief concern was occasioned by the maintenance of order, and the prevention of hunger riots or Bolshevism.

158

Of all these events we in Geneva, during the course of our negotiations, knew only those matters which had appeared in the newspapers. We read Andrássy's note on the evening of October 28th in the *Journal de Genève*, and on the following evening we read the first news from Prague which had reached Switzerland by way of Vienna, and which gave a fairly accurate account of what had taken place. We also heard of the violent revolutionary manifestos and fighting at Budapest, where the events formed a striking contrast to the comparative calm prevailing at Prague.

It was on October 30th that we received fuller details of what had happened at Prague and, in particular, of the proclamation of independence there. At the same time arrived the first reports that a special province comprising the German Bohemians had been formed, and that a separate Government had been set up for it at Liberec (Reichenberg). News then continued to arrive from Vienna concerning the events at Budapest, Cracow, Zagreb, Ljubljana, and also at Czernowitz, where a Rumanian National Committee had established itself and demanded independence for the Bukovina and Transylvania. On the same day we heard that the Supreme Austrian Command had ordered the evacuation of all the occupied territory, and from Paris it was reported that the Supreme Military Council was meeting to discuss the Armistice conditions for the Central Powers.

On the evening of October 31st we heard of the Armistice with Turkey, Karolyi's victorious revolution in Budapest, the increasing republican movement in Vienna, the demonstrations of the soldiers in the streets there, and the formation of a new national Government for German Austria. From Prague it was reported that all was quiet and that the National Committee had matters in hand as regards the economic situation, as well as communications and Press.

When we read all these reports we realized that our arrangements at Geneva, which, as we had surmised, would not be carried out until some future date, had now suddenly become a matter for immediate action. My greatest fear at that moment was that in Paris, at the negotiations on Austro-Hungarian affairs during our absence, arrangements might be made detrimental to our interests. I therefore hastened back to Paris with the feeling that my authority was now of wider scope than it had been on my departure. I was now the officially accredited representative of a nation and State, whose task it was to act as advocate for our historical heritage from the dismantled Empire.

In the course of the Geneva negotiations, and before my departure for Paris, I was repeatedly asked by the Prague delegates, in view of the extreme tension prevailing at home, to urge upon Masaryk the necessity for returning to Bohemia as soon as possible, as his authority was universally recognized. I was also to ask him to authorize Dr. Kramář to act as his deputy and sign State documents during the period which would elapse before his return. On reaching Paris I at once fulfilled both these requests, and also gave Masaryk a fairly detailed account of the course of the negotiations at Geneva. Masaryk thereupon communicated his approval of all that had been arranged there, and at the same time expressed his opinion on a number of personal questions. He also telegraphically authorized Dr. Kramář to sign State documents on his behalf. As regards an early return to Bohemia, he was rather doubtful. At that particular juncture he was engaged upon a discussion on important financial matters concerning our Siberian army and also our eventual financial co-operation with the Allied States in the near future. He was anxious to settle these matters at any cost before he left America. By the end of November all the important points had been settled, so that at the end of the first week of November Masaryk reached Paris on his return journey home.

XIX

CZECHOSLOVAKIA SIGNS THE ARMISTICE CONDI-
TIONS. THE FIRST DIPLOMATIC STRUGGLES
CONCERNING OUR FRONTIERS. THE END OF
OUR REVOLUTIONARY MOVEMENT ABROAD

(a) OUR SHARE IN THE ARMISTICE NEGOTIATIONS. THE
JURIDICAL AND POLITICAL SIGNIFICANCE OF THIS

159

The negotiations at Geneva had protracted my stay outside
Paris two days longer than was desirable. I did not reach Paris
until Friday, November 1st, and the early Allied negotiations
on the terms of an armistice with Austria-Hungary had begun
on the previous afternoon at Versailles. I regarded my absence
from the first meeting as a serious matter, since it might possibly
result in a real detriment to our national interests, both as
regards the formulation of the Armistice terms, and also in
respect of our juridical situation as an independent State
already recognized by the Allies.

The French Government, who had convened the Conference,
had not invited us to the first meeting as it should have done.
In addition to having been recognized by the Allies as an
Allied Government and nation we had received an express
undertaking in our agreements with France and England that
we were to participate in all Allied conferences where our
interests might be concerned. I therefore proceeded on the
morning of November 2nd to the French Foreign Ministry to
ascertain how matters stood, and to take immediate steps for
vindicating our point of view. I need hardly say that I was
dissatisfied with those who had convened the Conference, and
I made no secret of my opinion.

I gave Berthelot the first verbal reports on the Geneva
negotiations, and I informed him that I would supply the Allied
Governments with the written text of the Geneva declaration,
as well as a statement of our demand on the subject of the
Armistice with Austria. Finally, I emphasized how urgent it
was that a representative of Czechoslovakia should at once be

summoned to attend all further negotiations on the Armistice with the Central Powers. I added that our absence from these proceedings would make a very unfavourable impression in Bohemia and might produce results which would be unpleasant, both to us and to the Allies.

He proposed to deal with the matter unofficially, to which I agreed, and then returned to the Rue Bonaparte. Shortly afterwards I was invited by telephone to attend the meeting of the Great Powers at eleven o'clock that morning at the residence of Colonel House.

Berthelot's assistance immediately produced satisfactory results in every respect. Besides the main session of the Inter-Allied Conference (Supreme Military Council), which was held on October 31st and on November 1st, 2nd, and 4th, and which was attended by the chief political and military representatives of the Allied States (among those present were Clemenceau, Pichon, Leygues, Klotz, Lloyd George, Bonar Law, Balfour, Lord Milner, Colonel House, Orlando, Sonnino, Matsui, Hymans, Venizelos, Vesnić, General Foch, General Wilson, General Bliss, and General Robillant), conferences of the four chief Great Powers were held regularly every morning which supplemented the proceedings of the main Conference, and to which a number of military authorities, Prime Ministers and Ministers of Foreign Affairs were co-opted. It was to these proceedings that, as a result of Berthelot's intervention, I was invited by telephone, as I have mentioned above.

At midday on November 4th a special messenger from the French Foreign Ministry came to the Rue Bonaparte with an official invitation from Pichon for me to attend the plenary meeting of the Supreme War Council which was to be held on the same afternoon at Versailles.

160

I must confess that I was highly excited when, on the afternoon of November 4th, I took my seat in a motor-car decorated with our flag, and drove through Paris by way of St. Cloud and Sèvres to Versailles. When for the first time I entered the hall at Versailles where all the mighty of this world were assembled —mighty especially at that moment when they were settling the destiny of three Empires in Europe and Asia—and when I took my seat besides Vesnić and Venizelos, I could scarcely believe in the reality of what was happening. Three years previously I had escaped across the frontiers of Bohemia, crawling through the thickets to avoid being seen by the Austrian and Bavarian gendarmes, and staking the whole future on what destiny might bring. Now I was sitting in conference with the representatives of France, Great Britain, United States, Italy, Japan, Serbia, Greece, Belgium, and Portugal, to decide with them as to the fate of the Empires of Wilhelm and Karl, and to sign the terms of their capitulation.

The first meeting on October 31st had been attended only by six States, the four Great Powers (without Japan, which joined the latter meetings), Serbia, and Greece. The proceedings opened with a statement by Marshal Foch on the general situation at the various fronts, in accordance with which the military experts had prepared Armistice conditions to be submitted to the Conference. A discussion on this subject followed immediately, the first topic being the question of an armistice with Austria-Hungary. After certain differences regarding the occupation of Jugoslav areas by the Italian Army, when M. Vesnić expressed his reservation, and acquiesced only after having received an assurance that this arrangement involved no definite commitment with regard to the peace terms, the proposals of the military experts were accepted.

The proceedings continued at the second meeting on November 1st, the subject on this occasion being the Armistice terms for Germany. Belgium also took part in these negotiations. Much of the discussion was concerned with the Allied Note to President Wilson, in which the Allies expressed their two reservations regarding his Fourteen Points, i.e. on the freedom of the seas and on indemnities for areas devastated by the war. There were further differences between Vesnić and the Italian delegates concerning the surrender of the Austrian fleet to the Jugoslavs, and the settlement of this matter was postponed. At the third and fourth meetings, held on November 2nd and 4th respectively, discussions were continued on the Armistice terms for Germany, the final wording of which was then agreed upon. It was also decided that the terms thus settled should be transmitted to President Wilson, and that Marshal Foch should be authorized to negotiate direct with the German plenipotentiaries in the same way. The Armistice with Austria-Hungary, immediately after having been accepted, was forwarded to General Diaz, who received authorization to negotiate direct with the Austro-Hungarian plenipotentiaries.

161

The meeting of the Great Powers, which was held on Saturday morning at the residence of Colonel House in the Rue de l'Université, was attended mainly by the military leaders, Foch, Weygand, Sir Henry Wilson, the Italian general, Robillant, and the great European statesmen, Clemenceau, Pichon, Lloyd George, Lord Milner, Orlando, Sonnino, and Matsui. The main subject of discussion comprised the results of the signature of the Armistice with Austria-Hungary as regards the further conduct of the war against Germany. On behalf of the Czechoslovak Government I expressed my agreement with the Austro-Hungarian Armistice terms, and added a detailed statement on the chief demands which we had formulated at Geneva. After a fairly short discussion I secured the consent of the Allies. According to the agreement, on the following day I submitted them in a written form to the French Government, by whom they were transmitted to the Italian Commander-in-Chief.

Marshal Foch presented his proposals for the military arrangements involved by the occupation of the chief points on Austro-Hungarian territory. On the whole, these plans were in accordance with our requirements and our special demands, and could therefore easily be brought within the general scope of these proposals. It should be remembered that at this moment the Conference was not certain whether the German Government would accept the severe Armistice terms which had just been drawn up at Versailles, and from this point of view our participation was important. In his military plan Marshal Foch had taken Bohemia as one of the bases for an offensive against Berlin from the south, and he had asked the Czechoslovak representative to give his consent to this. He explained what measures he wished to adopt for the dispatch of troops across Austrian territory to Bohemia. It was, of course, his intention to use mainly our legionaries in France and Italy for this purpose.

Owing to the change of circumstances only a few of the demands which I submitted on our behalf were fulfilled. Communication to Trieste and also to France by way of Italy (later also by way of Switzerland) was secured for us. The first preparations were also made for the transport of our troops from France and Italy, transport of arms and war material by way of Italy and Austria was guaranteed, and decisions were made for the import of the most necessary food-stuffs. For mainly military reasons (there were also political ones) the capitulation of Austria-Hungary was not followed by any Allied military occupation. On the one hand there was considerable war-weariness among the Allies also, and then they took the views that after the revolution in all parts of the Empire, together with the capitulation of Germany, there was no need for any military occupation. After the Armistice with Germany I discussed the question of the food supply almost exclusively with Mr. Hoover and the American Government. The schemes for economic co-operation and financial help were gradually carried out, at least to a certain extent, during these negotiations.

162

The Armistice with Austria-Hungary, Germany, and Turkey formed the agenda at the eighth meeting of the Supreme Military Council between October 31st and November 4th. Full minutes of all these meetings were handed to me for my approval as the representative of Czechoslovakia. The text of the Armistice terms was placed before the Central Powers by Marshal Foch and the other military leaders also on behalf of the provisional Czechoslovak Government.

Of the new States, Czechoslovakia was the only one which participated in the Armistice negotiations. Poland was not admitted, and Rumania, although she had resumed hostilities, was also not invited. The Jugoslavs of Austria-Hungary had not yet been recognized as Allies by Italy and the other Great Powers, so that Serbia alone was represented at the Conference. At the meeting on October 31st M. Vesnić raised the question of the recognition of the Austrian Jugoslavs, but in spite of this the Conference took no steps in the matter.

From the above account it is clear that we were represented at the Conference on the basis of our juridical recognition and the treaties with the Allies which were signed before the collapse of the Empire. In the interests of historical truth I wish to point out that the events within the Empire and the *coup d'état* at Prague had no influence on this question. This is shown by the examples of the other Austro-Hungarian nationalities, quite apart from the fact that the Allied Governments at that time had no exact information as to the extent of the various upheavals within the Empire, and, from this juridical point of view, did not take them into account. At the meetings themselves not a word was said about the revolutions in Austria-

Hungary, and during the discussions concerning the Armistice with Austria the proceedings of the English delegation, for example, were based on the assumption that Vienna might not accept the terms, and that hostilities against Austria would then be continued.

As we shall see, this juridical status of ours was of considerable importance. Our situation was unique and was different from that of the Poles, Rumanians, and Jugoslavs. The Poles were not recognized by the Allies until February 1919, and the recognition of the Jugoslavs as a unified State was granted only during the signature of the Versailles Peace Treaty. Before our departure from Geneva it had been arranged that I was to transmit the results of our proceedings there not only to the Allies, but also to Masaryk and our military leaders. I also promised to keep in direct touch with Prague, and to supply our people there with the earliest possible news of subsequent events, if necessary, also asking them to communicate their instructions. Having therefore settled the matters connected with the Armistice negotiations, I began to deal with the further points of the Geneva agreement.

First of all, on November 4th, I notified the Allies of all the Geneva resolutions, and submitted to them the declarations which had been signed there. While still staying at Geneva I had supplied Masaryk with the first news about the negotiations with the Prague delegates, and on my return to Paris I had sent him a brief telegram concerning the results of the meeting. On the following day, November 4th, I sent a detailed report to Prague about my negotiations in Paris on the subject of the Armistice, and the assistance which was to be granted by the Allies to our people. I also reported to Prague Masaryk's approval of the Geneva resolutions, and insisted on the urgent need for maintaining order at home and absolute unity with us in Paris as the first condition for any further successful negotiations with the Allies concerning our cause.

(b) The Anniversary of Bílá Hora at the Front. The End of the War

163

Having completed these urgent tasks, I was anxious to visit our troops at the front as had been arranged before I left for Geneva. Colonel Philippe had informed me that General

Gouraud, with whose army our brigade had been incorporated, was preparing to make use of our troops for attacks in the front line somewhere about October 20th. It was our duty to be with our soldiers at the moment when they were about to engage in hostilities which were deciding the destiny of Europe. Now, after my return from Geneva, my visit had a still more immediate interest; our brigade had taken part in very severe fighting at Vouziers and Terron on the Aisne between October 19th and 25th, and its high military qualities received ample testimony in the army orders of the Supreme Command as follows:

> Under the energetic and skilful command of Colonel Philippe the Czechoslovak regiments Nos. 21 and 22 gave proof of the most admirable military qualities in the fighting from October 19th to 25th east of Vouziers. Resolute in attack, stubborn in defence, unwavering in the severe artillery fire, they brilliantly proved themselves equal to the tasks entrusted to them and satisfied their leader in every respect.

Accompanied by Major Fierlinger, who was then my chief military assistant, I started on the morning of Friday, November 8th, from Paris for the front section of General Gouraud's 4th Army, near Vouziers. At noon we reached a solitary house which formed the headquarters of General Gouraud and his staff. Only a short time before, during the attack on Paris, this house had been occupied by the Kaiser. General Gouraud received us courteously and with a sense of solemnity. The whole front was in movement, the Germans were retreating along the whole line, and the General's army had scored well-deserved successes.

The General prepared a simple but touching welcome for the Czechoslovak delegates. He invited us to a military lunch at which his staff and a number of our officers were present. During the lunch he spoke about Bílá Hora and our struggle for national independence, our defeat three hundred years ago, and our present victory in which we were participating on three fronts; he said that the servitude to which the nation had been subjected for three hundred years was ended that day by our great success, which would form a bond of friendship between our two nations. Only a short time ago, he said, the Kaiser had stayed in that house and helped to direct the operations which were to bring about the fall of Paris. That day he was welcoming there a Czechoslovak Minister who had come to greet his fellow-countrymen who were fighting to help in the liberation of France and thus also of their own country. It was a manifesto of victory, the terms of which would be handed by Allied Commanders-in-Chief perhaps to-day, perhaps to-morrow, or the day after, to the defeated Kaiser. "Three centuries of your servitude are revenged," concluded General Gouraud.

I replied to him with emotion as I looked through the windows at the gloom of the devastated fields, and reflected what hecatombs had been sacrificed, and how strange is the logic of events. The anniversary of Bílá Hora!

Shortly afterwards we rode out with a number of officers to see the troops. I came across our regiments a few kilometres behind the main front where they were drawn up in a rectangular formation. In a few words I conveyed to them greetings from Geneva, and informed them of what we had discussed and decided there. I also gave them a short account of the Armistice negotiations at Versailles, and told them that the old regime had already been overthrown in Prague and that we were free. "In accordance with an Allied resolution," I concluded, "you are going back to your own country to be prepared, if necessary, to continue the military operations there."

We had hoped that on November 8th we would proclaim the provisional Government at the front, but we already had achieved far more than this: a Government, the overthrow of the old regime at home, the downfall of the Empire and the dynasty, the approaching capitulation of Germany, the prospect of a return at an early date.

We completed the inspection of the brigade, during which General Gouraud decorated a number of our officers and men who had distinguished themselves in the recent fighting.

(c) Co-operation of the Provisional Government with Prague. November 14th, 1918, at Prague

164

After the events of October 28th at Prague I considered that our most urgent need was to establish permanent contact and an absolutely unified course of action with our people there. About November 5th and the following days rumours began to reach Paris, mostly from Vienna, that the National Committee was acting in a manner which suggested that it was opposed to us. There can be no doubt that the events in Poland, and partially also those among the Jugoslavs, had some bearing on these rumours which, however, were mainly to be attributed to the last efforts of the Austrophiles. There had been an evident conflict between the Polish Committee in Paris and the Warsaw Government. The Poles in the Allied countries, and to some extent those of Galicia, were unwilling to recognize the regime at Warsaw, to which the Allies had also adopted an attitude of marked reserve. The Jugoslavs were just then in the middle of negotiations about which their opponents were spreading pessimistic reports. Those in Paris were therefore anxiously awaiting the results of the Conference at Geneva between Korošec, Trumbić, and Pašić.

These matters were being followed very carefully by the Allied Governments, who naturally drew from them their own conclusions as to the future development in Central Europe, and formed their judgments about the political conditions of the liberated nations in the immediate future. In view of our proceedings at Geneva, I immediately refuted all reports alleging divergences amongst us. I also thought it necessary to inform Dr. Kramář in Prague about this, and to draw his attention to the danger underlying it. Here I must render a tribute to the absolute loyalty with which our politicians at Prague acted towards us during the critical days of the downfall of Austria, and after the return of our delegates from Geneva.

I was anxious to comply promptly with the demands of our Geneva delegates, and also to make all arrangements in Paris which would help to consolidate our conditions after the change of regime. My first step in this respect was to arrange for the transport of our troops from France and Italy to occupy those areas in which the new State encountered difficulties. For this purpose I had already, on November 9th, asked for the sanction of Prague to enable me to arrange with the French Government for the dispatch of a special French Military Mission to organize our future army. This course was rendered imperative by the interests and future policy of our new State. I immediately obtained sanction from Dr. Kramář for this purpose.

I then supplemented these proceedings by a new military agreement. In the sense of the Allied resolution that Marshal Foch should be Commander-in-Chief of all Allied armies, including those of the Eastern front if there were a continuation of hostilities against Germany, I asked for a formal arrangement between France and our Government, to hold good during the transition period while our State was in course of construction, to the effect that Marshal Foch should remain Commander-in-Chief of our armies on all fronts. On December 17th I submitted the matter to Clemenceau in writing, and on February 14, 1919, I signed a convention with France which was to hold good as long as Marshal Foch remained Commander-in-Chief of all Allied armies.

Finally, I turned my attention to the problem of maintaining the food supply at home with Allied help, and to the preparations for the Peace Conference. The problem of the food supply at this juncture was of vital importance to the new State, since it closely involved the maintenance of order and the protection of large areas from Bolshevism. The French Government and all the Allied representatives who were officially deputed for this purpose granted me, by progressive stages, full authority in these matters, so that little by little, with the help of our troops, I was able to contribute substantially towards the organization of the import of essential food-stuffs via Hamburg and Trieste. In these two ports the Allied Governments established missions which at that critical period rendered valuable services to our people at home.

The Americans in Paris, who were dealing with the provisioning of Czechoslovakia on behalf of the Allied authorities, showed themselves extremely considerate towards us, but in accordance with their instructions they demanded that from what we had or received we should render assistance also to the Germans and Austrians wherever there was a risk of Bolshevism, principally in Vienna. This was entirely in our own interests. I was anxious to show that the orderly elements prevailed amongst us, and I did not want the differences with our neighbours to loom too large at the moment of victory. I therefore made a point of promoting our help to Vienna also by means of food supplies. I further aimed at reducing to a minimum any friction which was likely to arise over our minorities and in connection with Slovakia.

As regards preparations for the Peace Conference, I began to make them at Paris in the early days of December; and in accordance with what I had arranged on this subject with our delegates at Geneva I instructed Prague also to begin preparations. The thoughts of the Allied circles in Paris were concentrated entirely on the Conference as soon as the Armistice had been signed, and if it was not convened until January, the reason was that they were anxious to settle beforehand a number of important matters, notably the details of how the work of the Conference was to be arranged.

At that period my co-operation with Prague was of a very gratifying character. As a result of the enthusiasm after the change of regime, and the unsparing recognition of what had been achieved by our movement abroad, our authority at home was practically unlimited. Prague accordingly complied promptly and readily with our wishes and suggestions. In his letter of November 15th Dr. Kramář paid a tribute to all the work which I had accomplished at Paris since my return from Geneva, and he announced that Prague gladly accepted my proposal concerning the French Military Mission. While agreeing with the course of action proposed towards the Germans in our country, he complained of a number of matters at home which needed adjustment. In particular, he said that there was a constant danger of Bolshevism also in the ranks of the Socialist parties, and that owing to our inadequate military resources we were being driven step by step from the Slovak regions by the Magyars. Karolyi's proceedings were becoming more and more dangerous to us, and it was essential to take some decisive step as regards the occupation of Slovakia. Conditions in the Teschen district, he said, were also unsatisfactory, owing to the action of the Poles. He concluded by emphasizing that the most important thing was to send our troops home as soon as possible, together with food supplies, and to urge President Masaryk to return to Prague with the least possible delay so as to exert his authority for consolidating our public opinion in social respects.

I continued, therefore, to attend to the settlement of all these difficulties of ours, but almost immediately afterwards it became necessary to engage upon our first diplomatic contest for the territory of the Republic, especially Slovakia. This first struggle was successfully concluded within the following two weeks.

165

The events at Prague connected with the convening of the revolutionary National Assembly, with the election of Professor Masaryk as President of the Republic, and with the appointment of a Government, produced an excellent effect in the Allied countries. At a time when chaos prevailed in Austria and Hungary, when no clear agreement had been reached between the Belgrade Government and the Zagreb National Committee, when in Poland there was still an active conflict between two tendencies represented by the Warsaw Government and the Paris National Committee respectively, the progress at Prague was regarded as a happy omen for the beginnings of the new Republic.

The Prague delegates of the National Committee had returned from Geneva on November 5th, and they had been received with the enthusiasm which marked the days inaugurating the new regime. The speech made by Dr. Kramář and the other delegates on their return, as well as the manifestos in the Press and at public meetings, testified eloquently to the great importance which was then attached to the Geneva negotiations, and to the fact that the passive resistance at home had joined forces with the liberation movement abroad.

Immediately after its return the delegation had begun, step by step, to carry out what had been agreed upon at Geneva. The members of the National Committee, who in the meanwhile had brought about the *coup d'état* at Prague, showed complete agreement with what had been decided at Geneva. It will be remembered that in conformity with the first law passed by the National Committee on October 28th, that body took over the administration of the Czechoslovak territories, and the State form was to be settled by the National Assembly jointly with the National Council in Paris. Before this could be done, the National Committee was held to exercise supreme authority within the State, while for external matters the nation and the new State were represented by the National Council at Paris, which in the meanwhile, by arrangement with the National Committee, had established itself as an interim Government.

In consequence of this, the presiding board of the National Committee, having made the necessary preparations after the return of the delegates from Geneva, convened the revolutionary National Assembly for its inaugural meeting on November 14th in the building hitherto occupied by the Provincial Diet. All the political parties sent their delegates, as previously agreed upon, the number representing each party being proportionate to its numerical strength. The total number of delgates was 249, of which 54 belonged to the Agrarian Party, 49 to the Social Democrats, 40 to the Constitutional Democrats, 28 to the Czech Socialists, 24 to the Catholic Party, 4 to the Centralist Socialist Party, and 1 to the Moravian Traders' Party. The Slovaks were represented provisionally by 40 members. The National Committee had laid stress upon the fact that the National Assembly was to exercise legislative power, and to have charge of the Government until the new Constitution had come into force and a definitive Parliament been elected.

Even at the very outset the revolutionary National Assembly, in spite of all difficulties, displayed an activity and an efficiency which showed that it was the product of a judicious convention, and also that each party and organization regarded it as their duty to co-operate in the prompt settlement of the most urgent questions which would enable the country to emerge rapidly from the chaos of revolution. This spirit was admirably manifested at the first meeting on November 14th. The National Assembly was opened by Dr. Kramář with an inaugural address, in which he referred to the victorious conclusion of the struggle. He returned thanks to all who had struggled and suffered, and to the Allied nations. He warmly welcomed the Slovaks from the former territories of Hungary, and towards the Germans who had not yet decided to take their seats in common with the Czechoslovak representatives, he undertook a commitment of national equality. He declared that the bonds were now broken by which the nation had been held to Austria and the dynasty, and that Czechoslovakia was now a free democratic Republic. T. G. Masaryk was then unanimously elected as its President amid unbounded enthusiasm.

Steps were next taken to elect the President of the National Assembly, the deputy chosen being F. Tomášek, who, having taken his vow of allegiance, welcomed the Slovaks, expressed the hope that the Germans would collaborate, and defined the future activity of the Assembly. After the deputies had taken their vows and the Vice-Presidents had been elected, Vice-President Bela, on behalf of the Slovaks, declared that they desired liberty which was neither Magyar nor Slovak, but only Czechoslovak.

The Government was then elected as the result of a joint resolution of all parties. This was done by unanimous vote. Dr. Kramář, who was elected President of the Assembly, while the members of the Government were taking their vows of allegiance, emphasized the historical significance of the day when, for the first time after three hundred years, a legislative National Assembly was again meeting. He also expressed the hope that the Germans would soon realize the necessity of co-operation.

These events were followed with particular attention in the Allied countries. After my return from Geneva I had informed Allied circles what would probably happen in Prague, and now my forecast was being carried out almost in exact detail. I had refuted all rumours of a conflict between us and Prague, and now the reports coming from there clearly demonstrated that we had been right. This was a circumstance which at that difficult period helped to strengthen our position among the Allies.

I attach to these Prague events, in their connection with the Geneva negotiations, a considerable political and historical significance. Here I do not wish to engage in a controversy about the various theories on this subject. I am merely recording the facts, and it will be for the impartial jurist and historian to examine them all and pronounce a detached judgment.

The formal and solemn severing of all bonds with the former Empire and dynasty, the proclamation of the Republic, and the election of Masaryk as President, the manifestations in favour of the Allies, our movement abroad, Czechoslovak unity—all these proceedings on the part of the revolutionary National Assembly constitute an historic event directly associated with the Geneva negotiations and the *coup d'état* at Prague on October 28–30, 1918. Our revolutionary activity abroad had again merged with the policy at home and its opposition to the Habsburg monarchy.

(d) THE FIRST STRUGGLES FOR THE PROTECTION OF SLOVAKIA AND THE FRONTIERS OF THE HISTORICAL TERRITORIES. VICTORY OF OUR CAUSE

166

During those November days when in Germany and Central Europe everything was in a state of ferment, revolution, and chaos, when the Allies were making preparations for the Conference, when enemy territories were being occupied, and when there was a menace of Bolshevism in several countries, we in Paris were living in a state of tension, excitement, expectation, and impatience. The provisioning of Bohemia was not proceeding as rapidly as we should have liked and as we had expected from what the Allies had promised. The transport of our troops was also being continually postponed. I urged Prague to be patient, but I myself was not satisfied.

The dissatisfaction and the alarm amongst us were increased daily by the events which began to develop in Slovakia about November 15th. Károlyi, who had taken charge of the Government in Hungary, realized that it would be possible to make an attempt to preserve the integral character of Hungary only on the basis of certain assumptions. He conscientiously did everything in his power, perhaps somewhat more skilfully than it would have been done by Tisza, Apponyi, Andrássy, or Weckerle. In this respect the Magyars did a serious injustice to this politician and his associates who, amid the welter of revolution, were desperately endeavouring to save for Hungary what at that time nobody else could certainly have saved. With this end in view Károlyi promptly decided upon a policy of racial justice. He contemplated special ministries for the Ruthenians, Slovaks, and Rumanians, he contemplated also administrative reforms on the lines of regional racial autonomy, he had already made practical experiments in this respect, and had announced to the world that future Hungary would for evermore abandon the impossible Chauvinistic policy of former Hungary. This was the programme of his revolutionary National Council, which was publicly proclaimed as early as October 25, 1918.

His second good tactical step consisted of his negotiations with the Allies. Seeing the inevitable advance of the Allied army from the south, and fearing a Serbian invasion of Hungary, he began promptly to negotiate with General Franchet d'Esperey, the Commander-in-Chief of the Eastern Allied Army, his purpose being to secure Allied influence for preventing Serbian troops from entering Hungary proper. In this he was successful, as the Allies soon caused the Serbians to withdrawn from the Banat beyond the Danube. Then began the Allied negotiations with Károlyi for the maintenance of order in Hungary.

Thus, between November 7th and the 12th, discussions took place between Károlyi and Franchet d'Esperey, the result of which was the arrangement of a special Armistice signed at Belgrade on November 13th. These proceedings were somewhat irregular, as the Armistice terms for Austria-Hungary had been arranged at Versailles between October 31st and November 4th, and they had been duly signed on the Italian front in the name of the whole Empire on November 3rd. These terms applied in their full extent to Hungary also, and the revolution which had broken out there made no change in this respect.

The States which had newly arisen (for example, the new Austria and the new Hungary) had not hitherto existed from the point of view of international law, as they had not been recognized. The negotiations with their authorities had, for the time being, been only of a local character designed for the maintenance of order in the locality concerned and without any political implications. Of the new States, Czechoslovakia was the only one which existed on a basis of international law. Serbia and Rumania had only their old territory, the problems involved by their new areas not having been settled. The juridical situation of Austria, Hungary, and Poland was altogether vague and uncertain.

M. Clemenceau, in granting permission to General Franchet d'Esperey to arrange a special Armistice, assured me by telegram on November 12th that this Armistice was not to affect any political questions. Nevertheless, by Article 17 of the Armistice, it was stipulated that for the time being the whole of Hungarian territory, except Croatia-Slavonia, was to be left under the local administration of the Magyar authorities. This article was then interpreted by the Magyars as an Allied recognition of the integral character of Hungary, and was adduced as an argument against the occupation of Slovakia by our troops and officials. The dispute arising from this was very serious, difficult, and dangerous, both juridically and politically, and it cost us much labour and anxiety. The question of Károlyi's Armistice, however, gave me an opportunity of settling this point once and for all, and securing an Allied decision which was of far-reaching importance to our territorial questions and also to our internal consolidation.

As I have already mentioned, Károlyi made use of all possible ways and means of saving for Hungary whatever could be saved. Several times he applied to the Allies with proclamations, telegrams, and personal appeals, emphasizing very skilfully that there should be no resolution creating a prejudice with regard to the integral character of Hungary and its administrative unity until the signature of the Peace Treaty. Everybody will understand what it would have meant for the territorial demands of the oppressed races in Hungary if that country had continued to be occupied by the Magyars until the signature of the Trianon Peace Treaty, i.e. August 1920. He also endeavoured to obtain a special Allied permission for Hungary to judge impartially the frontier question, and in this connection he emphasized that Transylvania, Slovakia, and the Ruthenians of Hungary desired to remain with the Magyars. He also broached the question of a possible plebiscite. His intervention with President Wilson in this respect was particularly important, and all these proceedings could not fail to have a considerable influence on the Allies. I had many opportunities of observing this in Paris, and it cost me much labour to counteract the effects of it in good time.

Dr. Kramář had sent me news from Prague about these matters, and had called for prompt help against what the Magyars were doing. The signature of this special Armistice had acted like a bombshell amongst us and also in Slovakia, and it was, moreover, accompanied by serious military movements on the part of the Magyars.

Under the immediate influence of the revolutionary events in our country and in Hungary, a successful attempt was made, on the initiative of Dr. V. Šrobár, to occupy various Slovak local areas with small garrisons of irregular military contingents supported by the Sokols, and also to obtain charge of the public administration. On November 4th Czechoslovak troops, numbering about 1,100 including also gendarmes, occupied Senica, Jablonice, Boleráz, Zohor, and Svatý Jan, while on November 9th this process was extended so as to include Mad'arská Ves, Stupava, Děvínská Nová Ves, and other localities. After November 10th the Magyars recovered from their first surprise, and hurriedly prepared two of their divisions, besides mobilizing several levies of recruits. They began a counter-attack upon our garrisons, and everywhere they carried out a policy of terrorism. On November 14th they drove the Czech contingents from Trnava, advancing on Žilina, and before very long the small body of Czech troops had been forced to retire as far as the Moravian-Slovak frontier. Many of our people now began to regard the occupation of Slovakia, and still more its incorporation in the Republic, as problematical. The Prague Diet was very alarmed, but the Government, having no resources for a campaign, or any regular troops which could be sent out for help, was practically powerless.

These events caused the question of incorporating Slovakia in our Republic to assume a juridically controversial aspect, and having had my attention drawn to these matters by Prague, I had to make an attempt to secure from the Allies a settlement on principle before the Peace Conference. As we shall see later, a settlement favourable to us was reached, and no further difficulties arose on this point. A month later an analogous question concerning the German regions of Bohemia had to be considered, and the settlement was again in our favour.

Károlyi, continuing his very skilful tactics, and judging that he was fully covered by his Belgrade Armistice, sent a special note to Prague on November 17, 1918, protesting against the occupation of Slovakia. Dr. Kramář replied to him on the following day, his argument being the one acknowledged by Paris, to the effect that the Czechoslovak State had been recognized by the Allies even before the change of regime, and this recognition applied also to the territories inhabited by the Slovaks. The Magyar Government could not therefore arrange an armistice on behalf of Slovakia, which was an integral part of the Czechoslovak State. Dr. Kramář then informed me of what had happened, and asked for immediate intervention. In this way the struggle for Slovakia was transferred to Paris.

From the second half of November onwards I was daily occupied discussing and negotiating this matter with military circles and politicians. As on previous occasions, I first saw Berthelot, who at once recognized our point of view as being the right one, and I then approached Pichon, Clemenceau, and Marshal Foch, as well as representatives of Great Britain and the United States. I pointed out to them that the Magyar action would inevitably result in a new armed conflict, sooner or later. In the course of these proceedings, it became obvious that there was a definite difference of opinion between the military and the political circles. The politicians regarded General Franchet d'Esperey's Armistice as a blunder, since it had been arranged in a manner which might prove prejudicial to some of the Allied wishes. After some hesitation it was acknowledged that the blunder must be rectified. I accordingly asked that the exact significance of Franchet d'Esperey's Armistice should be interpreted, and I also insisted that at the same time the frontiers should be fixed between the Magyars and ourselves so as to be a guarantee against any further surprise action, and also a proof that Slovakia did actually belong to us. I went into this matter on several occasions with Marshal Foch, who agreed to my suggestions, and finally proposed that I should settle a line of demarcation, which he would notify to Budapest, and behind which the Magyars would be compelled to withdraw. I therefore indicated what I regarded as a suitable line for this purpose, and then sent an official report on this dispute to M. Pichon asking him for a definite statement of the Allied point of view, which would then be taken by the Magyars and ourselves as definitive and binding. My report was sent on November 25th, and two days later I received a reply from M. Pichon, which contained the following:

> In your letter of November 25th you drew my attention to the conclusions arising from the Armistice negotiated with Count Károlyi on November 13th, and running counter to the Armistice with Austria-Hungary which the Allies signed on November 3rd.
>
> In view of the fact that Count Károlyi wished to draw incorrect conclusions from this document . . . I have the honour to inform you that the Minister of War has just sent precise telegraphic instructions on this matter to the Commander-in-Chief of the Eastern Allied Armies.
>
> In confidence I may mention that these instructions provide for the immediate withdrawal of the Magyar troops from the territory occupied by them without authorization.

This successfully concluded the first part of our struggle for Slovakia by which our right to that territory and the juridical ineffectiveness of Károlyi's Armistice were fully confirmed.

167

Immediately after the change of regime, Dr. Emil Stodola was appointed as our delegate at Budapest, and towards the end of November, at his own request, he was replaced by Dr. Milan Hodža. The first Allied Military Mission, directed by Lieutenant-Colonel Vyx, reached Budapest on November 27th. At the first interview between Dr. Hodža and Lieutenant-Colonel Vyx on November 29th, the latter spoke emphatically against our occupation of Slovakia, which, he said, was contrary to the Belgrade Armistice. He added that our action there would do us great harm at the Peace Conference. Dr. Hodža rightly pointed out that as an Allied State, recognized by the Great Powers even before the collapse of Austria, we were entitled to occupy Slovakia, and he asked Lieutenant-Colonel Vyx, in view of the fact that Paris was duly informed of our attitude in this respect, to obtain direct instructions from Generals Henrys and Franchet d'Esperey. But before any news of the negotiations in Budapest had reached Paris, my intervention there had been effective, with the result that Lieutenant-Colonel Vyx received due instructions from the Ministry of War, these having been originally drawn up by M. Pichon. On December 3rd he transmitted them to Károlyi in a very emphatic communication which reproduced our point of view in its entirety. On the following day Lieutenant-Colonel Vyx notified Dr. Hodža officially of the Paris resolution, and Dr. Hodža transmitted this to the Government at Prague in the following terms:

The Czechoslovak delegate to-day received this communication from Lieutenant-Colonel Vyx:

The Czechoslovak State has been recognized by the Allies. Its troops are recognized as Allied troops. The Czechoslovak State, therefore, is entitled to occupy the Slovak territory in the capacity of a belligerent Power, participating in the fulfilment of the Armistice which stipulates the occupation of the territory of the former Austro-Hungarian monarchy.

The Magyar Government is requested to withdraw its troops from Slovak territory.

From the news which reached me from Prague, it would appear that the first set of instructions supplied to Lieutenant-Colonel Vyx provided for the evacuation of Slovakia, but he did not receive any precise indication of the frontiers to which the Magyars were to conform. As I have mentioned, in the course of my negotiations at the Quai d'Orsay between November 20th and 25th, I had suggested a line of demarcation for Slovakia, consisting of the Carpathians, the River Morava, the Danube as far as the Ipola, from the Ipola to Rimavská Sobota, from Rimavská Sobota in a direct line to the confluence of the River Už with the Bereg, and from there along the course of the Už to the Carpathians. Moreover, I had been informed that these details had been telegraphed to Budapest. Dr. Hodža pointed out to Lieutenant-Colonel Vyx that if the evacuation line was not defined, difficulties would arise, and he therefore asked him to obtain further instructions from Paris immediately. He also at once applied to Prague, urging the authorities there to intervene in Paris, telegraphed to me by way of Salonica, and besides this wrote a letter to me direct. As the result of the telegraphic demand from Prague, I again intervened in the requisite sense, emphasizing the need for sending precise and emphatic instructions to Budapest on the subject of the demarcation line, and also insisting upon the prompt evacuation of Slovakia.

In the meanwhile, Dr. Hodža, fearing the possibility of further complications, reached an agreement on December 6th, 1918, with Dr. V. Bartha, the Magyar Minister of War, for establishing a provisional line of demarcation, to hold good only until fresh instructions arrived from Paris. They then communicated the details of this agreement to Lieutenant-Colonel Vyx, who at once reported the matter to Paris. I myself heard nothing about the Hodža-Bartha arrangement, either from Prague or Budapest, and this circumstance considerably complicated the situation.

My attention had been drawn to this fundamental question at the Quai d'Orsay at my very first negotiations there on the evacuation of Slovakia (after November 20th), and several times towards the end of November and at the beginning of December, when the Prague Government had exchanged telegrams with Károlyi and had sent Tusar to Vienna and Dr. Emil Stodola (later Dr. Hodža) to Budapest. When on November 29th I again discussed these questions with M. Pichon, he reminded me of it in emphatic terms. The American delegation who approached me officially in the matter was equally dissatisfied, and demanded that we should not enter into any negotiations either with Vienna and Budapest or with Berlin.

I drew the attention of Prague to this opinion of the Allies first of all telegraphically, and then in a series of detailed letters between November 27th and 29th. I also informed Prague telegraphically of the American *démarche*, when it was repeated on December 10th, during the stay of President Masaryk in Paris.

A second matter which was equally unpleasant was the Budapest agreement on a provisional line of demarcation. At the Quai d'Orsay and among the military authorities they were annoyed with us because we had no right whatever to make any arrangements with the Magyars on territorial questions, such a proceeding being possible only if carried out jointly by the Allies. In addition to this, they began to object to the demands of my line of demarcation because Károlyi was claiming that between him and the representatives of the Czechoslovak Government there had been a special agreement about a line of demarcation which was said to correspond approximately to the legitimate demands of both sides.[1] Károlyi argued that it was therefore impossible to expect the Magyars to evacuate the whole territory as far as the line which I had demanded in November and which Paris had then sanctioned. It will be seen that Károlyi was successfully

[1] The provisional agreement applied to Slovakia without Bratislava, without the Danube plain, without Košice or its environs, and without the most eastern portion of Slovakia.

endeavouring to take advantage of the Budapest agreement, in spite of the fact that it was provisional on instructions from Paris.

These topics caused considerable agitation at Prague, as might be supposed during such a period of uncertainty and alarm. The revolutionary National Assembly discussed them on several occasions, and the leading Czechs and Slovaks realized great potential danger in the situation. The Magyar Government had here proceeded very skilfully. Its first move was to try and negotiate with the Slovaks without the Czechs or the Prague Government, indicating that it was willing to make concessions if it negotiated with the Slovak National Council, but not if it had to deal with the Czechs. In this connection I should point out that towards the end of November there were several members of the executive of the Slovak National Council at Budapest besides Dr. Hodža, and Károlyi was endeavouring to bring the discussions on to autonomist lines in the interests of Hungary's territorial integrity by negotiating only with the Slovaks, without the Czechs and against them. In the National Assembly and in the Press at Prague there were utterances which showed that this development of affairs had caused much concern there. For this reason, on December 1st, the Prague Government issued a statement through the official Press bureau that nobody was authorized to carry on negotiations with the Magyar Government on any subject, and the parliamentary club of Slovak deputies issued a public declaration on the same subject. Dr. Kramář acted according to the demands of the situation. On December 10th he made a statement in the National Assembly to the effect that the occupation of Slovakia did not form a subject of negotiations between the Czechoslovak and Magyar Governments, that nobody had been authorized for this purpose by the Czechoslovak Government, and that Tusar and Hodža, our representatives in Vienna and Budapest respectively, were occupied exclusively with liquidation duties.

I handed this declaration to the authorities in Paris as soon as it reached me, and again asked for the evacuation to be effected as far as the line agreed upon in November. After wearisome and vexatious negotiations at the Quai d'Orsay, I received an assurance that the line of demarcation agreed upon in Paris would be kept to. Accordingly, the Magyar Government was officially notified by Lieutenant-Colonel Vyx to this effect. In acknowledging the receipt of the note, however, the Magyar Government stated that they would not accept the passage relating to the frontiers, as it did not agree with the historical facts of the case, and that they regarded the establishment of this new line as a brutal and arbitrary act. They therefore insisted upon the line of demarcation arranged on December 6th between Dr. Bartha and Dr. Hodža. Nevertheless, the Magyars were compelled to evacuate Slovakia as far as the line arranged by me in Paris.

I have emphasized the details of this interesting struggle because I regard these events as a logical continuation of our revolutionary activity abroad, and also because the settlement of two far-reaching territorial questions was practically reached before the Peace Conference. Thus concluded our first diplomatic incident concerning our controversy with the Magyars about Slovakia.

168

If I here refer to frontier questions and show how we secured the right to occupy nearly all our later State territory long before the decision of the Peace Conference, this will perhaps be the right place for me to add something about the analogous proceedings with regard to our historical areas, especially those with a mixed Czech and German population. The occupation of this territory was also expressly accorded to us on the basis of our war-time recognitions. But I will narrate the course of these events in their due order.

On December 13th Dr. O. Bauer, the Austrian Minister of Foreign Affairs in Renner's Government, sent the French Government and the other Allied Governments a protest against the attempt to retain the Sudetic Germans within Czechoslovakia, and he demanded that a plebiscite should at once be arranged. Three days later, in a new note, he demanded that the frontiers between Austria and Czechoslovakia, and between Austria and Jugoslavia, should be settled by a special process of arbitration.

Having been informed of this matter, I at once intervened with the French, English, and Americans, both verbally and in writing. I submitted a memorandum based upon our juridical position as a recognized Allied State with historical frontiers, and I further pointed out that around us, in Germany, Vienna, and Hungary there was a menace of Bolshevism. I also mentioned that, with a view to consolidating our economic affairs rapidly, we were preparing a currency reform, but all our plans were frustrated by the fact that hitherto not even our provisional frontiers had been defined. It was therefore, I said, unconditionally necessary to confirm, at least for the time being, our historical frontiers, since upon this depended the peace and order around us in Central Europe. The step taken by the Austrian Government provided a good opportunity of doing this.

M. Pichon agreed that my argument was right and promised to reply to the Austrian Government in this sense. Then on December 21st M. Berthelot gave me, as an official reply to my communication, the copy of a note which M. Pichon, as a result of our intervention, had handed the Swiss Legation in Paris for transmission to the Government at Vienna. This note is so important, both from a juridical and a political point of view, that I reproduce it here *in extenso*:

The Swiss Legation kindly handed the Ministry of Foreign Affairs two notes from the Government of German Austria on December 13th and 16th respectively.

The first of these notes protests against the intention of the Allied Powers to embody the Germans from Bohemia and Moravia within the Czechoslovak State. It declares that these Germans desire to separate from the Czechoslovak State, and proposes an immediate plebiscite for the purpose of settling the whole situation. The second note demands that the question concerning the frontiers of German Austria with Czechoslovakia and Jugoslavia respectively should be submitted to decision by arbitration.

These demands cannot be accepted by us.

The questions of the frontiers here at issue cannot be settled otherwise than by the Peace Conference, and for this purpose must be investigated by the Allied Governments at a very early date.

The French Government, however, takes the view that the Czechoslovak State, in accordance with the recognition granted to it by the Allied Governments, must have as its frontiers, until the decision of the Peace Conference, the existing frontiers of the historical provinces of Bohemia, Moravia, and Austrian Silesia.

As regards Slovakia, its frontiers must be established thus: The Danube from the present western frontier of Hungary to the river Ipola, thence along the course of the river Ipola to the town of Rimavská Sobota, then in a straight line from west to east as far as the river Už, and thence along the course of the river Už to the frontier of Galicia.

General Franchet d'Esperey called upon the Hungarian Government to withdraw its troops beyond these frontiers. This notification has been complied with. These frontiers have thus, in reality, been already respected.

S. PICHON.

The negotiations with the English were more difficult, but I succeeded nevertheless in obtaining their consent also. They promised that they would make the same arrangements as the French in the matter, and a few days later the British Embassy in Paris informed me that the British Government had taken steps in the sense of the English note.

It was the Americans who caused the greatest difficulty. I discussed affairs with Colonel House and his entourage, comprising Captain Lippman and Major Bonsal. Already at that time the Americans were paying close attention to all arguments which were based upon the historical frontiers of the new States. Those working with Colonel House told me that they feared to create prejudicial results in this matter. If they acknowledged our historical frontiers, what were they to say to the Poles, who were making an analogous claim, but with whose demands it was impossible to comply? They were not opposed to our point of view, but they were unwilling to commit themselves before the Peace Conference, for if they were to give their consent to the occupation of the territories demanded, that would be tantamount to a settlement of the whole question. Finally, however, they too gave their consent when I entered into a definite commitment that the Czechoslovak Government would unconditionally accept the decision of the Peace Conference as final.

It will be readily understood how wide was the scope of these decisions, and it was natural that under such circumstances I felt optimistic about the Teschen question. As early as December 22nd I telegraphically notified Dr. Kramář of this decision, and two days later I sent him a special communication containing the texts of my statements to the Allies as well as of their decisions as to our right to occupy the territory in question. Our Government thereupon carried out the occupation in due course.

169

The transport of our troops from France and Italy was unexpectedly delayed. The first resolutions for their prompt removal were passed at a moment when it was thought that hostilities would have to be continued against Germany from the south. When the Armistice with Germany was concluded, the Supreme French Command had no further interest in the matter and kept putting it off, more particularly as the French themselves had to cope with difficulties of transport, food supply, the occupation of the Rhine area, etc.

From the middle of November I was in continual touch with the French General Staff about these questions. I had first settled a regular transport plan with Colonel Philippe, which I then submitted to General Alby, Chief of the General Staff at the Ministry of War, but neither the General Staff nor Colonel Philippe would allow our regiments to leave France without complete preparation, new equipment, new uniforms, and unless they were reorganized in such a manner as to set a model standard at home. To this I had to agree.

With the Italian regiments the matter was even more troublesome. The first difficulty was due to the fact that at the last moment before the Italian offensive the division had received a new general. On October 21st a telegram suddenly reached me from General Diaz stating that he was obliged, for reasons of organization, to remove General Graziani from the command of our division, and that he proposed General Piccione as his successor. I was not altogether surprised at this, as I knew that there had been disputes between Graziani and the Supreme Command. Nevertheless, I was at first unwilling, for reasons of principle, to agree to this proceeding. By the terms of our agreement with the Italian Government the Supreme Command was not entitled to take stuch a step unless the matter had been first arranged by a preliminary agreement with us. But I knew that our division was about to take part in important operations at the front, and I therefore telegraphed my provisional consent in order that no crisis might arise in the command of our troops, with the possibility of a resulting disaster in the field. I intended to discuss the matter during my visit to Italy, but the development of events made this superfluous.

When the Armistice was signed, and we were to prepare our regiments for departure, this naturally tended to impede the smooth working of our plans, just as it had done in France. In Italy, however, the postponement was caused notably by a fresh decision to prepare a whole corps for us, and from the enormous number of new prisoners who had been captured after the victory at Vittoria Veneta to organize new militia regiments so that it would be possible to return to Bohemia with a fully equipped army comprising units of every kind.

Under these circumstances I decided, after consulting with

Prague, to send at least a military mission there at short notice for the purposes of military organization. I appointed as its chief Lieutenant-Colonel O. Husák, whose battalion had distinguished itself in the final stage of the hostilities at Terron. Husák selected a number of our best officers and N.C.O.'s from France, supplemented them by a few Italian officers, and left for Prague towards the end of November. He was received there with enthusiasm, and at once started organizing our home army.

It was not until about Christmas that the transport of our regiments from France and Italy, after my repeated efforts in Paris and Rome, began to make any real progress. The regiments from France were sent to Bohemia and Moravia, while those from Italy occupied Slovakia.

(e) MASARYK'S RETURN TO PRAGUE AS PRESIDENT. END OF
THE REVOLUTIONARY MOVEMENT ABROAD

170

On November 20th President Masaryk left New York on his way back to Prague to take up the duties to which the liberated nation had called him. On November 29th he reached England, and spent a few days in London, where he was welcomed as the President of a new State. He took the opportunity of meeting a number of prominent statesmen, such as Mr. Balfour, Mr. Churchill, Lord Milner, Sir Eyre Crowe, Sir William Tyrrell, and others, and then left for Paris, where he arrived on December 7th. Here he visited MM. Poincaré, Clemenceau, Pichon, and Berthelot, as well as various foreign diplomats, such as Colonel House, Mr. Sharp, Trumbić, Vesnić, Venizelos, Take Jonescu, etc. He remained in Paris for a week. On December 8th he visited our troops at Darney, where they were already preparing to return home. This was at the time when on behalf of the Czechoslovak Government I had participated in the official visit of the French Government to Alsace-Lorraine. After our return to Paris we together went through all the necessary preliminaries to the Peace Conference, and agreed upon our whole procedure.

I recall a number of points which struck me during Masaryk's visit to Paris on this occasion. Thus, he made no secret to me of the anxiety which he felt when he thought of the work awaiting him at home. He agreed that we had successfully overcome the first period of our difficulties, but he emphasized that we were now faced by the second period, involving the work of elaborating the State at home, and in many respects this would be far more difficult. And when I reminded him of the authority and popularity which he enjoyed, and which would make everything possible, he only made a deprecatory gesture with his hand and remarked: "We shall see."

He also pointed out what I ought to do, and how I should prepare for my return, adding his ideas of what my political future was to be. To this I said nothing: the matter was still new to me, and I had not given any thought to my political future. I had always merely fulfilled my duty, and work which creates, work which challenges, has always been my element.

During this time in Paris the President often looked tired and nearly always preoccupied. A sentence has remained fixed in my mind which he uttered on several occasions, and which he repeated to the soldiers at Darney: "We have reached the top, but it is easier to reach the top than to stay there." I could see why he was anxious, and the reports which we had in Paris at that time about the early difficulties of the Republic did not relieve his anxiety.

On the evening of December 14th, accompanied by M. Clement-Simon, the first French Minister in Prague, President Masaryk left Paris for Prague via Italy. At Padua he stopped to visit the King of Italy and our Italian troops, and then, accompanied by General Piccione, the new commander of our legionaries in Italy, he resumed his journey to Prague, where he arrived on December 21, 1918, almost by the same route as the one by which, four years earlier, on December 18, 1914, he had left Prague on his adventurous pilgrimage around the world.

The nation welcomed him with enthusiasm and emotion, with unbounded gratitude and hope. He was referred to as the people's liberator, and rightly so, for his life's work marks him out as the last of our great revivalists. He brilliantly completed the task of national revival in the spirit of Komenský, Palacký, and Havlíček.

President Masaryk took up his quarters in the castle at Prague in the same serious mood which he had shown on his arrival in Paris. This can be understood only by those who consider the great scope of his undertakings during the war, and the responsibility both as regards present and future which devolved upon him at that juncture.

By the return of President Masaryk to Prague on December 21, 1918, our liberation movement abroad was, in my opinion, completed. The President returned, for the time being, alone. Our troops from France and England arrived home again slowly in batches during the following months, and helped to maintain order at home, besides providing protection against possible dangers from outside, particularly with regard to the events in Hungary. The Siberian troops had to make further sacrifices to our cause and to that of the Allies. They were unable to return mainly for technical difficulties, but also for political reasons, as the course of events made it imperative for them to remain in Siberia until further notice. In view of the peace negotiations, our Government agreed to this course, and thus our troops in Siberia contributed to our successes at the conference in Paris.

At the moment of victory on the Western front and at home, Štefánik was touring Siberia for the purpose of maintaining order among our volunteer troops, who by now were becoming impatient. Like Štefánik himself, they felt isolated, and were eager to see their homes again. It had long been Štefánik's plan to return to Slovakia in an aeroplane, but he was unable to carry out his intention until May 4, 1919. This was to be his last journey. By a tragic irony of fate his aeroplane crashed when he was approaching the frontiers of his country, and he was thus not destined to enter Czechoslovakia alive.

After the President's departure I was unable to leave Paris, although the members of the Government had summoned me to Prague. At this time I was overwhelmed with work arising from the situation in Slovakia, and the approaching Peace Conference also entailed a daily increasing amount of labour. This was the beginning of my new activities for securing peace and the post-war reconstruction of Central Europe. This period was no less exhausting and difficult than had been the war itself.

Thus I did not return home until a whole year later, on September 24, 1919, after four years of toil and struggle abroad, during which there had been no respite and no moments without anxiety.

X X

FINAL REFLECTIONS

171

INTERNATIONAL public opinion to a preponderating extent considers that the responsibility for causing the outbreak of the war rests mainly with Austria-Hungary and Germany. The underlying motives of their war policy were of a twofold character. Austria-Hungary aimed at checking the Serbo-Croatian process of unification and the struggle of Serbia to gain further national territories from the Turkish heritage. Austria-Hungary, moreover, desired to preserve a free path to Salonika, and thus prevent the Jugoslavs from achieving their idea of national unification and liberation. This was because the influence of a Serbian success on the other nations within the Empire in their struggle for liberation would have been a menace to the continued existence of the Empire, and in any case to the supremacy of the Germans and Magyars. This was feared by Budapest, just as much as by Vienna. The humiliation of Serbia was accordingly to act as a means for arresting the progressive inner decay of the Habsburg Empire, or at least its transformation on the lines of the demands made by the various races inhabiting it.

In the last twenty years immediately preceding the war the principle that the Habsburg Empire could maintain itself only by dualism denoting the complete supremacy of the Germans in Cis-Leithania and the absolutist dictatorship of the Magyar nobility in Hungary, had become an axiom among the most powerful circle who controlled the pre-war policy of Austria-Hungary. The foreign policy of the Empire was also in accordance with this idea, which resulted, too, in the dependence of Austria-Hungary upon Berlin. Altogether, the internal policy of Austria-Hungary was decided mainly by the plans and general course of its foreign policy. These political principles were adhered to by the authoritative circles in Vienna and Budapest when the war broke out. A few divergent views of the heir apparent, Franz Ferdinand, although they were of considerable importance, produced no change in the line of foreign policy and the general plans of Vienna and Budapest as regards the Balkans.

In comparison with Germany, Austria-Hungary did not outwardly produce the impression of a State inspired by the will to power. It lacked the strength of a national idea, it was without Prussian militarism or sense of order. The unity and influence of the Catholic Church helped it somewhat, and the same applies to the coercive Magyar regime which in many respects outstripped Prussianism.

Politicians who identify themselves with the philosophy of power, but have not the necessary man-power to put it into effect, are known to make up for this deficiency by the Machiavellian view that in the interests of success all methods, however immoral or ruthless, are permissible. That was the guiding principle of pre-war Austria-Hungary towards its nationalities. For that reason I used to agree with those who preferred Germany to former Austria-Hungary.

172

The manner in which Germany and also the Habsburg Empire conducted the war was in accordance with the whole spirit underlying the development of pre-war Germany. The infringement of Belgian neutrality, submarine warfare, the bombardment of open towns, the use of poison gas, etc., all indicate a mentality animated by the principle that necessity knows no law and that the end justifies the means. The German military successes, which undeniably demonstrated the enormous strength of the nation, urged the leading circles still farther in this direction, and although the Allied strategy, both political and military, was less systematic, it was less mechanical, it reckoned more with the individual, and altogether it took greater account of the moral factors involved in the matter at issue.

It is from this point of view that further facts must be emphasized which corroborate the divergent characters of the two opposing camps. The war began with the provocative ultimatum to Serbia; London's proposal to mediate was not accepted, and the invasion of Serbia by Austria-Hungary became an accomplished fact. Shortly after that, Belgian neutrality was infringed by Germany. These circumstances imparted a special character to the war from the very beginning, and necessarily affected any judgment of it. They enabled the Allied propaganda to wield a strong moral weapon against the Central Powers, and as a further result the Allies formulated their decision to restore and liberate small States and nations.

The idea of destroying German militarism led logically to the transformation of Europe, mainly Central Europe, in such a way as to provide guarantees that there could be no repetition of what had led to the outbreak of the war. This latter purpose involved the introduction of genuine constitutionalism and a free regime, first in Germany and then also in the Habsburg Empire. It involved, too, the liberation of Poland and the granting either of greater rights or complete freedom to the Slavonic nations of the Habsburg Empire, besides bringing about a readjustment of the Balkans. Thus gradually—and it must be added, very gradually—there began to be evolved in the Allied countries a new outlook on the fundamentals and the underlying meaning of the war. This line of thought culminated in the Allied reply to President Wilson in the famous note on November 10, 1917. Here all the ideas which had been hitherto proclaimed sporadically were arranged in a systematic scheme. This process was supplemented by the Russian revolution, which naturally perturbed the whole of Europe, and to an enormous extent changed the opinions, plans, wishes interests, and needs associated with the war. The spreading and acceptance of these ideas was considerably promoted by our movement and that of the other oppressed nations.

Although the Peace Treaties did not strictly reproduce these principles, they nevertheless embodied their main ideas. Our own national traditions, our age-long contest for freedom of opinions, our democratic ideals as expressed in our reformation and national revival, and our political struggle during the nineteenth century, predestined us for the Allied camp from the very beginning.

Our own nation, both before and during the war, was in the camp of Western Europe by its historical development, the whole of its psychology, and its philosophic conceptions, by its spiritual and social structure. It was the only nation in Central Europe which had fully (I emphasize the word "fully" to indicate the contrast with the German reformation) passed through the spiritual revolution experienced by Western Europe in its political and social upheavals from the Hussite period to the end of the nineteenth century, even though in many particulars it was not so far advanced as the Western States. Here I do not wish to repeat in detail what is already sufficiently well known about our spiritual, political, and social revolution from the Middle Ages until modern times. It is a process associated with the names of Hus, Žižka, the Taborites and Bohemian Brethren, Chelčický, Komenský, Havlíček, and Palacký, and in it our nation opposed Rome, the Habsburgs, and our conservative neighbours, the Germans.

It was not merely its immediate political interests which led our nation into the camp of Western Europe. On the contrary, the whole of its cultural development conditioned its political struggle and its political interests during the war. Between the two there was no conflict. That struggle in which our direct political interests and our spiritual and cultural development were entirely identical had been continued until the most recent times. Our revivalist endeavour and our development in the eighteenth and nineteenth centuries were actuated by the same characteristic ideas as our spiritual revolution, shaping, in addition, the new social structure of our nation, which was brought about by our struggle against the Austro-Hungarian surroundings in the nineteenth century. It was a struggle on the part of the small Czech farmer, town-dweller, and workman to assert himself, and to achieve independence in spirit and in material affairs. The whole of our bygone political and economic struggles had been waged against the same opponents as in the Great War.

Thus, there was no divergence between our spiritual development and our actual political interests during the war. Nor is there any divergence to-day. It is in this sense that I interpret also the philosophical factor in our history. This is not the proclamation of an aimless external Western drift in our cultural and political life. I am not, and never have been, in favour of a mechanical Westernizing as opposed to the Eastern tendency. I have been, and still am, in favour of a European and, in fact, a world-wide outlook as a means towards developing a strong Czech national spirit with world-wide standards. I shall not here attempt to formulate a theoretical policy which may perhaps be based upon noble ideas, but lacks any vital foundation, and does not take into account stark political realities. My purpose is to seek a synthesis of interests and ideas, of life and theory, with a due regard to the future, both in respect of potent ideas and material needs.

The Great War was a phenomenon of such enormous scope,

involving such a mass of political, economic, moral, psychological, and other elements, that any formula as to its essentials and its significance must necessarily be of a very general character. If, therefore, we desire to form a correct estimate of what the significance of the war was, we must not merely investigate the political and other causes which brought it about, but also how it was conducted, which moral and material factors, which main ideas, and which main interests were victorious during its progress; and, finally, what positive result it produced, why and how it ended, and also what its aspect is from the point of view of the post-war crisis. In this connection we must first and foremost emphasize the fact that the war was not merely a conflict of liberated nationalist movements. Its basis was far wider, although this element was also contained in it.

The war can best be characterized by means of its results. It destroyed four great absolutist empires; three of them it transformed into republics, after having swept away their dynasties, while from the fourth one, the Habsburg Empire, it created six new national States. It destroyed the dynasty, the Government comprising the aristocratic and military elements, and, in fact, all the absolutist remnants of the old regime. It solved the problem of conferring unity and independence upon Poland, Czechoslovakia, Jugoslavia, as well as Rumania, Greece, Albania, the Baltic States, and Finland. It completed the national unification of Italy, settled the Alsace-Lorraine and the Schleswig-Holstein problems, and promoted several questions relating to the British Empire, influencing its constitution in the spirit of the self-determination of States and nations. Moreover, for the first time, it imposed a system of Colonial mandates, which again denotes an advance on the lines of self-determination.

The war also revived or evoked the question of independence or self-administration in the case of several Asiatic nations, the question of the freedom of the seas, of universal disarmament, a universal court of justice, and the League of Nations. Within all States where hitherto the old regime had fully or only partially held sway, the war imparted a strong democratic character to the political institutions, and brought about a great expansion in the socialistic movement. Through the Russian revolution it gave prominence to questions concerning the social structure of present-day States, and enforced the solution of universal economic problems on the lines of economic justice within the State and also between individual nations. The idea of a fair distribution of economic resources among States and nations was ventilated by the war, even though it has not been settled.

173

Thus the war, which in the course of time became an expression of an immense struggle for the successive democratization of humanity in all directions of human activity, brought about or emphasized a number of fundamental questions affecting the post-war world which themselves are often regarded as the main bases of the war.

In the life of each separate country this process was exhibited mainly by the democratic character which was imparted to the political institutions in all the new States, as well as in all the former absolutist or semi-democratic States. It was shown also by the manner in which the aristocratic and military classes were deprived of their influence, and the last remnants of the feudal regime were removed. It led also to the strengthening of the control over the executive power by legislative bodies, and to repeated attempts at a more satisfactory system of representation. In many cases this tendency brought about extremist actions which often caused violent reactions, such as Fascism. Such reactions are temporary and transient. Human experience extending over thousands of years has not discovered a better system of government than democracy. Every divergence from it has compelled those societies which have already enjoyed it to return to it with a rapidity corresponding to the violence with which it had been removed.

In international politics the democratizing development of present-day society, accelerated by the war, was shown chiefly in the proclamation of the principle of national self-determination, the establishment of new national States in Europe, and a marked tendency towards decentralization and autonomy in the case of heterogeneous States or empires. Here a special part was played by the idea of nationality as an ingredient of the democratizing process during and after the war as a whole, which in some quarters was inaccurately regarded as being more or less the basic factor determining the character of the war itself.

The idea of nationality is the product of modern times, a

result of the Renaissance and Reformation, and of the humanitarian philosophy of the French Revolution, which proclaimed the rights of man and the citizen. It applies the principles of democracy not only to the individual, but also to the nation as a whole. Our own national revival derived its theories of national liberty from the humanitarian philosophy of the French, just as the other Slavonic nations did, and just as certain other nations derived from it the principles of their national unification. In a word, humanitarian philosophy is the basis of modern democracy, which in its turn is the source of a nation's claim as a whole to political, economic, and cultural liberty. Being a struggle of Western democratism against Central and Eastern European absolutism, the war necessarily in its results became the culmination of European development during the last century in the struggle for the independence of subjugated nations.

174

It has been asserted that those who regard the underlying meaning of the Great War as a struggle to impart a democratic character to the modern world on the basis of humanitarian ideals, disparage or inadequately estimate the idea of nationality which was brought into play to so large an extent by the war, and do not properly estimate what is known as nationalism. This criticism was levelled in certain quarters against President Masaryk's conception of the war.

A nation as a collective entity in the present-day world can be something only by its ability to elaborate its system of national culture. This national culture, which includes political, economic, social, artistic, moral, and spiritual elements in general, remained a great and permanent feature in the history of mankind only as long as it corresponded with humanitarian ideals. Therefore all national cultures must strive after agreement with these ideals, which cannot be dispensed with, and must not be combated. They can and must vie with each other in the contest for moral values. I regard patriotism as love for culture of one's own nation and respect for the culture of another nation. There is no such thing as a common human culture; there are only national cultures.

I did not fulfil my national and human duty in the struggle for national independence because I regarded the collective entity of the nation as a factor which is self-sufficing and constitutes an end in itself. I fulfilled this duty simply because I regarded it as a dictate of humanity for every individual just as every collective entity to live without unnecessary restrictions and to develop a national culture.

For him who believes in the ideals of humanity, every step, every act, every sentiment is a service to humanity, to the nation, and to the progress of his own individuality at the same time. Such service and such labour do not await nor demand recognition or reward. They are an end in themselves, giving the individual the maximum of satisfaction and the maximum range for expressing his personality. Such labour is regularly accompanied and sanctified by religious faith.

From an economic and social point of view the war brought into prominence within every country the question of social and economic justice. It emphasized the question of socialism, in which at the same time it brought about a profound crisis, most strikingly manifested in the struggle for communism.

The war came at a moment when, in the countries of Western Europe, democratic tendencies had already made headway in economic and social policy. But the Great War was the first war of the masses; tens of millions of people in Europe and America were engaged in it, so that the conduct of the war became a matter directly affecting the masses, who made terrible sacrifices to it as regards their property, health, and lives. The consequence was that little by little they insisted upon a share in the decisions as to their destiny, and in return for their sufferings secured recompense mainly in an economic and social respect. They desired to have a decisive word in the future as to their density, and they realized that in so doing they could secure an influence on the economic life of the State, and could jointly control it in accordance with their requirements.

The wave of socialistic ideas gained an unexpected impetus after the war. It is true, of course, that this result was largely brought about by the common war-time sufferings of the masses, but it would be an error to suppose that the democratization of Europe which was brought about by the war will be transitory. Our own State, which is industrial in character, and our people, which through its social development comprises two main classes, the agricultural and the artisan, inevitably succumbed to this influence less than other States which were politically less advanced and industrially less developed.

Here it must be emphasized that side by side with socialism, and sometimes against it, agrarianism developed strongly in a number of States, chiefly as a result of the important function of the farmer as a prime producer during the war, and then, too, in consequence of agrarian reform which, wherever applied, increased the number of independent farmers, and established a powerful class of agrarian democracy. This accounts also for the post-war weakening of the urban bourgeois element in all States where this process was carried out. The conservative element of this bourgeoisie was replaced in a number of States by the increasing influence of a Catholicism which is acquiring democratic tendencies.

175

In an economic respect the striving towards democracy and justice, which formed one of the tendencies of the war, may be traced in the circumstance that, as I have already mentioned, for certain countries, such as Germany and Great Britain, the war represented, to a marked extent, a struggle for economic supremacy and for the freedom of the seas. Here the war merely indicated problems, and threw light on certain aspects of them, but did not solve them at all. These problems, which are difficult and delicate, are still awaiting a satisfactory solution in their entirety.

When the League of Nations was founded, it was thought of as a possible body for dealing with these matters. For example, during the discussion on colonies, the question of general economic reorganization came up indirectly, and the problem of over-population with the cognate question of colonization was touched on now and then during discussions, but was not, and could not be, settled. These are all matters which the war only skirted, leaving their settlement to future disputes and struggles. These questions also form part of the present-day tendency towards the democratization of society, and cannot be settled otherwise than by the application of democratic principles. As nations and States agree, and will continue increasingly to agree, on the subject of territory, disarmament, minorities, the international use of rivers and seas, so they will be compelled to agree on the division of economic output, on markets, on raw materials, on the emigration of surplus population, on economic contact with backward States and nations. These are, and will continue to be, the most immediate and also the most important tasks of the post-war world.

But I do not cherish any illusions or exaggerated hopes as to international democratization and the idea of democratization in general as a panacea which will secure the permanent peace and welfare of mankind. Even democracies are not always free from tendencies towards expansion and imperialism. And as regards the failings and difficulties of the League of Nations, I am acquainted with them perhaps better than many critics of the League, just as I know the actual measure of its influence to-day.

I assert, however, that the process of democratization is one through which the present-day development of mankind is passing and will continue to pass, that it involves the perfecting of the present-day organization of the world, that it is a step, if not towards perfection and lasting happiness, at least to something better than we had before the war and than we have to-day. It limits the evils of the past, and reduces their dangers for the future. That in itself is a great deal. Therefore I am an adherent and a champion of this process, of these ideas, of this development, although I am well aware that it will not solve definitely either the problem of the social structure of the community, or that of the final relationship between States and nations, from which war will perhaps never be entirely eliminated. I regard this process, however, as a proper development towards a more lasting peace, and that is where I seek the progress which the Great War rendered possible.

176

The war conveyed all these lessons to us Czechoslovaks with particular emphasis, because its meaning was identical with that of our national revolution which accompanied it. It would be absurd to expect a small nation such as ours to undertake precarious experiments for the purpose of showing others what they should do. That is not its mission, nor has it sufficient internal resources for such a proceeding. But it would be digging its own grave if it did not properly appreciate the meaning of the development of Europe and the world at large.

We were successful in our struggle because we adjusted our movement to the scope of world events. We rightly joined our struggle with the struggle of universal democracy, without considering on which side there was a preponderance of strength. We formed a correct estimate of potential developments and of the factors which were working, on one side or the other, in our favour or the contrary. We never acted in a time-serving spirit by counting first on one side and then on the other, nor did we ever swerve from our basic line of action. And nevertheless our policy was not that of the gambler or the visionary, but it was a policy which deliberately took into account the actual facts of the case, which worked laboriously from day to day, which built up its successes step by step.

We might have made the same mistakes as Ferdinand of Bulgaria or Constantine of Greece. Under the influence of certain well-known tendencies amongst us we might have "staked everything on the Russian card," but we were careful not to commit such errors as these. Our philosophico-historical conception of the war, and our conception of politics in general, gave us a proper indication of what we were to do and how we were to do it. In this lay our strength and, to a large extent, the secret of our successes.

What we achieved in the war was not due to the Tsar's declaration on our behalf in 1914, nor to the fact that our legionaries became involved in warfare with the Bolsheviks, nor to the fact that on October 18, 1918, President Wilson once and for all settled accounts with Austria-Hungary. What brought us victory was that from the very beginning we rightly surmised the probable development in Europe and throughout the world; that we rightly estimated the various factors involved, and by unremitting daily toil cultivated, influenced, and directed them in channels which contributed to our success; that we were able in good time, at least partially, to counteract the forces hostile to us. Altogether, our victory cannot be reduced to terms of simplicity by ascribing it to this or that isolated fact; it is a complex blend of numerous elements.

It was Masaryk's greatest merit that at the very outbreak of the war he was able to form a correct judgment of affairs, and to arrange his whole activity accordingly. A philosopher of democracy, of the social and national idea, he became the leader of our revolution and the organizer of our whole movement, not only because the development of events brought him to the forefront, but chiefly because his whole previous record enabled him during the war to act as an embodiment of our aims and endeavours, our ideals and wishes. Few nations have had the good fortune to be able at a decisive moment of their history to associate themselves unreservedly, with absolute confidence and certainty, with a leader who so unmistakably symbolized the ideals of the age and their great political, social, economic, and moral struggles, the ideals of the future, the traditions of his nation, and its immediate desires, and who at the same time was able so effectively to draw up a programme of his political and spiritual intentions. For this reason the leader of our victorious revolution was styled the nation's liberator, and it is by this name that he will be known in our history.

The circumstances were thus favourable to us. Our time had come, and it was only a question of what we ourselves would do. It can safely be asserted that our nation fulfilled its duty during the war. Abroad, the vast majority of our people, either of their own accord or in answer to our call, entered our armies. We were waging a war, and for this purpose we had to have troops. For this reason we started organizing a large national army at the first possible opportunity; for this reason we attached so much importance to it, and we exerted all our energies to securing its sanction and recognition.

The military share of victory is generally estimated by the numerical strength of the troops engaged in hostilities, and by the number of losses which they sustained. If on this basis we compare the millions of French, English, and Italian casualties, or the hundreds of thousands of lives lost by Serbia, Belgium, and Rumania, with our own losses sustained in the Allied ranks, we see that our positive military participation, assessed from this point of view and irrespective of our passive resistance at home, was not considerable. At the same time, our action in Siberia was certainly of great importance to the Allies. And the mere fact that we had three armies, that there were about 150,000 men who of their own accord were willing to sacrifice their lives for their ideals, must be regarded as having very significant implications.

I have intentionally omitted to discuss to what extent each of the Allies individually contributed to the success of our struggle. I have limited myself to giving an account of what each of them did for us and how they did it. In our struggle for liberty each of the Allies occupied its particular position in accordance with its views and interests. They did not present us with our liberty as a gift, but let me add that we ourselves would never have won our liberty by our own strength and labour. It was a joint achievement. Every Czechoslovak is under an obligation always to bear this in mind.

177

The Czechoslovak people greeted the hour of their liberation with such enthusiasm and such hopes that those familiar with collective psychology felt some concern for the moment when the nation would resume its normal life. And, as a matter of fact, the enthusiasm, the unbounded hopes, the great faith that a new life, a new world, and a semi-paradise were arising gradually began to change into a feeling of disappointment among many of our people when normal life and the current political struggles of parties and persons were resumed. Each individual had formed his own idea of what liberty would be like, and had expected from it a fulfilment of his own personal wishes, and the same applies to the majority of the political parties.

There was an impressiveness about this belief even if it was somewhat naïve and superficial. But the hardships of the war were at an end, and this fact alone worked upon the imagination of those who had suffered so much that it seemed to them as if they were about to enter paradise. And the idea of national liberty, a liberty the concrete effects of which in daily life were realized by few, manifested itself to the various classes, parties, and individuals first and foremost in its most ideal form.

The humdrum routine of daily life, however, with its clash of interests and opinions, with its conflicts of classes, parties, and persons, then had to be faced, and almost immediately people forgot those memorable days of the struggle for liberty, when adversaries embraced one another, when men's chief thought was of their common labour for the national cause, when enthusiastic tribute was rendered to the unselfishness and arduous perseverance of those who had fulfilled their duty at the darkest hour. The daily struggle of interests and aspirations brought with it a sense of disillusionment in various quarters, which was all the more unjustified according as it sought to burden others with the responsibility.

The events of the last twelve years have nevertheless strengthened my optimism—an optimism based upon the realities of life, prompted by imagination, grappling with hardships and injustices, and leading the spirit to a labour permeated with the desire for ideals; in short, a firm, active, and uncompromising optimism.

REFERENCES

(1) Published in English as *The Making of a State*. (George Allen & Unwin. 21s.)

(2) At that time aviation had hardly started and the plans of the pan-Germans seemed to me nothing more than childish phantasies.

(3) At these meetings it was decided that Dr. Lev Sychrava should go abroad. He left Prague in the second half of September and was the first of the Czechs who proceeded abroad with expressly revolutionary aims.

(4) This refers to the battle at which the Czechs were defeated in 1620.

(5) After a long search I found these documents unharmed in 1922.

(6) The Ministry for Foreign Affairs at Vienna had sent it to the Ministry of the Interior, whence Machar had obtained it through Kovanda.

(7) My information about the police was obtained from Jan Hájek, with whom I had been in touch ever since my stay in Paris. He was employed at the headquarters of the *gendarmerie*, and supplied very valuable and copious information, for which he ran many risks.

(8) One of our double postcards was seized by the authorities and after being deciphered it served as a piece of incriminating evidence in the proceedings which ensued. The fact that this was the only postcard which was seized in this way shows that on the whole our arrangements worked well.

(9) Dr. Rašín was arrested a few days later.

(10) Masaryk pointed out that circumstances might make it necessary to take active measures at home; for example, to organize manifestos of dissatisfaction, demonstrations, a secret printing press like that used in Belgium against the Germans, the dissemination of illicit newspapers, reports, etc., but it must be done cautiously and at the right time, and there must be no unnecessary rushing into provocative acts which would lead to persecution. Masaryk always emphasized these points.

(11) Dr. Kramář expressed this view to me in very emphatic terms.

(12) At that time, during the investment of Cracow, the enthusiasm for the Russians was at its height among all sections of our population.

(13) Captain Voska's activities in America, with the assistance of the American and British authorities, belongs largely to another aspect of our revolutionary movement. It was described in detail by President Masaryk in his memoirs.

(14) With reference to all these reports I should like to make the following observations:

1. They were sometimes intentionally written in an optimistic tone, in order to prevent our people at home from losing courage at a period of Allied military defeats. On other occasions they were given a somewhat pessimistic colouring when we wanted them to produce a definite reaction in Prague, i.e. more activity against Austria or other measures which we demanded.

This will explain some of the strong terms which I used from time to time.

2. They contain a number of inexact details either about military successes or diplomatic negotiations on both sides. I reproduced the items of information as I received them, and I did not always have the advantage of first-hand sources.

3. Mistakes occur in a few details of facts, but I always defined accurately the policy of ourselves, the Allies and Central Powers as a whole. In the same way I gave an accurate estimate of various individual events. Moreover, I received prompt and accurate information about all the main events.

4. There are some details which are repeated in nearly all the reports. This applies particularly to the wish that we abroad should not be repudiated by our politicians at home, that they should not relax their revolutionary activity—since not even the Allies would give us something for nothing—and that at all costs a continuous communication should be maintained between Prague and us.

(15) I set off for Holland on the very next day and spent Christmas Eve suffering from seasickness on the steamer. On the day after I met Dr. B. Štěpánek at Amsterdam. On this trip I spent two weeks in Rotterdam, where I lived under the name of M. Leblanc. The English authorities took me for an Austrian spy and would not let me return to London. When, finally, with great difficulty I did manage to land in England I was arrested, taken to London and imprisoned. Masaryk's intervention led to my release, and on January 11, 1916, I returned to Paris. I may mention that this was not the last occasion upon which I was imprisoned by the Allied authorities. The English locked me up three times—in each case only for a short period until matters were cleared up—and the French twice.

(16) In my third report to Prague, which was based upon the notes I took at that time, I wrote as follows on the subject of Masaryk's discussions with Briand:

" Professor Masaryk then came to Paris and discussed matters with a number of influential politicians. He was received by Briand who said to him verbatim: We French have always entertained keen sympathies for the Czech nation, and these sympathies have been strengthened by the war. I assure you that France will not forget your aspirations, which we share, and we shall do everything in order that the Czechs may obtain their independence. We will not speak about the details now, but as far as the chief point of your claim is concerned we are in agreement.

Deschanel, who to-day is powerful and influential, expressed himself similarly. We have France entirely on our side."

(17) Quoted from the notes which I took at the time. Protopopov was then on his well-known journey in Western Europe.

(18) In his pamphlet entitled In the Czech Service (Prague 1921), Dürich, speaking of Crkal (p. 29), says that I recommended him for the journey to Russia. I never recommended Crkal to anybody. From the first moment when I saw his work and attitude in the colony at Paris I was consistently opposed to him. All of us in the secretariat of the National Council, with the exception of Dürich, shared this point of view.

(19) From my daily notes during 1916 and 1917.

(20) Our purpose in arranging this sham arrest was to avert the suspicion of the Austrian authorities from people who were apparently being interfered with by the Allied authorities. In this way we succeeded in sending home a number of important messages.

(21) This was my second meeting with Milyukov. I had met him for the first time at Paris on May 29, 1916, when, as a member of the Russian Parliamentary Delegation, he was making a tour of the Allied countries of Western Europe with a number of his colleagues. This delegation on which Protopopov, then Minister of the Interior, was also serving caused considerable agitation in London and Paris on account of its political views and demands. On that

occasion I had visited Milyukov and Shingaryev, the two cadet leaders. They had made statements to me on war aims and their views of the Czechoslovak question which had then been a great encouragement to us. Milyukov's declaration, in particular, produced a strong and decisive effect, because we were in the early stages of organizing our political movement.

(22) At the time of Mackensen's offensive against Serbia the number of Austro-Hungarian prisoners there was said to have been about 35,000, of whom about 25,000 were Czechoslovaks. These figures are only approximate, and some of our officers give other estimates. Those which I quote here I regard as being approximately correct. The number of 4,000 of our prisoners in France was ascertained by the National Council, but it is certain that there were Czechoslovak prisoners in France of whom the secretariat of the National Council had no record.

(23) The difficulties which we encountered in our work even at this time, in spite of the fact that we were in regular touch with the authorities, and enjoyed a certain esteem and confidence, as representing an important political factor, is shown by the obstacles which I was perpetually encountering on my journeys from Paris to Masaryk in London. As General Secretary of the National Council I was being invited by the French authorities to headquarters and to the ministries. Negotiations were carried on with me regarding military and political affairs, I was supplied with reports and telegrams from Russia on the subject of our prisoners and troops, and also with reference to Štefánik's mission there. After events of any importance, or when I had received any urgent news, I generally proceeded to Masaryk in London to discuss with him what our next step was to be. On all these journeys the same difficulties with passport, visas, and control were always recurring. Having a Serbian passport and being obliged to state that I was travelling to the Allied countries for the purpose of discussing Czechoslovak questions, I everywhere aroused the suspicion of the authorities, by whom I was usually regarded as a spy. I have already mentioned that on a number of occasions I was arrested and imprisoned. A typical instance of this occurred in connection with the reports on our military movement which were sent to me from Russia by Štefánik in October 1916. On October 19, 1916, after visiting the headquarters at Chantilly, I left with my military documents for London. At Southampton I was stopped, subjected to an extremely unpleasant examination, and then imprisoned. The documents, which in the eyes of the English authorities formed a striking proof that I was a spy, were confiscated. It was only after long and difficult proceedings, which were followed by an apology on the part of the English authorities, that I was released. Once I was arrested at Havre and on another occasion in Paris. These difficulties continued until the proclamation of a provisional government. Even in the spring of 1918, when I had left London after my negotiations with Mr. Balfour on the subject of our recognition, Mr. Wickham Steed had to intervene at Southampton on my behalf. He pointed out to the police official that although they were now treating me as a suspicious person they would before long be placing visas upon passports signed by me. To-day it is pleasant to recall all this, but during the war it was very far from amusing. It wasted time, energy, health, and nerves.

(24) In this connection there is an interesting telegram which was sent on November 5, 1916, by Karl from the Austrian headquarters at Teschen to Burian. In this telegram, which explains more than could be told on many pages of description, Karl expresses himself as follows :

"The Emperor informed me to-day that Hindenburg proposes to make a *démarche* only after the Ploesci-Bucharest line has been taken. On raising objections I received the answer that the suitable moment must be chosen by the Field-Marshal. My impression is that the Foreign Office has been completely thrust aside and that there is a complete military dictatorship holding sway. The Kaiser is entirely uninformed about the lamentable economic situation of Germany and the war-weariness of his nation, which no amount of subterfuge could disguise. To-morrow I shall make another attempt to win over Hindenburg and Ludendorff in favour of accelerating the *démarche* which, I think, displeases them. Hohenlohe is doing all that is possible."

(25) During the discussions in the National Council with Dr. Sychrava and Osuský, the latter expressed the fear that the Allied Note to President Wilson might mention only the Czechs and not the Slovaks. In the course of my negotiations with the Ministry I convinced myself that our point of view in this matter was, on the whole, well understood. Nevertheless, throughout the proceedings I more and more insisted on the necessity for a formula which would comprise the Slovaks, for I was afraid that if this were not done it would cause difficulties within our movement.

(26) When the note was published in London Masaryk sent me the following telegram on January 12, 1917: "The success is unexpectedly great. Inform me whether we owe it to Briand. It will now be possible to state the fact in the papers. Your share in the success will also be appreciated."

In Vienna they knew that Russia had no initiative or share in the whole of the movement against Austria-Hungary. This pleased them, and they supposed that the whole matter was due to the initiative of the English Government.

(27) The Poles, in certain respects, received preferential treatment, mainly because, they started their volunteer movement a considerable time before the United States entered the war.

(28) In Russia, up to the time of the Bolshevik revolution, our army was not an independent fighting force, but was a constituent part of the Russian Army and took an oath of allegiance to Russia.

(29) From my notes taken during 1916 and 1917.

(30) On this occasion, just as previously, I was assisted by Barrère's whole entourage. Thus, throughout my stay in Rome, I was in constant touch with Charles Loiseau and his family, and it was again through Loiseau that I was able to communicate with the Vatican.

(31) In this sense I at once informed Masaryk, to whom, through Sir Samuel Hoare, I sent the following telegram: "I am returning to Paris but in three weeks I shall be back in Rome. I have completed all political negotiations here and we are beginning the organization of the troops. The result of our work is this: Complete recognition of the National Council, liberation of all interned civilians, establishment of Czechoslovak Labour Corps on second line of defence. Fear of reprisals on the part of Austria compels Italy to maintain certain reservations. The rights of our troops here will therefore be somewhat restricted. But on the whole the success is complete and in a short time will be supplemented.

(32) The former category included the Austro-Hungarian Ministers at The Hague (Szechényi) and Berne (Musulin) respectively, and Count Revertera. On the English side there was Sir Horace Rumbold, the English Minister at Berne, together with General Smuts and Philip Kerr, Lloyd George's secretary. The French representatives included Count Armand and Professor Haguenin, head of the Press Bureau in Berne. Of the neutrals should be mentioned the Swedish Foreign Minister at that time and, in particular, M. Loudon, who was then the Dutch Foreign Minister and who is now the Dutch Minister in Paris.

Among the second category may be mentioned Prince Djemal Tussun, and on behalf of the Austrians, Dr. Rostoworowski and Dr. Bader, together with Consul-General Montlong and Baron de Vaux. Of the staff of the French Legation at Berne may be mentioned Count de Châteauneuf, who, by all accounts, acted entirely on his own initiative and was not taken seriously. Such persons as Casella (the correspondent of the *Matin*) and Svatkovsky also were concerned in these matters on various occasions. An active part was taken in this respect by Parodi, who was then the confidant of Sir Horace Rumbold and who is now in the Secretariat of the League of Nations. Then there was a group of international pacifists, such as Professor Herron, Lammasch, and others.

(33) Mrs. Barton, a prominent Englishwoman resident in Switzerland, and a relative of Earl Balfour and Lord Robert Cecil. During the war she was in continual touch with Allied official circles.

(34) In fairness it should here be pointed out that in his consistorial pronouncement of January 22, 1915, Benedict did express his disapproval of the injustice perpetrated in the war. He then caused a confidential statement to be conveyed to the Belgian Government, indicating that though he had formulated his point of view in general terms, he had in mind the invasion of Belgium.

(35) "Aux Chefs des peuples belligérants."

(36) These three points in the Pope's note had already been emphasized in various forms in all Wilson's notes on the subject of peace aims, and both sides therefore regarded them as proposals acceptable to all, especially as they were expressed in such general and vague terms. On all the other points there was a fundamental divergency.

(37) The decree was published in the Press on the day after the first meeting between General Smuts and Count Mensdorff-Pouilly.

(38) For the same reasons, as we shall see later, it was my particular care that when our movement was recognized by Great Britain in August 1918, this uniformity of all our military forces should be expressly emphasized.

(39) At that time Wilson had no official knowledge of the London Pact.

(40) In his speech on October 24, 1917, just before the serious reverse at Caporetta, Sonnino was still unable to say anything final and decisive on this subject. He continued to express himself vaguely on fundamental questions, saying, for example, that Italy was not concerned with dividing up the Habsburg Empire.

(41) When the first reports on the establishment of our army in France reached Rome, Deputy F. Arca made a speech in the Italian Parliament on our revolutionary movement and demanded that it should be supported as resolutely in Italy as in France. Qualtiarotti, the vice-president of the Chamber, associated himself with Arca's speech and sent me also a congratulatory telegram to Paris.

(42) By the terms of the statutes which had been signed, neither the French Government nor the High Command had the right to settle the matter without our consent.

(43) The text of this official report runs as follows: "La commission des affaires extérieures, après avoir examiné les documents et recueilli les témoignages relatifs aux conversations de paix engagées et poursuivies par l'Autriche-Hongrie en 1917 et 1918, constate que ces conversations n'ont offert, à aucun moment, l'occasion d'une paix acceptable pour la France et pour ses Alliés."

(44) The question of a joint declaration by the Allies in favour of the oppressed peoples had at this moment made such progress in Paris, where

they were much more decisively opposed to Vienna, that Pichon, realizing the danger of disagreements (Wilson's declaration on the claims of Italy and the London Pact), proposed that a joint Allied programme on this subject should be drawn up. There was so much uncertainty and disunity on this point, and also so great a fear that it might lead to disagreement between the Allies, that a decision was made for each of the Allies in the meanwhile to proceed independently in this respect.

(45) After my conversations with Clemenceau I then believed that all our troops would be transferred to France in three months.

(46) This Article runs as follows: "The Emperor is Commander-in-Chief of the armed forces; he declares war and makes peace."

(47) This declaration, which was made on December 23, 1917, runs as follows: "The question of the State allegiance of national groups having no State independence, cannot, in the view of the Quadruple Entente Powers, be adjusted on inter-State lines. This question should be settled as the case arises by each separate State with its nationalities independently by a constitutional process."

(48) In May and August 1918 Dr. Štěpánek sent to Paris two reports in which he gave us a detailed account of his scheme for getting away from the Dalmatian islands to Italy with important political and military news by means of a submarine. The scheme would have demanded proceedings on the part of the Allies which we could not have asked for at that time, more particularly from Italy, which was very mistrustful in these matters. I replied to this effect in my report to Prague on June 14, 1918. Dr. Štěpánek, nevertheless, with remarkable courage, managed to cross the Adriatic in an ordinary boat with his friend Giunio, towards the end of October 1918, at a moment when the Empire was on the point of collapsing. He was first stopped in Italy, but then reached Paris where he took part particularly in the negotiations arising from the differences among the Jugoslavs. In November he returned from Paris to Prague as one of the first envoys with news about preparations for the Peace Conference.

(49) This report probably referred to the first conflicts of our transport divisions at Penza and Samara with the local Soviets.

(50) As far as I have been able to ascertain, the idea of concentrating or transporting our army by way of Archangelsk and Murmansk first made its appearance in an official document of the British War Office on April 1, 1918. From that date onwards the French military authorities also took it into account. It is first quoted in the French official documents on April 20th. A similar plan emerged in Russia also about the same time, whether under the influence of the telegrams from Paris and London, or independently, I do not know.

(51) The divergency of views between England and France as to the employment of our Russian army was settled two weeks later at the Franco-British Conference in London, where an official resolution on this subject was passed in accordance with our ideas.

(52) Clemenceau's remarks on this occasion included the following: "I want to have all your troops in France. I consider them first-rate soldiers. We will give you a declaration and will acknowledge your independence. You must be independent because you deserve it. You can rely on me not to leave you in the lurch."

(53) As soon as Masaryk, who was in Washington at the time, received the text of this document he sent Pichon a telegram of thanks.

(54) At that time I had no exact information as to the total number of our troops in Siberia. But having news in Paris that as our army proceeded eastward it was continually increasing in numbers by the arrival of fresh prisoners, we estimated its size as being far beyond what it actually was. That is why I erroneously mentioned so high a figure. At that time the maximum number of our troops was somewhere about 80,000.

INDEX